D0554255

The Age of Aspiration

The Age of

Aspiration

___

Power, Wealth, and Conflict in Globalizing India

Dilip Hiro

THE NEW PRESS

NEW YORK
LONDON

Requests for permission to reproduce selections from this book should be mailed to:
Permissions Department, The New Press, 120 Wall Street, 31st floor, New York, NY 10005.

First published in India as *Indians in a Globalizing World* by
HarperCollins Publishers India, Noida, 2014
This revised edition published in the United States by The New Press, New York, 2015
Distributed by Perseus Distribution

LIBRARY OF CONGRESS CATALOGING-IN-PUBLICATION DATA

Hiro, Dilip.
    [Indians in a globalizing world]
    The age of aspiration : power, wealth, and conflict in globalizing India / Dilip Hiro.
        pages cm
    "First published in India as Indians in a globalizing world, by HarperCollins Publishers
India, Noida, 2014"—Title page verso.
    Includes bibliographical references and index.
    ISBN 978-1-62097-130-7 (hardcover : alkaline paper)—ISBN 978-1-62097-141-3 (e-book)
1. India—Economic policy—1991– 2. India—Social conditions—1947–
3. Globalization—Social aspects—India. 4. Social change—India. 5. Power (Social
sciences)—India. 6. Wealth—Social aspects—India. 7. Political culture—India.
8. Social conflict—India. 9. East Indians—Great Britain. 10. East
Indians—California. I. Title.
    HC435.3.H57 2015
    330.954—dc23

                                                                    2015013943

The New Press publishes books that promote and enrich public discussion and understanding
of the issues vital to our democracy and to a more equitable world. These books are made possible
by the enthusiasm of our readers; the support of a committed group of donors, large and small;
the collaboration of our many partners in the independent media and the not-for-profit sector;
booksellers, who often hand-sell New Press books; librarians; and above all by our authors.

www.thenewpress.com

Composition by Westchester Book Composition
This book was set in Adobe Caslon

Printed in the United States of America

2   4   6   8   10   9   7   5   3   1

Contents

Map 1: India

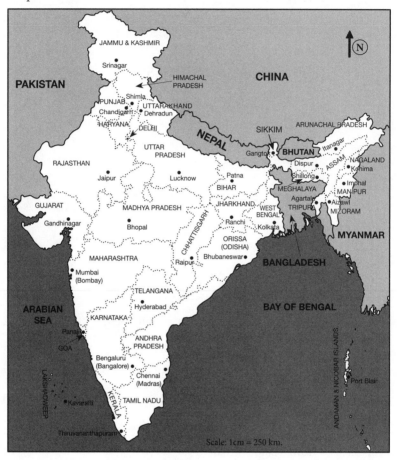

Map 2: Main Area of Maoist Influence

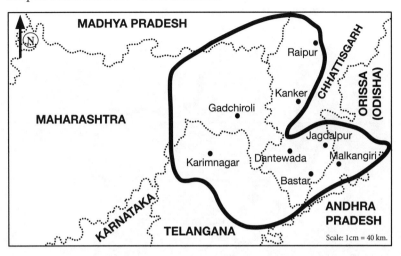

Map 3: Silicon Valley, Northern California (USA)

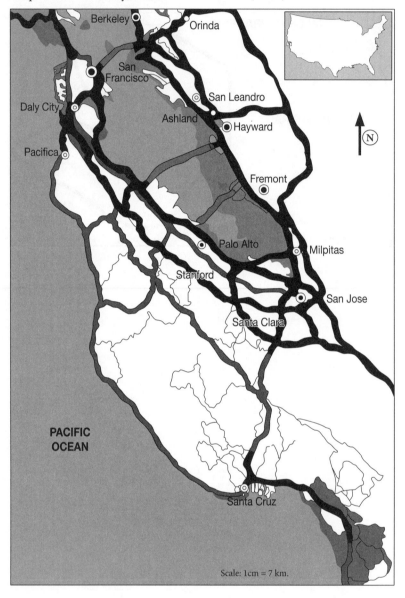

Map 4: United Kingdom

NORTH
ATLANTIC
OCEAN

NORTH
SEA

Glasgow

Ayr

Belfast

IRISH
SEA

Scunthorpe
Halewood
Rotherham
Ellesmere Port
Wrexham
Wolverhampton
Castle Bromwich
Solihull
Gaydon

Greater
London
Maidenhead
Slough
Egham
Port Talbot
Basingstoke

ENGLISH CHANNEL

○ Site of an Indian
company establishment

Scale: 1cm = 65 km.

Preface

It is hard to challenge *Fortune* magazine's recent claim that globalization has been the "world economy's central storyline"[1] for the last two decades. From cell phones to shopping malls, globalization—which Nobel Prize–winning economist Joseph Stiglitz defines as the "closer integration of countries and peoples of the world"[2]—has penetrated and transmuted the lives of hundreds of millions of Indians at home as well as abroad, particularly in the United States and Britain. It has created new wealth in India, boosting economic expansion, and it has fostered a powerful consumerist culture.

The dramatic transformation is aptly captured in the role reversal of the heroes of Indian cinema (known worldwide as Bollywood) over the past decades. Bollywood is a staple of mass entertainment and, as such, reflects and reinforces the nation's concerns, aspirations, and values. The movie *Guru*, inspired by the life of the late industrial magnate Dhirubhai Ambani, father of India's current topmost billionaires, Mukesh and Anil Ambani, was a smash hit in 2007. In it, Gurukant "Guru" Desai, played by Abhishek Bachchan, is portrayed as a ruthless, lawbreaking businessman who overcomes the economic hurdles created by the state, moored in central planning, to become a towering business magnate. This relentlessly pro-capitalist film presents Gurukant as a visionary, a harbinger of popular private enterprise as it is raucously lauded in today's media. Produced at the cost of Rs 150 million ($3 million), *Guru* saw a box-office gross of Rs 812 million ($16.2 million), collected at the new multiplexes that have sprouted up across India to cater to the expanding middle class as well as the affluent Indian diaspora.

By happenstance, the sea change is reflected in the roles played by the Bachchan family. Abhishek's father, Amitabh, became a popular larger-than-life "angry young man" in the 1970s thanks to his roles as a hero from a poor background in such films as *Deewar* (Wall) and *Sholay* (Flames). The affluent in those films were either unscrupulous businessmen or exploiting landlords.

The first signs of change appeared in the 1990s. As the scholar Vamsee Juluri observes in his book *Bollywood Nation: India Through Its Cinema*, the movies of this period "held aloft the family as the ideal symbol of morality through the wedding as the ultimate expression of consumer power, but beyond that they forgot all about angry young men and toiling peasants."[3] More recently, a crop of "multiplex movies" has appeared. An abiding feature of these films is the flaunting of a character's net worth in cash, Juluri observes—a sharp contrast from the movies of yesteryear, when affluence was suggested by a palatial house or an imported car. The new leitmotif is in tune with the clientele of the multiplexes, whether the cinemas are independent or housed in glitzy shopping malls. The admission price itself excludes working-class patrons, to the smug satisfaction of the prospering customers.

Just as a film like *Guru* could not have been conceived, much less produced, a quarter century ago, it would have been unthinkable to visualize someone like Narendra Modi, a politician with the flagrant backing of big business, moving into the official residence of India's prime minister, as he did in May 2014.

India has undergone a profound transformation in the past two decades, and in this book I present a record of this change. I examine what has become of India and its diaspora since 1991, when, facing the prospect of defaulting on its sovereign debt, the nominally socialist Indian government introduced a new economic policy that brought India into accordance with the neoliberal economic policy ascendant worldwide at the time. This economic big bang has had enormous financial, political, and cultural impacts on Indians at home and in the post-1991 Indian diaspora in the United States and Britain. Over the past few years, I have interviewed many people in India and abroad to assess the impact that globalization and the new economic policy have had on their lives. This has enabled me to construct a narrative that combines three major elements: the personal experiences of my interviewees; a picture of how globalization works in the production and sale of goods and services, communication, and finance; and a broad assessment of how the democratic system of a multiethnic, multireligious mega-nation of 1.25 billion people is coping with the opportunities and tensions arising from the onset of the new economic policy. In other words, I have described the state of the nation after a quarter century of the economic liberalization at home and globalization at large.

Four decades ago, I performed a similar task for my book *Inside India Today*. I spent nineteen months traveling in the subcontinent, with a brief break in my London home. Covering almost all the constituent states of the republic, I conducted formal and informal interviews in the capital of each state as well as two villages in each respective state. Since I am familiar with the languages spoken in northern, central, and western parts of the country, I conversed with my subjects there directly. Elsewhere, I used an interpreter. In villages, I talked to landless laborers, poor and middle-income peasants, rich farmers, landlords, and artisans. In cities, I interviewed menial workers, industrial proletariat, petty traders, white-collar employees, professionals, and government bureaucrats. I chatted informally, changing the direction of the conversation as I went along. My aim was to obtain firsthand information about the socioeconomic status of my subject, as seen by him, and his social and political views in a fairly simple, direct manner.

I followed a similar technique while interviewing journalists, academics, political leaders, party workers, trade unionists, and industrialists. But my questions in their cases were designed primarily to seek their views on, and analysis of, the social order and political events. These recorded conversations thus became a source of information and analysis.

During the first half of the 1970s, India's national literacy rate was 34 percent, and the majority of urban dwellers were illiterate. A landline telephone, provided exclusively by the Post and Telegraph Ministry, was a luxury that only the richest landlord could afford. Television was nonexistent, and a transistor radio was a novelty beyond the reach of most villagers. The moneylender, charging usurious interest rates, was a fixture in all rural settlements. Thatched huts and houses of unbaked bricks were commonplace, and voluntary housing segregation based on Hindu subcastes was the norm. Petty government officials extracted bribes from villagers. The overall political consciousness of rural dwellers was low. During election campaigns, vote-buying was a common practice among the competing candidates, with the leader of a subcaste delivering vote banks to the one offering the largest amount of cash. In urban centers, there were few cars, and almost all of these were locally manufactured Ambassadors, based on the 1956 (British) Morris Oxford model.

Four decades later, the national literacy rate had doubled, and three out of five villagers were literate. They could easily read a newspaper in their native language, although practically none of them did. Cell phones were common in villages, with competing telecommunications companies charging rock-bottom rates. Color television was accessible in rural areas, though only a minority could afford a TV set, so watching television was now a group activity, with neighbors gathering around a set in the evening. Along with transistor radios, it was the main source of news for villagers. Voluntary housing segregation remained intact, but it was rare to come across flimsy huts or houses of unbaked brick. Moneylenders did not figure as much in the lives of agriculturists as they did before. Agricultural banks, founded by the central government to provide credit to those who possessed land, had made a difference. Despite far better communication systems available in rural areas, the overall political consciousness of the inhabitants remained low. The petty bribing of bureaucrats continued, and electoral malpractices had reached obscene levels. Election campaigns, even for local offices, consumed hundreds of thousands of rupees. In cities and large towns, traffic jams had become commonplace due to insufficient investment in road infrastructure and an extraordinary upsurge in car purchases, fueled by easy mortgages. (With the annual sales of the Ambassador plummeting to a derisory 2,200, the management of Hindustan Motors suspended its production in May 2014.)[4]

My extensive research for *Inside India Today* gave me a firm grounding in the Indian state and society. It has enabled me to quickly plug into the social and political significance of current events in India during my subsequent brief visits. When I began my research for this book in 2008, my previous work had prepared me thoroughly to study the changes and challenges that the new economic policy and globalization had wrought.

I introduce this book with a brief economic history of independent India leading up to the acute crisis of 1991 and the steps taken to defuse it. As a founding signatory to the World Trade Organization (WTO), India was required to abide by all of the organization's rules by 2005, the scope of which, since it morphed from the General Agreement on Trades and Tariffs into the WTO in 1995, now included services and intellectual property. From 2006 to 2011, India achieved an annual economic growth of around 8 percent (except in 2008–9), breaking out of its previous band of 3 to 5 percent. From 2012 onward, GDP growth fell below 5 percent in an environment of high inflation and a series of jaw-dropping corruption scandals. This energized the opposition Bharatiya Janata Party (BJP), which went on an offensive against the Congress Party–led coalition government. By projecting Narendra Modi, the son of a tea seller, as its prime ministerial candidate against Rahul Gandhi, born into the privileged home of two former Congress premiers, the Bharatiya Janata Party shaped the campaign for the 2014 parliamentary poll. Generously funded by big business, BJP leaders mounted an electoral blitzkrieg the like of which had not been witnessed by Indians before. Their subsequent victory heartened business circles. Among other things, it reversed the fall in property values, particularly in the satellite towns that had grown up around India's megacities, such as Delhi. There, the city of Gurgaon is in the lead. It was a clear favorite among Indian experts in information technology returning from the English-speaking West.

Gurgaon embodies all that is admirable and deplorable about India since the onset of the new economic policy. It illustrates the disjunction between the dynamism of private enterprise and official lethargy and corruption; the subversion of the welfare laws by bureaucrats and businesspeople; the stark contrast between the exponential rise in private land and property values and the glacial advance in infrastructure and public services—as well as the huge opportunities offered by the construction boom to the crooked to transform their untaxed, illegal profits into legitimate white money, a process that is attracting a growing number of nonresident Indians. This is the substance of the first chapter.

The next two chapters deal with the growing presence of India-based corporations in Europe and North America in traditional industries—steel and aluminum, cars, and pharmaceuticals—and in the sector of information and communication technology, as well as the expanding Indian diaspora in Britain and the United States in the wake of the new economic policy and globalization. Chapter 2 covers Britain, whose commercial and political links with the Indian subcontinent span two centuries. In chapter 3, I focus on the rising presence in Silicon Valley of Indian expatriates with postgraduate degrees from prestigious American universities and the reasons for their advancement. This is interlinked with the success that India's tech firms have had in undercutting their Western competitors by getting the bulk of their orders by Western clients fulfilled in India at vastly reduced costs. These success stories, however, are irrelevant to the vast majority of Indians, who live in villages.

These typical Indians have gained the least, if at all, from the new economic policy and globalization. That is the substance of chapter 4, which contrasts the condition of marginal peasants with rich farmers by presenting appropriate case studies. It also covers such subjects as the Green Revolution and genetically modified crops, as an update on the technological and social developments in agriculture.

The continued fall in the average ownership of agricultural land by villagers—triggered by population growth and the static level of cultivated land—has accelerated the migration of laborers to urban centers and a subsequent rise in the number and size of city slums. The boom in urban construction is another major attraction for rural workers. The details are laid out in chapter 5, which covers slums of three types: inner city, suburban, and along riverbanks. Irrespective of their location, these underprivileged communities suffer from high crime rates and an unholy collusion between lawbreakers and corrupt cops.

Chapter 6 deals with corruption of a higher order. It outlines the links between the Congress Party and rich businessmen since the pre-independence era in both public and private sectors. It also deals with the measures taken to combat sleaze and the inadequacy of such provisions.

The subsequent chapter covers the Naxalite, or Maoist, movement, whose resurgence is directly related to the onset of neoliberal policies and the globalization of capital that has blurred the distinction between domestic and overseas multinational corporations. The chapter traces the movement's history since 1967. The Maoists' base in the mineral-rich east-central region, inhabited by the tribal people—the most exploited community in India—has proved too strong to be crushed so far. The Modi administration's relaxation of the regulations to protect the environment and the interests of the indigenous tribal inhabitants, in order to benefit mining companies, is likely to boost local support for Maoists. The earlier governments' failure to end the Maoist insurgency needs to be viewed against the wider national environment of democratic politics.

Among the peculiarities of Indian politics is the protest tactic of a high-profile personality fasting unto death in order to pressure the government into addressing a grievance or implementing a reform. Chapter 8 dwells on this and other unique features of Indian democracy that have come into play to cope with the fresh challenges thrown up by the new economic policy and globalization.

Chapter 9 is a record of how villagers, forming 70 percent of the national population, view themselves and politics in general. The mood of those living in settlements near expanding cities is upbeat, despite the corruption and opacity of the bureaucracy and police. The mood is the opposite in villages located far away from urban centers, due to the fall in average landholding and the neglect of agriculture by predominantly city-dwelling politicians.

The final chapter outlines the possible scenarios for Indians at home and abroad.

In my conversations with villagers, I found that they continue to express land area in the traditional measurement of a *bigha* (related to an acre), thus ignoring the official adoption of the metric system in 1962. However, what a bigha means varies from state to state. For example, in Rajasthan it equals 0.625 acre, or 0.24 hectare, whereas in Uttarakhand it means 0.25 acre, or 0.1 hectare. By contrast, metric weights are used universally, with 1 quintal equaling 100 kilograms.

The exchange value of the Indian rupee has varied from Rs 4.79 to US$1 in 1950 to Rs 60 to US$1 in 2014, with the figure being Rs 17.50 just before the new economic policy in mid-1991. For the recent period, I have used the flat rate of Rs 50 to US$1, with the earlier decades calculated differently.

Globally, statistics are expressed in millions, billions, and trillions. But in India, statistics are expressed in lakhs (one lakh=100,000) and crores (one crore=100 lakhs=10 million). For the sake of consistency, I have opted for millions and billions.

A foreign word, written in italics at the first mention, later appears in roman.

The epilogue is not indexed.

As before, it has been a pleasure to work with Carl Bromley, the editorial director of The New Press. The task this time was to revise and update the initial version of this book, printed by an Indian publisher in the previous year for sale only in the subcontinent.

Dilip Hiro
May 2015

Introduction

On the evening of May 21, 1991, everything seemed normal in the passenger sections of Bombay's Sahar International Airport, which lies on the outskirts of Santa Cruz, a suburb of India's commercial capital. By contrast, the airport's cargo section was filling with policemen in dark blue uniforms. There was frisson in the air, even though it was viciously humid thanks to the moisture coming in from the nearby Arabian Sea. The staff at the cargo section was expecting goods they had never officially handled before: standard gold bars straight from the vaults of the Bombay-based Reserve Bank of India, the country's bank of last resort.

One enclosed truck arrived in the middle of the night bearing two hundred shining gold bars, weighing 2.5 tons and guarded by pistol-wielding guards—and then another. The bars were carted to the freighter of the Air India Cargo, chartered by the Reserve Bank and destined for London Heathrow Airport via Cairo and Geneva. Being a turboprop plane, the freighter had a limited capacity for cargo.

All told, the Reserve Bank delivered nearly 3,800 gold bars, weighing forty-seven tons, to the Bank of England, keeping only 1,600 bars in its vaults. Later, this remaining treasure was flown to the Union Bank of Switzerland via the Geneva International Airport. By the end of that month, the currency reserves at the Reserve Bank of India were down to $600 million, barely enough to pay for three weeks of essential imports. (Normally, such reserves should cover a minimum of six months' imports.) India's central bank had mortgaged its entire gold reserves, worth $605 million, as collateral to raise an emergency loan of $2.2 billion from the International Monetary Fund.

May 21, 1991, was a day of shame for India as a nation. At the individual level, it was equivalent to the moment when an Indian householder, looking crestfallen, carries a satchel containing his wife's gold jewelry to the pawnbroker's for cash to buy groceries—a distressing admission that his family finances have collapsed. In the event, this heartrending national ignominy came to be associated, unfairly, with Prime Minister Chandra Shekhar, the sixty-four-year-old socialist politician noted for his good looks, enhanced by a trimmed beard.

In November 1990, when Shekhar assumed premiership as the leader of a minority faction in parliament, backed by the much larger contingent of the Indian National Congress (henceforth, Congress Party), he inherited an economy in dire straits. Inflation was running at 17 percent, and the country's foreign exchange reserves had plunged to $1.2 billion. As the value of the Indian rupee started slipping in exchange markets, the Reserve Bank struggled to slow the slide by spending its meager foreign currency reserves. The threadbare reserves sent alarm bells ringing in the Shekhar government. In the midst of the deepening crisis, Rajiv Gandhi, leader of the Congress Party parliamentarians, decided to withdraw his party's support for Shekhar. Shekhar resigned on March 6, 1991, but he stayed on as caretaker prime minister until after the general election in May.

In the interim, Shekhar approached the International Monetary Fund (IMF) for a loan, with India's gold reserves offered as collateral. Yet their value was not enough to cover all that was needed. Since 1980, India's foreign loans had spiraled from $20.5 billion to a record $72 billion, making it the largest debtor nation after Brazil and Mexico. Looking frantically around for other sources, the government recalled the emergency aid promised earlier by Japan and Germany. By adding that sum to the credit offered by the IMF, India managed to avoid defaulting on its sovereign debt.[1] When the news broke of the wholesale mortgaging of the nation's gold, politicians and the public were outraged. In India, gold enjoys a cultural status much higher than its material value, bordering on the mythical. But the deed was done.

The first stage of the parliamentary election on May 20, 1991, passed without incident. But the following day brought horrific news. In the course of electioneering in the southern state of Tamil Nadu, Rajiv Gandhi was assassinated by a female suicide bomber, a militant Tamil, opposed to his policy of providing military support to the Sri Lankan government's campaign against irredentist Tamils. The rest of the general election was moved to mid-

June. The Congress Party leadership passed to Pamulaparti Venkata Narasimha Rao, a rotund, jowl-faced lawyer and lifelong party member. Though his party won only 244 seats out of 542, he managed to become the prime minister with the help of small factions that were not included in his cabinet when he formed his government. He gave the job of finance minister to Manmohan Singh, an Oxford-trained economist and a former deputy chairman of the Planning Commission.[2] Together, they drastically altered the economic development model that India had been following for the past forty-four years.

Enlightened Policies Gone Awry

In 1947, British India was partitioned into India and Pakistan, with each acquiring an independent status. Both countries became founding members of the General Agreement on Tariffs and Trade, sponsored by the United Nations. It was a multilateral agreement to regulate cross-border trade in goods, with the aim of reducing tariffs and other trade barriers and eliminating preferences, on a reciprocal and mutually advantageous basis. Since 1947, India has been ruled most of the time by the leaders of the Congress Party. In the mid-1930s, they had prepared a blueprint for India's economic development. After independence, they implemented land reform, albeit haphazardly, and laid the foundation for rapid industrialization.

Guided by the Congress Party luminary Prime Minister Jawaharlal Nehru (in office 1947–64), a handsome and charismatic social democrat, India launched its first Five-Year Plan in 1951. In the same year, the parliament passed the Industrial Development and Regulation Act, which required an entrepreneur in any industry to acquire a license to do business. This was done to ensure the best possible use of limited capital, technology, and management skills in the context of a national policy of self-reliance and import substitution. It was necessitated by the paucity of foreign exchange due to the meager exports of Indian goods.[3]

In 1956, the Industrial Policy Resolution was adopted by the bicameral parliament,[4] which assigned to the public sector industries of such basic and strategic importance as coal, iron and steel, aircraft manufacturing, shipbuilding, and oil extraction and other mining. Another industrial category, which included machine tools, heavy chemicals, and fertilizers, was assigned to the mixed public-private sector, with the rest assigned to the private sector. On April 1, 1956, a comprehensive Companies Act came into force. But, given the propensity of the glacial Indian bureaucracy toward corruption and negativity, the beneficial intent of the official policy became grievously distorted. A licensing system to make an optimum use of the scarce resources of capital and managerial skills ended up as a corrupt "license-permit-quota" regime run by a nexus of senior civil servants, elected politicians, and a handful of influential business houses. Periodic rule changes and new parliamentary legislation to cope with scarce foreign exchange provided additional leverage to bureaucrats in order to tighten the already stringent regime in the industrial sector. The Foreign Exchange Regulation Act of 1973 was one such law.

The efforts of the Mumbai-based Tata Consultancy Services to import an advanced Burroughs computer from the United States were chronicled by Subramaniam Ramadorai, the company's CEO, in his book *The TCS Story . . . and Beyond.* Between submitting an application for an import license to the Department of Electronics and clearing the computer through strict customs procedures on arrival in Mumbai, Tata had to complete seven intermediate steps. These included forwarding copies of the application from the Department of Electronics to the ministries of finance, commerce, and industries; getting approval from the Monopolies and Restrictive Practices Commission; and calculating the import tariff, which often exceeded the price of the machine. The finance ministry's approval to give Tata access to foreign exchange to pay for the equipment was tied to Tata's commitment to export twice the import cost over the next five years. Failure to do so could have resulted in a government confiscation of the imported machine. "Every stage had its own challenges, mostly because this was all being done for the very first time in India and the existing laws were open to interpretation by government officials who were unfamiliar with computers," notes Ramadorai.[5]

Until 1961, India's policies on trade and foreign investment were quite liberal. After that, it advised foreign companies to acquire local participation in their existing equity. Many foreign companies reacted negatively. PepsiCo Inc., for instance, ceased operations in response. The next year, the government officially prioritized domestic industry and economy, and it stuck to this mandate until 1977. This protectionist policy in an early stage of industrialization was not peculiar to India. Almost all the currently industrialized nations erected tariff walls to help nurture their nascent industries at home.

The drought of 1965–66, coupled with a ballooning budget deficit caused by war with Pakistan in September 1965, fueled inflation. At the urging of Washington and the World Bank, the government of Indira Gandhi (r. 1966–77, 1980–84), daughter of Nehru, devalued the Indian rupee by a whopping 57.5 percent in June 1966 to increase exports to pay for imports of food.

Later, due to the split in the Congress Party, Indira Gandhi's faction lacked a majority in the popularly elected Lower House (*Lok Sabha*, or People's Council, in Hindi) of the parliament. To stay in power, she relied on Communist members of parliament. Pressured by them, she piloted the Monopoly and Restrictive Trade Practices Act through the chamber in 1969. This act aimed to prevent the concentration of economic power, control the rise of monopolies, and protect consumer interests by outlawing monopolistic, restrictive, and unfair trade practices. The companies that dominated their respective industries had to obtain governmental approval to expand, appoint directors, and acquire, establish, or merge with another firm. Her government also nationalized fourteen major commercial banks and instructed them to aid small businesses and rural agribusiness. This act specified that a company with revenue of Rs 200 million ($25 million) could not expand without clearance from the government.[6]

The Foreign Exchange Regulation Act of 1973 required foreign companies that owned more than 40 percent equity in their Indian operations to get the permission of the Reserve Bank of India to continue their business in the country. The Reserve Bank was and remains the primary instrument to execute the government's financial policies. The new law also made it mandatory for foreign firms to include local participation in their equity. Fifty-four Western companies, including IBM and the Coca-Cola Company, ceased operations by 1978. Nine more companies followed in 1980–81.[7]

In the 1970s, India's trade deficit worsened due to the second oil shock of 1979–80, when Iran's petroleum shipments ceased worldwide due to the Islamic revolution there. While the shortage pushed up the cost of oil imports, the higher prices of India's exports eroded their competitiveness. To overcome the widening trade deficit, the government of the newly elected Indira Gandhi approached the IMF for a loan after issuing an Industrial Policy Statement, which streamlined licensing and amended the Monopoly and Restrictive Trade Practices Act to simplify business transactions. In late 1981, the IMF granted India a loan of $5 billion, to be repaid, with interest, in ten years.

Economic liberalization gathered pace during the rule of Indira Gandhi's son, Rajiv (in office 1984–89), after her assassination in 1984. His administration instructed the Reserve Bank to relax its rules about external commercial borrowing by private companies. Its later decision to increase the output of such consumer durables as refrigerators led Indian firms to borrow from Western banks. The net result was a threefold rise in India's external commercial borrowing during that decade.

The government itself raised loans from foreign commercial banks at high interest rates to finance its budget deficits. These banks approved of Rajiv Gandhi's administration contracting the public sector sharply from 1988 onward. This contraction, coupled with market reform, made the Bombay Stock Exchange bullish. Annual inflation dropped to single digits, and Western multinationals, which had shunned India before, started moving in. India's loans from the World Bank also rose sharply during the second half of the 1980s.

The defeat of Rajiv Gandhi's Congress Party by the United Front coalition of opposition groups in 1989 led to two prime ministers in as many years. The second premier, Chandra Shekhar, assumed the high office in November 1990 as leader of a small faction of MPs; Gandhi's Congress Party backed him without joining his cabinet. The subsequent political uncertainty came at a time when various small loans granted by foreign banks to the Indian companies started maturing.

Externally, the Kuwait crisis, caused by Iraqi President Saddam Hussein's invasion of the emirate in August 1990, led to the doubling of India's oil payments and the loss of $3 billion in remittances from Indian expatriates in Kuwait and Iraq. These workers, holding Indian passports, were officially classified as nonresident Indians. The same status applied to all other Indian nationals settled abroad. The turmoil caused by the Kuwait crisis led the nonresident Indians to transfer their funds from India to Hong Kong and Singapore. India's credit worthiness plunged. Western banks refused to grant any more loans to the Indian government or private companies.

The year 1991 was a milestone in world history for multiple reasons. It began with the Second Gulf War and ended with the collapse of the Soviet Union. In the wider context, 1991 marked the end of a chapter in the globe's economic history, which China inaugurated in 1978 with Chinese leader Deng Xiaoping's economic reforms, which allowed private enterprise and foreign investment in the People's Republic of China. In the intervening period came deregulation in the United States under President Ronald Reagan (in office 1981–89); the decision of the European Union (EU) to create a single market; the fall of the Berlin Wall in 1989, which opened the gate for eastern European nations to join the EU; and the conversion of the Association of South East Asian Nations into a free-trade zone. The disintegration of the Soviet Union spelled the end of central planning in its fifteen constituent republics.

After 1991

The New Industrial Policy, announced in July 1991 in Delhi, drastically reduced the license-permit-quota regime, the so-called "License Raj." It abolished import quotas, slashed tariffs from over 100 percent to 25–36 percent, and ended industrial licensing except for enterprises in defense and national strategy. It limited public-sector monopoly only to security, national strategy, nuclear power, and railways. In the service sector, it allowed private companies in banking, insurance, telecommunications, and air travel. Foreign companies were allowed equity up to 51 percent (up from 40 percent) in thirty-four industries. During the five-year tenure of the Narasimha Rao government (1991–96), the average annual GDP expansion was 6.7 percent.

To distinguish itself from the Congress Party, the Bharatiya Janata Party (BJP) stressed *swadeshi* (Hindi: made domestically), or self-reliance, in the economic sphere. This chimed well with the followers of BJP who supported the party's earlier call for Hinduization—popularly called *Hindutva*—in the cultural sense. In the 1998 general election, it emerged as the largest group and formed a coalition government that lasted only a year.

It was only after the 1999 parliamentary poll that the BJP was able to lead a stable coalition cabinet. It underscored its commitment to the new economic policy and globalization by cutting tariffs further, lowering barriers to foreign direct investment, and redefining swadeshi as "competing effectively in the global economy." This sophistry was meant to mask the fact that the predominantly Hindu business houses had started to fund the BJP as a serious alternative to the Congress Party when they noticed its surging popularity among Hindus, which it gained by playing up the highly charged religious card. The party had in return transformed itself into an advocate of market economy. Earlier, the Foreign Exchange Management Act of 1999 had allowed freer movement of capital in and out of India. To expedite privatization, the BJP-led government established the Ministry of Disinvestment.

India's involvement in the information and communication technology industry provided glittering material for glossy newsmagazines in the United States that were keen to applaud the rise of the world's largest democracy as it accelerated its drive into a market economy and globalization. At home, the (minority) English-language newspapers and magazines went into overdrive, declaring India an "Information Superpower" deserving some kind of global status. Such claims flew in the face of the following fact: the tech industry provided direct and indirect employment to less than 1 percent of the national workforce of 487 million people, in a country where half the households lacked electricity and only 5 percent had a landline telephone connection.[8]

All the same, the GDP expansion in fiscal year 2003 broke out of the traditional 5 to 6 percent band to hit 8.2 percent.[9] The BJP coined a beguiling phrase: "India Shining!" Sure of winning a fresh mandate from voters, it brought the general election forward by several months, to April–May 2004.

BJP leaders had not foreseen that the opposition Congress Party, led by its freshly confident president, Sonia Gandhi, would adopt the leftist parties' critique. She argued that the benefits of the improved growth rates were being skimmed off by the top 5 percent of the population, leaving 70 percent of Indians stagnating, surviving on less than $2 a day. The election gave the have-nots a chance to register their protest. They did.

They favored the opposition Congress Party, which emerged as the largest group but lacked a majority. Backed by the fifty-nine-member Communist-led Left Front, which forewent cabinet posts, the Congress Party led a coalition government under the title of the United Progressive Alliance (UPA), with Manmohan Singh as the prime minister.

The Singh government's dependence on the Left Front led it to balance its concessions to domestic and foreign companies with measures to lift the living standards of the indigent masses. An example of the pro-poor measure was the National Rural Employment Guarantee Act, which guaranteed one hundred days of wage employment per year to every rural household. This provision proved beneficial to the bulk of the voters, and the Congress Party saw an increase in its popularity. Its share of parliamentary seats rose from 145 to 206 in the 2009 general election, with the strength of Congress-led UPA rising from 218 to 262—just ten seats short of an absolute majority. In contrast, the size of the Left Front halved to twenty-eight MPs. With a few independent MPs joining the UPA and the twenty-seven MPs of the regional Dravida Munnetra Kazhagham (Tamil: Dravidian Progressive Federation) allying with it, the incumbent Singh was released from the Left Front's pressure. As a result, his second administration turned increasingly neoliberal. The emergence of the Gandhi-led National Advisory Council, consisting of nonpartisan, pro-poor experts and functioning within the ruling circle, was a feeble alternative to the Left Front.

Therefore, affluent Indians enjoyed greater riches. The number of billionaires shot up from twenty-seven in 2008 to fifty-six in 2013. Likewise, there was an upsurge in the number of millionaires, up from 193,000 in 2009 to 248,000 in 2013. According to a study by the London-based *WealthInsight*, a financial magazine that tracks the world's rich, India's high-net-worth individuals—those possessing assets worth $1 million or more—own nearly 65 percent of the nation's $1.3 trillion in individual wealth. This is more than twice the rate for the rest of the world.[10]

The increased concentration of wealth accentuated the problem of corruption in politics and government, resulting in scams of ever greater proportions in the public as well as private sectors. The ballooning of graft was related to the ease with which money could be transferred across borders thanks to the globalization of finance and the exponential rise in the use of the informal worldwide *hawala* system. A spate of mega-scams came to light during Singh's second administration and created popular anger and disgust.

While the corruption scandals received massive publicity, what went largely unnoticed was the overall result of nearly two decades of the new economic policy. The actual number of Indians below the poverty line *rose* by 5 percent. While India accounted for one-sixth of the human race, it was home to a quarter of the global poor.[11]

In the domestic political arena, a spate of colossal corruption scams provided high-octane fuel to the opposition BJP, which launched a full-frontal assault on the government. By dithering on the introduction of a bill for an anti-corruption ombudsman, called the Lokpal, the Singh cabinet made itself doubly vulnerable. The decline in annual GDP growth to 5 percent in fiscal year 2012 (ending in March 2013), equivalent to half of the figure attained three years earlier, added to its woes. The standing of both the Congress Party and its regional ally, the Dravida Munnetra Kazhagham, plunged precipitously.

The BJP leadership combined its attacks on the government with highlights of their economic scheme, called the Gujarat Model, named after the state ruled by BJP Chief Minister Narendra Modi since 2001. The Gujarat Model was a compendium of Modi's policies and his governance style, which bordered on authoritarianism. But its exact definition was hard to fathom.

Modi's Controversial Rise

The Gujarat Model had its admirers and detractors. The former argued that the Modi government was business friendly but did not promote crony capitalism. Though Modi was all for private enterprise, he was not an out-and-out pro-marketeer. Nonetheless, all agreed that he was an ardent believer in economic freedom, which meant minimal state regulation, if any. He was also opposed to providing subsidies for food and fuel. While all governments in Gujarat, irrespective of the party label, had encouraged investment and industrial development, Modi had led the campaign for investment vigorously from the front. Under his watch, the state had enjoyed a consistent GDP expansion rate of almost 9 percent. And, given the average annual agricultural growth of 8 percent (a figure disputed by nonpartisan experts), his supporters claimed that the Gujarat Model was pro-poor.[12]

Modi's critics emphasized the favors that he had bestowed on such corporate barons as Ratan Tata and Gautam Adani. To encourage Tata Motors to relocate its Nano plant from West Bengal to Gujarat in 2008, the Modi government lent the company Rs 95.7 billion at 0.1 percent interest on its own investment of Rs 29 billion, to be repaid in monthly installments over twenty years.[13] In 2005, it began extending to the Adani Group thirty-year renewable leases on twenty-eight square miles (7,350 hectares) of land at 1¢ to 45¢ per square meter, to be used for the Adani Port and Special Economic Zone, the largest Special Economic Zone in India. Adani then subleased parts of this land to other companies for as much as $11 per square meter.[14] In addition, the Modi government bent all the rules to award the Adani Group a lucrative contract for supplying electricity, resulting in an estimated loss of Rs 23.63 billion over twenty-five years to the public treasury.[15] As for helping the needy, among India's large states, Gujarat had the worst record in implementing the National Rural Employment Guarantee Act.[16]

The 2014 poll shaped up as a contest between the Congress Party's vice president, Rahul Gandhi, the Cambridge University–educated son of Rajiv and Sonia, and Modi, the prime ministerial nominee of the BJP. A management consultant by training, the forty-three-year-old Gandhi, a scion of the

Nehru-Gandhi family, lacked administrative and organizational skills. In stark comparison, Modi, the son of a tea seller in Vadnagar, a small town in North Gujarat, was a self-made politician who had been the chief minister of Gujarat since 2001.

Modi was an ardent Hindu nationalist, having joined the Hindu chauvinist organization Rashtriya Swayamsevak Sangh (Sanskrit: National Volunteer Union, or RSS) as a child of eight. In his teens, he helped his elder brother run a tea stall near the local bus stop, a fact he would highlight during the 2014 election campaign, reveling in the moniker of *chaiwalla* (Hindi: tea seller) to emphasize his humble origin—an electoral asset. In 1970, at the age of twenty, he became a full-time *pracharak* (Hindi: campaigner) of the RSS in Ahmedabad. He obtained an extramural degree in political science through distance learning from Delhi University in 1978. Five years later, he acquired a master's degree in political science from Gujarat University. In 1985, RSS leaders assigned him to the BJP, the then five-year-old political arm of the RSS. He rose through the ranks. As the party's secretary in Gujarat, he devised the strategy for the state election in 1995 that led to its victory. He was promoted to general secretary of the organization at the BJP's central office in Delhi three years later. This gave him nationwide exposure, and as a skilled organizer he shored up the party's fortunes in several states. At the same time, he masterminded the election strategy in Gujarat that led to the BJP's win in 1998. As a top party official, he was in tune with the BJP-led government's neoliberal policies.[17] When Gujarat's chief minister Keshubhai Patel decided to step down due to failing health in October 2001, Modi was parachuted in to succeed him by the party's national leaders. Given his Spartan lifestyle, he soon established himself as incorruptible, in contrast to his predecessor.

On February 27, 2002, a railway coach carrying Hindu devotees and their families returning from a pilgrimage to the holy city of Ayodhya caught fire just after leaving the railroad station of Godhra in North Gujarat, incinerating fifty-eight people, including thirty-five women and children. Because of an earlier altercation between a Muslim group and the Hindu travelers at the station, Muslims were immediately blamed for the deaths.

The fire triggered widespread violence and rioting in Gujarat, with the Muslims in Ahmedabad bearing the brunt. After the initial bloodletting, with included arson and the destruction of Muslim shops, intermittent violence continued for more than two months. Altogether, 790 to 2,000 Muslims lost their lives, as did 254 Hindus, with 223 people reported missing.[18]

More than five hundred mosques and prayer halls were damaged, while seventeen temples suffered the same fate. Nearly 61,000 Muslims and 10,000 Hindus lost their homes.[19] "Official statistics provided in June by the Police Department, now under new administration [that is, a new commissioner who, as a member of the central Indian Police Service, gets appointed or transferred by the Home Ministry in Delhi], show that the State of Gujarat, governed solely by the Bharatiya Janata Party, failed to take elementary steps to halt the horrific momentum of violence," reported Celia W. Dugger in the *New York Times*. "The day after the train attack, police officers here in Ahmedabad did not arrest a single person from among the tens of thousands who rampaged through Muslim enclaves, raping and looting as well as burning alive of 124 Muslims."[20] When asked if he wished he had handled the riots any differently, Modi told Dugger that his greatest regret was not handling the media better. In her interview, recorded on a videocassette, Dugger remarked that Modi did not show "any regret or [express] any empathy for those who had been slaughtered in his State, on his watch."[21]

Modi lost his moral standing in Britain, the European Union, and the United States. They cut off all official contacts with his government. His application for a diplomatic visa in March 2005 was rejected by the United States, which also revoked his existing tourist and business visa. Katrina Lantos Swett, vice chairwoman of the U.S. Commission on International Religious Freedom, explained that this was a forensically researched decision based on questions about Modi's level of involvement in the 2002 communal violence in Gujarat.[22] And yet, in Gujarat, under Modi's leadership, the BJP improved its majority in the State Assembly by ten seats, raising the total to 127 seats in the December 2002 poll.

To refurbish the tarnished image of his state, Modi hit upon the idea of holding a summit of investors in Ahmedabad. The first such event, called Vibrant Gujarat, was convened in September 2003. The government claimed that seventy-six memorandums of understanding, worth $14 billion, were signed.[23] Vibrant Gujarat became a biennial feature and received wide and favorable coverage in the media. It provided Modi a highly publicized opportunity to woo Big Business, a move that would pay him a handsome political dividend a decade later.

At the third Vibrant Gujarat summit in January 2007, focused on the state's thirty-three Special Economic Zones and attended by the CEOs of such corporations as the Tata Group, Reliance Industries, Adani Group, ICICI Bank, Royal Dutch Shell, and General Motors, officials announced the signing of memorandums of understanding worth $152 billion. Brothers Mukesh and Anil Ambani (the richest and third-richest resident Indians), Ratan Tata, and Gautam Adani competed with one another in praising Modi for the speed and predictability of obtaining clearances and permits for their projects from his administration. There was no mention of the sale of the state's wasteland at nominal prices to large corporations as well as the government's generous soft loans.[24]

The ghost of Godhra and the anti-Muslim riots continued to haunt Modi. Its latest iteration was a petition to the Supreme Court in 2006 submitted by Zakia Jafri, the widow of Ehsan Jafri, a Congress MP who, along with sixty-eight others, was burned to death in a housing complex in Ahmedabad[25] because of the deliberate negligence of the local police. It argued that by failing to act swiftly to stop communal riots Modi failed to discharge his constitutional duty. In March 2008, the Supreme Court formed a Special Investigation Team, chaired by R.K. Raghavan, a former director of the Central Bureau of Investigation, to probe Jafri's claim. In April 2009, responding to another petition by Jafri that claimed Modi and another minister had been complicit in the killing of her husband and sixty-eight others, the Supreme Court instructed the Special Investigation Team to investigate her complaint. Almost a year passed before they got around to questioning Modi. In its report to the Supreme Court in May 2010, the team stated that it found no evidence to substantiate the allegations against Modi. A salient reason for this conclusion was that in the intervening eight years a good deal of hard evidence had been lost or deliberately destroyed. On September 12, 2011, the Supreme Court announced that it would cease monitoring the case, since a constitutional issue was no longer involved. It transferred the file to the local magistrate's court in Ahmedabad.

Welcoming the news, Modi tweeted, "Allah is great," and announced a three-day fast as a gesture of reconciliation with the Muslim community.[26] The start of his fast on September 15, his sixty-first birthday, marked the launching of his campaign to become BJP's prime ministerial candidate.

The Special Investigation Team submitted its final report, absolving Modi of any wrongdoing, to the local court in March 2012. Jafri immediately filed a protest petition. While the fate of her petition remained undecided, the British government reversed its stance on Modi. In October, British High Commissioner Sir James Bevan met Modi to "explore opportunities for closer co-operation."[27] Two months later, the BJP won 116 seats out of 182 in the Gujarat Assembly elections. With that, the chance of Modi being named as the party's prime ministerial candidate improved. All the same, to clear his name at the national level, he found a way of wriggling out of taking responsibility for what had happened under his watch by offering an inappropriate analogy. "If someone else is driving a car, and we are sitting in the backseat, if a puppy ends up under the wheels would it be a sad thing or not?" he remarked in his interview with Reuters in July 2013. "Of course it would. . . . If something bad happens somewhere, it is natural to be sad."[28]

On September 13, Modi was adopted as the BJP's prime ministerial candidate. In late December, the Ahmedabad magistrate's court rejected Jafri's protest petition and agreed with the conclusion of the Special Investigation Team that there was no evidence against Modi in the case. This opened the door for the United States to reestablish official contact with him. U.S. Ambassador Nancy Powell met him in Gandhinagar on February 13, 2014. "The meeting was part of the U.S. mission's outreach to senior leaders of India's major political parties in advance of the upcoming national elections," stated the U.S. Embassy in Delhi.[29]

By then Modi was in the thick of electioneering for the Lok Sabha, the Lower House of Parliament.

An Electoral Battle like No Other

"Mission 272 Plus"—referring to the number of seats the BJP needed to win an outright majority in the Lok Sabha—was waged with an extraordinary combination of precision and thoroughness. The campaign combined extensive use of social media with traditional advertising in a way that forged party leaders, cadres, volunteers, and professional advisers into a seamless and formidable whole. Accomplishing the titanic task of appealing to 814 million voters in 543 constituencies required enormous sums of money, which Big Business eagerly poured into the party's coffers. Centered around Modi, dubbed the Chief Executive Officer of India Inc., this meticulously planned exercise would engender the most egregious personality cult in independent India. Modi's visage—with his neatly trimmed white beard, receding white hairline, and rimless spectacles—became ubiquitous.

Having suffered two successive defeats at the polls, BJP leaders installed an IT cell at its head office in Delhi in 2010. It became known as the National Digital Operations Cell, or N-Doc. It established a database of nearly one million people who had, over the years, contacted the party across various platforms. To make the best use of these potential foot soldiers, N-Doc focused on 155 urban constituencies, labeled "digital seats," which could be won by deploying a large cyber army. Five thousand volunteers were assigned to each constituency. They were turned into campaigners, equipped with party badges, Modi caps, and T-shirts, ID cards, pamphlets, and voter lists on their cell phones, which would later be installed with a ringtone proclaiming "*Modi Aane Wala Hai*" (Hindi: Modi is set to come). In addition to canvassing, these volunteers—most of them RSS members—were deployed to collect donations for the "Modi for PM" fund and to coax undecided voters, often in informal discussions over tea.[30] Party strategists were confident that above-average voter participation would favor the BJP. This would indeed turn out to be the case. The record 66 percent voter turnout exceeded the historic average of 55 percent by 11 percentage points. With most of the new votes going to the BJP, it was handed an absolute majority in the Lok Sabha in the first-past-the-pole electoral system. (Nonetheless, the overall vote for the BJP was only 31 percent, which was 2 percent less than its score in 2009.)

In these 155 constituencies, the BJP central office sought and secured the assistance of nonresident Indians living in the United States and other Western nations who were members of the Overseas Friends of the BJP. It received substantial backing from the four-thousand-strong Overseas Friends corps in America. According to its president, Chandrakant Patel, the Overseas Friends had hired volunteers, half of whom would fly to India to campaign for the BJP in their native constituencies. "The others will make/send at least 200 calls and SMSes every day from the U.S." The Overseas Friends had received voter lists of these urban constituencies from the BJP central office in Delhi.[31] Since the relatives and friends of nonresident Indians were invariably middle or upper-middle class, the nonresidents' calls from the United States helped to reduce the abstention rate among such voters who by and large considered politics a dirty business and often did not bother to vote.

Between January and the end of April 2014, the eighteen chapters of Overseas Friends in the United States organized over two hundred Narendra Modi tea parties. One such assembly in mid-February, at an Indian tea stall in Ortega Park in Silicon Valley's Sunnyvale, drew sixty professionals working for such IT behemoths as Microsoft, Apple, Oracle, and eBay. The ostensible subject under discussion was the role of technology in improving governance in India.[32] The Indian employees of eBay, which was founded by Pierre Omidyar, had a particular interest in such a meeting. They knew that Jayant Sinha, a fellow nonresident Indian, had resigned his partnership in the Omidyar Network, a philanthropic investment firm with assets of $730 million, and returned to India. He had done so with the intention of winning a seat in the Lok Sabha as the BJP candidate. He was the son of Yashwant Sinha, who was finance minister under BJP Prime Minister Atal Bihari Vajpayee from 1998 to 2002.

Before joining the Omidyar Network, the balding, portly, fifty-year-old Jayant Sinha served as the managing director of Courage Capital, a hedge fund. He had acquired that position after twelve years of service with McKinsey & Company, a multinational management consultancy, where he rose to become a partner. Earlier, he had capped his undergraduate degree from the Indian Institute of Technology in Delhi with an MBA from Harvard Business School.

After his return to India in January 2014, Sinha worked with Ajit Kumar Doval—the founder of the Vivekananda International Foundation, a think tank affiliated with the ultranationalist Rashtriya Swayamsevak Sangh—to organize a closed-door meeting between Modi and Indian and foreign investors and leading infrastructure companies and banks on February 27. The scramble for invitations became so acute that he and Doval froze the list at 250 participants a week before the meeting, which by then included Morgan Stanley, JP Morgan, the London-based Nomura Investment Bank, and Credit Lyonnais Securities Asia.[33]

Modi's words at this meeting had a tonic effect on Big Business at home and foreign institutional investors abroad. On February 28, the Indian bourses' barometer, the National Stock Exchange Index, crossed the 21,000 benchmark, closing at 21,120, its highest level in five weeks. This was an early and unmistakable sign that Big Business was backing Modi.

With Yashwant Sinha pulling the strings, the BJP's central leadership adopted Jayant Sinha as the party's candidate for the constituency hitherto represented by him in the eastern state of Jharkhand. It overruled the objections of local BJP activists critical of Jayant Sinha's twenty-seven-year absence from India while he advanced his technocratic career in the United States.[34] To overcome the resistance of party workers, Sinha discarded his Western business suits for a long saffron shirt and pajamas as he canvassed for votes in the countryside.

Riding the Modi wave nationwide, he won the contest with a majority of 159,000 votes and was appointed a junior minister of finance. And, within months of Modi becoming the prime minister in May, Jeff Bezos,

Satya Nadella, and Mark Zuckerberg—the respective CEOs of Amazon, Microsoft, and Facebook—would visit Delhi and meet Modi.[35]

Modi's speeches drew huge rallies between mid-September 2013 and May 12, 2014. During this period, he addressed 457 rallies in twenty-five states. Each venue was selected with great care; each speech was given all-India exposure. As Modi spoke (in Hindi), a member of the N-Doc IT cell relayed the telecast live on the BJP's YuvaiTV. The N-Doc team in Delhi edited the speech in small clips for YouTube and tweeted Modi's key statements. The speech could also be heard live on cell phones through an automated number for a nominal fee. In addition, Modi addressed eight hundred rallies in hologram, where his lifelike performance was greeted by the audience with awe and disbelief.[36]

The content of each of Modi's speeches was tailored to each audience he addressed. N-Doc asked all new volunteers to write what they wanted Modi to do as the prime minister. This information was then passed along to two dozen researchers in Gandhinagar, Gujarat's capital, who prepared material for each of Modi's addresses. Over time, a standard format of the Modi speech emerged, driven by a wish to appeal to the highest number of his listeners. It started by praising the people of the region, referring to their glorious past. Then followed a few lines in the regional non-Hindi language. After that, Modi turned to local problems, contrasting the audience's struggles with the great achievements of the BJP-ruled states—Gujarat, Madhya Pradesh, and Chhattisgarh. He lambasted the poor performance of the Congress-led government in Delhi. "Congress and corruption are twin sisters" was Modi's favorite one-liner. Another was "We want a Skilled India, but Congress has created a Scam India in ten years." Modi set the agenda, hammering away his primary theme that good governance and development were the two issues on which his party was fighting these elections, while studiously avoiding communal tensions. "Give me a strong government, I'll give you a strong India," he would shout, to thunderous applause.[37]

In stark contrast, the Congress Party campaign, fronted by Rahul Gandhi, was hackneyed and confused. Late in the day, its organizers realized the electoral potential of social media. Even then, their exploitation of this avenue boiled down to highlighting parts of the party's election manifesto. They lacked a scheme to build and convert the people in their database into active canvassers.

Overall, the size and passion of the Congress Party rallies lagged behind the BJP's. Rahul Gandhi was no match for Modi's oratory in Hindi. He failed to feel the pulse of the masses. His organizational skills were poor. He was widely described as inept. Though neither he nor Manmohan Singh was corrupt, the stench of the mega-graft scandals of the Congress-led government was too overpowering to be countered by their personal integrity. As if these handicaps were not enough to put the Congress Party at a severe disadvantage, it found itself overwhelmed by the BJP's advertising avalanche. The BJP rented 1,500 billboards across the country for three months at the cost of Rs 25 billion ($500 million). It bought the most prominent advertising slots in fifty top national and regional newspapers and filled them with four to five daily advertisements until the end of the election, at the cost of Rs 5 billion ($100 million). The budget for magazines was Rs 1.5 billion ($30 million). The TV advertising budget of Rs 10 billion ($200 million) was used to buy 2,000 spots per day across the Hindi, English, and regional news, general entertainment, and sports channels.[38]

According to a media planner at Madison World, which managed BJP's advertising account, "Planned spends on all media, including print, television, outdoor, internet and radio would be close to Rs 4,500 crore [$900 million]. The party has set aside additional Rs 500 crore [$100 million], which would be used, depending on the need to shore up the campaign in critical constituencies and states in the last few days of campaigning." In marked contrast, a senior BJP leader claimed that his party would spend Rs 7.5 to 8 billion ($150 to $160 million) on advertising. The media planner at Madison World added, "The strategy, apart from carpet bombing voters with the BJP's message, is to block out all other political parties across the print, television, online and offline media irrespective of cost."[39] Little wonder that according to the Centre for Media Studies, Modi received 7.5 times more TV coverage than Rahul Gandhi.[40]

Apparently, BJP leaders, advised by some of the best Indian brains in public relations, made an astute use of the billions of rupees that filled their party's coffers. By outspending their Congress rivals by an estimated 4:1 ratio, they achieved an end-result variously described as a political tsunami, a peaceful revolution, and a democratic asteroid.

A Political Tsunami

The BJP surpassed its "Mission 272 Plus" by eight seats, increasing its size nearly two-and-a-half fold. With the junior members of the BJP-led National

Democratic Alliance (NDA) gaining 54 seats, the winning coalition had the backing of 334 MPs. The victors were jubilant, describing the result as a tectonic shift that marked the end of the politics of the Nehru-Gandhi dynasty and the birth of an era of initiative and accomplishment.

Notably, the BJP did not have a single Muslim MP,[41] nor did any of its NDA partners.[42] Of the twenty-three cabinet ministers, seventeen had their roots in the Rashtriya Swayamsevak Sangh.[43] Only one of the ministers, Najma Heptullah, was Muslim. A member of the Rajya Sabha, the Upper House of Parliament, she was elected by the State Assembly of Madhya Pradesh. On assuming her post as Minister of Minority Affairs, she declared that Muslims were not a minority and that they were not entitled to welfare, which the Congress-led government had granted them.[44]

The hammer blow to the Congress Party reduced its strength to forty-four, nine short of the minimum required to be named the official opposition—an excruciatingly humiliating status for a party that had ruled independent India for four-fifths of its sixty-seven-year history.

Predictably, the stock markets were euphoric. Over the previous two months they had been rising strongly in anticipation of the Modi victory. On May 16, when the victory became reality, Sensex, the Mumbai benchmark stock exchange index, ended at an all-time high of 24,121. Over the previous six months, foreign investors had poured more than $16 billion into Indian stocks and bonds, taking the total to almost $280 billion and raising their stake in Mumbai-listed equities to 22 percent. This strengthened the Indian rupee, which closed below Rs 59 to US$1, an eleven-month high.[45]

Given Modi's promise to support the construction of roads, ports, and power plants, the infrastructure companies were particularly bullish. But that sentiment also spread to the real estate sector, which had turned bearish as the annual GDP growth rate slipped below 5 percent. Reversing the long-established upward trend, the property prices in the thriving National Capital Region declined by 8 percent in 2013 compared to the previous year. The rent for a three-bedroom apartment had fallen by 7 percent during 2013.[46] Besides the Union Territory of Delhi, the National Capital Region comprised the fast-expanding satellite towns of Gurgaon, in Haryana, and Noida and Greater Noida, in Uttar Pradesh. Noticing the sharp fall in the popularity of the Congress-led coalition government, Rao Inderjit Singh, the MP for Gurgaon and a veteran Congress leader who had served as a cabinet minister in Delhi, resigned from his party and joined the BJP in September 2013. He got reelected as a BJP stalwart and found a seat in the Modi administration as a junior minister.

Gurgaon was the undisputed leader of the satellite settlements around Delhi that had emerged in the wake of the impressive economic expansion during 2006–11. It was a clear favorite with the Indian information and communication technology experts returning from the United States and Britain.

1

Gurgaon: Shining City with a Dark Underbelly

"Westin," reads a massive sign embossed on a curling, multistory building, its white exterior shining in the sun, as the visitor approaches Gurgaon. The word is mysterious and oddly alluring. Is it the name of an IT corporation? Or a glitzy shopping mall? Neither. It turns out to be the name of a five-star luxury hotel of the Starboard chain, still in its infancy. Aside from its aluminum-foiled appearance, its unique feature—as I would discover later—is to offer rooms that cater specifically to the single woman traveler on a corporate expense account. Located near the elevators to minimize the distance a guest has to walk, these marble-floored rooms are furnished with special makeup tables inside spacious bathrooms. To ensure additional safety to women occupants, these rooms are serviced exclusively by female staff.

Gurgaon is New India in miniature, with all its achievements and failures. A close study of the Poster City reveals a mismatch between the glacial and corrupt bureaucracy and the vibrant private sector. It provides ample evidence to show how a nexus of public officials and predatory businesspeople distort or torpedo welfare measures passed by lawmakers in response to popular demand. It is a city where a boom in land and property values sits oddly with lackadaisical advances in public services and infrastructure. Above all, the relentless drive to build residential and commercial properties is being exploited blatantly to turn illicit gains into legitimate earnings. This ploy has come in handy not only to resident entrepreneurs but also to an expanding body of nonresident Indians, mainly in the United States and Britain.[1]

But scrape the surface ever so slightly and you discover a dark, Dickensian underbelly. Gurgaon claims the third-highest per-capita income in India. Yet

21

an unskilled worker there earns about a third less than in Pune, a provincial city in the state of Maharashtra. A typical corporate executive working for a Western multinational in Gurgaon has seen his or her salary raised fivefold in as many years, while the wages of his or her housemaid have remained frozen. The affluent in this boomtown are not sharing their phenomenal gains with the underclass. A worker in a clothing factory earns Rs 2,500 ($50) a month, whereas the average monthly paycheck of a CEO of a multinational is Rs 600,000 ($12,000). The differential of 240:1 between the highest and the lowest incomes verges on the obscene. The benefits of the boom have gone to those at the top and the middle, leaving the bottom stagnating.

Plotting the trajectory of Gurgaon from a minor provincial town to a thriving city of 1.5 million yields a rich mine of insights that can be applied to India as a whole. The principal one is the mismatch between the traditional sloth and corruption of government officials and the energetic drive of the private sector in search of higher profits. The next in importance is the explosive rise in the value of land and residential and commercial property which sits uneasily with the lackluster progress in infrastructure and public services. At the root of this development is the upsurge in construction due to accelerated urbanization and the rising living standards of the middle classes. The phenomenal growth in construction has enabled the dishonest to turn their ill-gotten fortunes into legitimate wealth easily and on a much larger scale. The news of a dramatic upsurge in property values in urban areas started attracting a growing number of nonresident Indians to invest in real estate at home, particularly after the 2007–8 banking crash in the West, which drastically depressed share prices in Western bourses.

Metamorphosis of Old Gurgaon

From a small, nondescript town, surrounded by half a dozen villages, Gurgaon (Hindi: village of guru) has come a long way in two decades. The twelve-fold population growth to the present 1.5 million is only a minor part of its meteoric rise. Today, it is the Indian headquarters of such multinationals as Coca-Cola, Pepsi, Honda, Ericsson, and Nestlé. It has more neon-lit malls with multiplex cinema screens per square mile than any other Indian city. It has been garlanded with such titles as the Millennium City, the Showcase City, and the Skyscraper City. While the first sobriquet is time-bound, and the second far too self-glorifying, the last one is a concrete fact that no pair of eyes can deny. More than just the number of residential tower blocks, rising ever higher, that have mushroomed, it is the variety of architecture in this ever-expanding sprawl that awes and intrigues the visitor.

The DLF Gateway Tower—the gleaming settlement's landmark near the eight-lane toll plaza at the Delhi-Haryana border—is hard to miss. A twenty-story cylindrical structure of tinted glass and concrete with a sideways slice at the top, it resembles a giant half-smoked cigarette. Equally ostentatious is the nearby Leela Kempinski Hotel, a slim rectangular structure, rounded at one end, with its rooms overlooking the lush Rajokri Gardens of Delhi. These turn out to be exceptional—most of Gurgaon's skyscrapers look like concrete weeds sprouting from the soil, often unpainted eyesores. But here and there is an eight- or nine-story structure embellished with a colorful façade, capped with a curvaceous white umbrella, and fronted by lawns, shrubs, and elegant palm trees.

Among the corporations, the Cyber City office of Ernst & Young India Limited—specializing in assurance and tax transactions—is iconic. Set amid vast green lawns, the bland monotony broken by irregular pools of clear water, it is a multistory, transparent structure. Consisting of seven elliptical floors, the tinted-glass building is designed to provide shade during certain hours of the day as determined precisely by its latitude and longitude. This is achieved by extending the floor plates as they go up in order to shield the floor directly below from the intensity of direct sunlight. The strikingly innovative design enables indirect sunlight to create the ideal reflected lighting during office hours, thus eliminating the need for artificial lighting and reducing energy consumption.

Aircel, a cell-phone operator, makes its presence felt even by a casual visitor. A huge AIRCEL sign—white letters against a blue background and topped by its logo of three expanding brackets symbolizing soundwaves—is painted on a slanting concrete slab that bridges the pavement of National Highway 8 and the top of a multistory office, and it leaves a lasting impression even when viewed from a speeding car or auto-rickshaw.

Contrary to its title, the DLF Square is not a square in the conventional sense. It is the name of a vertical building ninety meters (ninety-eight yards) high, its twenty-two floors encased between four robust pillars, with walls made of large square blocks of black plastic. It is home to many company offices.

The term "DLF" is seen and heard so often that it has become part of daily discourse in Gurgaon, identified as easily by a corporate CEO as a rickshaw puller. The name DLF Limited evolved in 2006 after a series of changes.

Formed from two tributaries—the Delhi Land and Finance Limited, established in 1946, and American Universal Electric (India) Limited, established in 1963—this soon-to-be gigantic corporate entity was unveiled as DLF Universal Electric Limited in 1979, then as DLF Universal Limited two years later. Now DLF Limited operates through a maze of some forty subsidiaries, one of which is the DLF New Gurgaon Homes Development Private Limited.

A Multilayered Saga of the DLF

With an annual turnover of Rs 97,900 million ($1.48 billion) in 2013–14, a market value of nearly Rs 275,000 million ($4.17 billion), and an estimated land bank of 17,450 acres in thirty-two cities, DLF is the world's largest listed real estate corporation. (The average agricultural landholding of an Indian is 3.3 acres.)[2] With its initial public offer (IPO) in May 2007 covering only 13 percent of its shares, the vast bulk of the equity was held by its chairman, Kushal Pal Singh, and his family. The oversubscribed IPO won Singh—looking dapper in his well-cut suits with the trademark maroon silk kerchief in his breast pocket—a much-coveted write-up in *Time* magazine. The post-IPO surge in share value made him the globe's wealthiest property owner in 2008. In 2011, according to *Forbes*, he was India's eleventh-richest person, with an estimated net worth of $7.3 billion in 2010. In October 2014, the Securities and Exchange Board of India found DLF guilty of not properly disclosing to investors material information about certain subsidiaries at the time of its IPO, and it banned the company and six of its executives, including Singh, from accessing the capital market for three years. This verdict caused a 28 percent decrease in DLF share prices in one day. Despite this, DLF remained the country's most valuable listed real-estate corporation.[3]

Born in Bulandshahr, Uttar Pradesh, in 1931 into a Hindu family of lawyers and army officers, the tall, athletic, square-jawed Kushal Pal Singh started his career as a commissioned officer in the Indian Army, following his education in aeronautical engineering in Britain. He then tried his hand at manufacturing before turning to real-estate development.

The stratospheric rise of Singh is more than just another story of a novice businessman joining the billionaire's club. It highlights the runaway expansion of the construction industry which, along with the information technology and telecommunication sector and the business process outsourcing sector, has been the main engine of India's rip-roaring economic growth over the past decade.[4] A critical examination of Singh's success lays bare the anatomy of modern India: galloping corruption in the public and private sectors; the nexus between politicians and businesspeople, and their ill-disguised chicanery; the ballooning of underground black money; the growing role of nonresident Indians as independent agents in transforming black money into white by investing in residential and commercial property in India; and the rapid widening of inequality among Indians at home.

The founder of Delhi Land and Finance Company, in 1946, was Singh's father-in-law, Chaudhary Raghvendra Singh, a former civil servant. Like Washington, DC, India's capital is a Union territory. But whereas Washington measures sixty-eight square miles, Delhi covers 573 square miles, divided almost equally into urban and rural areas. Over the next decade after founding his company, the elder Singh bought farmland around the city and established about twenty residential colonies to satisfy the needs of the wealthy Hindu and Sikh refugees who emigrated from Pakistan after the partition of British India in 1947. A decade later, the Indian parliament passed the Delhi Development Act to ensure a planned expansion of the capital. The new Delhi Development Authority turned land development into a state monopoly. This limited DLF's business to the projects already approved or in progress before 1957.[5]

In the absence of a male child of his own, Chaudhary Raghvendra Singh persuaded his son-in-law Kushal Pal Singh, married to his elder daughter, Indira, to leave the army and enter his business, which he had renamed DLF United Limited. The young Singh did so in 1960. The next year, Kushal Pal Singh combined his American Universal Electric Company, a joint venture between Universal Electric Company of Owosso, Michigan, and the resources of the elder Singh's family, to manufacture small electrical motors. Later, his Willard India Limited collaborated with ESB Incorporated of Philadelphia to produce automobile and industrial batteries.[6]

Excluded from property development in Delhi, Chaudhary Raghvendra Singh turned his attention to the thirty acres of land he had bought in the district of Gurgaon, whose capital, Gurgaon, was identified as a satellite town in Delhi's Master Plan of 1962. But, again, his hopes were dashed. The passage of the Haryana Development and Regulation of Urban Areas Act in

1975 banned commercial development of agricultural land. The main reason for this was to maintain India's self-sufficiency in food. The law placed the authority for urban development and regulation into the hands of the Haryana Urban Development Authority.

Advised by his father-in-law, a despondent Kushal Pal Singh prepared to sign a share transfer form. "Just as I got ready to sign away my stake in DLF, Tayal [Y.S. Tayal, chief financial adviser], who was a mild-mannered person, cleared his throat and spoke," Singh writes in his autobiography *Whatever the Odds: The Incredible Story Behind DLF*. "He said, 'Once your signature is on that paper, you will lose DLF forever. So before you sign, please think about it carefully.' However, he cautioned that . . . [DLF's] financial health was extremely poor." That got Singh to reassess the situation. "[Tayal] continued: 'I will be retiring from DLF in a few weeks, so I can speak my mind freely. . . . Once all of you sign all the share transfer forms and accept the cheques, it would mean that your family will get permanently disassociated from DLF forever.'" Singh got the message. "In a flash, I realized the truth of what he was saying and the implications of giving away my DLF share-holding."[7] If he, his wife, and his sister-in-law had signed the transfer papers, they would have received Rs 4.6 million ($92,000). In late 2011, at the time of the publication of Singh's autobiography, the Singh family owned a 78.6 percent stake of DLF shares, worth Rs 269,163 million ($5.383 billion). A 58,500-fold appreciation!

In the mid-1970s, the Singh family's manufacturing firms were also not faring well. So, in 1979, it merged American Universal Electric (India) Limited with DLF United Limited to form DLF Universal Electric Limited.[8] This had only a marginal impact on the family's dwindling fortunes, so the young Singh turned to the elder Singh's land in Gurgaon district.

"I was hungry [in 1980]," Kushal Pal Singh said in his interview with *Time* magazine in 2007. "And the best things in life are done when you are hungry for more business."[9] He started acquiring small plots of farmland near his father-in-law's holdings in the way the elder Singh, lacking sufficient funds, had done: buy now and pay later, with interest—even though, at Rs 5,000 (then $625) an acre, the purchase price was modest. He was meticulous about giving interest checks to the vendors on the first of the month, without fail, which earned him the trust of farmers, who were innately suspicious of the motives of city slickers. This would provide a vital building block for Singh's future plans.

1981, a Landmark Year

The year 1981 proved to be crucial for several parties in this tale. It witnessed the bailout by the central government of Maruti Limited, a car-manufacturing company. Established in the early 1970s but bankrupt by 1977, Maruti was originally formed by Prime Minister Indira Gandhi's son, Sanjay, who died in June 1980. Scandal followed Maruti. No car was ever assembled during Sanjay Gandhi's lifetime. *India Today* called it Sanjay's "small car racket."[10] But the revived Maruti Udyog Limited started constructing its factory in Gurgaon, then home to 141,000 people. It signed a joint-venture agreement with Suzuki of Japan, who owned the bulk of the shares, and produced its first automobile in 1983, which would become the dominant brand in India's fast-expanding car market.

Deploying a variety of tactics, Kushal Pal Singh managed to expand his total farmland to 150 acres by 1981. Individual farmers were reluctant to sell their holdings, though they owned only small plots. For centuries, these farming families had relied exclusively on agriculture for their sustenance. "Convincing them to sell their land was not easy," Singh recalled many years later. "I sat with them, discussed various topics and had endless glasses of milk, tea or buttermilk. . . . Over time I virtually became a part of each family and was soon involved in settling family disputes, arranging school admissions. . . . It helped create a relationship of mutual trust and respect."[11] Since most of the farmers were Ahir Yadavs by caste, with a minority being Gujjars, they were susceptible to pressure by their caste headmen, whose loyalty could be bought. Indeed, at election time, it was customary for these leaders to haggle with different candidates to extract the maximum cash for delivering their vote banks.

On the morning of May 12, 1981, seated on a *charpoy*, a string cot, under an acacia tree next to a well, the forty-nine-year-old Singh recited his well-rehearsed set of reasons why the rural interlocutor with whom he shared the rickety charpoy should part with his land near Gurgaon. Just then, a four-wheel-drive Jeep drove up the nearby dirt track. It suddenly sputtered to a halt close to the charpoy. While the driver opened the hood to release the steam from the Jeep's overheated radiator, the sole occupant of the vehicle disembarked. A tall, handsome, well-built man, dressed immaculately in a long white shirt and tight pajamas, the passenger turned out to be Rajiv Gandhi, the elder son of the country's prime minister, Indira Gandhi. Unlike his younger brother, Sanjay, who died when a test plane he was flying crashed, Rajiv was a trained pilot with Indian Airlines. After his brother's death, he quit his job and entered politics. He got elected to parliament from Sanjay's constituency and became president of the youth wing of the ruling Congress Party. That morning, he was in the vicinity of his farmhouse on the outskirts of Mehrauli, a village midway between Gurgaon and Delhi.

Gandhi wondered aloud what Singh was doing in "a desolate place" like Mehrauli during that time of year, when hot winds blast from the desert of Rajasthan. Singh explained his purpose. Rajiv, who had heard of DLF, asked why he had not put to use the land his company already owned. The hurdle was the Haryana Development and Regulation of Urban Areas Act, replied Singh. It defined an urban area as one that included land within three miles of a municipal area and barred the use of agricultural land for nonagricultural purposes. (The way around the latter limitation was to get agricultural land reclassified as nonagricultural land by bribing the bureaucrats and/or their political masters, a strategy that Singh would have been loath to share with Rajiv Gandhi, who would later win the sobriquet of "Mr. Clean.") "Laws can be changed, right?" remarked Gandhi. "We've been trying for years now without any success," replied Singh.[12]

This was not quite correct, as a written testimony by DLF Universal Limited would later reveal. An official statement of DLF cited by the *Economic Times* read: "1981: DLF Universal Limited obtains its first license from the State Government of Haryana and commences development of the 'DLF City' in Gurgaon, Haryana." The truth lay midway between Singh's much-touted conversation with the late Rajiv Gandhi and the claim made by his company a quarter century later. Whereas DLF received its first license to build in 1981, the DLF City project, requiring three thousand acres of contiguous land, was actually launched later.

"The real challenge, however, was to acquire contiguous tracts of land from families that in some cases had thirty signatories," Singh told *Business Today* magazine in 2002. "Even if one member opposed selling the ancestral land, the deal wouldn't go through."[13] This was hardly an insurmountable problem. Over time, Singh seems to have won over the cooperation of several *patwaris* (Hindi: record keepers), the land-recording officials, and he left it to the patwaris to break the resistance of intransigent landholding villagers.

How did DLF obtain a license to build on agricultural land? "The fact that you need a license from the state government to build makes it a political decision; that's where corruption creeps in," explained Mohan Tikku to me.

A slim, gray-haired retired journalist, he had been a resident of the National Media Center in Gurgaon since 1995. "In those days [1979–85], the late Bhajan Lal was the chief minister of Haryana. Issuing a building license was at his discretion under the [lawful] discretionary powers of a chief minister.[14] He made a lot of money that way."[15]

But, for a builder, that was just the beginning. "The next stage in the process is dealing with various agencies," continued Tikku. "The town planning, the urban development, the sanitation department, the power connection, the fire safety, the water supplier, the electrical wiring safety, and so on. Each of them has to give its approval and a certificate of satisfaction, right down to the final occupation certificate. Even when the builder has met every requirement and rule, he faces bureaucratic delays. So he has to pay 'speed money'—bribe. And all bribes are in cash, which means builders have to have plenty of cash on hand. All the officials store their bribes in cash. That's how black money multiplies. In the end, the price of the building goes up. But there are plenty of buyers among those politicians and bureaucrats who have collected piles of bribe money. They are eager to turn this black cash into white money. So they buy these overpriced properties by paying mostly in cash and only partially by check. And the acquired real estate becomes a white capital asset."[16]

In other words, permitting private developers to construct residential and commercial properties in the urban areas of Haryana and elsewhere in India led to an accelerated pumping of "speed money" into the country's economy, increasing the size of the already considerable pool of underground black money. When property development was carried out by governmental or quasi-governmental organizations, there were far fewer opportunities for the ministers or bureaucrats to extract bribes from such entities.

As for politicians in general, the ones from modest households were more drawn to lucre than those from privileged families. Bhajan Lal (1930–2011), a stout, snub-nosed, jowly-faced man with metal-frame glasses and a golden yellow turban, was born into a humble rural family. He started his political career as president of a village council, or *panchayat*. He reached the pinnacle of power in Haryana as the leader of the anti-Congress Janata Party when he was forty-nine. He defected to the Congress Party of Indira Gandhi after she returned to power in Delhi in 1980. In Rajiv Gandhi, her only surviving son, Bhajan Lal saw a rising political star. Given Kushal Pal Singh's access to Rajiv, Bhajan Lal was overly generous to the DLF, particularly when it meant filling his pockets with backhanders.

DLF forged ahead so long as Bhajan Lal remained the chief executive in Haryana, until July 1985. Tellingly, DLF's official account describes 1985 as the year when the company initiated "plotted developments"—the first such plot being in Gurgaon—and consolidated the development of DLF City as a township. By then, following the assassination of Indira Gandhi in October 1984, forty-year-old Rajiv Gandhi had become the prime minister. He was intent on smoothing the path for the companies such as DLF to enter the lucrative urban property market.

However, a hurdle appeared for DLF in the person of Bansi Lal, who succeeded Bhajan Lal. A slim, bespectacled man with a receding hairline and a bulbous nose in an oval visage, Bansi Lal was a veteran politician. It was he who had shepherded the 1975 Haryana Development and Regulation of Urban Areas Act through the state assembly. He was incensed to discover how his predecessor had mangled the law to favor DLF and other private developers. *India Today* magazine reported in May 1986 that Bhajan Lal's government had "twisted the law in every possible way" in giving licenses for more than 4,150 acres in Gurgaon to private realtors. Further details appeared in the *Times of India* on August 16. Using his discretionary powers, Bhajan Lal had issued more than five hundred building licenses to private developers, including DLF, Ansal Housing and Construction Limited, and Unitech Group. He did so by shredding the rules laid out in the 1975 Act and by neglecting to verify the companies' claimed ownership of land, which they often started buying *after* getting the licenses.[17]

Bansi Lal canceled 189 building licenses, including many of DLF's. Singh appealed to Rajiv Gandhi to intervene, which he did. But, confident of his support among the state's lawmakers, Bansi Lal ignored the prime minister's advice. For the two years that he was the chief executive in Haryana, DLF was forced to hibernate.

By contrast, Bansi Lal, a committed progressive, vigorously pursued the long-established policy of encouraging the formation of group housing societies or cooperatives to build residences. One such organization was the National Media Center housing cooperative, formed in 1982 by journalists, academics, doctors, and artists. It bought twenty-two acres of land from the inhabitants of Nathupur village, on the outskirts of Gurgaon. It was under Bansi Lal's watch that the foundation stone was laid for the center in 1986.[18]

In Chandigarh, the capital of Haryana, Bansi Lal's six successors were political lightweights who altogether lasted a mere four years in office. This instability enabled Singh's DLF to accelerate the building of DLF City on the three thousand acres it had managed to acquire while still meeting the legal obligation regarding the economically weaker sections of the community. "The Haryana law requires that any building project by a private company must reserve 20 percent of the housing for the economically weaker sections of society," explained Tikku. "That meant constructing one-room tenements costing Rs 20,000 ($400). The idea was to provide decent accommodation to domestic servants, sweepers, rickshaw pullers, guards, peons, messengers, and the like. Given the large size of the economically weaker sections in Gurgaon, the authorities resorted to a lottery. The likes of DLF and Ansal lost no time to approach the lottery winners with cash. They were temped and sold their rights to realtors."[19] Thus DLF and other leading private developers succeeded in defeating the egalitarian intentions of the state government. (This pattern recurs with other welfare measures on the statute books, as subsequent chapters will show.) The realtors combined these small plots and built multistory tower blocks. Prices shot up. They enjoyed a bonanza, as did the original landowners, though on a more modest scale. The latter built two-story tenements on the land they retained and rented them out to the menials and migrant workers from other states.

With Rajiv Gandhi as the prime minister in Delhi, DLF's prospectus brightened as never before.

Rajiv Gandhi, the Early Liberalizer

As an engineering student in Cambridge and London for five years, followed by a twelve-year stint as an airline pilot, Rajiv Gandhi maintained his interest in technology and modernization. His marriage to Antonia (Sonia) Maino, an Italian Catholic, further helped Westernize his thinking and behavior. As a result, he was more open to loosening the thirty-year-old framework of centralized economic planning that he inherited. He made cautious moves in that direction.

He increased support for science, technology, and associated industries by cutting taxes and tariffs on computers, aircraft, and defense and telecommunication equipment. "The telecom revolution, the precursor to the IT revolution that has done so much to boost India's economy and its reputation, took place [under Rajiv Gandhi]," noted economist Ramgopal Agarwala, a former World Bank official, in his interview with Mark Tully, a British journalist living in Delhi. During his time, "there was also some relaxation of the [bu-reaucratic] License-Permit Raj, and plans to relax its grip further had been drawn up too."[20] Agarwala's assessment was shared by many industrialists and businesspeople. "Economic liberalization started in 1988," recalled Deepak Jolly, the burly public relations vice president of Coca-Cola, in Gurgaon. "Small changes happened from 1988 to 1991, like a public sector company could be privatized 100 percent."[21]

Among those who benefited from the Indian government's relaxed import policies was Kushal Pal Singh. His company was able to import some parts for a 1,678-mile gas pipeline being built by GAIL (India) Limited from General Electric (GE) Company, a labyrinthine conglomerate and the sixth-largest corporation in the United States, with a presence in more than one hundred countries. That in turn led to Singh's introduction to Jack Welch, the tall, balding, narrow-eyed CEO of GE, in New York in 1986, and Singh's subsequent appointment as GE's national adviser in India. It was in that capacity that Singh organized Welch's first trip to India in 1989. On that trip, Welch met Rajiv Gandhi.[22] Though Rajiv Gandhi's Congress Party lost the general election in November 1989, his two successors, who altogether served for only a year and a half, left intact his policy of welcoming Western corporations and favoring the private sector.

Post-Rajiv Economic Deregulation

Rajiv Gandhi's assassination during the run-up to the general election in May 1991 shook international investor confidence in India. His plans for further economic liberalization after his expected electoral success fell by the wayside. The Congress Party leadership passed to seventy-year-old P.V. Narasimha Rao. A bald, square-jawed, plump man of medium height, often dressed in a long shirt and dhoti, he was a contrast to Rajiv Gandhi in more ways than one. A lawyer by training, he had been a politician all his life. His formidable parliamentary skills helped him to complete the full five-year tenure of his office as prime minister even though his party was twenty-seven seats short of majority in the Lower House.

Within a month of his assumption of supreme power, his government found that the country's reserves in foreign currencies would barely cover imports for one month. He approached the International Monetary Fund for a major bailout. In return for this emergency aid, his administration agreed to devalue the Indian rupee by one-fifth and reform the economy at a brisker pace. This new economic policy of liberalization, privatization, and globalization was introduced in July 1991.

To Kushal Pal Singh's profound delight, Bhajan Lal returned as Haryana's chief minister in the same month that Rao assumed office, a post that Lal would hold for the next five years. This was the golden period of DLF, when Chaudhary Raghvendra Singh's jocular quip that "DLF stands for Damn Lucky Fellow" was transformed into a phenomenal business reality. With land prices spiraling upward, Kushal Pal Singh decided to abandon the construction of stand-alone townhouses and instead started building residential tower blocks. DLF completed its first condominium project, called Silver Oaks, in DLF City. It contained six hundred apartments. Singh's penchant for British names could be attributed to the few years he had spent in Britain as a student, but he was not the only realtor slavishly adopting such British or American monikers. Residential buildings sprouted up with names like Beverly Hills, Hamilton Court, Manhattan Apartments, Regency Park, West End Heights, and Windsor Place, and there were new office blocks called Royalton Towers, Icon Pinnacle, Plaza Tower, and Gateway Tower. In 1993, Singh's standing in the corporate world was as high as the fifteen-story Silver Oaks. At GE's headquarters in Fairfield, Connecticut, he was promoted to a member of the corporation's International Advisory Board, a position that would help propel his company to a higher plane.

As trade liberalization gathered pace after the formation of the World Trade Organization (WTO) in 1995, it became easier to transfer illicit funds abroad. In 2010, the publication of the meticulously researched figures about capital outflow from India by Washington-based Global Financial Integrity (GFI) shocked the nation. According to the GFI document, entitled "The Drivers and Dynamics of Illicit Financial Flows from India: 1948–2008," illicit assets worth $462 billion were transferred out of India through tax evasion, crime, and corruption. "The report also shows that these illicit outflows contribute to stagnating levels of poverty and an ever widening gap between India's rich and poor," said GFI director Raymond Baker. Indian companies and the superrich stashed cash overseas to avoid taxes and hide ill-acquired gains, thus widening inequality and depriving the poor of crucial resources, which the government could have used to provide sorely lacking public services. "In this report we clearly demonstrate how India's underground economy is closely tied to illicit financial outflows," explained GFI lead economist and the report's author, Dev Kar, a former IMF official. "The total present value of India's illicit assets held abroad accounts for approximately 72 percent of India's underground economy." High-net-worth individuals and private companies were the primary drivers of illicit flows out of India's private sector, and the fact that 68 percent of India's total illicit capital loss occurred *after* the economic reforms of 1991 proved that deregulation and trade liberalization contributed to or accelerated the transfer of illicit money overseas.[23] In early 2012, Central Bureau of Investigation director Amar Pratap Singh revealed that about $500 billion of illegal money of Indians was deposited in tax havens abroad, and that Indians accounted for the largest number of depositors in Swiss banks. This figure was based on the findings of the report by the Supreme Court–appointed committee on black money. The funds originating in tax evasion and crime proceeds were funneled to various tax havens through multiple routes.[24]

There has been a long-standing linkage between black economy and real estate in India, and the accelerated construction and sale of high-value property led to runaway expansion in black money. With the entry of Dubai-based Emaar Properties into India's real-estate business in 2005, in partnership with the Delhi-based MGF Developments Limited, the inflow and outflow of capital got mixed up.

But DLF had several advantages over its competitors. In 1996, it unveiled Phase III of its Gurgaon project and built its first office complex, the DLF Corporate Park. A far greater prize came Kushal Pal Singh's way the following year, when he persuaded Jack Welch to set up GE Capital International Services as the India-based business-processing arm of GE Capital.[25] It boosted the growth of GE businesses in India and contributed to the country's progress by giving its Gurgaon-based subsidiary access to GE's vast intellectual resources in the technology and IT sectors.

Once GE—a company that has the distinction of being the longest continuous listing on the Dow Jones Industrial Average[26]—set its footprint in Gurgaon, other major multinationals followed. These included American Express, Bank of America, Coca-Cola, Ericsson, IBM, Microsoft, Nokia, and Oracle. The subsequent arrival of the highly paid officials of these corporations, earning upward of Rs 6 million ($120,000) a year, raised the demand for high-value residential housing, which benefited DLF as well as other leading builders.

"Coca-Cola moved its headquarters from Mumbai to Gurgaon in 1998," recalled Deepak Jolly. "Land prices in Mumbai had risen so high that the company could not expand its headquarters there. Gurgaon was comparatively cheap, and there was lot of space. Also, here our employees could own good, spacious houses, unlike the cramped, expensive accommodation in Mumbai. And Gurgaon is near the modern Indira Gandhi International Airport, which is a big help for our senior executives. Since 1992, the building of skyscrapers has been allowed. Also, with some areas in Gurgaon named as Special Export Zones with tax rebates, there is an opportunity to export."[27]

In 1999, the central government decided to connect India's four leading metropolises—Delhi, Mumbai, Chennai, and Kolkata—by a six-lane highway. The proposed National Highway 8 would link Delhi with the nation's commercial capital of Mumbai and pass through Gurgaon. The completion of the highway system in 2003, followed by the widening of National Highway 8 two years later, proved a strong tonic for the city.

"Y2K, the millennium bug, gave a big push to IT companies in Gurgaon because Western corporations began associating India with information technology rather than spiritualism or yoga," said Tikku. "After that, call centers here expanded rapidly. Among the sixty-odd center firms, the leaders are Genpact, Accenture, Convergys, and EXL. Altogether these firms have contracts with about 2,000 Western companies."[28]

Return of the Tech-Savvy Indian Expatriates

Encouraged by this connectivity, in 2004 Kushal Pal Singh undertook the development of DLF Cyber City, a ninety-acre integrated IT park. That year, India achieved a healthy 7.5 percent expansion in its GDP. The economic upsurge led many qualified Indians who were working in America and Britain, particularly in IT, to return home. By 2006, more than 35,000 expatriate Indians returned from the United States to settle in Bangalore, then the country's booming high-tech center. Another thirty thousand Indian expatriates from Britain flew back home. This inflow increased to the point where the Ministry of Overseas Indian Affairs started issuing Overseas Indian Citizenship certificates in January 2006; they handed out forty thousand in the first six months.[29] This document provided the holder all citizenship rights, except the right to vote, while retaining his/her foreign nationality. The reverse flow was a reflection of the fact that, by 2005, India accounted for two-thirds of the global market in offshore IT and 46 percent of global business process outsourcing.[30] At the higher end of outsourcing, medical tests in America were now analyzed by Indian radiologists and pathologists.

These returnees sought the same comforts they enjoyed in the West. They found them in such newly built Gurgaon colonies as the Nirvana Country, built by Unitech Group, which was ready for occupation in January 2007. It contained houses with air conditioners and Italian marble floors, and twenty-four-hour access to water and electricity. Fenced off by high walls and privately guarded, the colony reproduced the sanitized charm of Western suburban life. The returnees found the prices of the apartments—starting at $180,000 (or Rs 9 million), two hundred times the average annual income of an Indian—easily affordable. The realtor sold all 250 apartments within two hours; more than two-fifths of the buyers were Indian returnees.[31]

There were multiple reasons behind this homeward move. On a personal level, they wanted their children to grow up in India, speak Hindi, and have Indian friends. They knew that, with many Indian companies keen to have footprints abroad, there was growing need for Indians with specialist knowledge and experience to help them navigate the overseas world successfully. Among them was Shiv Dayal, a native of Delhi, a bespectacled man of medium build with a luxuriant thatch of pomaded black hair. After earning his MBA from London Business School in 1995, he worked in the mergers and acquisitions divisions of JPMorgan Chase & Co., a financial services firm,[32] and Dresdner Kleinwort in London and New York. He dealt with merger, acquisition, sale, privatization, equity raising, and private equity transactions for clients in North America and Europe as well as Russia, India, South Korea, Saudi Arabia, the United Arab Emirates, and Brazil. He also advised some investors to funnel venture capital into the Indian IT sector. On his return home, he set up Langham Capital in Delhi and established its research department in Gurgaon.

By then, Gurgaon had become a city of gated communities, tiered by income. Cooperative housing society complexes were at the low end of this new hierarchy, and the fourteen-story Aralias luxury condominiums along DLF Golf Course Road, selling for Rs 100 million ($2 million), were at the top end, with buildings like DLF's Princeton Estate ranked in between. For the most part, cooperative housing society complexes tended to cater to specific groups, private or official. "The Defense Ministry takes a poll of its officers as to where they'd like to settle down after retirement," explained retired Major General Prince Jit Singh Sandhu, an elegant Sikh in a business suit, turbaned, with his combed white beard tied into a knot under his chin. "Some choose Chandigarh, others near Kolkata, but many opt for Gurgaon. Therefore we now have the Jalvayu [Hindi: Water and Air] complex of the Air Force and the Navy, built in 2001. It has 1,200 apartments. Another complex built by the Army has 700 flats."[33]

The rank of a gated residential complex depends on the procedure for letting in a visitor and the frequency of security cameras installed on different floors. A simple wave-through by a bored-looking sentry signifies low grade, whereas a tight procedure involving a written entry in a register and the issuing of a pass by a guard indicates a higher level.

Hierarchy of Self-Contained Islands

The nine residential tower blocks and forty individual houses built by the housing cooperative society of the Power Welfare Organization—allied to the state-owned Power Grid Corporation—began to fill from 2003 onward. Like all gated communities, this complex, home to two thousand people, is surrounded by a wall and has a nominal guard presence at its entrance gate. It has its own diesel-fueled generator to ensure uninterrupted power supply during frequent and prolonged electricity cutoffs (up to seven hours a day), and its own tube well to supplement the inadequate water supplies provided by local authorities. There are plumbers and electricians on call around the clock. Besides the basement parking, the complex has its own gym, a small park, two general stores, and an auditorium. Uniquely, it also has its own high school, which provides instruction up to the twelfth grade and admits students from outside the compound. The universal aim of the realtors is to minimize the contact of the complex dwellers with outsiders.

Those who paid Rs 2 million ($40,000) for a three-bedroom apartment in 2003 found their property revalued at Rs 12 million ($240,000) less than a decade later. The upturn had been particularly sharp since the downturn in the New York and London stock markets during the Great Recession of 2008–9, which encouraged nonresident Indians to invest in property in places like Gurgaon, with an annual return of 50 percent or so. This was a stark illustration of how affluent Indians had become integrated into a global economy.

During that decade some original owners rented their property. Among such tenants were Ira Acharya and her husband, Pravan Jha, their two young sons, and Jha's parents. In their early forties, both Acharya and Jha were IT executives, each with sixteen years of experience. A fair-skinned woman of medium height, with large, expressive eyes, Acharya, often dressed in colorful *salwar kameez*, obtained a master's degree in computer applications from Delhi's Jawaharlal Nehru University. She joined Tata Consultancy Services as a software engineer and rose to become a leader of a group of teams with an aggregate strength of two hundred employees.

Established in 1968, Tata Consultancy Services is the number one Indian technology company offering IT services, business solutions, and outsourcing. Whereas most of its 220,000 employees were based in India, as of 2012, more than 90 percent of its earnings came from abroad—a remarkable example of globalization. Tata has half a dozen offices in Gurgaon, each one focused on a different aspect of its multifarious operations.

A tall, dark, broad-shouldered man, Pravan Jha was director of technology at Aricent Technology Company of New Jersey, which specialized in software development in telecom systems. He started as a software engineer at the annual salary of Rs 70,000 ($1,400) and graduated to earning Rs 2.5 million ($50,000) a year. His wife's annual gross pay was roughly half that much. The income tax on their collective earnings of Rs 3.7 million ($74,000) was about a third of the total and was deducted from their paychecks. The breakdown of their monthly budget was 30 percent for income tax, 30 percent for food and drink, 20 percent for rent and utilities, 5 percent for education, 5 percent for entertainment, 5 percent for insurance, and the rest toward their savings. This is roughly how an upper-middle-class family in America spends its earnings.

Avid newspaper readers, Acharya and Jha bought the *Times of India*, *Indian Express*, and *Dainik Jagran* (Hindi: Daily Awakening) every day. "Recently, middle and upper classes have been disturbed by the corruption scandals," remarked Jha. "But politics and politicians are no different from the society in general. Look at Gurgaon, a city of fifteen lakhs [1.5 million]. It has many avenues for spending money, but very little by way of cultural uplift. There are only two bookshops and one theatre. There are expensive restaurants where a meal for me and my wife with aperitif and wine would cost about Rs 5,000 [$100]. That's what a security guard earns working a twelve-hour shift for a month."[34]

Compared to the laid-back guards at the lowly Power Welfare Organization complex, the ones at DLF's Princeton Estate were regimented to follow a strict protocol. Besides noting down the vehicle registration number, a guard

wrote the details of the main visitor in a register, equipped to produce car-
bon copies, and handed him a counterfoil.

Thus armed, my companion and I proceeded to the fourteen-story tower
block C-3 in our taxi. Refreshingly, the surroundings were free of the debris
that is a hallmark of most buildings outside the gated complexes in Gurgaon
as well as Delhi. On the ground floor of C-3, there was yet another guard
with a register. (Almost invariably, these heavily suntanned guards are slim,
mustached, and dressed in dark blue pants and a light blue shirt embroidered
with the security company's logo, and sometimes equipped with walkie-
talkies.) The solid concrete walls, painted off-white, looked pleasant, and the
elevators were robust and clean.

At the door of apartment 34, Kalyani Kapur received us. A dark-eyed,
wide-browed woman in her late thirties, her intelligent countenance framed
by sleek black hair, she spoke with great confidence—as one should expect
from someone who led a workforce of two thousand. She was the head of operations and business at iGATE-Patni Computer Systems Ltd., located at a
five-acre site in Noida, a satellite town east of Delhi. Born of Kashmiri
Hindu parents settled in Delhi, she obtained a science degree from Delhi
University, followed by postgraduate courses in international marketing
and dialer administration at Miami University. She then worked for an IT
company in Irvine, California, before returning to India after her marriage
broke down, where she joined iGATE-Patni Computer Systems.

Her firm had a contract with JPMorgan Chase Bank[35] to provide customer
information service through its call center. "Like all other employers in
India, JPMorgan Chase and iGate-Patni do not give their employees any
entitlements, and there is no such thing here as state unemployment benefits," Kapur explained. "So the local employees are strongly motivated to keep
their jobs. Their efficiency is high, far above their American counterparts. At
the same time, they are paid one-third of U.S. salaries. At my call center a
typical agent is in their mid-twenties. Often being married, they are keen to
keep the job even though it brings only Rs 30,000 [$600] a month, with
overtime."

As someone who had studied and lived in California, how did her life in
Princeton Estate compare with the one in an American suburb? "Here we
have a swimming pool to ourselves, a small park for jogging, a fitness center,
and a community center," said Kapur. "We have our own health clinic with
a doctor and a nurse. Recently, we formed a housing committee to look after

the communal part of the complex—keep stairs clean, ensure street lights are working, and so on. We pay only Rs 300 [$6] a month for that. There is even a [Hindu] preacher who comes around every Sunday morning to deliver a marigold garland that has been blessed by the deities. He gets Rs 300 [$6] a month from us. A car wash costs Rs 500 [$10]. A part-time cleaner gets Rs 1,200 to 1,500 [$24 to $30] a month and a part-time cook Rs 1,500 to Rs 2,000 [$30 to $40]." But, she added, private education, necessitated by substandard government schools, was expensive. "For my son, in the fourth grade, the fees are Rs 80,000 [$1,600] a quarter, or Rs 320,000 [$6,400] a year, which is almost the starting salary of a technical engineer. But he is at a school where the classrooms are air-conditioned—and also their buses."[36]

The stress all along, from schools to apartments, is to insulate the users, as much from the physical environment as from their less privileged fellow citizens. Unitech Group's online prospectus for its detached houses in the Nirvana Country complex baldly recommended the properties to "those who want to distinguish themselves from the masses."[37] The officials of the Residents Welfare Associations in these enclaves often instruct children and women not to go beyond the precincts of their complex.

At the highest end of luxury condominiums, residents of the Aralias tower block, next to the Gurgaon Golf and Country Club, are the beneficiaries of extra security afforded by surveillance cameras on each floor, and they also enjoy a panoramic view of a scenic eighteen-hole golf course composed of manicured lawns interspersed with small lakes and streams.

Elysian World of the Gurgaon Golf Club and Rubicon Bar

Upon entering the 142-acre site, past the ubiquitous guards, the visitor is transported to a world far removed from the dusty, sun-baked environment of snarled roads, screaming horns, hazardously designed traffic roundabouts, and belching diesel generators stacked on roofs, to the heart of a replica of the garden county of Kent in southeast England. A wide, smooth driveway, bifurcated by well-cut privet hedges laced with white electric wires that are studded with tiny colored bulbs, and flanked by center-lined palms and fluttering flags of multiple colors, leads to a three-way junction. A brief drive to the left ends at the Club House's semicircular porch. Up the polished stone steps, behind an ornate wooden door, lies a large, sumptuously furnished room with comfortable sofas facing wood-paneled TV sets. Framed certificates of excellence adorn the walls—Asian Golf Monthly Awards, declaring the Gurgaon Golf Course the best in Asia—next to the pictures of the winners of the DLF Masters, Hero Women's Indian Open, and Avantha Masters. The two floors above contain a restaurant and bar, called the Eagle's Nest, furnished with a pool table.

Designed by the world-renowned American golf champion Arnold Palmer, this course—eight years in the making—opened for business in 1999. It is exclusive. "The entrance fee is Rs 1 million ($20,000), which includes some deposit," said Sunam Sarkar, the robustly built, mustached sales director of Apollo Tyres. "For Indian residents, the membership is Rs 100,000 ($2,000) a year. Now it is open only to those who live in a DLF property."

Across the spacious main room, there is an open-air platform several feet above the ground, carpeted with azure, red, scarlet, and magenta swathes of irises, lilies, and geraniums. The platform is furnished with tables, chairs, and huge umbrellas. Sipping a caffè latte while looking across at one of the five artificial lakes with fountains and ducks, the incredibly deep-green golf course embellished with strolling peacocks, and the wooded Aravalli Hills range in the distance, you might well feel like a visitor to a European spa town. "Unlike the century-old Tollygunge and Bengal Clubs in Kolkata and the Yacht Club in Mumbai, this place is not used for making business deals," averred Sarkar. "Business deals in Gurgaon and Delhi are done in five-star hotels."[38]

Though Sarkar did not say, what he probably had in mind was the Rubicon bar at Leela Kempinski Hotel, the ultimate in opulence and elegance. A discreet alcove in the hotel's glitzy lobby leads the affluent customers through a tunnel, lit by ruby-colored lighting, into an intimate lounge bar. The cumulative impact of the décor, the lighting, the Chesterfield wing chairs, the glitter of twinkling, crystalline amber liquids, and the exquisite metallic latticework—designed meticulously by Spin Design Studio of Tokyo, specialists in restaurants and bars—is to engender a feeling of well-being and temporal success in its guests. They can sit at the counter of the low-slung bar, Japanese style, or occupy winged chairs and alcoves near the floor-to-ceiling windows facing the Gurgaon-Delhi Expressway, for deal making in the strictest confidence.

The choice of drinks is virtually limitless: there are vodkas, cognacs, and seventy-five brands of whiskey, including some from Japan; 1,500 wines in the hotel's state-of-the-art, see-through cellars, from the astronomically priced French wines to the humbler varieties from Chile; and numerous cocktails, which vary from day to day, depending on which fresh ingredients have been flown in. Money is no object. Each time a prospering businessman imbibes a peg of Ladyburn 1973 Vintage Single Malt Scotch Whisky, costing Rs 4,000 ($80), he drinks up a month's wages of his cleaning maid.[39]

While the state government of Haryana derives almost half of its total revenue from this twenty-four-square-mile urban sprawl, it has been woefully deficient in providing Gurgaon with adequate infrastructure and public services. For example, the city's police contingent is only one-fifth the size of the private security-guard force.

Creaking Infrastructure

The 1975 Haryana Development and Regulation of Urban Areas Act mandated private realtors to build pathways, lighting, and sewage within the gated complexes. They did, but the state authorities failed to construct linking roads, sewage disposal systems, and drainage; supply adequate water from reservoirs; and provide uninterrupted power from the provincial or national grid. "We pretty much carry the entire weight of what you would expect many states to do," claimed Pramod Bhasin, the elegantly dressed former CEO of Genpact and its predecessor, GE Capital International Services, in his interview with the *New York Times*. "The problem—a very big problem—is our public services are always lagging a few years behind, but sometimes a decade behind. Our planning processes sometimes exist only on paper."[40]

The most obvious result was pockmarked feeder lanes without sidewalks. Even thoroughfares, carrying heavy traffic, were neglected. The two-mile-long Mehrauli-Gurgaon Road, lined with shopping malls, was treacherous due to numerous potholes, some of them deep depressions. In the absence of sewage mainlines, particularly in the newly built sectors, sewage flowed into vacant plots. The dazzling interiors of the corporate offices in Cyber City were reached via streets that were often waterlogged.

The old village of Wazirabad—now transformed into Sectors 52 and 56 of Gurgaon, which is divided into sixty-eight sectors—was the exception. Here the main street was upgraded to a smooth, metallic finish. "This has very little to do with the local or state authorities," said retired Major General Sandhu. "The infrastructure in Wazirabad here has been funded by the World Bank. Underground sewage has been built but not commissioned so far." Yet some of the manholes in the main street had gone missing. "The manhole is wide enough to swallow a stray child, and large enough to break the springs of even the sturdiest vehicle," remarked Sandhu. "And imagine an unsuspecting pedestrian crossing the street during a moonless night when the street lights are off."[41]

Outside the gleaming modernist office of a multinational company—air-conditioned, humming with banks of computers, with power backup assured by giant diesel generators on the roof[42]—it was a common sight to find a couple of stray cows foraging in dumped waste between tower blocks, or a stray goat urinating in the street. The spiritual uplift generated by the sight of the residential high-rise condominiums in the Sushant Lok neighborhood sinks again at the sight of uncollected mounds of garbage nearby. A children's park in the Palam Vihar area had been turned into a dumping ground by contractors who gathered trash from other areas and unloaded it there. Elsewhere, empty plots were a fair game not only for the contractors but also local residents. There was hardly any sign of a parking facility in Udyog Vihar (Hindi: Place of Industry), which is home to some two thousand manufacturing units of various sizes, with an annual turnover running into hundreds of millions of dollars. From an upper story of the landmark DLF Gateway Tower, looking southward, one could make out a long row of shacks made of rusty, corrugated metal sheets next to a dilapidated culvert—a remnant of the old village of Nathupur—near a stagnant pool of water. Not far from the very expensive Galaxy Hotel, just off of National Highway 8, stood Raj Cinema—next to a slum.

The unplanned and often unauthorized boring of tube wells by private developers to satisfy the needs of the rich had led to a fast-depleting groundwater table. To compensate for this, the realtors started drilling deeper than the officially permitted limit. The resulting overextraction of water caused the flooding of basements in residential blocks, as well as surrounding agricultural plots. When the complaints of the suffering landholders in Tigra village in Sectors 65–68 went unheeded by the local municipality, they petitioned the High Court in the spring of 2011. Thus challenged, the concerned municipal official revealed in November 2011 that he had ordered the sealing or dismantling of 442 illegal tube wells, thereby highlighting the private developers' scandalous violation of the law.[43]

Tigra was the latest in a series of villages to undergo urbanization. Many other villages, including Chakkarpur, Nathupur, Sikandarpur, and Wazirabad, had already been reduced to a fraction of their respective original sizes.

Original Villages Turned into Slums

The impact of globalization on India is vividly conveyed in the case of Chak-karpur, located to the east of Old Gurgaon, delineated by National Highway 8. Once a medium-size village with the lands of its inhabitants spread over sev-eral square kilometers, Chakkarpur was turned into a slum barely half a square kilometer in area, squeezed between two thoroughfares and a housing estate for the skilled workers of the Maruti Suzuki car factory. The bulk of the land had been transformed into DLF City Phase 1, which housed, inter alia, the landmark JMD Tower, the upscale Lifestyle International department store, and the pioneering Sahara Mall, emblazoned with the logos of apparel shops, gift boutiques, and fast-food eateries. The huts in the slum, made of wooden walls and corrugated sheet roofs, provided shelter to the nannies and security guards who served the residents of the luxurious apartments surrounding it.

While the multistory condominiums had the convenience of gushing water taps throughout the day, the slum dwellers nearby queued to buy water from tankers because the communal taps, dependent on electrical pumps, often ran dry due to frequent outages. When water did flow, men and boys bathed in the cold water from buckets. During nighttime power cuts, the glimmering lights of the high-rise blocks gave the slum a penumbral appearance. Scenes such as these dramatically illustrated how private affluence and public pen-ury coexisted within a shouting distance.

These slum dwellers were almost invariably outsiders who had drifted to Gurgaon in search of work, often from outside Haryana. As for the original villagers, after selling their lands to DLF in the 1980s, most of them upgraded their modest houses, then built rows of small rooms of bricks and concrete blocks next to their cattle stables, which they rented out. But their gains were dwarfed by the astronomical rise in DLF's assets. The land that DLF had bought from the original villagers at Rs 8,000 (then $1,000) an acre was now worth about Rs 250 million ($5 million) per acre.

The one-room tenements sprang up not only in Chakkarpur but also Na-thupur, Sikandarpur, and Wazirabad, as well as Dundahera, on the north-western edge of the city. The demand for these dark, unventilated rooms, each measuring about ten feet by twelve feet, came from an estimated floating pop-ulation of nearly 200,000 people who labored as unskilled or semiskilled workers for construction sites, garment factories, and wealthy households, and as security guards in offices, factories, gated complexes, shopping malls, and hotels.

This laboring class was to be found as much in Chakkarpur and Nathupur as in Dundahera, with its landmark fifteen-foot-tall, orange-painted statue of Hanuman, the Hindu monkey god, on the eastern side of the road leading to the small Palam airport on the edge of Udyog Vihar. Beyond this congested, potholed road lay a narrow lane, or crooked alley. The air was thick with the smell of open drains and human feces. Small heaps of household garbage lay scattered in pathways, providing a feast to swarms of flies, mangy dogs, and an occasional cow.

Behind the modest, flyblown shops of greengrocers, butchers, general store owners, and confectioners, run by immigrants from other states, stood two- and three-story buildings. While the lower floors consisted of small, poorly ventilated rooms with damp walls and peeling paint, each fetching a monthly rent of Rs 1,500 to 2,500 ($30 to $50), the top floor, with larger, better-maintained rooms, was the domain of the landlord.

Karan Lakhan, one of the occupants on the ground floor, was a thirty-eight-year-old Hindu, with a wife and three children, who belonged to the blacksmith subcaste. A reedy-looking man, he was mustached, with thin eyes and a large nose. Born into a landless peasant family in a village in Bihar, the poorest Indian state, he arrived in Delhi in 1996. After a couple of years as a construction worker, he joined Gopal Clothing Company, one of the first factories to open in Udyog Vihar. "The company makes all sorts of clothes— denim jeans and jackets, cotton tops, twill pants, denim shirts and skirts, children's clothing, T-shirts and all," he said. "First I worked in the fabric relaxing and shrinkage department as a helper. Gradually I moved up the scale and joined the cutting section. For the past five years I have been a cutter. My shift is twelve hours, seven days a week. I get one day off every fortnight. And I earn Rs 8,000 [$160] a month. The monthly rent eats up Rs 2,000 [$40]. That includes electricity but we only have one bulb and a TV. And power is off every day for two to four hours. We get tube well water supplied by the municipality. But during summer, water gets scarce." How did he see the future of his children? "I am sending them to school even though it costs money. I am lucky I can afford it. Half of the kids in Dundahera get no education at all." Why? "Their parents can't afford even proper clothes for them, much less books and things." Did he send money home? "I try, but I can manage no more than Rs 1,200 [$60] a month. Gurgaon is expensive."

For its day-to-day needs the Lakhan family was well served by local shops. But when he had to buy a sari for his wife, Sita, a small, dowdy woman, or shoes for himself or his children, they went to the down-at-the-heels Nathupur market.[44]

The Proletariat's Bazaar

To reach the Nathupur Market, I exited the main highway, lined with state-of-the-art buildings and shopping malls, drove briefly along Sikandarpur Road, and turned left into a dusty, rugged lane sprinkled with sharp-edged stones, lined with signs painted in English on steel panels of different sizes—Shagoon Tent House, English Wine & Beer Shop, Om Shakti Estate Agents—typical of a thriving Indian provincial city. Past a string of lesser property agents along a wayward path strewn with trash—debris, torn papers, polythene sheets, crushed stones, broken glass, and dust—I turned a corner and entered the Nathupur Market. At a fruit juice stall, a lanky attendant was pressing sugarcane between two wheels powered by a diesel engine. The row of shops beyond the stall included a tiny kiosk stocked with *paans*,[45] cigarettes, and chewing gum, an open-air kitchen serving food, a shop displaying vividly colorful spices, a ready-made apparel store, and a sole tailor working a Singer sewing machine with his feet at the threshold of a cell-phone repair shop.

When a muddy patch in the jagged pathway slowed me down, I noticed on my left a narrow side lane with rickety stalls. On my right was a breach filled by a wide gate, beyond which lay a spacious courtyard. It was the property of the original Nathupur's headman, now dead, according to his son, Amit Kumar, standing by the gate. A big, broad-shouldered man with close-cropped hair, in a T-shirt and pants, he wore dark glasses and an earring. "In this bazaar the original farmers retain the ownership of the land," he said in fluent English. "They rent these shops, which are run by people from outside Haryana." I asked him how long he thought Gurgaon's boom would last. "The construction of high-rise office blocks is almost over," he replied. "And the building of the residential tower blocks has slowed. But the Delhi Metro project only came in 2009. It'll go on for some years. After that will come proper sewage and drainage. So we'll be on the roll for another ten to fifteen years."

For the present, though, the overall scene was mixed. Sunil Mandal, at the paan-and-cigarette kiosk—measuring eight feet by ten feet—was downcast.

"My income has fallen because most of the big buildings have been finished, and many construction workers have gone back to their villages," he bemoaned. A twenty-three-old man of medium height, slim, with a trimmed black mustache and a gap between his front teeth, he was wearing a white shirt, black trousers, and brown sandals. Born into a small peasant family in a village in southern Bihar, he completed the eighth grade at the age of fifteen but did not stay to help his father work the one and a half acres of land meant to sustain a family of seven, excluding Sunil's wife. "I married when I was twenty-one," he said, rather shyly. "But she's staying with her parents. There'll be another ceremony before she comes to live with my parents."

How did he end up in Gurgaon? "I noticed that the people of my village coming back from Kolkata or Delhi were wearing good clothes and shoes," he recalled. "I decided to follow their path. My village is twelve hours by railway from Kolkata and eighteen hours from Delhi. My uncle Avnish Mandal was working in Delhi as a house cook. So I chose Delhi."

At first, he worked in a garment factory as a helper, earning Rs 2,500 ($50) a month for a daily eight-hour shift. "After I had paid Rs 1,000 [$20] as rent, and spent Rs 800 [$16] on food, there was very little left," he said. So he moved to Gurgaon, borrowed some money from his uncle, and took over a cigarette kiosk. "Here I make Rs 6,000 [$120] a month on a turnover of Rs 24,000 [$480]. The shop rent is Rs 2,000 [$40], my room rent Rs 1,000 [$29]. Food costs Rs 800 [$16], and other expenses Rs 700 [$14]. That leaves me Rs 1,500 [$30] a month, which I send to my parents in the village."

Several shops up the street, Majnun Khan sat at the front of his eatery next to cauldrons of rice, lentils, and curried goat meat, a pile of thin chapatis, a pot of yogurt, and a bowl of salad made of sliced onions and green chilies. His customers, seated on wooden benches at the back, ate with their hands. An attractive, athletic-looking man of twenty-five, oval-faced, with a luxurious head of hair, Khan arrived in Gurgaon five years ago from Meerut, forty miles east of Delhi. Power outages were a major irritation to him. "When electricity is off, we just sit around, doing nothing," he complained. Why not buy an inverter, whose batteries store power during the normal supply then run during an outage for up to six hours? "My God, the cost!" he replied to my suggestion. "The minimum price is Rs 5,000 [$100], then you have to pay for the extra wiring and sign up for an annual maintenance contract."

I was curious if the construction slowdown had affected his business. "Not really," he replied. "Mine is a poor man's restaurant. The average bill is only about Rs 60 [$1.20]." What about those who spend Rs 2,500 ($50) on a meal? "Ah, all those living in luxury apartments. They have become rich through dishonest means." How did he know? I asked. "I have seen it with my bare eyes. They ask you to do something and then they don't pay you for that. And that's how they make money, by exploiting others."[46] Exploitation, however, was not limited to individuals or private companies. It was practiced by the Haryana government, no less.

The State as an Exploiter

Many times, the state authorities cheaply acquired panchayat land—meant for common use by villagers—for public utility purposes by invoking the colonial 1894 Land Acquisition Law, then sold or leased it to private developers at vastly inflated prices.

For instance, in 2001–2, the Haryana Industrial and Infrastructure Development Corporation and the Haryana Urban Development Authority acquired 351 acres of panchayat land in Wazirabad for Rs 700 million ($14 million) for building utilities and industries. Since 253 acres were officially registered as forestland, and the rest as part of the environmental Aravalli Plantation Scheme, the government should have preserved it as a green zone. In any case, it failed to implement its public utilities plan. Instead, in 2009, it sold the requisitioned land to DLF for Rs 17 billion ($340 million) to develop it into a residential, commercial, and recreation complex.[47] Ostensibly, the state made a clear profit of Rs 16,300 million ($326 million). But DLF gained far more, since the market value of this land was Rs 40 billion ($800 million). Besides breaking its promise about constructing public utilities, the state allegedly violated the environmental law by allowing the development of forestland as commercial property. Encouraged by local social activists, the villagers objected and took their case to the Supreme Court, which appointed a Central Empowered Committee on environment to investigate. Following its report in January 2011, the Supreme Court passed a landmark verdict. It ordered that all land earmarked for common use by villagers be restored to panchayats. It also directed the chief secretary of the Haryana government, the topmost bureaucrat, to prepare a plan to evict unscrupulous trespassers who had grabbed land using force or political influence.[48]

"The government must release a map or a tentative plan while acquiring land for public utility purposes," said Amina Shervani, a founder member of the Haryana branch of the Upjau Bhumi Sanrakshan Andolan (Hindi: Fertile Land Conservation Movement) in the Gurgaon area. "This will not only ensure that villagers are convinced about the proposed development but can also keep a tab on the changes in plans made by the government."[49] Later that year, this organization was one of the signatories to a letter urging transparency in the acquisition of land and consultation with the people to be displaced, sent to Jairam Ramesh, Minister for Rural Development in Delhi, who was in charge of drafting a federal law on land acquisition.[50] Such activists came mostly from the socially conscious middle class. But, for every Shervani, there were thousands of middle-class residents of Gurgaon who had unwittingly benefited from the encroachment on fertile agricultural lands.

But this class was not homogeneous. It was divided into lower, middle, and upper categories, with call-center agents at the bottom and experienced corporate middle managers at the top. A typical call-center representative, age twenty to twenty-five years, working night shifts for fifty hours a week, earned Rs 15,000 ($300) a month, including incentives. His or her basic monthly salary of Rs 8,000 ($160) was almost twice that of a junior engineer working for the state-owned railways. (Nationwide, the average per capita income was Rs 4,500 [$90] a month.) Yet these employees were sometimes pejoratively called "upwardly mobile cyber-coolies," working in air-conditioned, white-collar sweatshops.

Call Centers: Where Globalization Gets Personal

Call centers form the core of business process outsourcing, the contracting by companies of certain processes or operations to a third-party service provider. With 110,000 call-center employees, divided almost equally between men and women, Gurgaon has emerged as the leader in this field. It was therefore not surprising when in 2009 the local MP, Rao Inderjit Singh of the Congress Party, was elected chairman of the Parliamentary Committee on Information Technology. Four years later, sensing the rapid disappearance of popular support for his party, he defected to the Bharatiya Janata Party. He was reelected as a BJP candidate in May 2014 and found a seat in the Narendra Modi government as a junior minister.

Since the business conducted by Indian call-center agents, or reps, is almost wholly with the English-speaking peoples of North America, Britain, and Ireland, the millions of calls daily received and made by these centers in Gurgaon and elsewhere in India can be viewed as cultural interaction on a gigantic scale. The smallest call center in Gurgaon is a team of six people sitting behind their computers in an obscure office, and the biggest and oldest is Genpact, along St. Thomas Marg. Its ten thousand employees work around the clock, seven days a week, on several open-plan, air-conditioned floors, serving mainly the myriad constituents of General Electric.

Roughly two-thirds of Gurgaon's call-center workers commute from Delhi, many of whom are women who live with their parents. Rents are high in Gurgaon, and the suburb lacks cheap and reliable local transport. Therefore, companies such as Genpact, Accenture, EXL, and Convergys run fleets of vehicles to transport their staff, often deploying cars like the Toyota Qualis, a boxy car with space for fifteen passengers. Genpact's 350 white vans, cars, and sport utility vehicles log roughly 60,000 miles a day.

Call centers receive inbound calls that require answering queries about goods or services and solving problems encountered by customers. Outbound calls focus on selling services or goods. Before they start taking calls, prospective agents undergo training lasting one week to three months. During this period, they are forbidden to speak any Indian language. They are also instructed not to use the phrase "call center," reveal their location, or tell the local time when pitching a sale or dealing with a customer.

Their training has three components: vocal, cultural, and technical. The purpose of voice training—covering accent and diction—is to eliminate mother-tongue influence. The major differences between the pronunciations in the standard North Indian English and its American counterpart revolve around the letters *t*, *d*, and *r*. North Indians are instructed to soften their *t*s and *d*s, and roll their *r*s. Since the Indian habit of rounding of vowels is jarring to the American ear, it needs correcting. A word like *Africa*, pronounced in the United States as "Ahfrca," comes out as "Afreeka" in India. The trainee learns primarily by listening carefully to accent tapes and intoning most commonly used words, such as "pleasure." Voice training is especially important for those recruited to make a sales pitch.

Culture training is directed at a particular English-speaking country. For the United States, for instance, training would involve learning the names of all fifty state capitals. More importantly, trainees also learn the current colloquialisms, often drawn from chat shows on television—*cool, up to speed, dude, clunky, guys, go-getter, no worries,* and *geek*—and gain familiarity with popular TV programs. Some overly enthusiastic Indian teachers urge the trainees to eat American fast food and listen to American music. To prepare the trainee to handle queries from customers of varying ages and diverse backgrounds, some instructors divide customers into different categories—eccentric, arrogant, bumpkin, quarrelsome, prudent, assertive, and sweet-tempered—and teach different ways to handle them. This requires the trainee to build up an emotional repertoire, like a professional actor. The de-Indianizing process is capped by the name change. Mehul becomes Max; Jha, Jones; Fazal, Fred; Sarbjit Singh, Sally Singer; Radhika, Regina; Sundri, Sandra; and Shyam, Sam.

Next comes the technical training. When it pertains to a product—a computer, a vacuum cleaner, an oven, an electric drill—the trainee needs to understand either its inner workings or be able to follow the troubleshooting procedure displayed on his or her computer. If the trainee is rendering a service, this can range from debt collection or credit-card queries to airline ticketing problems—or even persuading the person at the other end of the line to switch gas or electricity suppliers or sign up for a cell-phone contract.[51]

High Attrition, Varied Experiences

Whether they are engaged in outbound or inbound calls, call-center agents work under immense pressure. A 2006 survey of 230 Indian call-center employees at three leading companies—Accenture, Convergys, and Wipro—showed that a typical agent served 180 customers a day, far above the American agent's average of 75 customers.[52]

A 2005 report by economist Babu P. Ramesh, based on a survey of 280 employees at six call centers in Noida and sponsored by the state-funded V.V. Giri National Labour Institute—"Employment and Employment Relations in IT Enabled Services and Tele-working"—was so critical of their working conditions that the institute's management was successfully pressured by the government to stop distributing the document. The report showed that the long hours and relentless surveillance led to health problems and burnouts. Supervisors monitored the employees for the number of calls they handled, the average time spent on each call, and the gap between calls. Closed-circuit cameras and electronic timers recorded the time that agents were away from their computers, including the minutes spent in the toilet. They were required to remain pleasant, courteous, and attentive, especially when dealing with irate callers. As a result, many of them suffered "Burn Out and Stress Syndrome," the report concluded.[53]

With the average call-center agent lasting only about two and a half years on the job, leading business process outsourcing companies conduct ongoing recruitment drives. It is not uncommon to see in upscale parts of New Delhi such store-front notices as "Walk-In for Instant BPO Spot Offers: No Money [to pay], No Catch!" With improved diction and English accents, call-center agents nowadays easily find employment in airlines, hotels, and retail trade, where salaries have inched up to the level of BPOs.

Individual experiences vary. As a first job for high school or university graduates, call-center employment has its merits. It invests them with purchasing power, familiarizes them with the latest technologies, brings them into contact with Western people, and affords them the opportunity to buy expensive clothes, restaurant meals, and drinks in bars, where there is free mixing of the sexes. The downsides are long, unsocial hours, unbearable pressure at work, and little or no prospect of career advancement.

Large BPO companies such as Genpact and Convergys have their own cafeterias, gyms, health clinics, and ATMs. Genpact even has its own private ambulance. These firms pay well, so they are more demanding of their employees than others. "I just finished university and thought it'd be fun to work at a call center," said Jyoti Shekhar, a twenty-one-year-old woman from South Delhi. "But it has turned out to be more like a jail. The early glamour of free cabs and meals is gone. I am on inbound calls and handle about one hundred during a shift. Shifts start with two beeps on computer screens. When calls start, the numbers start flashing on our common switchboard as agents pick them up, one after the other. My shift is from four a.m. to one p.m., so the company car picks me up at 2:30, in the middle of the night. By the time I get home it's three in the afternoon. Six days a week. At work I am allowed only five minutes to go to the toilet. If somebody misses a call, a manager from America phones to complain about me. My starting salary is Rs 8,000 [$160] basic. I live with my parents, so I keep it all. I buy designer clothes and [an] iPhone and DVDs."

Sajan Sanghera, a man of medium height and build, looking older than his twenty-five years, is also an inbound agent, a member of an eight-person team headed by a leader. "The callers are often irate because they have been waiting for a long time," he said despondently. "The team leaders randomly listen in to calls to check the accent, alertness, grammar, and punctuation. Any mistakes you make go on a warning card. And after you get a certain number of warnings you are sent to a counselor or dismissed. If somebody in my team disconnects a call, he gets fired. If somebody is late back from the break even a tiny bit, his incentive gets canceled. That can hurt if you live in Gurgaon, which is expensive, or if you have to send money to your elderly parents."

Reps who make outbound calls can earn higher sums because they get incentive payments based on the debts collected or the sales made. The downside is that if they fail to sell, they get dismissed. Since they have to use automatic dialers, they cannot control when to call.[54] Sometimes a rep ends up with four hundred calls per ten-hour shift, with many numbers not responding.

"On average I receive thirty to fifty calls in a nine-hour night shift," a twenty-two-year-old male employee of Hewlett-Packard told a reporter for the online magazine *Gurgaon Workers News*. "Some of them take thirty minutes, most less. The company tells you off if you take more than thirty minutes. The basic wage is 10,500 rupees [$210], but there are incentives. We are supposed to sell things, from software programs to computers. For example, if a guy calls because of a virus problem then we are supposed to sell him a virus software after having solved the problem. I sell stuff for 1,000 to 2,000 dollars a month, but I get only 2 percent of that—1,000 to 1,500 rupees [$20 to $30]—incentives for that. The rest is for HP [Hewlett-Packard]."[55]

On top of working long hours and night shifts, BPO workers sometimes encounter racial abuse from customers in America and Britain. The tall, fair-skinned Promod Mehra remembered being called "you dusty boy" in a drawl—typical of Americans from the Deep South—by an irascible caller having a problem with his vacuum cleaner. Having initially spurned the caller's challenge to tell him where he was, Mehra had conceded that he was "in India." Arati Mishra, a Hindu Brahmin, was shocked to have an Englishman, struggling with his computer, shout "You Paki!" at her.[56] She managed to maintain her composure and calmly guided her abuser to repair the flaw in his machine.

A study of one hundred women working night shifts in call centers, published by the Mumbai-based *Economic and Political Weekly*, revealed that 40 percent of them suffered from indigestion, backaches, and eyestrain.[57] Yet today, almost half of the call-center agents are women, with a majority of them earning more than either of their parents.

Dating between colleagues at work is common. Males treat their female coworkers as equals. Yet there is a feeling that by working night shifts, a woman agent lowers her value in the matrimonial market. To counter this perception, some BPO companies allow their female employees' families to visit them during working hours.

As for men, about two-fifths take up correspondence courses to improve their educational qualifications. But most find the extra effort too strenuous to continue. The ambitious among them find their way into knowledge process outsourcing (KPO), which includes market, business, or investment research, intellectual property and legal support services, and data and financial analysis. The pressure to perform is far less intense here than in the BPO industry.

In medium- and large-size BPO companies, over time, a culture of camaraderie develops among call-center reps who share accommodation and socialize together. Going out to a Pizza Hut or the nearest shopping mall for a meal has become a popular group ritual. Among other things, this makes lowly agents socially equal to their bosses as well as to the software and technical engineers. A shopping mall has acquired a social status in New India's booming urban centers that it lacks in the United States or the United Kingdom. "The shopping mall represents the new Indian mindset of indulgence, of spending, of enjoying oneself, of enjoying your money," beamed Preeti Reddy, the consumer and retail vice president of KSA Technopak India Private Ltd., a management consultancy firm in Gurgaon.

Shopping Mall: A Glitzy Symbol of Globalizing India

Much praise is lavished on shopping malls for their air-conditioned comfort, the provision of a wide range of goods, and for being a one-stop family entertainment arena. "Be it a candle night [sic] dinner or shopping in bulk, Gurgaon shopping malls promise everything under one roof," enthuses Martinez Collins, an expert on real estate in Gurgaon.[58]

The chaotic scenes of drivers fighting for scarce parking space while struggling to avoid the people crowding around the entrances—particularly along the "Mall Mile" of MG Road, which has eight shopping malls—illustrate the growing popularity of the malls as well as the grotesquely flawed planning by public authorities. Parking space in the basements of the MG Road malls are able to accommodate only 40 percent of the customer-carrying vehicles, which leads to a near-perpetual gridlock on this thoroughfare on weekends.

Yet the estimated fifty thousand people—including some from New Delhi—who patronize the malls over the weekend stand apart from the bulk of Gurgaon's population. The clientele of these shopping malls consists of young professionals—doctors, lawyers, accountants, academics—as well as middle and top corporate managers, factory foremen and supervisors, successful businessmen, retired military officers, and middle- and high-level bureaucrats.

Such was the composition of the patrons of Ambience Mall, popularly called Ambi Mall, during my visit there on a Saturday afternoon in March 2011 along with Sandhu, a retired major general. One of the newest establishments of its kind, Ambi is located near the Delhi-Gurgaon Expressway toll plaza—its many lanes divided into "Tag Only," "Cash," and "Toll Card"—and has a vast parking lot.

In the hierarchy of the forty malls in the city, Ambi lies midway between the upscale DLF Emporio and the rock-bottom Sahara Mall. Its three floors contain two hundred retail stores, specialty shops, car showrooms, restaurants, and pubs, with a mix of global brands, national brands, and local retailers—from Marks & Spencer, Debenhams, and Next to Pantaloons, Reliance Trends, Jumbo Electronics, and Big Bazaar Hypermart. Almost all of the stores are huge and have striking interiors. A wide variety of cuisine was on offer, ranging from IndiJoe and Sahib Sind Sultan to Aromas of China, Asia 7, Punjabi Grill, and Nirula's Potpourri to KFC and Pizza Hut. During our visit, Sandhu and I had to queue for seats at Punjabi Grill. Surveying the diners in the food court, Sandhu said, "After the meals, many families will go to one of the cinemas in the multiplex."

Going to the movies is the one custom that transcends all classes and castes in India. Yet neither Sandhu nor anybody else around expected to see a chauffeur, much less a gardener or construction worker, at the box office of the multiplex. As at all shopping malls in Gurgaon, security guards were posted at strategic points in the Ambi to ensure not just safety for the stores and restaurants but also to bar the entry of any riffraff into the complex, in order to preserve its carefully crafted image of high value.

"Is Ambiance Mall world-class?" asked Sandhu as we walked to the parking lot. "I don't know about the world at large," I replied. "But it comes near to what is available in Britain."

2

Britain: A Magnet for Indian Companies

Britons first arrived in the Indian subcontinent as employees of the East India Company, a trading firm established by a royal charter by Queen Elizabeth I in 1600. By the time the industrial revolution got under way in Britain in the second quarter of the nineteenth century, the Company had acquired a substantial political-administrative presence in the subcontinent and maintained an army there. Because Britain's soil was unsuitable for growing cotton, it was the task of the Company to ensure a steady supply of the staple to Britain's highly mechanized mills. When the British government assumed direct control of the Company in 1858, it inherited this role. A complementary part of Britain's policy was to discourage the native manufacturing industry in India. Unsurprisingly, therefore, the Indian National Congress, formed in 1885, came to visualize political independence as a prerequisite for rapid industrialization.

After independence was achieved in 1947, however, impoverished India lacked sufficient capital and technological expertise to establish a solid industrial base. The first state-owned iron and steel mill was built in 1959 in the West Bengal town of Durgapur by a consortium of thirteen British engineering firms called Indian Steelworks Construction Company. The project was financed by a loan of £103 million from the British government.[1]

The continued paucity of foreign exchange due to India's poor export performance proved a barrier to expanding its manufacturing base. It was only toward the end of the twentieth century that several new factors converged to help India acquire a surplus in its foreign trade: namely, computerization, the

Internet, real-time trading across international boundaries, financial globalization, outsourcing across borders, lowering of tariffs worldwide, and the
emergence of a generation of highly qualified Indian engineers in high-tech.
Healthy reserves of foreign currencies, however, were not enough to enable
Indian companies to search for advanced technologies or access larger markets in the West. For that, they needed massive loans from Western banks.
For historical reasons, an aspiring Indian corporation's first port of call abroad
was Britain, which was also the gateway to the much larger European Union.
The historical link between Indian and British business is encapsulated in the
story of the Tata Group conglomerate.

Modest Origins of the Tata Group

After spending ten years as an employee of his father's trading company,
which supplied cotton to textile mills in England, Jamsetji N. Tata (1839–
1904) branched out to build what would ultimately become the Tata Group.
Among his crowning achievements was the construction of India's first
textile mill, in the central city of Nagpur, in 1877, and the construction of the
landmark Taj Mahal Hotel in Bombay in 1903. His ambition to build
the first steel mill in India was kindled during a visit to Manchester in 1867,
where he was exploring the possibility of establishing a textile mill back
home. He was struck by British writer Thomas Carlyle's assertion, in a public
lecture, that "the nation which gains control of iron, soon acquires control of
gold."[2] Years later, this sad-eyed, long-nosed, richly bearded Indian Zoroastrian, often donning a rounded pyramidal hat, finally, after much effort,
began planning the first steel mill in India. No British steelmaker wanted
to cooperate with him, as they were hostile to the idea of a British colony
acquiring a steel plant of its own. Profoundly disappointed, he sailed to
America. There he sought and secured the assistance of steel-manufacturing
consultants in Pittsburgh and New York.[3]

India's first steel mill was commissioned in 1907, three years after Jamsetji's
death, under the leadership of his son Sir Dorabji Tata (1859–1932). It was
named Jamshedpur, after his father, and became a veritable company town
for Tata. It remains a giant steel city to this day. Exactly a century later, in
2007, Tata Steel acquired the London-based Anglo-Dutch Corus Group plc,
which owned all of Britain's mills. It was poetic justice on a grand scale. The

Tata Group emerged as the largest employer in Britain's declining manufacturing industry, having acquired through Corus Group—a merger itself of British Steel and the Dutch Hoogovens group in 1999—all of Britain's functioning steel plants, as well as the plants that manufactured the prestigious Jaguar and Land Rover cars.

In the mid-1990s, Britain's services industry approached India's information technology companies to cope with the millennium bug scare and address the pressing need to immunize computer systems from crashing on January 1, 2000. The contracts secured by India's IT firms exposed their managers to Western companies and their management practices. In return, these firms showed Western businesses that India was a reliable source of low-cost, high-quality services. This development coincided with the passage of India's Foreign Exchange Management Act, which aimed to encourage foreign trade and investment, and the relaxation of the Reserve Bank of India's earlier, more restrictive rules on the outward flow of Indian capital.

When the colossal speculative bubble around the dot-com industries burst in July 2000, Indian IT companies remained virtually unaffected, because only a few were then listed on U.S. or British stock exchanges. But over the next dozen years, the situation changed radically. By 2012, there were about seven hundred Indian companies operating in the United Kingdom—with thirty-five of these based in London—altogether employing more than ninety thousand people.[4] Seventy were listed on the London Stock Exchange, half of them on the Alternative Investment Market, a submarket established in 1995 to allow smaller companies to float shares in a more flexible regulatory system than in the main market. Once online facilities became widely available in the United Kingdom by the mid-2000s, it took only twenty minutes to set up and register a company online, and thereby acquire access to 500 million consumers in the European Union. Since 1979, there had been no restrictions on the movement of capital into or out of Britain. According to Ernst and Young's European Investment Monitor, India became the third-largest inward investor in the United Kingdom in 2010–11, a slip from its position as the second-largest in 2007 (in terms of projects).[5] In India, the British High Commission treated visa applications by Indian businesspeople favorably and speedily. It issued 350,000 visas a year—a world record. Britain launched a same-day visa service in Delhi and Mumbai in May 2013; India was the first country in the world to be accorded this privilege.[6]

Mittal, the Richest Man in Britain

In 2001, the HCL Group (originating as Hindustan Computers Limited in 1976) entered into a joint venture with the Frankfurt-based Deutsche Bank AG to purchase the British Telecom–owned Apollo Contact Centre, an IT services company, in Northern Ireland, for $11.5 million. Within four years, with a workforce of 2,350 people, the HCL Group became the largest Indian employer of Britons in the United Kingdom. "Western bankers' attitudes towards India and Indian companies changed sharply after 2001," said Lord Paul, the eighty-year-old founder of the London-based Caparo Group, which has an annual turnover of $900 million.[7] That manifested itself in the rise of Indian investments in Britain. With twenty-eight new Indian companies investing in the United Kingdom in 2003–4, the total number of Indian businesses in Britain rose to 480.[8]

In April 2004, the popular British perception of India as an impoverished nation received a jolt. During that month, Lakshmi Niwas Mittal (b. 1950), a steel tycoon, born in a village and holding an Indian passport, set a record for the world's most expensive house purchase.[9] Though his corporation—Mittal Steel Company NV, a public limited company with steel mills operating globally—was registered in Rotterdam, Holland, he and his directors conducted business from their Berkeley Square office in Central London—his homebase since 1997.

Mittal paid $128 million for a four-story neo-Georgian mansion with eighteen bedrooms at 18–19 Kensington Palace Gardens, adjacent to Kensington Palace, the London residence of the late Princess Diana. It had a garage space for twenty cars, Turkish baths, a ballroom, an oak-paneled picture gallery, a sculpture by the world-famous Henry Moore, and a jewel-inlaid basement pool. One of its earlier owners had turned the two adjacent houses into one and furnished it with marble floors and pillars from the same quarry that was mined to build the famed Taj Mahal.

Two months after purchasing the house, Mittal lavished £30 million ($54 million) on the marriage of his daughter Vanisha to Amit Bhatia and set another global record, earning him headlines in the international media. The five-day-long event, which started with a ring ceremony at Versailles in Paris, continued at the seventeenth-century Vaux le Vicomte château in front of an audience of over a thousand guests, who included the richest and most glamorous among Indians at home and in Britain.[10] Earlier that year, *Forbes* magazine estimated Mittal's net worth at $6.2 billion, which made him the richest person in Britain, a title he held until 2011.

India's impressive economic growth in 2003 and 2004 impacted financial journalists covering India in the British news media. "It was in 2004 that the *Financial Times* stopped referring to Indians as a part of a blob called 'Asians' and started reporting on the Indian and the Chinese diaspora instead," said Dr. Shefaly Yogendra, a London-based consultant in technology policy and strategy with a doctorate in technology policy from Cambridge University. "The upsurge in the Indian economy and the purchase of the most expensive residential property on the planet by an Indian national signaled a turning point for how India changed its brand image as a nation and as a trading partner and an investor in Britain."[11] This was also the time when there was a shift in the perception of Indian culture, with its Bollywood cinema getting favorable write-ups in the British media.

The Central Role of Western Banks

According to Grant Thornton LLP, a London-based financial advisory service, 50 percent of India's outbound investments in the early 2000s were in Europe, and only 25 percent in North America. Nearly a quarter of the merger and acquisition deals involving Indian companies were in the IT sector.[12] This suggested that India's manufacturing corporations were also active abroad. For instance, Bharat Forge, one of the world's biggest makers of specialist forged parts for vehicles, bought Scottish Stampings, based in Ayr, Scotland, to get better access to Western markets and advanced technology. Eleven other Indian manufacturers also acquired a foothold in the United Kingdom.

Flush with profits, many large Indian corporations went on an acquisition binge. Initially, these companies scoured smaller companies at home. Later, they extended their investigations overseas in order to acquire the latest technology, enter new markets, and secure natural resources, particularly fossil fuels. They also wanted to acquire reputed Western brands to fill gaps in their business portfolios. During the first half of the 2000s, the net outward foreign direct investment by Indian companies was quite modest at $8.2 billion. That figure jumped ninefold, to $74.3 billion, during the second half of the decade.[13]

It was not until the mid-2000s that India's banks were able to play a meaningful role in cross-border acquisitions by the Indian firms. Before then,

Indian banks lacked this capacity. As Vikram Kadam, an India-born senior executive in the corporate and investment banking section of Paris-based BNP Paribas SA, in London, explained, "Often to clinch an acquisition deal, a company has to raise a loan. The main lending bank needs good syndication capacity. If it agrees to raise $1.5 billion for a client, it would most likely start with $100 million of its own and take five months to put a syndicate together. But if it is required to raise the whole amount in a month, then it may have to invest $500 million of its own. Indian banks' syndication capacity is limited. Until the early 2000s, they were short of foreign currencies because they lacked business in foreign countries as well as experience in Western markets. Also, the Indian rupee was not fully convertible."[14] Full convertibility of the rupee for capital accounts could have led to excessive capital inflows from non-Indian sources, causing inflation as well as the rupee's appreciation, which would have reduced exports. Conversely, a massive withdrawal of foreigners' investments in the Indian currency would have reduced the foreign exchange value of the rupee and made imports expensive, thereby hurting the country's economic growth. So when it came to acquiring foreign firms, an Indian company had to approach large Western investment banks, which had foreign currencies and good syndication capacity, and could raise capital more cheaply through the bond market than any Indian bank could.

As it was, keen to enter the vast, untapped market in India, Western banks were eager to invest. "But because India does not allow the sale of local banks to foreigners, Western banks chose to fund Indian companies' foreign [and domestic] acquisitions, to get involved in their M&A [merger and acquisition] deals," explained Kadam. By 2005–6, all major Western investment banks stopped doing business in India through their Hong Kong or Singapore branches, and instead set up their own offices in India. They were welcomed by Indian firms, which were often unfamiliar with the domestic laws and rules under which a Western business operated. They knew, though, that a typical Western investment bank could lend large sums of money. They also knew the rules for a takeover of a local company by a foreign entity and for a proper valuation of the target firm. Their standard contract with an acquiring Indian company covered the mechanics of a takeover, the financing arrangement, examining the accounts, and advising which law firm to hire.

What are the factors that an investment bank considers for financing a buyout? "First of all, it examines the cash flow of the acquiring firm to judge its ability to repay the loan," explained Kadam. "It measures the risk involved after the acquisition. Say, if it is the mining of iron ore, then it studies ore prices over a number of years. It notes the total revenue of the acquiring firm as well as the ratio of interest to its operating revenue, called interest coverage ratio, ICR. It notes the amount of capital it has in order to withstand losses and for how long. It examines its level of debt. Last but not least, it evaluates the general standing of the company. In India, for instance, the Tata Group stands apart from all others, including the Reliance companies run by the superrich Ambani Brothers and the London-based Vedanta Resources." In a 2011 investor poll by the Mumbai-based Equitymaster Agora Research Private Limited, the Tata Group was voted the most trustworthy among India's corporate houses by 61 percent of those polled, well ahead of Infosys Technologies, which came in second place with 17 percent.[15]

Like General Electric Company in the United States, the Tata Group is a conglomerate of disparate firms, ranging from tea and coffee production to salt packaging, automobile manufacturing, steelmaking, and management consultancy. But its ownership is such that it stands apart from any other conglomerate. Tata Sons, the parent holding company, has only 34 percent of the equity of its operating subsidiaries, with 66 percent held by charitable trusts set up by Tata family members. For instance, the Sir Dorabji Tata Trust and Allied Trusts give grants to the organizations in natural resource management and rural economy, urban poverty and livelihoods, education, health, civil society, governance and human rights, media, art, and culture.[16] In 2011, the global sales of the conglomerate were £54 billion ($86.4 billion), with sales in Britain at £20 billion ($32 billion), 37 percent of the total.[17]

On the Indian side, everything about a merger or acquisition had to be cleared by the Reserve Bank of India. It has a section called External Commercial Borrowing to guard against excessive commercial borrowing in foreign currencies. Such borrowing by private Indian companies in the 1980s was one of the main reasons for India's acute foreign exchange crisis in 1991. "However, an Indian company can easily circumvent the ECB framework by setting up a shell company registered outside India," explained Kadam. "For instance, Tata Sons Ltd., the holding company of the Tata Group, can establish Tata Europe registered in the UK or Luxembourg. But a shell company has to pay higher interest than the parent company to raise capital even when they have the same credit rating."

2006: The Landmark Year

During India's fiscal year ending in March 2006,[18] the investments made in the United Kingdom by Indian companies exceeded the £134 million ($266 million) that British corporations invested in India.[19] In the first nine months of 2006, Indian firms accomplished 115 foreign acquisitions with a total value of $7.4 billion, compared to $1.1 billion in 2000, according to *The Economist*.[20]

On October 20, 2006, the boards of Tata Steel, Tata Steel UK (a Tata Steel subsidiary), and Corus Group—then the world's third-largest steel producer—announced an agreement on the terms of a recommended acquisition of all Corus shares at 455 pence a share in cash by Tata Steel UK. Two weeks earlier, Corus shares had closed at 407 pence apiece. Tata Steel UK sent the relevant documents to Corus shareholders on November 10. It was a bold move on the part of Tata Steel—with its annual production in 2005 of 8.7 million metric tons—to acquire a European corporation with nearly three times its output.[21]

But there were compelling reasons for the amalgamation of the two steel companies. Enjoying self-sufficiency in iron ore, Tata Steel's cost of production, at $160 per metric ton of steel, was the second lowest in the world.[22] By contrast, Corus was scouring far and wide for a reliable, steady supply of iron ore at reasonable prices, against the backdrop of the exponentially rising demand from China. As for Tata Steel, from 2004 onward it had launched a drive to diversify abroad. Within two years, it had acquired NatSteel in Singapore (annual output of 2 million metric tons), Millennium Steel in Thailand (annual output of 1.7 million metric tons), and two steel-rolling mills in Vietnam. The economic logic was to ship low-cost steel slabs to finishing plants overseas for conversion into value-added products in high-end markets.[23]

The driving force behind these initiatives was Tata Steel's chairman Ratan Tata (b. 1937), a great-grandson of Jamsetji N. Tata. After graduating from Cornell University with a degree in architecture in 1962, he started his career in the Tata companies on the shop floor of TISCO. After working in several other Tata firms, he was appointed managing director of National Radio and Electronics Company in 1971. Four years later, he completed the Advanced Management Program at Harvard Business School. In 1981, his uncle Jehangir Ratanji Dadabhoy Tata promoted him to chairman of Tata Industries, which included Tata Consultancy Services, with a remit to promote new ventures in high technology. Immediately, Tata Consultancy Services imported its first IBM mainframe to Mumbai. Once Rajiv Gandhi became the prime minister in 1984, his policies gave a fillip to Indian companies that wanted to make a mark in the high-tech sector. A son of Feroze Gandhi, a Zoroastrian, Rajiv had a soft spot for the Tata Group, founded by Indian Zoroastrians.[24]

When the robustly built Ratan Tata, endowed with a strong visage and natural gravitas, succeeded his uncle as the CEO of the Tata Group in 1992, the conglomerate had an annual turnover of $8.5 billion. These firms had prospered immensely behind high tariff walls and barriers to foreign capital investment prior to 1991. Of the eighty companies of the Tata Group, he found that eleven produced 85 percent of revenues and 90 percent of profits. He reorganized the conglomerate by leaving such low-return industries as cement and toiletries, and instead focused on seven core sectors: metals and minerals, automotive and engineering, chemicals, agrobusiness, hotels, IT, and power. When he discovered that the stake of the Tata Group's holding company Tata Sons had become diluted to "single figures" in some cases, he set out to rectify the situation.[25]

Whereas his buyouts in southeast Asia had gone smoothly, his bid for Corus ran into choppy waters. Brazil's largest steelmaker, the São Paulo–based Companhia Siderúrgica Nacional (CSN), which had already proposed merging with the Corus Group in 2002, now became a rival suitor to Tata Steel on November 17, 2005, by offering 475 pence a share in cash.

Tata Steel countered with a bid of 500 pence a share. The dogfight inflated the price of Corus shares to 506 pence on November 23, the highest since May 2000.[26] CSN countered with an offer of 515 pence, an offer that won the recommendation of a jubilant Corus board.[27] But then, Tata Steel promised further improvements in its terms. On December 18, the Takeover Panel, the British regulatory authority on takeovers, decided to conduct a rarely exercised auction option on January 30, 2007, to settle the matter.

Tata Steel and CSN leaked inside information to trusted journalists to underscore its financial superiority over the other. The value of Corus equity rose further. On January 19, it hit a record 544 pence. On that day, Brazil's leading financial daily revealed that Citigroup and UBS AG in Brazil had agreed to increase their lending for CSN by 10 to 20 percent, and that Barclays, Goldman Sachs, and ING Bank, operating from abroad, had put together a package of nearly $8.3 billion in secured loans, a revolving credit facility, and a high-yield bridging loan. In addition, CSN claimed to have access to its own cash reserves of $2 billion. Altogether, these would easily cover the $10.5 billion needed to buy Corus at 550-odd pence per share.[28] For its part, Tata Steel revealed that its directors had authorized its white-haired CEO, B. Muthuraman, to take the offer as high as 600 pence per share.

On January 30, the closing price of Corus at 4:30 p.m. London time— ten p.m. in Mumbai, 2:30 p.m. in São Paulo—was 563 pence. In London, the panel's two officials sat in front of their computers in their office above the London Stock Exchange complex, with the members of the small committee on manufacturing available online in their respective offices.

In Mumbai, flanked by Ratan Tata and Koushik Chatterjee, the company's chief financial officer, Muthuraman sat in Tata's office on the top floor of Bombay House, a modest four-story building in the city's business center. They were in a buoyant mood. A few hours earlier, they and the other directors of Tata Steel had announced a 41 percent leap in net profit for the quarter ending in December, with revenue up by 20 percent at almost $1 billion.[29] Though, as the CEO, it was Muthuraman who was authorized to submit the bids, the ultimate decider was Chairman Tata. Copiously briefed on the background of CSN's brash and wildly successful CEO Benjamin Steinbruch, he was anxiously aware of the steely grit of his younger Brazilian rival across the oceans. He calculated that Steinbruch would battle him to the last.

In stark contrast to the Tatas' modest headquarters in Mumbai, Steinbruch was ensconced in a conference room on the twenty-second floor of the swanky, CSN-owned glass-and-concrete skyscraper at Avenue Brigadeiro Faria Lima, 3400, whose thirty-seven floors were occupied by leading industrial and financial companies. Steinbruch, hunched over his computer, was flanked by his CFO, Alberto Netto, and the company's controller, Rog Dos Santos.

The basic rules of the auction decided by the Takeover Panel were that the bidding figure had to be raised by a minimum of five pence in each round, with a maximum of nine rounds spaced an hour apart. The auction started at 563 pence. Following each bid, the rivals called the auctioneer in London to ensure that their messages had been received and to confirm their terms. An hour's break gave the suitors enough time to redo their sums. After the first jump of ten pence, the bids went up in increments of five. Between the fifth and sixth rounds, Steinburch and his colleagues fortified themselves with *canja* (Portuguese: chicken soup) and *pão francês* (Portuguese: French bread). To shore up their flagging energy during their customary sleeping hours, Tata and his co-directors munched on chocolate bars and sipped sweet coffee. In the eighth round, Muthuraman offered 608 pence a share in cash.

It was six a.m. on January 31 in Mumbai, but only half an hour past midnight in London. Having been deprived of sleep for the past twenty-four hours, Tata Steel's top officials were feeling the strain. They had ended up paying almost 50 percent more than their 407 pence offer from October 5, 2006, when Tata Steel announced its intention of an alliance with the Corus Group. Now they had to wait another interminably long hour to find out if Steinbruch was daring enough to trump their latest offer.[30] When that hour finally passed without another shot being fired by their nemesis in São Paulo, they relaxed.

They were eager to broadcast their hard-won victory, but the Takeover Panel's rules barred them from doing so. Only its executive was authorized to announce the final outcome of the auction. It was two a.m. in London when the executive, advised by the committee on manufacturing, declared Tata Steel the winner. By the time it issued a statement, it was eight a.m. in Mumbai. Tata Steel's luminaries likely rushed back to their homes and collapsed in their respective beds, confident of an exalted place in the corporate history of India. In the final analysis, it was Ratan Tata's vaulting ambition, his all-consuming urge to win, and his innovative, labyrinthine plan to assemble what was an unparalelled sum in India's private enterprise chronicle that enabled Tata Steel to swallow a Western corporation three times its size.

Breathless TV news broadcasters in India gushed at the birth of the country's first Fortune Global 500 multinational corporation,[31] entering the much-coveted list in the 401st place. Steel magnate Lakshmi Mittal applauded the second biggest acquisition in the industry and the largest takeover by an Indian company overseas. These high-profile acquisitions, achieved in the glare of global media, led ArcelorMittal and Tata Steel to accelerate and expand their drive to acquire huge swathes of iron-ore-rich terrain in the central-eastern region of India. They accomplished this by getting the indigenous tribal inhabitants evicted from their land. Since the land was the only means of livelihood for these people, such actions would eventually swell the ranks of the rebellious Maoist movement.[32] For the present occasion, though, the mood was unabashedly self-congratulatory. "The Indian corporate sector is doing well and increasingly looking globally," said Muthuraman. "I believe it's an important step, a milestone." Echoing his sentiment, India's finance minister, Palaniappan Chidambaram, averred that the successful bid reflected the newfound confidence of Indian industry. It was indeed the coming of age of India's corporate sector—on the world stage, no less.

There were other factors at work in this deal besides the economics of shipping low-cost steel slabs to plants overseas for conversion into finished products—the economic rationale that had guided Tata Steel's earlier forays in southeast Asia. "Corus is a unique opportunity for us in terms of scale, location, and culture," beamed Tata. "This is a key part of our global strategy."[33] The point about culture was critical. That was why Tata immediately announced that he would leave the running of Corus—employing more than fifty thousand people, led by CEO Philippe Varin—to its present managers. The combined annual output of nearly 28 million metric tons would catapult the enlarged Tata Steel to the position of fifth-largest steel producer in the world, from its previous ranking of fifty-sixth in a list of 120.

None of this countered the negative view that most financial analysts in India took, arguing that Tata Steel had forked out too much for Corus. Tata's shares slumped 11 percent overnight. Irrespective of the view of India's financial markets, senior management of the Tata Group, the parent of Tata Steel, had the urgent task of financing the deal once Corus shareholders had accepted the Tata offer. On April 2, following clearance by the High Court of England and Wales, Tata Steel completed its acquisition of Corus Group plc. The net funding for this deal finally came to $12.9 billion, a dauntingly huge sum for the Tatas. The complex, multi-national financial arrangements that Tata Steel made to accomplish this feat aptly captured the true extent of how globalized capital had become and how blurred the distinction was between Indian and foreign capitals. It threw a penetrating light on the crucial role played by the Western banking giants.

Ratan Tata rallied not merely Tata Steel but also its wholly owned subsidiaries: Tata Steel UK Ltd., Singapore-based Tata Steel Asia Holding Private Limited, Tulip UK Holdings, and Tulip Finance Netherlands BV, a private limited company. Initially, the deal was financed by a cash infusion of $2.7 billion from Tata Steel—funded by a combination of its own cash resources and syndicated loans—to Tata Steel Asia Holding. In addition, Tata Steel Asia Holding raised bridge loans of $2.5 billion, and Tulip UK Holdings raised an unsecured loan of $600 million, which was invested as equity in Tata Steel UK Limited. Later, to fund the balance of the contingent consideration[34]— an additional payment due under the acquisition—Tata Steel UK Limited, through its wholly owned subsidiary Tulip Finance Netherlands BV, raised secured loans of $4 billion and bridge loans of $3.1 billion. These loans were raised without recourse to Tata Steel, the parent body.

On April 17, the board of Tata Steel approved the long-term financing for acquiring Corus as follows: equity capital from Tata Steel, $4.10 billion, and long-term funding/quasi-equity, $2.66 billion, giving a total of $6.74 billion; and nonrecourse long-term debt[35] at Corus, $6.14 billion.[36] The $6.14 billion nonrecourse debt at Corus, consisting of a bridge loan and revolving credit facility, was arranged by Credit Suisse (Swiss) in the lead, followed by ABN-Amro (Dutch) and Deutsche Bank (German). The loans were distributed as nonrecourse—that is, secured by collaterals—to be serviced out of the cash flow and other assets of Corus. These loans, with maturing periods of five to seven years, were raised without recourse to Tata Steel.[37]

This arrangement deeply impressed British bankers. "After Tata Steel's takeover of Corus," remarked Lord Paul, "there was a big change in Britain's financial markets toward India and Indian companies."[38] That made it easier for other Indian corporations to acquire assets in the West with the assistance of Western banks.

Tata Steel had a long-established distribution network in India and southeast Asia. These regions had thriving automobile industries, heavily dependent on sheet steel, which was expected to provide a foothold to Corus products in expanding markets in the coming years. In reality, this happened sooner than anticipated due to the 2008–9 Great Recession in the West, which lowered sales of cars in Europe by about a third and with it the demand for sheet steel on that continent.

Singed but Not Burned

India felt the heat of the 2008 economic slump in the West but did not get burned. It maintained its GDP growth at 6.6 percent in the fiscal year ending in March 2009. During that same period, Britain's GDP shrank by 4.7 percent. Overall, Indian companies had healthy cash flows and ample funds to invest abroad. During the first half of 2008, Indian corporations bought twenty UK firms.[39] During this period, India's foreign exchange reserves were healthy, at $311.8 billion, number five in the international table after China, Japan, Russia, and the Eurozone. During the fiscal year ending in March 2009, outward investment by the Reserve Bank of India had remained steady at $18.58 billion.[40]

But in the run-up to the general election in May 2009, Congress Party leader Sonia Gandhi argued that the ongoing "economic upheaval" in the West could "grievously affect the most vulnerable sections of our society," and that her party had partially insulated India's poor from becoming "victims of the unchecked greed of bankers and businessmen." In that context, she said, "Let me take you back to Indira Gandhi's bank nationalization of forty years ago. Every passing day bears out the wisdom of that decision. Public sector financial institutions have given our economy the stability and resilience we are now witnessing in the face of the economic slowdown."[41] In a world where neoliberal economics held commercial and ideological sway, the freshness of this argument, backed by evidence, stood out.

In the fiscal year ending March 2009, the Indian government had over 70 percent shares in depository banks. Capital ratios in banks were 12 to 13 percent, much higher than in Britain and America. The banks' nonperforming loans amounted to 1 percent of the total. Yaga V. Reddy, the Reserve Bank governor from September 2003 to September 2008, believed in regulating the financial sector because of his belief, as expressed to the *New York Times*, that "if the bankers were given a chance to sin, they would sin." He restricted a bank's exposure to a particular sector or a particular client. To curb speculation in land prices, he ruled out virgin-land purchases by banks. He raised risks on lending for the construction of shopping malls and other commercial properties. He instructed banks to set aside extra capital for every loan they granted. When he noticed U.S. banks setting up off-balance-sheet vehicles to hide debt, he virtually banned the practice in India. This led local banks to hold onto the loans they had made, which reduced their capacity to lend funds to their aspiring clients, since the banks could no longer sell their debts to Wall Street in the form of securities. The upside was that, unlike American or British banks, which had become lax about recovering their loans, Indian banks became keen to see their loans repaid.[42] Whereas the banking shares in America went into freefall in 2008–9, those in India held up so well that, in February 2009, the market value of the State Bank of India exceeded that of Citigroup, the largest bank of the United States.[43]

The successor to Reddy at the Reserve Bank of India continued his policies, which had the backing of the Congress-led coalition government that assumed office after the 2009 Lower House elections, with Manmohan Singh as the prime minister. Reversing the BJP-led administration's policy, the Singh cabinet decided not to reduce its majority stake in state-owned companies.

As the post-financial crisis recovery phase in the West started to pick up in the latter half of 2009, the GDP expansion in India accelerated. Indeed, during the first quarter of 2010, the country achieved a record growth rate of 11.2 percent.[44] During this period, India emerged as the most profitable market for Standard Chartered Bank, surpassing Hong Kong in 2010. In July of that year, the Tata Group became the largest manufacturing employer in Britain. Its fifty thousand employees across forty towns and cities exceeded the nearly forty thousand people working for BAE Systems plc, the giant aerospace and arms manufacturer.[45] This was a reflection of the steady deindustrialization of Britain, resulting from the policies of the Margaret Thatcher government from the mid-1980s onward. Nonetheless, the primacy of the Tata Group in Britain's manufacturing industry would have delighted the late Jamsetji N. Tata to no end.

In 2011, the market capitalization of the Tata Group was in the range of $35–40 billion, with almost half of its assets outside India. In this conglomerate, Tata Consultancy Services (TCS) had come to loom large. On revenue of $10.2 billion it made a profit of 21.6 percent. With only one-tenth of its earnings originating in India, it was truly international. Its worldwide staff of 223,000 in more than forty countries represented ninety-nine nationalities—quite an achievement for a corporation that hired its first non–Indian national in 1994. Half its total sales were in North America and a quarter in Europe. Of the remaining 25 percent, the Middle East accounted for 10 percent and Latin America the rest. For a corporation that originated in Mumbai as the Tata Computer Centre in 1965, using rented IBM 1401 computers to punch cards, mainly to serve TISCO, a sister concern, TCS's subsequent prosperity astonished many.

TCS: The Jewel in the Tata Crown

TCS started exporting its services abroad in 1971 with a programming contract in Iran. Three years later, it imported the first machine built by Detroit-based Burroughs, a rival of IBM, and signed an agreement with that company to sell Burroughs computers. Pressed to earn foreign exchange to be able to pay for the import of U.S. computers, TCS tried hard to get contracts in America. Its rock-bottom service charges lured Burroughs to assign it the task of writing the code for Burroughs machines for several U.S.-based clients, making it the first Indian firm to penetrate the American market. In

1976, it imported its first large mainframe Burroughs computer to receive software exports, and began offering services for hardware installation, support, and maintenance work for the Burroughs range of computers in India. In 1979, it secured its first non-Burroughs contract in the United States, with American Express, after a three-year struggle by Subramaniam Ramadorai, the resident manager of its New York office.

Though TCS opened an office in 1977 in Britain, where it worked with ICL, another rival of IBM, the Indian government did not allow the company to execute sales on its own until 1979. Despite the low fees it charged for its services—compared to the rates offered by British or American IT companies—it failed to overcome the widely prevalent reluctance of locally based European firms to do business with an Indian company.

"Such stalwarts as IBM and Accenture had a long track record," explained Abhinav Kumar, the Brussels-based public relations manager of TCS Europe. "They possessed a prestigious and widely recognized brand. They had strong relationships with their clients rising up to the level of the board of directors."[46] It was not until 1981 that TCS signed its first substantial contract in the United Kingdom, with Western Trust & Savings Ltd. in Plymouth, a retail bank with twenty-eight branches.

"In the first decade of TCS, it was very difficult to get foreign exchange where the top priority was given to food imports," said Amur S. Lakshminarayanan, the slim, silver-haired, bespectacled CEO of London-based TCS Europe. He joined the company in 1983 and took charge of the Western Trust project in 1992, when the Internet began to penetrate the mainstream of business in the West and India. "That led us to devise a different way of operating. We broke up the value chain and figured out what to do in India and what not. We devised a way where we did some aspects of the job at a Western site and others we did in India. Those employed back home were highly motivated and worked long hours in order to keep their jobs. That way we had the best of both worlds. Or to put it in business terminology, we had global backing in terms of manpower and IT capabilities."[47] The key to the near-vertigenous ascent of TCS lay with the fact that three-quarters of its work was done in a low-cost country, India, whereas in the case of competing companies such as IBM and Accenture, the proportion was reversed. In the absence of unemployment benefits or any other element of the modern state welfare system in India, white-collar employees were left with no option but to put in long hours without overtime pay.

Over the years, an operating pattern emerged. If a job required a team of fifty engineers, it was divided into three segments: those who worked at the European head office in London, others who worked with the client at its premises, and the third batch in India.

A far more senior TCS executive was Ramadorai, a bald, broad-shouldered, bespectacled man. He joined the firm in Mumbai in 1969, set up its office in New York seven years later, and climbed the hierarchical ladder to become its CEO in 1996, an office he held until his retirement in 2009. "Our 'developing nation' attitude led to us being enormously creative when it came to finding hardware solutions and replacement parts," he wrote in his book *The TCS Story . . . and Beyond.* "This was a contrast from today's 'use and throw' approach. . . . We had to make do with less. Foreign exchange was scarce; import procedures were complex and time-consuming and import duties punitive. Almost all our equipment had to be imported. . . . So we had to innovate to survive."[48] Thus India's prospering software industry—a vital source of its foreign currencies for the past decade and a half, and a major contributor to its impressive GDP growth—owes its existence to its acute deficiency in foreign currencies in earlier times, when companies like TCS had to earn foreign exchange to pay for the importing of a new machine. "Doing more with less became part of our DNA. Our technical competence was tested because with both memory and disk capacity in short supply, we had to build applications in the most optimal way with what we had. At the same time our export obligations meant that quality could not be compromised."[49]

Despite all this innovation by IT companies like TCS and Infosys, India provided negligible business for them in the 1970s and the first half of the subsequent decade. Actually, it was only in 1986 that TCS was established properly as a wholly owned subsidiary of Tata Sons Ltd., the holding company of the Tata Group, with Nanabhoy Palkhivala as its CEO and chairman. In 1989, it developed an electronic depository and trading system called SECOM for SIS SegaInterSettle AG (Swiss Central Securities Depository). At the time, this system was by far the most complex project undertaken by an Indian IT company.[50]

By the time Ratan Tata became the CEO of Tata Group in 1992, TCS had three thousand employees. But it was only in 1995 that he replaced Nanabhoy Palkhivala as chairman of TCS. Presciently, TCS built its business around migration from one system or language to another and designed tools to automate this process. That enabled it to adopt an assembly-line approach toward correcting the Y2K code, which led to its building of a software factory in Chennai in 1998. Its software tools automated the conversion process and enabled third-party developers and clients to deploy them. By so doing, TCS handled 600 to 700 million lines of code. The burgeoning Y2K business quadrupled the TCS revenue during 1995–99, to $420 million. In the process, it gave greater visibility to India and Indians in the minds of Western corporations.

In 1999, TCS saw an outsourcing opportunity in electronic-commerce and related solutions and set up its e-commerce division with ten people. Within five years, e-commerce was contributing half a billion dollars to the annual turnover of TCS.

The next important date in the history of TCS was August 2004, when it became a publicly listed company—much later than its rivals, Infosys Technologies, Wipro Technologies, and Satyam Computer Services. Its IPO, issued at Rs 850 ($18.75) a share, was oversubscribed 7.7 times and raised $1.17 billion. The splitting of one share into two in August halved the price of a share, thus drawing increased investor interest, which raised the market value of the parent company, Tata Group. Indeed, it was on the back of the glittering performance of TCS that Tata Steel went on to outbid its Brazilian competitor, CSN, for the ownership of the Corus Group.[51]

It was not until 2004 that TCS management set up its marketing department, for which it had not seen any need previously. At the same time, it split its operations into eight major divisions: banking, insurance, life sciences, manufacturing, public sector and government, retail, telecom, and transport.[52] In TCS's drive to enhance efficiencies in its own internal IT and communications systems—a recurring theme in its management consultancy work— its directors introduced the systems it had recommended to its clients. With over one hundred thousand employees on its payroll in 2008, TCS became one of the top ten global IT software and services corporations. Its revenue exceeded $5 billion, with a profit margin of 20 percent.

What explained the phenomenal rise of TCS? "We are a one-stop company," said Amit Gupta, the man in charge of telecom in Gurgaon, in November 2011. "We provide everything our potential customer is looking for. We are customer focused. Therefore 95 percent of our business now consists of repeat orders. The gap between TCS and other companies is growing because we are very efficient. And we practice corporate social responsibility."[53] In London, Abhinav Kumar cited several major reasons: low cost; assured delivery; flexibility due to a large pool of technical staff in India who enable TCS to operate twenty-four hours a day; a stronger work ethic among Indians than among Western competitors; and seasoned managers who have risen from the bottom and therefore have extensive operational experience.[54]

The financial tsunami, which started in September 2008, caused the FTSE 100 index in London to plummet 31.3 percent by the year-end (a record), with similar declines in Paris and Frankfurt. In New York, the Dow Jones Industrial Average plunged almost 34 percent in 2008, its worst year since 1931. Standard & Poor 500 tumbled 38.5 percent, and the tech-heavy NASDAQ dropped 40.5 percent. Western companies became cheaper to buy. But with the value of the financial sector slashed by a perilous 57 percent in 2008, the Indian companies found it was an uphill battle to raise loans from Western banks. Therefore, outward Indian investment dropped to $13.7 billion in the fiscal year of 2009–10. A pick-up to $16.84 billion followed in the next financial year. Later, between April and October 2011, the outward investment from India soared to a record $20 billion plus.[55]

The headlines in the financial media in India and the West centered around such Indian corporations as Essar Energy, which bought Shell Oil's giant Stanlow oil refinery in Merseyside in 2010; Tata Motors, which acquired Jaguar and Land Rover plants in 2007; and Mittal Steel, which acquired Arcelor in 2006. But small and medium-size Indian firms operating in Britain or North America remained below the popular radar. This was particularly true of the 180 companies that had invested in Britain's IT sector.[56]

Travails of Small Indian Firms

Historically, aspiring Indian and Pakistani entrepreneurs found themselves at a disadvantage when they decided to set up a business or a workshop in the United Kingdom. Until the 1962 Commonwealth Immigration Act, Britain was open for permanent settlement to anybody from the Commonwealth, which included India and Pakistan. The new law introduced a system of work vouchers, which the aspiring immigrant had to obtain at the British High Commission in his or her country before traveling to the United Kingdom. These vouchers were to be issued only to those who had received higher education. The resulting increase of professionally qualified Indians settling in Britain rectified to some extent the pre-1962 preponderance of rural immigrants from Punjab. Nonetheless, the general impression of Indian immigrants as unskilled or semiskilled workers persisted. Therefore, the only way an enterprising Indian settler could break away from his taxing, low-paying manual or semiskilled job was to live frugally and build up his savings or join a syndicate to raise the capital for a private enterprise. The overall perception of the Indian subcontinent as an indigent region acted as a further damper on the typical British bank manager.

The situation eased somewhat when a fair number of affluent South Asians arrived in the United Kingdom from East Africa, particularly Uganda, in 1972. Most of them were traders, civil servants, and professionals. But some were successful businessmen and industrialists. As part of the "economic war" that Uganda's President Idi Amin launched against non-Africans, in August 1972 he ordered sixty thousand Asians who lacked Ugandan passports to leave the country within three months. Some thirty thousand, holding British passports, arrived in Britain, penniless. Among them was Manubhai Madhvani, whose company had set up sugar, oil, and textile mills in Uganda, which were confiscated by the government. Though deprived of their properties, these expelled Asians retained their university degrees, business and professional skills, and the communal network. "They helped each other to help themselves," wrote Madhvani in his autobiography, *Tide of Fortune: A Family Tale.* "You can take someone's money, but you cannot take their know-how."[57] Little wonder then that six of the ten richest Asians in 2006 who had their assets exclusively in Britain were from Uganda and Kenya.[58]

It was against this background that within three decades the size of the middle class among British Asians increased to about 12 percent—on a par with the native population. The emergence of the first generation of Asian children educated exclusively in Britain—with their above-average performances in schools and universities—helped to change the view of this new generation held by British bankers.

At the same time, back home, India's IT firms made their mark by tackling the millennium bug in the computer systems of well-known British companies, including banks. The year 2000 thus became a watershed for those Indian settlers who wished to raise bank loans. When it came to setting up an IT firm in the United Kingdom, however, very little capital was needed. The basic requirements were qualified engineers and technicians, and local contacts capable of attracting clients who had had no previous dealings with Indian firms. There, the key to success lay with localization. "The only way an India-based IT company can succeed in the UK or any other Western country is to get localized, to grasp the business and other culture of a Western country," said Manik Dey in Slough, a bustling settlement of 140,000 about twenty miles west of London. According to the 2011 census, Slough was the most ethnically diverse town in Britain, with its 45 percent white population only marginally exceeding Asians, at 40 percent, and most of the rest being Afro-Caribbeans. South Asian immigrants had gravitated toward Slough for job opportunities and bright prospects for business. Their contemporary prosperity could be judged by an exotic index—the number of reported thefts of gold jewelry, since gold was the precious metal in which they traditionally invested their savings. In 2011, these thefts accounted for a third of all the nine hundred burglaries.[59] This was a far cry from the late 1930s, when the metamorphic change to this rural settlement caused by the establishment of a vast industrial estate had so upset the lovers of countryside that John Betjeman, a budding poet who would become the nation's Poet Laureate in 1972, had penned a poem titled "Slough," which began: "Come friendly bombs and fall on Slough."

A mild-mannered, moon-faced, bespectacled man in his mid-forties, Manik Dey was the CEO of Ontrack Systems (UK) Limited, a wholly owned subsidiary of the Kolkata-based Ontrack Systems Limited. "There are three ways to achieve localization. Learn the business culture of a Western country yourself, which takes a long time. Or set up a joint venture with a British IT company. This requires much research and probing, and then you must know how to work profitably with your local partner. Another way is to hire white British IT engineers, hoping they will attract contracts. But in general it is difficult to get a qualified white engineer or a technician to work for a small or medium-size Indian company. You have to pay them above-average salaries. And you will still need networking and/or effective marketing. Even then, it takes a couple of years to get established and turn a profit." Some Indian IT companies, he added, employed only Indians. "That is not a wise policy. You need a good mix of Indians and locals who can help to bring in business."[60]

The experience of his parent company, Ontrack Systems Limited, was a case in point. A private limited company specializing in software development and e-commerce solutions, Ontrack was established in 1988 by B. Hari (aka Hari Balasubramanian), an electronics engineer from Calcutta University, and S.V. Ramani, a commerce graduate from the same institution. Early on, they realized that Europe was the second-largest software export destination for Indian software, after the United States. To gain the advantage that accrues to the trailblazer, they opened an office in central London in 1995 for their subsidiary Ontrack Systems (UK) Limited. But their unfamiliarity with the British business culture and the absence of any network proved to be the hurdles they could not readily overcome. In 1998, they managed to enter into a joint venture with a small local firm in Holland. With the help of their Dutch partners, they gradually became accustomed to the European business culture, an essential step for future growth.

In Kolkata, to overcome the problem of high turnover of their technical staff in a very competitive industry, Hari and Ramani turned Ontrack Systems Limited into a public limited company in September 2001. The listings on India's stock exchanges enabled them to offer stock options to employees to retain their loyalty. The debilitating turnover of the technical staff dropped sharply, which led to more efficiency and higher profit.

Thus assured, both professionally and financially, the founders resurrected their British subsidiary. Their first employee was Manik Dey, then serving as the head of operations for an Indian software firm in Britain. He struck an innovative deal with PersonalMedic Limited, a firm founded in February 2002 by a doctor, Simon Wallace, and his two business partners. In exchange for a 50 percent stake in PersonalMedic's equity, Ontrack Systems (UK) Limited agreed to develop a software application for PersonalMedic to store the entire health record of a person on a smart card or floppy disk. This gave it a head start in software application services in the healthcare sector. It "would provide OSL with additional revenues since a firm long-term software development agreement has been signed between these companies," predicted Ramani.[61]

While the British subsidiary's technical staff designed software solutions, the far larger staff at the product development center in India did the follow-up at a minimal cost to the parent company. Countering the general downward trend in the software industry in the West that followed the bursting of the dot-com bubble in July 2000, Dey managed to secure contracts with some UK-based clients who had strong interests in the oil-rich region of the Middle East. "For the year ending in March 2002, the turnover for our company in Holland and Britain was less than €1 million," said Dey. "It went up to €3.6 million three years later and kept rising until the credit crunch of 2008–9."[62]

Meanwhile, realizing the importance of supporting the Arabic language software development, Dey opened an OSL (UK) office in the Fujairah Free Zone in the United Arab Emirates, rather than in the expensive cities of Dubai or Abu Dhabi. A firm believer in "localization," he appointed a UAE national as the general manager. In Britain, despite the extra effort and cost required to hire white British technical staff, he assembled a racially mixed team in his office.

In Kolkata, founders Hari and Ramani pursued the twin strategy of "buy-and-build"—that is, achieve growth within the company while also acquiring other firms. In 2005, they converted their Dutch joint venture, Ontrack Systems BV, into a wholly owned subsidiary. It soon became profitable.

When business started to pick up in 2010, Dey hired more staff. By 2012, his office in Slough had forty employees, including white British sales and operational chiefs, compared to ten employees in the Bilthoven, Holland, office, which was administered by a Dutch national. Though the European subsidiaries employed only 23 percent of the total company staff of 220 in 2012, they generated more than 70 percent of the revenue, despite the fact that Ontrack's service charges were often lower than its British competitors'.

The healthy profits generated by Ontrack Systems Limited in Europe enabled Hari and Ramani to make acquisitions in Australia and Silicon Valley in 2011.[63] Silicon Valley had emerged as the unchallenged capital of high-tech products (faster and faster silicon chips powering smaller and smaller microprocessors, the brains of computers), high-tech services (business-to-customer, business-to-business, and customer-to-customer), and management consultancy for raising the efficiency and profitability of organizations by establishing a proper mix of high-tech goods and services.

The achievements of these companies came in the wake of the improved trade balance of India—and the loans they were able to secure from Western banks for acquiring or merging with Western companies. In the financially globalized world, these banks were seeking avenues for higher returns all over the world while paying close attention to the risks involved.

On the crucial point of localization, those highly qualified Indian engineers—who went on to acquire advanced business administration degrees from prestigious American universities—readily found professional acceptance in California's up-and-coming Silicon Valley.

3

The Indian Diaspora in America's Valley of Fortune

The contributions made by Indian immigrants in the San Francisco Bay Area's Silicon Valley were of a different order from the ones they made in Britain or other regions of the United States. The prospering Valley became a magnet for Indians in the late 1970s in part because the novelty and innovation of the high-tech revolution in the Bay Area created a rising demand for qualified engineers. Another factor was the climate of the region, more akin to what is typical in India, except for the monsoon season.

Over the next few decades, this group played a vital role in strengthening the links between the economies of the globe's most prosperous nation and a developing country struggling to improve its modest rate of economic expansion. The process produced two interrelated developments: it helped accelerate the high-tech revolution in the United States, and it turned India into a leading hub of software products and services that would be exported to Western destinations to the tune of many billions of dollars. This was a departure from the traditional Indian exports of minerals and other raw materials, and it helped to boost the country's current trade account and ease the pressure on its currency's foreign exchange value.

Much more important than the salubrious climate of southern California were the attitudes of the local white businesspeople and entrepreneurs. "Silicon Valley was more of an even playing field because it really just started in the '70s," recalled Satjiv Chahil, who climbed the ranks at Apple Computer Inc. (later Apple Inc.) in the late 1970s to become its vice president for worldwide marketing. "The entrepreneurs were from the '60s and '70s—the flower children—and were much more open-minded. They didn't have so much of the racial bias that would keep Indians down [elsewhere]."[1]

This occurred in the wake of the 1964 U.S. immigration law, which discarded the principle of dividing the annual three hundred thousand immigrant quota for a foreign country according to the percentage of American citizens originating there in the 1920 census—which favored European immigrants—and replaced it with a "special skills" priority for those professions and trades in which America was deficient. This law removed the measly quota of one hundred people for India in place before 1964.[2]

By 2010, the Bay Area was home to about half of the 528,000 Asian Indians in California.[3] For historical reasons, in the United States the term "Indian" needed to be qualified. In the early 1960s, when I worked for an American corporation in Baltimore, I was described by my colleagues as an East Indian, to distinguish me from an American Indian. With the arrival of hundreds of thousands of Indian immigrants in the United States, the authorities needed to coin a more specific term. They settled for Asian Indians, which clearly demarcated them from American Indians, now identified as "Native Americans." Asian Indians played a critical role in advancing the information and communications technology industry in the Santa Clara Valley, which came to acquire the title of Silicon Valley after the element silicon used to produce semiconductors, which became the indispensable component of all electronic products.

Nationwide, Asian Indians accounted for 5 percent of the 40.4 million immigrants to the United States in 2011—up 150 times from their population of twelve thousand in 1960, which represented less than 0.5 per cent of 9.7 million immigrants.[4] The communal profile of Asian Indians in the San Francisco Bay Area stood out. The median income of an Indian household was $107,000 a year. Three-quarters of the adults had at least a bachelor's degree—three times the national average—and 70 percent were in management or professional positions.[5] These settlers were part of the larger Indian diaspora in the United States, the richest ethnic group in the country in 2005. Their annual median household income—$68,771—was almost 50 percent higher than the national average.[6]

A study by AnnaLee Saxenian of University of California, Berkeley, published as "Silicon Valley's New Immigrant Entrepreneurs" in 1999, showed that by the mid-1990s a third of the Valley's science and engineering workforce was foreign-born. A quarter of its engineers—28,000 people—were Indian, with a majority holding postgraduate degrees. By the end of the decade, when the high-tech boom neared its peak, 774 of the 11,443 companies in this sector that had been founded over the past two decades had Indian CEOs.[7]

In India, the post-1991 era is seen as a period when Indian business and technological prowess was released from the tight embrace of the Indian state. But none of this would have happened if India had not followed the state planning adopted by the social democrat Jawaharlal Nehru, who became India's prime minister after its independence in 1947, and who stressed higher education in science and technology as the foundation for the country's systematic industrialization. Almost all Indian engineers working in Silicon Valley had acquired their undergraduate degree at an Indian Institute of Technology (IIT), and many had obtained a postgraduate degree in business administration at an Indian Institute of Management (IIM), both of these institutions being in the public sector. The first IIMs were founded in 1961 in Ahmedabad and Calcutta (later Kolkata) in collaboration with the Harvard Business School and the Sloan School of Management at the Massachusetts Institute of Technology, respectively. It was Narendra Patni, an MBA of the Sloan School of Management, whose company, Data Conversion Inc., incorporated in Massachusetts in 1972, pioneered the commercial offshoring of services, starting with low-cost data encoding on paper or magnetic tape in India to be transmitted by telephone for printing in the United States.

Scaling IIT Heights: A Herculean Task

The first Indian Institute of Technology, established in 1951, was nothing more than an upgrade of an earlier technical college in Kharagpur, 120 miles southwest of Kolkata. It was only after 1956 that the Indian government adopted a plan to establish new IITs throughout the republic. But, lacking enough foreign exchange to import expensive equipment and teaching staff, it approached the Paris-based United Nations Educational, Scientific, and Cultural Organization (UNESCO) and friendly foreign governments for help. Once UNESCO agreed to assist by channeling funds provided by the Soviet Union to pay for the equipment and experts, construction for the second IIT, at Powai, a suburb of Mumbai, started in 1958.[8] During his visit to Mumbai in 1960, Leonid Brezhnev, chairman of the Presidium of the Supreme Soviets, the de jure head of state in the Soviet Union, planted a sapling at the Powai campus. The campus spread out over 550 acres and included twenty-four departments, centers, and schools, which would come to include information technology and management. During his visit to the Powai IIT in December 2010, Russian president Dmitry Medvedev said, "Doubtless the ties that were established back in the 1950s have not disappeared. They used to be stronger."[9] After 1958, three more IITs followed in as many years. Then there was a long hiatus, which was broken in 1994 with the construction of IIT Guwahati in the state of Assam.

Entrance to an IIT became the dream of almost every aspiring Indian high school student. The competition was so tough that only one out of thirty-four applicants to the IIT in Bombay gained entry. Since 1958, the competition has become even more intense. Aspiring IIT students and their parents realized that American corporations valued IIT graduates highly, and that being hired by an American company was the ticket to lifelong affluence not on offer anywhere else on the planet. It would catapult them from their existence in a congested apartment in a noisy neighborhood of an Indian city to life in a light and bright two-bedroom bungalow with a garage and lawns in front and back on a quiet street in the San Francisco Bay Area, worth at least Rs 13 million ($260,000). Instead of using the overcrowded public transport or decrepit taxis, they would drive a Ford Fusion or Nissan Altima on sleek highways and well-maintained side streets. If unmarried, their value in the matrimonial market would shoot up. Their parents were not daydreaming. Their expectations were quite realistic, as borne out by statistics. Between 1955 and 2004, nearly 25,000 IIT graduates settled in America.[10]

The minimum age for entry to an IIT was seventeen, and the maximum age was twenty-five. It cost the student's parents about Rs 35,000 ($700) a year for room, board, and tuition. That was less than one-fifth of the actual expense—the Indian government paid the rest. Little wonder that, at the age of sixteen or so, students often enrolled in privately run coaching classes, where they were drilled for the IIT entrance test, consisting of math, physics, and chemistry. The exam was incredibly demanding, and so was the four-year course leading to a Bachelor of Technology or Engineering degree. "Put Harvard, MIT and Princeton together, and you begin to get an idea of the status of an IIT in India," remarked Rebecca Leung of CBS's *60 Minutes*. "It is dedicated to producing world-class chemical, electrical, and computer engineers with a curriculum that may be the most rigorous in the world."[11]

In 2012, almost 520,000 high school seniors took the entrance exam. Just over 10,000 passed—less than 2 percent. By contrast, Harvard admits about 10 percent of its applicants. Acceptance by an IIT is strictly on merit. For example, even Rohan Murthy, son of Nagavara Ramarao Narayana Murthy,[12] a former CEO (1981–2002) of the Bangalore-based giant software corporation Infosys Technologies, known as the Bill Gates of India, failed to pass the IIT entrance test in 2003. Later, Cornell University in Ithaca, New York, accepted him, and he majored in computer science. "I do know cases where [Indian] students who couldn't get into computer science at IITs, they have gotten [a] scholarship at MIT, at Princeton, at Caltech," noted Narayana Murthy.[13]

U.S. corporate management teams, particularly in the fast-growing high-tech industry, were quick to note the high quality of IIT graduates, and they went on a recruitment drive. "Microsoft, Intel, PCS [Personal Communication Service network], Sun Microsystems—you name it, I can't imagine a major area where Indian IIT engineers haven't played a leading role," said Vinod Khosla, a thin, gray-haired, gaunt-faced partner at a leading venture capital firm, Kleiner, Perkins, Caufield and Byers, in 2003. "They are favored over almost anybody else. If you're a WASP [White Anglo-Saxon Protestant] walking in for a job, you wouldn't have as much preassigned credibility as you do if you're an engineer from an IIT."[14]

The resulting exodus of IIT graduates—followed by those of the IIMs—became a sore point in India. "Some people would say we are like subsidizing factories, which produce largely for the higher end of the American employment market," said E.M. Rahim, a Mumbai-based journalist. "You don't have to be crudely nationalistic to raise this question. There's a demand here, and these guys are simply not available."[15] India's brightest engineers, educated at great expense by the taxpayers of a poor, developing nation, were being exported to the globe's richest and most technologically advanced country.

Yet the Indian government had no means of staunching this outflow. It was required by the Supreme Court to issue a passport to every law-abiding citizen, which meant that a qualified IIT or IIM graduate was free to leave the republic and work abroad. To their credit, most of the Indian expatriates in the United States maintained close contact with their families back home, sending them part of their earnings, and they also invested in new houses and offices being built in Indian cities and satellite towns,[16] and sometimes nongovernmental organizations.

Indian corporations seeking investment also benefited from this reciprocal relationship with American tech companies. Having purchased with borrowed funds a prestigious Western company in a new or long-established industry, an enterprising Indian corporation could find itself unable to refinance its debt on time because of the credit crunch in the West. In this case, it invariably turned to investors in India to bail it out. And Indian investors came to its rescue, almost without fail. This afforded Indian corporations a gold-plated alternative to Western credit not available to their Western counterparts.

Slightly more than half of the software services India exported were bought by American companies, for a total value in 2011 of $67 billion.[17] These included information technology enabled services, also known as offshore IT, and business process outsourcing, wherein Western companies outsourced call-center operations, accounting, payroll processing, and primary research, as well as data analysis and data mining. Together, these services are sometimes identified by their acronym, ITES-BPO (Information Technology Enabled Services–Business Process Outsourcing).

Over time, other unforeseen advantages began accruing to the Indian economy as engineers, entrepreneurs, and executives traveled back and forth, particularly between San Francisco and Bangalore, in southern India. A former British military cantonment city with a salubrious climate, Bangalore was home to 1,700 software companies in 2005.

This was the end result of two parallel processes, one inside Silicon Valley and the other outside, involving both the newly arrived high-tech industry and traditional businesses. As the subsequent survey in this chapter will show, Silicon Valley's Indian diaspora has proved a key resource for both the United States and India, making a vital contribution to America's high-tech industry and exporting to the homeland much of the energy, creativity, and experience that has made Silicon Valley the world's technology star. The notable examples in the non–Silicon Valley category are Indra Nooyi at PepsiCo, Ajay Banga at MasterCard, and Rajat Gupta, who set the record by becoming the first India-born executive to head the New York–based McKinsey & Company, a multinational consultancy company, in 1994.

Cross-Fertilization

All these high flyers had one thing in common: they possessed a master's degree in business administration either from an IIM in India, set up in coordination with a reputed American business school, or a prestigious American university. That is, they had imbibed the business culture of the United States. Rajat Gupta, for example, was a graduate of IIT, Delhi, with an MBA from

Harvard Business School. He joined McKinsey & Company in New York in 1973 and served as head of the firm's branch in Stockholm eight years later. After being promoted to a senior partner in 1984, he was appointed chief of the Chicago office in 1990. Realizing the opportunities that India's 1991 economic liberalization offered, he urged the directors to open an office there, which they did in 1993. The India branch thrived because it had the advantage of being the trailblazer. Nine years later, he was elected the managing director for a three-year term and was reelected twice. Under his leadership, the company doubled its workforce, which operated in forty countries. But, as a director of Goldman Sachs investment bank during 2006–10, he let his greed fog his judgment. He conveyed boardroom secrets to a billionaire hedge-fund owner, Raj Rajaratnam. Gupta was found guilty of securities fraud and conspiracy and sentenced to two years in jail in October 2012.

By comparison, the rise of Ajay Banga (aka Ajaypal Singh Banga), a bearded and turbaned Sikh, was slow and unglamorous. Born into the household of Lieutenant General Harbhajan Singh Banga in the western city of Pune in 1960, he was educated at various garrison towns. He finished his university education at IIM, Ahmedabad, associated with Harvard Business School, in 1981. He then joined Nestlé USA and worked there until 1994, when he moved to PepsiCo's restaurant division. He was involved in the launching of the corporation's fast-food franchises, which then included Kentucky Fried Chicken, in India. His first target was Delhi. Facing much bureaucratic and local business resistance, he succeeded against heavy odds. In 1996, he moved to Citigroup, where he became head of the U.S. consumer assets division in 2000. His salesmanship skills remained sharp. In 2003, he was seen in Flushing, New York, inaugurating a Gold Roshni (Shining Gold) promotion scheme during Diwali, the Hindu-Sikh Festival of Light, offering exquisite gold jewelry to those who opened new accounts at the bank.[18] He became the CEO of Citibank's Global Consumer Group in 2005 before being promoted to Asia-Pacific CEO in 2008. His big break came two years later, when MasterCard's board of directors appointed him the company's president and CEO.

Far more striking was the example of an Indian woman reaching the pinnacle of an American multinational that is a household word in more than two hundred countries and territories. In October 2006, Indra Nooyi—with an MBA from IIM, Kolkata, and a master's degree in public and private management from Yale School of Management—became the CEO of PepsiCo, the globe's second-largest food and beverage corporation with 185,000 employees. A portly woman with short hair and an easy smile, she joined the corporation in 1994 after working for Motorola and for a consulting firm for seven years. She was promoted to chief financial officer in 2001.

Born into the household of Anant Krishnamurthy, a bank accountant, in Chennai, the capital of Tamil Nadu, she went to an all-girls school run by the Roman Catholic Church, where she was a member of the cricket team. Her mother, Shantha, was a strong influence. She encouraged her to aim high, starting with achieving a perfect score on her math exam papers. When her application for admission to Yale University was accepted in 1978, her parents, surprisingly, allowed her to travel to the United States on her own. "It was unheard of for a good, conservative, south Indian Brahmin girl to do this," she recalled many years later. "It would make her an absolutely unmarriageable commodity after that."[19] It was during her stay in America that she met her future husband, Raj Kishan Nooyi, an engineer like her. But unlike her, he was not a Tamil, nor was he a Brahmin by caste. He carried the name of his village in the state of Karnataka. Their marriage, solemnized according to traditional Hindu custom in 1980, has endured. They have two grown-up daughters. Her husband has been very supportive of her vaulting ambition. Soon after becoming the top executive at PepsiCo, she offered counsel to ambitious businesswomen: "Pick the right husband," she said. "I did. And here I am."[20]

In a long interview with the Delhi-based *Economic Times*, she mused about her life in the United States. "When I first started in my summer job [in Connecticut], I didn't have money to buy business suits. So you just wear a saree, because that is a necessity and it just did fine. What I would not do is flaunt my Indianness by wearing a saree to work every day, because it distracts from the job. . . . When in Rome do as the Romans do. Social events are different . . . I have never worn a saree to board meetings." She added, "I think I have never shied away from the fact that I am an Indian, and I don't intend to, but you can be at home with both cultures."[21] Her religious roots remained intact. In her office, she kept an idol of Ganesha, the Hindu god with an elephant head, worshipped as the harbinger of good fortune.

Nooyi's love of cricket led her to take an interest in baseball. "That was the year [1978] when the Yankees were going through an incredible season," she continued in her *Economic Times* interview. "I fell in love with the Yankees then. But then I also discovered that in business, the language of business is sports. So, people would talk about 'I do not want to get singles, I want to get [a] homerun.' And the next morning, everybody in business analyzed the game and unless we were the part of the whole process, we felt very left out. So I combined my love for, or an urge to have an affiliation to, the bat-and-ball sports, with the Yankees' incredible season with this language of business. Things came together."[22]

Interviews in the U.S. media followed. "PepsiCo did not have a woman in the senior ranks, nor a foreign-born person who was willing to think differently," she told Simon Hobbs of CNBC.[23] As a former management consultant, she was given to forming long-term visions, which the PepsiCo top management had lacked before. As the CEO, she succeeded in swaying the rest of the board of directors with her vision, and thus helped position the corporation for growth in China, the Middle East, and India.

A penetrating insight into the secret of her dizzying ascent in the American corporate world was provided by her hard-knuckle, competitive capitalist values. "Disruption is now our friend, not our enemy," she declared. "If you don't disrupt yourselves, the competition will." Along with this went a drive to keep innovating. "The minute you've developed a new business model, it's extinct, because somebody is going to copy it."[24]

After her appointment as chairperson of PepsiCo in 2007, *Forbes* magazine ranked her the third most powerful woman in the world in 2008. "It was overwhelming, honestly," she told Simon Hobbs of CNBC TV. "Incredible privilege and incredible responsibility. I realized I was going from a quasi-private person to a completely public figure. People build you up too fast and they have to realize that I'm [only] human."[25]

She maintained her position as the most powerful businesswoman in America in *Fortune*'s list from 2006 to 2010. She retained her ties with India, whose government bestowed upon her the country's third highest award, the Padma Bhushan (Hindi: Lotus Ornament), in 2007. Two years later, she held PepsiCo's board meeting in Mumbai, the second such gathering outside the United States, pointing out that India was one of the corporation's top three markets. PepsiCo had started bottling its soft drinks there in June 1990, three years ahead of Coca-Cola. "We want to show them [the other directors] the glory of India and the issues in India so that we [can] propose solutions," she said. "You cannot just import Western solutions to India. You have to crack solutions, which are right for India, right for its people, and right for its farmers."[26] In 2012, *Forbes* magazine included her among the world's ten most powerful women, one rank behind Sonia Gandhi, president of the ruling United Progressive Alliance in India.

Vinod Khosla had such personalities in mind when he pointed out that "Some of these people who have reached the higher echelons in the corporate world in the U.S., they have persuaded their corporations to start operations in India, whether it's Texas Instruments, whether it's General Electric, whether it's Citibank."[27]

An innovator and entrepreneur by instinct, Khosla capped his IIT undergraduate degree in electrical engineering in Delhi, and a master's degree in biomedical engineering from Carnegie Mellon University, with an MBA from Stanford University, Silicon Valley's creative hub, in 1980. After briefly working for Daisy System, an electronic design automation company, in 1982, he cofounded Sun (an acronym for the Stanford University Network) Microsystems along with three of his Stanford classmates. It was funded by a board member of the venture capital firm Kleiner, Perkins, Caufield and Byers, founded a decade earlier. As Sun Microsystems' first CEO and chairman, Khosla pioneered open systems and processors based on reduced instruction-set computing architecture for microprocessors. This was a giant step in simplifying computing, and it lead to the evolution of the desktop computer, a technology that would have an enormous impact on hundreds of millions of individuals worldwide.

Other Indian innovators followed. Cirrus Logic, established by Suhas Patil in 1984, became the leading supplier of personal computer graphics chips, audio converters, and chips for magnetic storage products. Brocade Communications Systems, cofounded by Kumar Malavalli in 1995, emerged as the leader in storage area switching, thus setting the scene for broadband communication. And the twenty-eight-year-old Sabeer Bhatia, along with Jack Smith, introduced Hotmail, the world's first free e-mail service, on American Independence Day, July 4, 1996.

Behind these successes lay such groundbreaking contributions to technological innovation as the Ethernet, the Pentium microprocessing chip, and the truly revolutionary fiber optics. In each of these, Indian scientists and engineers played a central role. Kanwal Rekhi, a cofounder and CEO of the San Jose–based Excelan Inc. in 1982, pioneered Ethernet networking technology, one of the basic building blocks of the Internet. While working for Intel Corporation, Vinod Dham invented the Pentium P5 microprocessor in March 1993. It became the largest selling processor.[28] The arrival of fiber optics in the communication industry heralded a new era. For this, most credit goes to Narinder Singh Kapany, an Indian physicist. In 1954, he conducted the first successful experiment with light beams inside bent glass tubes and achieved total reflection of light—the basic principle of fiber optics—while studying at the Imperial College of Science and Technology, London, where he obtained his doctorate a year later. He then migrated to the United States, where he founded Optics Technology Inc. in 1960, the same year that the term "fiber optics" appeared for the first time, in an article he penned for *Scientific American*. The replacement of copper with fiber optics in telephone cables speeded up telecom traffic; soon the instant transmission of words and images became commonplace.

Following the example of Khosla, who left Sun Microsystems to become a partner in the venture capital firm Kleiner, Perkins, Caufield and Byers in 1986, many of these innovators and entrepreneurs opted for the role of venture capitalist, investing in and supporting a new generation of start-up companies.[29] Later, Khosla set up his own venture capital company, in part to offset the racism that some Indian entrepreneurs faced when approaching established white venture capitalists, not all of whom had grown up as flower children. Earlier, such discrimination had compelled some Indians to find white partners to act as their delegates.

The High-Tech Boom

As the dot-com boom accelerated in the United States and elsewhere in the Western world from 1996 onward, the number of Indian millionaires in Silicon Valley blossomed like wild flowers in what the people of Indian origin fondly christened the Valley of Fortune.

Noticing the absence of venture capitalists and entrepreneurial drive among qualified engineers in India, Khosla and other successful entrepreneurs, corporate executives, and senior professionals from South Asia established The IndUS Entrepreneurs (TiE), a nonprofit organization, in San Jose soon after Delhi launched its New Economic Policy in July 1991. Its aim was to foster entrepreneurship globally through mentoring, networking, and education, with special focus on the Indian subcontinent. By the late 1990s, it was an important part of the Indian network in the Bay Area, which included the Silicon Valley Indian Professionals Association and the Indian Women's Business Association. "The mentor relationship can help a firm survive and avoid drastic mistakes," remarked Havani Kola, who built her company Media Kola from scratch in 1997 with the assistance of her business contacts. "I called many [Indian] CEOs when I reached a dilemma, and most were generous with their time."[30] During the next two decades, TiE acquired 15,000 members, including 2,500 charter members, across seventeen countries. According to Sean Randolph, a Bay Area expert on high-tech industry, "The largest contingent outside the US is in India, supported by active links to the mothership, TiE Global, in Santa Clara."[31]

During this period, another phenomenon had come into play: the cycling of knowledge in the high-tech sector between America and India. By then, such U.S. megacorporations as Cisco, Google, Intel, and Oracle staffed the top levels of their otherwise locally recruited outfits in India—often engaged in research and development in Bangalore—with their Silicon Valley employees of Indian origin. The India offices of such Bay Area companies as IDG Ventures and Sequoia Capital were also led by returnees. Together, taking into account India's huge market with mainly low-income consumers, they strived to develop their specific brand of innovation, based on effective but low-cost services and technology.

Whereas Sequoia Capital, with a record of funding Apple, Google, YouTube, and LinkedIn, started operating in India in 2002, the comparatively small IDG Ventures, formed in 1998, opened for business in Bangalore and Mumbai four years later. Since then, demand for venture capital has shot up. During the first half of 2012, venture capital firms invested more than $787 million in ninety companies in India.[32] Companies such as Sequoia Capital, IDG Ventures, and Silicon Valley Bank not only lend capital but also their experience, networking, and hands-on support. Among those Indian firms that have benefited from this pool are the country's first consumer Internet company, Nauri.com; India's version of Expedia (MakeMyTrip.com); and Café Coffee Day, the local answer to Starbucks.

Little wonder that the San Francisco–Bangalore flight, started by Lufthansa in 2001 and dubbed "Bangalore Express," has always run to full capacity as entrepreneurs, employees, and investors travel back and forth. According to Randolph, San Francisco–Bangalore became one of Lufthansa's most trafficked routes and its second-largest long-haul market.[33] These high-tech businessmen (and, rarely, women), often in jeans and sweatshirts, traveled business class, and during the eleven-hour flight from San Francisco to Frankfurt, they gathered at the galleys for drinks. "They switch seats to get closer to people they want to talk to," reported Mehul Srivastave of *Businessweek*. "Entrepreneurs stalk venture capitalists, salesmen scope out new clients, and CEOs get bombarded with business cards."[34]

While Indian engineers and entrepreneurs had scored a fairly impressive list of highly publicized successes in high-tech industry, they had inevitably met with many more failures, which seldom grabbed headlines. Khosla had a string of stinking failures. These included Asera, BroadBand Office, Dynabook, Excite, @HomeNetwork, and Zambeel. But, when asked at a meeting of young Indian entrepreneurs in Bangalore in 2011 whether he ever feared failure, he replied, "Freedom to fail is a key ingredient in success. Try and fail, but do not fail to try."[35]

Khosla's bullish tone stemmed from the fact that he had amassed a personal fortune of tens of millions of dollars, which enabled him to seriously consider sponsoring a mix of "for profit" and "for social impact" ventures as well as to finance a few daring science experiments. "Any sufficiently advanced technology is indistinguishable from magic," he said, recycling a quote from the late science-fiction writer Arthur C. Clarke, author of *2001: A Space Odyssey* and *Rendezvous with Rama*, among others. "You can't tell what's crazy and so we encourage crazy. I often suspend disbelief and listen to a story that sounds crazy and impossible."[36] That was why he funded Khosla Ventures entirely with his own capital. Five years later, he took on Pierre Lamond, a French-American, who had been a partner in the Menlo Park–based Sequoia Capital, a long-established venture capital firm. By then, he was fully committed to help green energy start-ups in addition to IT start-ups.

In May 2010, Khosla Ventures made international headlines when, having raised $1.3 billion in capital, it hired Tony Blair, former British prime minister, as an adviser on an undisclosed retainer to offer strategic advice on investments in environmentally friendly or helpful IT technologies. "Understanding local and global politics is now important for us techie nerds," Khosla said with uncharacteristic self-deprecation. "This is where our relationship with Tony Blair can really help us. He understands far better than I ever will the political and geopolitical forces, as well as organizational behavior and social behavior and change."[37] In another high-profile move, in December 2012 Khosla Ventures added former U.S. secretary of state Condoleezza Rice and her consulting firm, RiceHadleyGates, as strategic advisers to help its portfolio companies "navigate government and regulatory concerns abroad," particularly in the alternative-energy industry.[38]

Whereas Khosla combined his technical prowess with a flair for enterprise and risk-taking, the white-haired Dr. Bala S. Manian (born Bala Subramanian) had the distinction of marrying his entrepreneurship with expertise in science, which covered optics, computer vision, and bioinformatics—an interdisciplinary field combining computer science, statistics, math, and engineering—to process biological data. Over a period of three decades, he singlehandedly set up a string of companies in Silicon Valley focused on life sciences and medical technology, then sold them at high premiums to large U.S. corporations. His age (he was born in 1946), and his habit of wearing spectacles with one lens blackened to hide his missing eye, made him stand out physically. With characteristic clarity, he summed up his long, successful career thus: "I am a scientist, entrepreneur, venture capital investor, still trying to figure out what drives me."[39] He is truly a man of many parts, whose multiple forays into various aspects of science, technology, and business flowered without exception.

Manian is also a man with a social conscience. A leading expert in the design of electro-optical systems, he holds more than thirty patents, many of which have been put to commercial use. In 1999, the Academy of Motion Picture Arts and Sciences gave him a Technical Academy Award for advancing digital cinematography. He became a venture capitalist and in 2002 turned his attention to India. By the end of that decade, along with his role as a venture capitalist he was the chairperson of the investment committee of India Innovation Fund.[40]

After he received an undergraduate degree in physics from Madras University and a postgraduate diploma in instrumentation from IIT, Madras (now Chennai), Manian obtained a master's degree in applied optics from Rochester University, followed by a doctorate in mechanical engineering from Purdue University. He worked as a research academic at Rochester University for four years. He moved to Silicon Valley in 1980. There he founded Digital Optics Corporation, an optical instrumentation and systems development company, which developed the first three-color laser, a film reader/writer system that enabled filmmakers to insert or merge special effects into movies using computerized digital imaging. After selling this company in 1984 to Matrix Corporation, he founded Lumisys and Molecular Dynamics in 1987. Five years after Lumisys went public, it was swallowed up by Eastman Kodak. In 1991, he established Biometric Imaging Inc. to produce cellular analysis instruments, then sold it to Becton Dickinson, a $3 billion medical device and diagnostic company, eight years later. Molecular Dynamics went public in 1993, and it was acquired by the multinational Amersham Biosciences Corporation in 1998.

"I have a PhD in mechanical engineering but dare not call myself a mechanical engineer," he said tongue in cheek in 2011. "I am a life science entrepreneur with no formal life science education. I have built many successful ventures in California, but I am still trying to get my bearings as an entrepreneur in India."[41] His survey of conditions in India led him to set up ReaMetrix, a biotechnological firm, in San Carlos, Silicon Valley, and Bangalore, to provide basic research and assay development services to biotechnology and pharmaceutical companies with the aim of producing affordable solutions for developing nations. He commuted between San Francisco and Bangalore every six weeks.

In December 2005, ReaMetrix in Bangalore, with the assistance of a team of Indian returnees, developed Tri-T STAT, a low-cost kit for testing HIV. But it was not until July 2009 that it was cleared by the Food and Drug Administration in the United States. It is now replacing the current liquid-based procedure in HIV detection kits—dependent on costly and complex cold chain storage—and drastically reducing the expense of HIV testing.

Whereas the likes of Khosla, Nooyi, and Manian hogged the media limelight for their outstanding achievements, there were hundreds of other Indian immigrants who had been winners of lesser import. Among them were Ashok Trivedi (b. 1949) and Sunil Wadhwani (b. 1953).

Nabobs of Networking

In the mid-1990s, the Indian high-tech corporation outside Silicon Valley that made a mark nationwide was the Pittsburgh-based Mastech Systems Corporation, a global provider of IT services and solutions since 1986. Compared to the average of 25 percent growth for large IT corporations in the mid-1990s, it expanded at twice that rate.

Its founders were Sunil Wadhwani and Ashok Trivedi. Wadhwani, a bespectacled, mustached man with a receding hairline, earned a master's degree in industrial administration from Carnegie Mellon University after receiving a bachelor's degree from IIT, Chennai. In 1981, he founded Urovalve Inc., a medical device manufacturing firm. Trivedi, a small-eyed, square-jawed man with a determined look, acquired a master's degree in business administration from Ohio University after receiving a postgraduate degree in physics from Delhi University. For the next ten years, Trivedi toiled at the headquarters of Unisys Corporation in Blue Bell, Pennsylvania, twenty miles north of Philadelphia, as a software specialist, marketing manager, and product manager. During this period, he attended the Owner/President Management Program at the Harvard Business School.

Longtime friends, Wadhwani and Trivedi would exchange business gossip over tankards of beer at a Pittsburgh bar. During one such session in early 1986, Trivedi lamented how his company was trying to shove bulky mainframe computers down the throats of clients who really needed networked personal computers. Wadhwani would recount similar complaints from fellow graduate business students at Carnegie Mellon University. They considered the idea of doing something positive, to set up their own firm. "The more we drank, the better the ideas got," Wadhwani would later tell a reporter from the New York–based *Inc.* business magazine.[42]

But when they presented their $350,000 unconventional business plan, which involved telemarketing software-development and support programs without setting up local offices in the areas they wished to serve, bank managers turned them down. So they ended up capitalizing Mastech Systems Corp, their new PC-networking-and-services business, with $100,000 raised by pooling their own savings and running up their credit cards. They operated from a ten-by-ten-foot room in Wadhwani's apartment in a Pittsburgh suburb and worked in a flexible manner, changing their roles to suit the need of the moment.

At $244,000, the firm's turnover in 1987 was decidedly modest. But their PC-networking business model held great promise, and the company had low overheads. When sales exceeded $20 million in 1992, Mastech earned thirty-first place on *Inc.* magazine's list of the five hundred fastest-growing companies in the United States, under the title of "Inc. 500." The founders smiled effusively as they held high the Mastech emblem. Their firm retained a place on the "Inc. 500" every year except one until 1996, when it went public on the back of an annual turnover of $123 million. Its $15 share opened at NASDAQ in December at 14 percent premium. It became one of the few IT companies listed on NASDAQ that had never borrowed venture capital—a fact that its founders often trumpeted, since it defied the well-trodden path of IT companies.

By 1996, Mastech had opened a software development center in Bangalore and became one of the earliest U.S. companies to do so. It also opened offices in San Francisco, Washington, D.C., Toronto, London, and Singapore. Of its 1,600 employees, less than 10 percent worked in the Pittsburgh area. Yet, as Wadhwani admitted in 1997, "It is a handicap, not being in the Silicon

Valley. The biggest challenge for a firm like ours is finding top quality managers."[43]

Still, with improved cash flow resulting from the NASDAQ listing, Mastech accelerated its already high-octane performance. "Upstart Mastech has carved out a chunk of the market against bigger rivals by offering a wide range of services and some of the lowest costs in the business," reported *Businessweek* on May 31, 1999. "The result is sales growth averaging 56 percent a year since 1995 to $390.9 million in 1998. That landed Mastech at No. 79 on our Hot Growth list." This led the magazine to honor Wadhwani and Trivedi as the "Nabobs of Networking."[44] The company's six thousand employees were spread globally from Japan to California, from Australia to the Middle East, in thirty-two locations serving more than nine hundred clients. Yet the founders stuck to their initial policy of shunning the showcase offices and large workforces of big IT competitors. "Linking its three software-development offices in India to the 400 people at the headquarters outside Pittsburgh [in Oakdale] lets technicians work on a project virtually around the clock," noted *Businessweek*.

Trivedi attributed his company's meteoric rise to two main factors. "We got global faster than most other companies [by establishing a subsidiary in Bangalore in 1993]; and we developed services faster than many other companies," he told Rediffusion, an Indian news agency, in October 1998. "We follow technology very closely and find ways of helping our clients to derive competitive advantage from that. That is what clients want . . . they say, 'How can you help me use technology so that I, General Electric, General Motors, IBM or Johnson & Johnson, can help myself to become more competitive?' That is what we do, help them."[45]

Long before Nooyi came up with outside-of-the-American-box ideas to boost the reach and revenue of PepsiCo, Trivedi deployed his non-American background to grasp the cultural and economic mores that differentiated non-Western countries from America, and amalgamated that perception with a resolve to maintain the best U.S. business practices alongside Mastech's company values. That was the key to the firm's galloping success in such diverse countries and regions as South Africa, Malaysia, the Philippines, the Middle East, India, Bulgaria, and Japan.

Mastech's revenue topped $492 million in 1999. On March 7, 2000, at the zenith of the dot-com bonanza, the founders changed the name of their company to iGate Capital Corporation. They announced that iGate Capital would consist of five units of existing Mastech and four new companies, each specializing in a particular area of e-services, such as teaching clients how to take an Internet business originally designed for 56k modem access and rebuild it into a broadband revenue earner, and to help corporations install wireless capabilities for their communications equipment. This turned iGate Capital into an Internet incubator rather than an IT services company and led to higher valuation of its stock, which was already at $50 plus per share. Overnight, iGate shares opened 25 percent higher. In retrospect, this proved to be the crest of the founders' achievements.

During the next year, the corporation expanded rapidly, running thirty-four offices in sixteen countries with over seven thousand employees. In March 2002, the founders changed the name to iGate Corporation and moved the principal executive office to Fremont, in the heart of Silicon Valley, to be able to recruit top-quality managers. By then, Fremont, home to almost 210,000 people, had become a popular destination for many expatriate Indians. Numbering about 39,000, they were the second-largest ethnic group after white Americans. They were settled in that part of California where the median household income was almost 50 percent higher than the national average of $49,800, according to the census of 2010.[46] Though Fremont is very much a generic California suburb—populated by flat, brown, single-story homes, with wide roads and big malls—for many Indians it is a "home away from home." It has dozens of Indian restaurants and shops. Its many temples and benevolent societies provide a rich variety of cultural activities. Undoubtedly, newcomers like Wadhwani and Trivedi found Fremont very congenial, both socially and culturally.

But neither the relocation of the executive office nor the name change made iGate immune to the downward spiral in which the IT industry found itself when the dot-com tide went into an ignominious retreat. By the end of 2002, the iGate share collapsed to a derisory $3, with annual sales squeezed down to $293 million and earnings per share a puny 12 cents. The turnover of $288 million in the following year reflected the continued stalemate.

Faced with the crashing winds of the American market, Wadhwani and Trivedi sought safe harbor in their home base of Bangalore, where they had founded a wholly owned subsidiary, iGate Global Solutions Limited. It was a move that the prestigious Tata Motors would follow later when the credit lines from the Western banks dried up.

As Fremont-based IT entrepreneurs, the duo had noted with a mixture of admiration and envy the stellar performance of Phaneesh Murthy, the global sales chief and company director of Infosys Technologies. A robustly built, jowly faced, bespectacled man with a trimmed mustache, Phaneesh Murthy was a high flyer. After capping his IIT in mechanical engineering in Chennai with an MBA from the IIM in Ahmedabad in 1987, he joined Sonata Software in Bangalore to handle product management. His brilliant performance there drew the attention of N.R. Narayana Murthy, the CEO of the eleven-year-old Infosys Technologies, whose annual revenue, at $2 million, had hit the buffers. After joining Infosys, Phaneesh Murthy argued that the only way the company could grow was by focusing on foreign sales, particularly with the United States. He displayed a rare combination of talents, having earlier made his name as a top-quality software programmer by designing India's first enterprise resource planning software, which integrated all the data and planning of an organization into a unified system. Accepting Murthy's strategy, the Infosys management set up the company's worldwide sales and marketing headquarters in Fremont in 1995 under his leadership.

It was a smart move. Infosys's rising presence in the international market helped its directors to make it the first Indian company to be listed on NASDAQ in March 1999. The exponential rise in its American sales lifted its aggregate revenue to $700 million by 2002. It would gain entry into the NASDAQ 100 index in December 2006, an event that Murthy failed to celebrate.[47]

In June 2002, Murthy stepped down as the global sales chief and company director in order to defend allegations of sexual harassment, stalking, and wrongful dismissal by Reka Maximovitch, a petite twenty-seven-year-old Bulgarian American who served as his secretary for fourteen months starting in October 1999. She alleged that she was pressured by Murthy, a married man, to have sex with him. Fearing the loss of her job, she capitulated and slept with him once. Regretting this lapse, she failed to turn up at the office the next day. She returned only after Murthy had assured her of putting their relationship on a "professional footing." This lasted for a while. Pressured again by Murthy, she resumed an intermittent sexual relationship with him until December 2000. When she refused to return to work after that, she was dismissed by Infosys. But that was not the end. Murthy started calling her at home and at her new employer's office. To stop this behavior, she obtained two restraining orders against him between January and June 2001, the first of which he breached. Finally, she filed a court case against Murthy in Oakland in December 2001.[48] The breach of the restraining order came as a shock to the Infosys board, who were not previously aware of it. Nonetheless, the board did not abandon Murthy after his resignation. It made an out-of-court settlement with Maximovitch almost a year later for $3 million.[49] Following Murthy's departure, the company's share price dipped by nearly 7 percent.

After leaving Infosys, Murthy teamed up with his wife, Jaya, to do a few consulting jobs before returning to Bangalore. He founded Quintant Services, India's first business process outsourcing company, in January 2003. Wadhwani and Trivedi contrived to recruit him by acquiring a majority stake in Quintant Services for $19 million through their Bangalore-based subsidiary iGate Global Solutions Limited. They appointed Murthy the CEO of their subsidiary.

They also sought Murthy's overall assessment of iGate. He told them that, with half of the corporation's revenue derived from providing staffing to its clients, their business model was flawed. But there was no quick-fix solution for ending the woes of the parent company. The inescapable fact was that high-tech industry did not have a neutral gear. It was either on its way down to becoming a has-been or on a steep upward curve, turning itself into an enticing target for a takeover by a leviathan of the industry.

The only way Wadhwani and Trivedi could keep iGate solvent was to start selling their overseas subsidiaries. In 2004, they disposed of their subsidiaries in Australia and Britain for $10 million, followed by the sale of their Canadian subsidiary for $11 million the next year. In contrast, their iGate Global Solutions in India, run by Murthy, steamed ahead in its efforts to attain outsourcing contracts from foreign corporations. These contracts helped the parent company improve its annual turnover, which inched up to $307 million in 2007.[50]

Next year came the banking crash in the West. Share prices nosedived. Corporate managers reduced their investments to the bare minimum. Having strived hard and succeeded brilliantly until the early 2000s, Wadhwani—now a member of the board of the Information Technology Association of America—and Trivedi, together owning almost half of iGate shares, thought it wise to pass on the baton to the younger and more energetic Murthy. In April 2008, Wadhwani stepped down as iGate's CEO and Trivedi stepped down as its president. Murthy took over as the CEO, based at the company's principal executive office in Fremont.

Within a few years, Murthy would merge iGate with Patni Computer Systems Limited, the second oldest IT consulting and services company of India, which claimed to have pioneered the concept of offshoring. What would distinguish the buyout of Patni—listed on the New York Stock Exchange—

was the involvement of private equity funds. The deal broke the pattern of banks being the sole financiers of such acquisitions.

As a rule, private equity firms focus on industries with high growth potential, such as IT businesses. By the same token, they are not much interested in traditional industries like steel and aluminum. Hence the funding for Tata Steel UK's acquisition of the Corus Group came from banks. In the case of iGate, the London-based Apax Partners, the seventh-largest private equity group in the world, funneled money into the takeover of Patni Computer Systems through its Australia-based Viscaria Proprietary Ltd. fund. To add a further distinctive element to this landmark deal, a vice president of General Electric Company, the sixth-largest corporation in America by revenue, played a subtle but effective backdoor role in swinging the end result in iGate's favor. These elements made iGate's acquisition of Patni Computer Systems the most multifaceted example of the globalization of capital in the early twenty-first century.

The Groundbreaking Fremont-Mumbai Bonding

In 2010 Murthy succeeded in reversing the downward trend of iGate, improving the record low annual sales of $193 million by almost $100 million and reporting a profit of $52 million. The share price soared to $25 in October 2010.

His success encouraged two partners of the giant Greenwich-based General Atlantic private equity firm to make a bid for Patni Computer Systems, then India's sixth-largest software corporation,[51] of which General Atlantic controlled 17.4 percent equity. Patni Computer Systems, cofounded as a private limited firm by Narendra Patni and his two younger brothers, Ashok and Gajendra, in Pune in 1978, had a head start when in 1979 it secured a $500,000 contract for developing a software package for a garment factory in Manhattan through the New York–based Data Basics Corporation.

By the time Patni Computer Systems went public in January 2004, with an IPO of Rs 230 ($5.15) a share, it had nine software development centers in India and twenty-one sales offices in North America, Europe, and Asia-Pacific. In 2005, it achieved the distinction of listing on the New York Stock Exchange. Its revenue leapt from $450 million in 2005 to $579 million in 2006 and its income from $61 million to $80 million.[52]

This tempted the younger Patni brothers, who each owned 15.2 per cent of the equity, to sell part of their stakes. But because they demanded a high premium, almost all the foreign private equity firms that had shown initial interest walked away. With the sales of Patni Computer Systems falling sharply because of the financial turmoil in the West in 2008–9, there was a hiatus in the bidding.

In spring 2010, Japan's Hitachi and the IT giant NTT vied for control of Patni Computer Systems with America's aggressively successful Carlyle Group, the world's third-largest private equity company; the Boston-based Advent International; and the London-based Apax Partners. The three Patni Brothers decided to sell their combined equity of 45.6 percent, but only at a premium of 20 percent or more, which reduced the number of suitors.

However, since the Carlyle Group–led consortium was interested only if it could acquire controlling stake in Patni Computer Systems, General Atlantic became the pivotal player. Its two partners succeeded in getting Murthy interested in bidding for Patni. Working with the iGate's co-chairmen, Wadhwani and Trivedi, he moved with his customary gusto and brought Apax Partners on board.

Murthy faced competition from the Carlyle Group–led consortium. It offered Rs 600 ($12) a share on two conditions: the Patni brothers must stay out of the IT business, and the bid price would be lowered if a subsequent audit of Patni Computer Systems' accounts showed further liabilities. The unconditional iGate-Apax bid was Rs 500 ($10) a share, while the current market price was Rs 489.

Finding the conditions of the Carlyle Group–led consortium unacceptable, the Patni brothers accepted the iGate-Apax offer of Rs 503.50 ($10.07) a share on January 3, 2011, amounting to $921 million. Indian law required iGate to buy an additional 20 percent stake at the same price, which meant a further investment of $301 million. At $1.22 billion, the deal became the biggest acquisition in the history of India's IT industry.[53] To pay for it, iGate secured commitments for debt financing of up to $700 million from the New York–based investment bank Jefferies & Company, Inc. and RBC Capital Markets, an investment bank of Royal Bank of Canada.[54] This transaction was once more a highly publicized example of the globalization of capital.

Murthy's stewardship of iGate would end in May 2013 when, following their investigation into another sexual liaison with a subordinate and her sexual harassment claim, the directors sacked him.[55] Eleven years earlier, he had been sacked by Infosys directors on similar grounds.

Whereas the glamorous high-tech companies stole the limelight, mergers and acquisitions in older industries continued, as Indian corporations constantly explored ways of leapfrogging technology by purchasing Western companies, succeeding sometimes with memorable buyouts. Such was the case with the Mumbai-based Hindalco Industries.[56]

Traditional Industries

Hindalco was part of the Aditya Birla Group, the third-largest multinational conglomerate, after the Tata Group and Reliance Industries Limited, with operations in nearly forty countries. It grew out of the textile mills built by Birla Brothers Limited, founded in 1919 by Ghanshyam Das Birla (1894–1983).

The Birla family hails from the same part of Rajasthan as Lakshmi Mittal and Ravi and Shashi Ruia. By acquiring Arcelor S.A., the European company with the second-largest steel output in the world, in 2006, Mittal—whose immediate family owned Mittal Steel, the number one steel-producing corporation by volume—earned himself the title "Raja of Steel." In 2010, the Ruia Brothers' Essar Energy bought the Stanlow oil refinery, the second-largest refinery in Britain, from Royal Dutch Shell. Despite the Birlas' diversification into apparel, cement, metals, petrochemicals, financial services, telecom, and IT services, and a workforce of 130,000 worldwide, the group remained a family firm.

Kumar Mangalam Birla, a member of the enterprising Birlas, became chairman of the group following the premature death of his father, Aditya Vikram Birla, in 1995, at which time the list of the conglomerate's companies included the thirty-seven-year-old Hindalco, producer of primary aluminum and copper. The twenty-eight-year-old Birla had obtained a commerce degree from Bombay University and an MBA from the London School of Business. What he lacked in experience he made up for with strategic vision and manic drive, combined with a radical departure from the management style of his predecessors. That is, he started rewarding merit rather than blood relationship and loyalty to the founding family—a bane of many of the leading Indian business houses. He gradually adopted the accounting and governance practices of the West, as the other competing conglomerates were also doing, particularly the Tata Group. This was a major factor in enabling him to expand the Aditya Birla Group—with annual turnover of $3 billion in

1995—to the point where his personal fortune had ballooned to $4.4 billion by the time he was thirty-seven.[57]

Birla was intent on making Hindalco a leading vertically integrated corporation—starting with alumina (aluminum oxide ore) and ending with beverage cans and automobile parts—by acquiring a Western company with an advanced technology and global presence. Hindalco, the cheapest producer of primary aluminum on the planet, had 60 percent share in the small but fast-growing Indian market for rolled products. Birla found that the Atlanta-based Novelis Inc. had all the attributes he was seeking. Operating aluminum sheet mills in eleven countries, it was the number one producer of rolled aluminum in Europe, South America, and Asia and number two in North America. Overall, it had almost one-fifth of the global market, with a clientele that included Coca-Cola, Anheuser-Busch, Ford, and General Motors. It also recycled more than 35 billion used beverage cans annually.[58] But the long-term, fixed-price contracts it signed with its customers for aluminum sheets reduced its profitability to a puny 1 percent on sales of $8.4 billion in 2005 against the background of rising costs in labor and primary aluminum. During January–September 2006, it lost $170 million,[59] which made its management open to takeover offers. That autumn, it willingly entered into talks with Hindalco and others.

On January 26, 2007, Novelis confirmed that it was negotiating with potential buyers for the sale of the corporation. The share price of $30 started rising. It hit $38.40 on February 10. The next day, Novelis announced that it had confirmed the sale of its shares with Hindalco in an all-cash transaction valued at $5.9 billion, including $2.4 billion of debt. Prone to using business-school speak, Birla said, "This buyout is in line with our long-term strategies of expanding our global presence across our various businesses and is consistent with our vision of taking India to the world."[60] This meant $44.93 in cash per Novelis share, a 17 percent premium on the previous day's closing price—or a thumping 50 percent premium on the closing price on January 25.[61] Novelis shareholders were jubilant, but Hindalco's Indian investors were not so pleased. They judged that Birla had overpaid. Hindalco shares plummeted by 13 percent, wiping $600 million off its market value. Birla was defiant. "When you are acquiring a world leader you will have to pay a premium."[62]

Like Tata Steel, Hindalco had to rally support from diverse sources to cough up so much cash at one go. The option of Birla selling his shares of the Aditya Birla Group's companies to raise cash was ruled out. His large-scale disposal of these shares would have deeply depressed share prices and undermined other investors' confidence in the conglomerate's financial health. However, like the Tata Group, the Aditya Birla Group had built up substantial assets in such countries as Australia, Brazil, Canada, China, Germany, Italy, Spain, and the United States. A little over half of its revenue originated overseas. It therefore enjoyed a good rating by Western banks. Birla was also able to convince leading bankers that creating a corporation as large as Novelis from scratch would cost $12 billion, twice the amount he was paying. Furthermore, he assured them that he would leave the current Novelis management intact—a repeat of what Ratan Tata had told the *Financial Times*.

Aditya Birla Group established a shell company called AV Metals Limited in Canada. It managed to secure a $2.8 billion loan from UBS (Swiss), ABN-Amro (Dutch), and Bank of America (U.S.). Half of this sum was in the form of a bond with an extortionate interest rate of 7.2 percent.[63] Aditya Birla Group's Canadian subsidiary Essel Mining and Industries contributed $300 million and Hindalco $450 million, which enabled AV Metals to pay $3.5 billion to buy all Novelis shares. With the addition of another $2.5 billion, consisting almost wholly of Novelis' debt, the grand total of $6 billion made it the highest Indian investment in North America and the second-largest foreign investment by an Indian corporation after Tata Steel's purchase of Corus. Novelis Inc. became the wholly owned subsidiary of Hindalco.

On the industrial side, this transaction, completed on May 15, catapulted Hindalco from the thirteenth-largest primary aluminum producer in the world to the fifth-largest vertically integrated aluminum manufacturer on the planet.[64] Recalling this fact would often make Birla's round, bespectacled face, topped with coiffured jet-black hair, break into a generous smile. It also pleased him to realize that other industrial tycoons now came to view him with an undisguised blend of admiration and envy.

But his smile turned to a scowl when the West's banking tsunami of 2008–9 froze Hindalco's credit lines from Western financial institutions, which made it unfeasible for the company to refinance the bridge loan it had raised. So Birla did what Ratan Tata had done: he offered Hindalco shares at a discount to the present shareholders. The effort raised $1.25 billion. In addition, he managed to raise a loan of $1 billion from a syndicate of twelve foreign banks against Hindalco's vastly increased assets of nearly $9 billion.[65]

What Birla shared with Ratan Tata, Indra Nooyi, Narendra Patni, and other high flyers was the imbibing of the management practices of successful

Western companies: maintaining an open business culture, rewarding talent, fostering innovation by adequately funding research and development, emphasizing client satisfaction, responding speedily to queries and complaints, and delegating authority.

Nooyi's Attempted Empathy with Indian Farmers

When it came to tackling public relations and marketing problems in India, Indra Nooyi, CEO of PepsiCo, proved particularly sensitive. From 2003, villagers and environment-friendly nongovernmental organizations in India started complaining that PepsiCo, as well as Coca-Cola, was consuming excessive groundwater in the manufacture of its beverages in areas already suffering water shortage. In the predominantly agrarian India, water is of vital importance to farmers, whose livelihood depends on adequate water supplies for their crops, and who are also therefore deeply interested in finding ways of conserving it.

As PepsiCo's CEO since 2006, and its chief financial officer for the previous five years, Nooyi prodded the board of directors to launch a nationwide program in India to achieve a "positive water balance" by the end of the decade. This meant PepsiCo India would return the same amount of water it consumed to the local communities by reducing its water use in the production of its beverages and initiating and aiding programs to achieve greater water access in local areas, chiefly through rainwater harvesting and small dam-building schemes.

Laudable as this move was, the actual progress was patchy. After being appointed the CEO of PepsiCo in October 2006, Nooyi took personal interest in the issue. Within months, she traveled to India to energize the company's positive water balance program. She tried to counter those who criticized her company's profligate ways of using water by describing her personal experience while growing up in Chennai. "I still feel guilty filling a bathtub with water," she said. "We at home didn't get much water growing up during the 1960s in the Indian coastal city of Chennai. I belong to a very middle-class family wherein we had to rise every morning between three and five—the only hours that the valves to the municipal water supply were turned on—and fill every bucket in the house. Two buckets were set aside for cooking, and two each would go to me, my older sister, and my younger brother. You had to think about whether to take a bath. As a matter of fact, you learned to live your life off those two buckets."[66]

It was unclear how effective this approach of hers proved to be in practice. However, in May 2010, PepsiCo claimed that its Indian subsidiary had reduced water use by 45 percent since 2005. It added that in 2009 PepsiCo India had used 5 billion liters of water but added 6 billion liters to the country's water supplies. According to Melanie Warner of CBS News' Money-Watch, the accountants at Deloitte Touche Tohmatsu had done the math regarding the company's claim of achieving positive water balance. They had arrived at this total by including the amounts of water generated by the construction of small dams and recharge ponds, rainwater collection on roofs, and collaborations with rice farmers to do "direct seeding" instead of growing rice seedlings in a nursery, which reduces water usage by 30 percent. "It's unclear," added Warner, "—as it always is with these environmental offset maneuvers—how much of a role Pepsi played building the dams and rainwater harvesters, or whether these things would have happened anyway without Pepsi."[67]

Such skepticism about corporate claims concerning environmental protection was certainly in order. But the one area where there was no room for speculation or second-guessing was the poor state of agriculture in India.

4

The Scandalous Neglect
of India's Agriculture

Those who fume at the disrepair of the streets and roads in India's urban areas often muffle their criticism after a foray into the countryside. Such was the case when I myself ventured out of Dehradun. Dehradun, the capital of the northern state of Uttarakhand, is a garrison city with a vast military cantonment and home to the headquarters of Oil and Natural Gas Corporation, the country's largest company by market value.

Chaperoned by a nongovernmental organization official, Arijit Banerji, my host in Dehradun, I boarded a four-wheel-drive vehicle with a sturdy, hawk-eyed driver at the steering wheel. The fifty-mile journey to the village of Rasulpur proved to be a stomach-churning, bone-crunching experience, akin to being vigorously shaken up inside a washing machine, despite the driver's dexterous handling of the treacherous thoroughfare—waterlogged in places and pockmarked with craters deep enough to slow down a tank.

The atrophy of rural roads captures starkly the state of the rural economy, heavily dependent on agriculture and such allied activities as horticulture, animal husbandry, and dairy farming. Between 1970 and 2013, the contribution of agriculture and related activities to the GDP plunged from 43 percent to 13.7 percent, a steep fall of two-thirds. Distressingly, a little over half of the country's labor force of 487 million produced less than one-seventh of the GDP in 2013.[1] The advocates of neoliberalism are blasé about this scandalous state of affairs. They attribute agriculture's relative decline to the rapid expansion in services and industry, particularly after the year 2000. By so doing, they inadvertently agree with those critics who lambast the government for downgrading the importance of agriculture, on which two out of three Indians still depend for their livelihood. In contrast to the blistering economic expansion during 2004–10, the improvement in the agrarian sector has barely kept pace with the rise in population, with agriculturists suffering a downturn in productivity and incomes. The worst victims were the landless laborers, which explains why, even in the most prosperous period, the annual reduction in poverty was a puny 1 percent.[2] In 2011, the year of the last census, more than a third of India's 1.2 billion citizens survived below the official poverty line of Rs 32 (64¢) a day in cities and Rs 26 (52¢) a day in the countryside.[3] According to the Multidimensional Poverty Index, developed in 2010 by the United Nations Development Program and Oxford Poverty & Human Development Initiative, 53.7 percent of Indians were poor.[4] The figures based on the findings of the 66th round of the National Sample Survey Office for 2009–10 showed rural and urban monthly averages of Rs 1,054 ($21) and Rs 1,984 ($40) per capita respectively, representing 65 percent (rural) and 67 percent (urban) living below the poverty line.[5]

Such statistics were not on the mind of Prem Singh Pawar—known as Prem Lala among his fellow villagers—the elected president of the *gram panchayat*[6] (village council) of Rasulpur, a settlement of two thousand souls. A slim man in his mid-forties, with sunken cheeks and a black mustache, he was neatly dressed in khaki cotton trousers and a checkered sweater over a white shirt. His family lived in an L-shaped house with an open courtyard, furnished with a bore well and a hand pump for water (one of twenty-five in the village), with verandas on both arms of the L, supported by wooden pillars and occupied by string cots in front of four rooms. The walls were embellished with gaudy posters. The most striking one portrayed Durga—a Hindu goddess whose multiple arms bear a trident, a scimitar, a sword, a mace, a bow, a conch shell, and a lotus flower—riding a tiger. An altogether different mood was conveyed by the image of Lord Krishna, painted in blue, playing a flute while his lover, the demure Radha, rested on his shoulder. His house was more spacious than that of his neighbors. In their case, a residence consisted merely of a living room, a bedroom, and a kitchen, with an outside latrine.

Pawar was a practical man with firsthand knowledge of what transpired in the portals of power. "The government spends too much money on towns and cities but not enough on villages," he growled.[7] As leader of the panchayat, which covered Rasulpur and two nearby settlements, with a combined population of six thousand, he had a set of rights and responsibilities. He was mandated to maintain the existing infrastructure and build any further additions, after they had been approved by the state authorities. He was authorized to supervise local markets. He registered births, deaths, and marriages in the area. He functioned alongside a *gram sevak* (Hindi: village servant), a civil servant appointed by the state government to act as a conduit between the state capital and the panchayat.

Pawar's budget was made up of grants from the state administration and the district council, called *zilla parishad*, which covered several "blocs," each bloc consisting of a clutch of rural settlements. The state government's grant to a panchayat was in proportion to the revenue it received from that community, including land revenue, which covered the costs of assessment and collection of revenue, periodic land surveys, the maintenance of land records, and such indirect taxes as value-added tax—known as sales tax in the United States. This ensured that the villages that were at the bottom of the heap remained there—a vicious cycle, with paupers unable to break the shackles of penury.

In practice, Pawar received his funds from his bloc development officer, a civil servant. Most of this money was channeled to building contractors and suppliers of goods and services, and this created opportunities for kickbacks. "As the panchayat president I have not made money for myself," said Pawar as he sipped sweet milky tea, surrounded by a group of curious villagers. "There is a temptation to spend some of the money given by the state government and put some in your own pocket. But it is better to be honest."

There is always an embezzling opportunity whenever money changes hands between an elected or appointed government functionary and a private contractor. In such instances, the sums range from substantial to colossal. In rural India, these transactions are primarily centered around building new infrastructure or repairing the existing one. The contractor increases his profit by using substandard materials and/or failing to meet the building requirements to which he had agreed. "Let us say a contractor has agreed to construct one kilometer of asphalt road for Rs 5 million [$100,000]," explained my Dehradun host. "He is required to build a meter-deep hard base, and then put gravel to a specified depth before pouring tar to produce a solid, smooth road. But he prepares a shallow foundation, unloads less gravel, and economizes on tar. He bribes the government inspector, who certifies that the work has been done as required. Come monsoon, and the seepage of rainwater through the unevenly asphalted layer makes the road surface crack. With traffic the cracks spread, the road breaks up, and you get potholes and loose gravel."[8]

Then there is the citizen's everyday experience of forking out petty bribes, euphemistically called "speed money." Here a civil servant demands—and receives—a fee from an applicant for doing something that is part of his routine task. In India, it is mandatory to produce copies of certain official certificates or documents to claim government benefits. For this, villagers have to approach petty functionaries. As someone who had been involved in an improvement project for Rasulpur for some years, Banerji had an inside track on the speed money. "The minimum bribe was Rs 50 ($1) to get a photocopy of a ration card for purchasing staples at subsidized prices, or a certificate declaring a household to be below the poverty line or belonging to the underprivileged Scheduled Castes," he said.[9] That is, obtaining one such photocopy wiped out half a day's earnings for a landless laborer who depended on the erratic chance of work on a daily basis to support his family.

Skewed Distribution, Land Hunger

As a villager without a plot of his own, a landless worker exists on the lowest rung of the rural economic ladder. One out of ten village households belongs to this category. The next rung consists of marginal peasants owning less than the national average of one hectare, or 2.59 acres, each. Such is the preponderance of marginal tillers that together with the landless they account for 80 percent of rural households today. Yet cumulatively they own merely 23 percent of the arable land. In 1971 only 60 percent of village households belonged to this stratum.[10]

The rate of pauperization accelerated after the introduction of the New Economic Policy in 1991.[11] The Gini coefficient[12] of land ownership holdings remained constant at 0.71 during 1971–92 but increased to 0.74 in 2003.[13] (A Gini coefficient of zero means perfect equality, where everyone has equal land or income, and a coefficient of one means that one person owns all the land or income.) As part of the International Monetary Fund (IMF) loan granted in 1991, India was required to reduce its fiscal deficit, then running at 8.2 percent of the GDP. The government drastically cut its investment in irrigation, water management, flood control and scientific research, power generation, and related rural needs. This reduction was not matched by a corresponding rise in investment by the private sector in these sectors.[14] Nor did the central and state authorities substantially increase investment in improving education and healthcare in villages. Pressured by the World Trade Organization (WTO) and the IMF, the Indian government started withdrawing market controls and curtailing subsidies for such inputs for cultivation as chemical fertilizers and diesel needed to run water pumps. Cash crops like cotton, vanilla, and black pepper became exposed to volatile international markets, an unnerving experience for Indian cultivators untutored in coping with wild jumps in prices. Due to the generous subsidies given by the federal government to American cotton farmers, among others, which were blatantly overlooked by the WTO, the international price of lint cotton—that is, seedless cotton—fell from $1.10 a pound in 1996 to 52¢ a pound a decade later.[15] This hurt cotton growers in India, the world's second-largest producer of the commodity in 2007.

What about the 20 percent of rural families who own 73 percent of the land? They fall into four categories: small farmers (one to two hectares), semi-medium (two to four hectares), medium (four to ten hectares), and large (ten-plus hectares). Where did Rasulpur fit into this matrix? "About 60 percent of the 320 families have some land, the maximum being ten bighas [2.5 acres, or one hectare]," averred Pawar. "And 40 percent have no land at all." These numbers gave Rasulpur the lowest rank in the hierarchy of landownership. Yet the land distribution in this settlement was typical. During my visit to Sisola, home to some five thousand people, located ten miles from Meerut in Uttar Pradesh, a state that accounts for one-sixth of India's population, I came across similar figures. The only difference was that the richest farmer, Sala-huddin, possessed seventeen acres (6.5 hectares) of land. He was the only one who could afford to buy a tractor, costing Rs 275,000 ($5,500), by raising a bank loan with his land as collateral.[16]

Since Rasulpur is in a region that gets generous rainfall—about eighty inches during the summer monsoon (June to September)—it is part of the 64 percent of the nation's cultivated land that is rain-fed, with the rest dependent on man-made irrigation. The downside is that the monsoon is quirky, and it limits cultivation to a single crop in a year. Therefore, total dependence on monsoon rains leads to low productivity.

"When you depend purely on monsoons, one bigha [0.1 hectare] yields three quintals [666 pounds] of sugarcane," said Pawar. "With assured [manmade] irrigation, we can double the crop. And if we also use a tractor and chemical fertilizer, then we can harvest eight quintals per bigha. In reality, we get only four per bigha because we depend on bullocks." The modern alternative to bullocks is a tractor.

A tractor first appeared in one of the neighboring villages of Rasulpur twenty years ago. Since then their number had risen to three. "By using a tractor we save time," remarked Shikha, Pawar's wife, who was decked in a flower-print cotton sari, undulating earrings, and a shining nose piece. "One hour by a tractor is equal to eight hours by two bullocks. These animals cost Rs 200 [$4] a day plus all the hassle of maintaining them. The rent for a tractor is Rs 1,500 [$30] a day. So the cost is the same as with oxen, but there is no hassle with a tractor."

Shikha's intervention encouraged an older man with a walrus mustache, dressed in a long bedraggled shirt and a dhoti, to speak. "For sugarcane you can get only one crop a year," he said. "Then the following year you have to do other crops which do not take out so much nutrition from the soil. Like you can plant wheat, pulses, groundnuts, mustard, or vegetables." Others nodded in agreement.

What was the source of water for these crops? I asked. "Tube wells." The first was drilled outside the village around 1991. Two decades on, it went dry because of the fallen groundwater level. The other well materialized seven years later. "It works intermittently because the electric supply is erratic," said Pawar fatalistically. "And when the power is on, the motor to run the pump is often out of order." Since this tube well was also linked to an overhead tank, connected to several communal taps, the supply of filtered water for drinking and other household purposes ceased.[17]

I asked why the villagers did not complain. "Who should we complain to?" retorted Pawar. "If you do not pay a bribe, the official will not look at your complaint. If you then go the police and wish to register a complaint against that official, they demand a bribe." In any case, irrigation water was not cheap. "If you want irrigation water, you pay a fixed monthly charge," explained the older man with a walrus mustache. "Then you pay for the water supplied per hour depending on when electricity is available."

Unreliability and costliness of the irrigation water was a subject that also came up in my interviews in Sisola, located in the Gangetic plain, where, unlike Rasulpur, nestled in the foothills of the Himalayas, the monsoon showered the region with only thirty-five inches of rain annually.[18]

In Rasulpur, being an elected officeholder was no guarantee that Pawar would be spared the venality of civil servants or bank managers. "If you want to get your bank loan application expedited, you pay a bribe so that your file is moved and signed, and the loan is granted," he said plaintively. "Each time your file is moved you pay. The bribe as a percentage of the loan varies."[19]

Rural indebtedness had increased in the wake of the New Economic Policy and the trade liberalization dictated by the WTO. During the first post-NEP decade, indebted farm households in India nearly doubled, from 26 percent to 48.6 percent.[20] In 2001, this figure in Andhra Pradesh was a staggering 82 percent. Their emphasis on export-led growth encouraged cultivators to switch from food crops to such fertilizer-intensive cash crops as cotton, coffee, sugarcane, groundnuts, pepper, and vanilla. As a result, the daily per capita availability of food grain plunged by about one-fifth, from 510 grams in 1991 to 422 grams in 2005. The trend continued. A study published in 2009 by the official National Nutrition Monitoring Bureau showed that 35 percent of Indians suffered from chronic hunger as measured by body mass index (BMI). The BMI is calculated by dividing a person's weight in kilograms by the square of his or her height in meters. BMIs below 18.5 indicate chronic hunger, those between 18.5 and 22 are normal, and anything above 22 indicates rising degrees of overweight.[21]

For marginal and small landholders, the move to cash crops was very risky. It meant a steep increase in agricultural costs and loans, and exposure to the vagaries of the international commodity prices, as determined by the colossal Western multinational trading corporations. When a cultivator in Kerala changed his crop from paddy to vanilla, the cost per acre rocketed from Rs 8,000 ($160) to Rs 150,000 ($3,000). An agricultural bank would only lend him up to half the value of his plot under paddy cultivation, not the far more valuable vanilla. Therefore, he ended up borrowing funds from traditional moneylenders, who charged a minimum of 2 percent interest a month. Once he had signed such a contract he got sucked into a vicious cycle of debt because of his inability to repay the loan in full.

A study by Cambridge University found a correlation between small or marginal farming, cash crops, and the suicide rate among agriculturists. Kerala, with a high proportion of marginal cultivators who had switched to cash crops, had the highest male suicide rate in India.[22] Such was also the fate of hundreds of thousands of Indian cotton growers who were driven to kill themselves because of unbearable indebtedness. Invariably, they were marginal or small holders in dry areas.

Cotton Belt Turns into Suicide Belt

The highest suicide rates are confined to five states—Maharashtra, Karnataka, Andhra Pradesh, Madhya Pradesh, and Chhattisgarh. These states account for a third of the national population. In India, committing suicide is a crime. State police keep records in which they note the probable cause of death. This data is collated by the National Crime Records Bureau of the Home Ministry in Delhi. Concerned about the farmers' suicides in their state, as revealed in April 1998 by Palagummi Sainth, the celebrated rural affairs editor of *The Hindu* daily, some members of the Andhra Pradesh Legislative Assembly demanded to see the records. They discovered that of the 1,800 suicides in Ananatpur district, three-fifths were attributed to "stomach ache"! This "ache," it transpired, was caused by a hapless peasant swallowing pesticide that was freely available from the state authorities.

From then on, annual statistics about these suicides started appearing in the media. By 2010, the total had ballooned to 250,000.[23] The number had risen sharply after 2001. In April of that year, the Bharatiya Janata Party–led coalition government in Delhi removed quantitative restrictions on imports two years ahead of the deadline specified by the WTO. Among other measures, it abolished price controls on agricultural produce. This plunged the peasantry into even greater penury. During 2001–6, there was a suicide every half hour.[24]

The cotton farmlands contributed the most to this human tragedy. The worst plagued was Vidarbha, the eastern region of India's second most populous state, Maharashtra, home to 3.2 million cotton-growing families. During 2001–5, the annual number of self-killings swelled ninefold to 445. The area was prone to droughts, and the deadly impact of the one in 2005 was felt in the following year.

In the summer of 2006, Prime Minister Manmohan Singh made a two-day trip to Vidarbha. Addressing the suffering families of Dhamangaon and surrounding villages, he said, "After what you have told me about the difficulties that you are going through, I understand that debt is a big problem." He failed to mention the gargantuan size of the collective debt. At Rs 266 billion ($5.3 billion), it averaged out to Rs 80,000 ($1,600) for a family of 5.4 members.[25] The average annual expenditure of the typical farm household with 2.59 acres of land was a little over Rs 32,500 ($650). Of that, it spent 60 percent on food and 18 percent on fuel, clothing, and footwear.[26] (These figures roughly tallied with the findings of the NSSO's 66th round survey in

2009–10, which showed that the average Indian farm household spent 55 percent on food and 18 percent on clothing and footwear.[27]) So the amount available for investment in cultivation was paltry. Appeals to Singh to cancel the distressed farmers' loans fell on deaf ears.

The farmers' dependency on extortionate loans arose after the Environment Ministry in Delhi granted the Monsanto Company, based in Creve Coeur, Missouri, the right to cultivate genetically modified *bacillus thuringiensis* (Bt) cotton seed in different parts of India. Bt cotton seed was spiked with the gene of a toxic bacterium to kill parasites and pests. Once these experiments proved satisfactory, it was left to individual state administrations to grant permission to Monsanto to market these seeds. The government of Maharashtra, the second-largest contributor of cotton to the national pool after Gujarat, did so in June 2005. The government-owned Maharashtra Hybrid Seeds Company Ltd. (Mahyco) partnered with Monsanto to patent Mahyco-Monsanto Bt cotton seed. Mahyco-Monsanto Biotech Limited sublicensed to many local seed companies in different states the right to produce and market this seed. Now state authorities had a vested commercial interest in promoting what its sublicensees' sales agents called the "magic seed," guaranteed to yield bumper crops free from parasites and insects.

But they were exorbitantly expensive, selling for Rs 1,800 ($36) per 450-gram bag, as against Rs 350 ($7) for a bag of the local hybrid seed. By exploiting its monopoly, Mahyco-Monsanto Biotech reaped huge profits from the sale of the Bt seed, part of which was pocketed by the seed retailer. A field study revealed that four out of five Maharashtra farmers had learned of the Bt cotton seed from seed dealers who made more profit selling it than any of the traditional non-Bt varieties. "We cannot afford planting Bt anymore," admitted Sumant Meshram, resident of the village of Hiwra. "But we cannot buy non-Bt seeds in the market either. The dealers tell us that there is no supply."[28] What was held back from the farmers was that these so-called magic seeds needed twice as much water as the traditional ones, partly because they took almost seven months to turn into cotton buds—versus the five months for the local varieties—and that they were infertile, forcing the cultivator to purchase a fresh batch every season.[29]

Agricultural banks gave loans of only Rs 12,000 ($600) per acre, even though the market price of the land was Rs 100,000 ($2,000). To purchase the much-hyped Bt cotton seed, a farmer was therefore compelled to borrow from traditional moneylenders by mortgaging his land. These unlicensed, unregulated lenders charged usurious interest rates, a minimum of 24 percent a year.

However, after Prime Minister Singh's visit in mid-2006, the Indian government announced a relief package for Vidarbha, costing Rs 37.5 billion ($800 million) over the next five years. It covered irrigation projects, new loans and extensions for old ones, and economic diversification. But it wasn't as generous as it sounded. The Rs 37.5 billion total was reached by including previously sanctioned projects; only half of it represented new funding. Even then the total funding translated into spending only Rs 2,300 ($46) annually for each cotton-growing family.[30] Little wonder that during the next five years the irrigated area in the region increased by a puny 2 percent.

There was no drop in the suicide rate. Indeed, between July 1 and July 15, 2006, at least sixty-two farmers took their lives. The glaring irony was that the landscape at the epicenter of these peasant suicides was peppered with massive advertisements on walls, billboards, and public buses displaying a smiling farmer as he showcased a huge crop of raw cotton. These signs were funded by the many sublicensees of Mahyco-Monsanto. At one point, it hired Nana Patekar, a Bollywood star who often played a street-smart, urban tough guy, to promote its seed. Besides his product promotion on TV, he toured his native Maharashtra giving addresses at farmers' rallies.[31]

As the founder of the Vidarbha Jan Andolan Samiti (Vidarbha People's Movement Committee), Kishor Tiwari, a balding, moon-faced engineer in his late fifties, monitored the rural deprivation from his office in the small town of Pandhar Kawada, one hundred miles south of the regional capital of Nagpur. "Millions of cotton growers and their families in the Vidarbha region are distressed because of slashed agricultural subsidies, dismantled price controls, and closed state-funded cotton procurement centers," lamented Tiwari in mid-2006. "Essential agricultural input costs of water and electricity have increased a lot. Farmers used to getting water and power for minimal charges for many years now face rising input costs, when the market prices of their produce do not cover their expenses. Last year [2005] cotton procurement price was Rs 2,500 [$50] per quintal [100 kg]. This year, affected by international market prices, the rate plunged to Rs 1,700 [$34] a quintal. Growing cotton at this price is a loss-making proposition."[32]

Unsurprisingly, following the bumper crop of 1,448 suicides in Vidarbha in 2006, the annual number settled down to an average of 1,260 for the next two years. The Indian government's offer of a Rs 100,000 ($2,000) grant to the family of a farmer who killed himself made little difference.[33] When drought struck Vidarbha in 2009, more than 2 million hectares were planted with Bt cottonseed, primarily because non-Bt seeds had virtually vanished from the market. But when the fledgling plants did not receive rainwater in time, cotton crops withered. The score of suicides in that year crossed the nine hundred mark.

In 2010, *Peepli Live*, a popular Bollywood movie, written and directed by Anusha Rizvi, a former journalist, was in effect a wake-up call to the nation's conscience on farmers' suicides. The movie tells a story of a heavily indebted family in the fictitious central Indian village of Peepli. The protagonist, Natha, something of a dreamer, is manipulated by his elder brother, Budhia, to kill himself so that his surviving family can qualify for government compensation. But the plan goes awry when word of the plan spreads. It attracts TV channels eager to exploit the "live suicide" by a now-reluctant Natha. With a by-election imminent in the area, politicians join the foray for their own ends. When the ruling party realizes that if Natha dies it will lose the election, it gets the village headman to kidnap him. As various parties try to locate the missing Natha, he escapes to Gurgaon, where he makes a living as a day laborer. The family loses its mortgaged land to the bank. As critics observed, it was not your "average Bollywood movie."[34] "A scathing satire on the country's apathy towards the rural class, and specifically towards farmers, *Peepli Live* employs a comic tone to tell a serious story," noted Rajeev Masand, the film critic of CNN-IBN television channel.[35]

None of this had any impact on the vagaries of nature. When drought struck Vidarbha again in 2011, the state's chief minister, Prithviraj Chavan, announced at the end of the year an aid package of Rs 2 billion ($40 million) as relief to dejected cultivators. But these funds were released only in May 2012.[36]

In between, in March 2012, there were nationwide demonstrations against Bt seeds on the tenth anniversary of their introduction. Protest was widespread in Vidarbha, with small and marginal farmers and the widows of the suicides burning sacks of cotton to dramatize their anger.

In June, a field study by the Council of Social Development on the impact of Bt cotton seed on cotton growers led it to conclude that lack of irrigation was a major cause for their suicides in Vidarbha. This chimed with Tiwari's repeated refrain that "Vidarbha is a classic example of the wrong selection of the Bt technology in dry regions. Most farmers who committed suicide there are Bt farmers."[37]

Earlier, at a function organized by Monsanto in Pune, the state's second-largest city after its capital, Mumbai, agricultural commissioner Umakant Dangat urged farmers to plant Bt cotton only in irrigated areas. On August 9, he followed this up with a sweeping announcement of an immediate official ban on the sale and distribution of Mahyco-Monsanto's Bt cotton seeds because the company was supplying "inferior quality seeds."[38] Maharashtra's lead was followed by Karnataka, whose government banned the sale of Mahyco-Monsanto's Bt and other hybrid seeds in March 2014.[39]

It was not just marginal and small cotton farmers who were driven to self-destruction. Even the medium-size landholders (four to ten hectares) were feeling the squeeze. Such was the case with Badruddin Jeewani in Pandhar Kawada, where the village market was lined with fertilizer and seed shops. Sipping a glass of milky tea in the pleasant November sun in 2012, he chatted with visiting social activists. "I now own a good sixteen acres of land," he told them. "Things have gone so bad that I had to sell almost ten acres in the last five years. There is no other way I could sustain my family. Cotton doesn't bring any profit now. If things don't improve soon, I will be landless."[40]

The Middle Layer

During my field research, I met a middle-size farmer, Koja Ram Parihar, at his farm near the Rajasthani town of Tinwari, twenty miles from Jodhpur, the prime city of the Marwar region, the ancestral land of the Mittals and Birlas. The owner of ten hectares (twenty-six acres), he was at the top end of the medium stratum in the rural hierarchy. Nationally, such landholders, forming barely 3 percent of village households, owned 30 percent of the arable land.

A slim man of medium height, the fifty-eight-year-old Parihar was an attractive man with high cheekbones, brown eyes, a prominent gray mustache, and sunburnt skin. Dressed in a white vest and a white dhoti, he smiled readily. He stated, disarmingly, that he was illiterate. His father, born into the gardener subcaste, owned twenty-four hectares (sixty acres). As the eldest of three brothers, he inherited twelve hectares (thirty acres).

He and his wife lived with the families of their three married sons, a household of fifteen people. Altogether, eight of them worked the land, which Parihar had prudently partitioned into different segments, each given to a different crop. A little over half was turned into fields of various vegetables, with garlic and onions as favorites because of the comparatively high prices they fetched. Another quarter was allocated to groundnuts, yielding him a profit of Rs 200,000 ($4,000) a crop. On the remainder, he planted cotton seed. The sale of raw cotton enriched Parihar by Rs 250,000 ($5,000). "Cotton crop needs a lot of attention," he said. "Cotton-picking is hard work, back-breaking."[41]

Did he know of the cotton farmers in Vidarbha committing suicide because of crippling debts? "Yes, I have heard," Parihar said vaguely. "Looks like they are buying expensive American seed. That needs lots of fertilizer and pesticide and water to get higher yields. The American seed is good for only one crop. Our seed is natural, which replicates itself. My yield is not as much as theirs. But a cotton merchant pays the same price for the commodity whether from the American seed or Indian."

Parihar was based in an area that had an average annual rainfall of a derisory thirteen inches. "I am independent of rain," he declared with a wave of his calloused hand. "I depend on one open well and two tube wells." How much did a tube well cost? "Drilling it and equipping it with casing, Rs 100,000 [$2,000]. Then you need a water pump, another Rs 70,000 [$1,400], and electric connection and cable and outside piping, add another Rs 100,000 [$2,000]. All told, roughly Rs 300,000 [$6,000]." He had supervised the whole process personally, from selecting the site to the inauguration ceremony conducted by the local Brahmin. Yet that was not the end. "Next to each tube well I erected a steel tank to store water," he continued. "That cost me Rs 100,000 [$2,000]. For getting irrigation water from the government you must have a meter, with the monthly rent of Rs 45 [$1]. The power bill for my two tube wells is Rs 4,200 [$84] a month. That is cheap because I signed up early on. Now metered water supply for two tube wells is Rs 9,000 [$180] a month. But power supply is only for five hours at a time, from four to nine in the morning and one to six in the afternoon."

For building up all these capital assets, did he raise loans from banks? "I avoid doing that as much as I can," Parihar replied. "Look at the State Bank of India. They give a loan of Rs 15,000 [$300] per bigha [0.625 acre] when the land is worth Rs 200,000 [$4,000] a bigha. And they charge 11 percent interest a year."

What Parihar told me about the government-owned all-purpose State Bank of India applied to agricultural banks as well. Earlier, during my stopover in Tinwari, I had walked into the year-old branch of the Oriental Bank of Commerce, a public sector bank specializing in agricultural credit, nestled between a general goods store and a barbershop. Its manager, Bhawar Lal, a dark, plump man in khaki pants and a white bush-shirt, facing a flat screen computer, told me that his brief was to help marginal farmers. He was authorized to grant a loan of up to 50 percent of the collateral, and he had pegged the price of one bigha at Rs 30,000 [$600]. He had no intention of raising that figure.[42]

At Parihar's farm, it was now mid-afternoon. We saw three of his grandchildren return from school. "All our children now go to school," he said proudly. "Things have changed. When my illiterate father died thirty-seven years ago, we lived in a mud house. Seventeen years later, I built that red brick house." He pointed toward a low, solidly built, sprawling structure some two hundred yards from where he sat on a string cot under a margosa tree. "We have color TV. And two months ago we got a TV dish. But the problem is that there is no electricity in the evening when we have time to watch TV." The TV dish shining in the afternoon sun was therefore more a status symbol than a utilitarian object of daily use.

Erratic power supply was the norm in rural India. In the village of Sisola, for instance, they had electricity for only twelve hours a day, alternating every two weeks. "It is from eight in the morning to eight in the evening, or the other way around," explained Salahuddin. "We have a refrigerator. We remove everything from it when the power is off. It is a nuisance, but what can we do?"[43] How did Parihar's present lifestyle compare with his father's? "In the early days, land was cheap and irrigation was cheap," he replied. "Now expenses are high. But in general, life is better than before."

At the top rung of the rural hierarchical ladder was the farmer who owned more than ten hectares. He belonged to that miniscule 0.6 percent of village households who possessed nearly 12 percent of all agricultural land. To meet a member of this class, I did not have to stray too far from Jodhpur.

Top of the Tree

Everybody in the village of Kuri Bhagtasni knew Hanuman Ram Jangid and his family. Among other things, in 2005 the Jangids had built a splendid house with a large screened porch, marble floors, piped water, and porcelain washbasins, and furnished it with a color television, chairs, and tables. The Jangid family had bought a Massey-Ferguson tractor as early as 1976. A quarter century later, they became the proud owners of a four-wheel-drive Jeep, which remained in fine fettle ten years on.

They could afford to build up such exceptional assets: the rural rich are exempt, nationwide, from income or wealth tax and capital gains tax. As elsewhere in India, landownership was obscenely uneven in Kuri Bhagtasni, a settlement of six hundred people, or 110 families. "Now only thirty to forty families are engaged exclusively in agriculture," said Hanuman Ram Jangid. "Most of them have five to ten bighas [three to six acres]; the maximum is fifteen bighas [nine acres]. The income of those dependent on agriculture is low, and their children are not going into it. In agriculture there is no work for five months in a year, so farmers and agrarian laborers have to find other work."[44] Earlier, he had told me that cumulatively the villagers possessed 4,500 bighas (2,800 acres), of which less than half was being cultivated.

For a forty-four-year-old stocky man of medium height and graying hair, Jangid was very energetic, making his points with vigorous thrusts in the air with his muscular right arm. After finishing his compulsory education at fourteen in 1981, he started assisting his late father, Dewa Ram Jangid—a heavily turbaned man whose color photograph dominated the sitting room— to manage the vast landholdings worked by hired laborers or tenant farmers.

Since a tenant peasant lacked agricultural property to offer as collateral, he could not receive a bank loan. So he ended up borrowing from better-off relatives who charged 2 percent interest a month. "If you fail to repay on time then the interest goes up," said Jangid in a voice devoid of any emotion. "That forces the tenant farmer to sell the gold ornaments of his wife, a heart-rending experience." Irrespective of class, Indians' attachment to gold borders on the mystical.

"Before the early 1980s we depended on rain and open wells, twenty-five to thirty meters [eighty to a hundred feet] deep, which yielded sweet water suitable for irrigation," recalled Jangid. "After thirty meters you hit sandy rock. Once past the rock, you get water that is salty and unsuitable for growing crops. Twenty years ago, an open well supplied enough water to irrigate forty bighas [twenty-five acres]. But not now. The water table has been depleted. Also, twenty years ago there was more rain than now. Tube wells started appearing in the early 1980s. One tube well irrigates twenty bighas [twelve acres]. Their number grew so large that around 2001, they started yielding saline water. Now there are two hundred tube wells in the area, capable of irrigating four thousand bighas [2,500 acres], but the cultivated land is down to half that figure."[45]

Tube-well irrigation was expensive. "Power supply is erratic," said Jangid languidly. "It is available for five hours at a time, and the timing varies from week to week. And if you decide to have your own generator then the cost shoots up. Most of us have diesel-fueled generators, which we use only in emergency. At Rs 500 [$10] an hour, it is very expensive to run your generator to pump water." This was in 2011, when the retail price of the subsidized diesel, the most popular petroleum product consumed in India, was about Rs 40 (80¢) a liter. That figure went up in September 2012, when the federal government cut the subsidy by about Rs 10 per liter. Starting in January 2013, there was a monthly reduction in subsidy, so that by the time Narendra Modi formed his BJP-led cabinet in May 2014, it was down to Rs 6 per liter.[46]

"We grow millet and oatmeal as well as guava and lentils," continued Jangid. "Before the late 1980s, harvests were good; there was more irrigation water than now. But on the negative side, we had pests and plant diseases, which is not the case at present. Also now we get subsidized fertilizer, even though the subsidy had come down recently. Last year [2010], with the subsidy of 50 percent, the price of potash fertilizer was Rs 522 [$11] for a bag of fifty kilograms. Now, with the subsidy slashed to 25 percent, the price had leapt to Rs 980 [$20] for a bag of fifty kilograms. By 2013, the subsidy will be removed completely." Did farmers like him complain? "Yes, we did. But the central government explained that [they] are under pressure by the IMF to reduce subsidies. There are bigger forces outside India twisting our government's arm, and imposing their will."

With the rising costs of agricultural inputs and electricity, land cultivation was becoming a loss-making proposition. "If you use tube wells and factor in the cost of power utilization and fertilizer, then you will spend Rs 100,000 [$2,000] on a plot of forty bighas [twenty-five acres]," said Jangid, impressively at ease with figures. "The yield will be forty quintals, putting your cost of production at Rs 250 [$5] per quintal. But the selling price is only about half that. So you will lose Rs 50,000 [$1,000] every season. Therefore, you decide to keep the land fallow." Later, driving his Jeep, he gave me a tour of his fallow land, overgrown with weeds.

This was a stark contrast to what prevailed in Punjab and Haryana. There practically every square inch of agricultural land was cultivated. The Punjab-Haryana region was the seed bed out of which had grown the Green Revolution. The term "Green Revolution" is shorthand for a combination of measures that include the provision of chemical fertilizers, credit, price incentives, marketing facilities, and technical advice—with high-yielding varieties of wheat and rice seeds at the core.

The Green Revolution Hits a Ceiling

At partition in 1947, independent India lost to West Pakistan large areas containing food surpluses. The ensuing communal violence and the uprooting of millions of people caused a huge loss of production in India's fertile northwest region. Therefore, India had to import food and pay for it in hard currencies drawn from its meager foreign earnings. Despite the emphasis that the first three Five Year Plans, starting in 1951, put on rural community development programs, land reclamation, and irrigation projects, food output reached a plateau of eighty to eighty-two metric tons a year during 1960–64.[47]

It was against this backdrop that the Green Revolution was launched in 1965, when an earlier pilot scheme was extended from the original fifteen districts to 114. This coincided with the arrival from the United States of the high-yield variety of seeds for wheat and rice. The subsequent increase in the yield of these grains encouraged more and more cultivators to adopt the new techniques. The area under cultivation with the miracle seeds exploded from 4.6 million acres in 1966 to 34.6 million in 1970. It covered about a third of the total wheat-growing acreage and one-seventh of the rice-growing acreage. Because of the expansion of the area under wheat cultivation and the increase in yield caused by the new techniques, wheat production doubled during these four years.[48]

Punjab and Haryana were the leaders of this revolution. These states had a large number of peasant proprietors, and their governments had invested heavily in building up an infrastructure of irrigation systems, roads, and electricity, and supported it with a reasonably efficient system of credit and distribution of new seeds, chemical fertilizers, and farming equipment. During the 1960s, in the Ludhiana district of Punjab, for instance, the land under irrigation increased from 45 percent of the total to 70 percent; the consumption of fertilizer rose from 18 pounds per acre to 242 pounds; and the wheat acreage under high-yield variety seed increased from 1 percent of the total to jaw-dropping 90 percent. The average yield of wheat per acre leapt from 1,385 pounds to 3,280 pounds.[49]

However, with four-fifths of the owner-farmers working plots of more than four hectares (ten acres), Ludhiana was far from typical. In the large wheat-growing states of Uttar Pradesh and Bihar, four-fifths of all cultivating households operated farms of less than eight acres (three hectares). They lacked the resources needed to secure a reliable source of irrigation, often a deep tube well, which became a common sight in the Punjab-Haryana region from the early 1970s, and which was the key to increased output.

Nationally, though, rice cultivation, which covered more acreage than wheat, was more important. The average landholding in the rice belt was much smaller than in the wheat zone. Therefore, the proportion of landowners, who lacked the resources needed to utilize the new technology, was much higher.

Francine R. Frankel, an American expert on Indian agriculture, conducted a study of the rice-growing region at the end of the five years of the Green Revolution and reached a conclusion that, astonishingly, remains valid four decades on. She noted that farmers with twenty acres or more in the rice belt had made "the greatest absolute and relative gains" by mechanizing farm operations and diversifying their cropping pattern, and those with five to ten acres had experienced "some improvement in net income," while the vast majority—"probably as many as 75 percent to 80 percent"—had suffered "a relative decline in their economic position."[50]

The Green Revolution continued to advance for almost two decades, but only in the areas that already had irrigation facilities, since this was the sine qua non for the success of the miracle seeds. "The new technology [of the Green Revolution] matured during 1980–83 to 1990–93 when it spread widely to more areas and encompassed more crops," noted Professors G.S. Bhalla and Gurmail Singh. "The result was a notable increase in the levels and growth rates of yields and output as well as in agricultural worker productivity in most states and regions. Thus during 1980–83 to 1990–93, the crop output recorded an unprecedented annual growth rate of 3.40 percent compared with a growth rate of 2.24 percent during 1962–65 to 1980–83."[51]

With this, India became self-sufficient in food. It no longer had to spend foreign currencies to import grains to feed its rising population, which in 1991 was 846 million, compared to 361 million in 1951.[52] However, this did not alter the grossly skewed consumption of food by Indians, with the upper middle and upper classes increasingly displaying the ill effects of excessive eating, such as overweight and obesity.

But the implementation of the New Economic Policy retarded the steady progress in this crucial field. After a meticulous study of the official statistics on the subject, Bhalla and Singh concluded, "From 1990–1993 to 2003–2006, the growth rates of both agricultural output and of land yields slowed compared to the pre-liberalization period. At the all-India level, while the output growth decelerated to 1.74 percent per annum from 3.37 percent per annum, the yield growth declined to 1.52 percent per annum from 3.17 percent per annum."[53]

As explained earlier, this nationwide setback was related to the central and state governments' slashing of investment in irrigation and water management, which reduced the profit margin of cultivators. On the regional level, resource-poor eastern India—including Assam, Bihar, Orissa (aka Odisha), and West Bengal—suffered more than the other three regions: northwestern (Haryana, Himachal Pradesh, Jammu and Kashmir, Punjab, Uttar Pradesh, and Uttarakhand), central (Gujarat, Madhya Pradesh, Maharashtra, and Rajasthan), and southern (Andhra Pradesh, Karnataka, Kerala, and Tamil Nadu).

The exception that proved the rule was the prosperity of the spice and condiment plantations in Kerala. Between 1990–93 and 2003–6, the value of the plantation produce of condiments and spices to aggregate agrarian produce more than doubled, from 16.7 percent to 36.3 percent. With trade liberalization creating favorable conditions for exporting these commodities, farmers increased the area and production of these crops.[54]

On the other hand, in the fertile northwest region, the absence of crop rotation to break the duopoly of wheat and rice, the lavish application of fertilizer and pesticide, and the excessive drilling of tube wells led to reduced efficiency. Farmers' profits shrank, the soil quality deteriorated, and the groundwater table fell dramatically.

The Plunging Water Table and Rainwater Harvesting

Of India's claimed 101 million acres (39 million hectares) of irrigated land as of 2009, three-fifths had come to rely on groundwater.[55] To monitor the situation, the Indian government had established the Central Ground Water Board in the Ministry of Water Resources in 1970. Over the nest two decades, state governments followed their lead by setting up their own groundwater departments.

By 2005, there were roughly 20 million individual wells in the country contributing to groundwater depletion. These included traditional open wells and hand pumps as well as deep tube wells.[56] Unlike in China, India had virtually no law on groundwater. Anyone could pump water as long as it lay under his or her plot of land. As a result, groundwater was being extracted from lower and lower levels and at a much faster rate than it could be replenished by rainfall. With an average annual rainfall of forty-two inches, India was not short of this precious gift of nature. But the amount varied widely from region to region. What most areas had in common was the loss of rainwater going down the drain or disappearing as steam.

The solution lay in capturing rainwater and storing it in containers above or below ground for immediate use, or to channel it into the soil for later extraction. This is called rainwater harvesting. It has been practiced in India and elsewhere in different ways since antiquity. In modern times, rainwater harvesting can be accomplished using rooftops, storm-water drains, wide paved or unpaved areas, or lakes and ponds. Individual households in towns and villages may store rainwater for their gardens, livestock, washing, and bathing. Given the alarming drop in the water table in the countryside, those who resort to rainwater harvesting opt for recharging ground water.

A typical rainwater harvesting system consists of a catchment area—the area that receives the rainfall, a coarse mesh to prevent the passage of debris, gutters to collect and transport the water to a storage container, and pipes to carry the stored water for reuse or recharge. If rainwater is filtered properly, it could be used for drinking. For a recharge, the storage tank has to be installed into the ground and connected to another tank with holes in its bottom. Here, two options are available: either the percolations of rainwater seep through the soil at shallower depth into recharge trenches, or the water percolates down much farther and joins the groundwater, as in recharge wells.

Faced with a severe drought in Andhra Pradesh, its chief minister Nara Chandrababu Naidu devised a water conservation mission code-named "Neeru Meeru" (Telugu: Water and You) in 2000. Its ten-point program included installing "rooftop rainwater harvesting devices in urban areas." Following a drought in Tamil Nadu in 2003, its government mandated installing rainwater harvesting devices in about half a million urban households, including those in the capital of Chennai. A survey of 759 households in the city by Chennai Metrowater in 2009 showed that the groundwater level had risen by three to six meters. Such a satisfactory result led Metrowater officials to conduct a random check for the maintenance of rainwater harvesting structures before the onset of summer monsoon season.[57] Thanks to the Kerala government's rainwater harvesting campaign and publicity by various media, rainwater harvesting is quite popular in that state.

Compared to the popularity of rainwater harvesting in the south, the situation in Punjab was bleak. Its people and politicians proudly broadcast the fact that though the state accounted for merely 1.5 percent of India's territory, it produced one-fifth of the nation's wheat and more than one-tenth of its rice.[58] But farmers seemed oblivious to the disaster that awaited them if they continued to overexploit the groundwater and deplete the table by a meter annually. "This state would turn into a desert in less than twenty years," warned a town-planning official in Jalandhar, requesting anonymity, in his interview with Anju Agnihotri Chaba of the *Indian Express*. According to the Soil Conservation Department, more than 65 percent of the rainwater was "going to waste" every year.[59]

A few years earlier, the state government's local bodies department made it compulsory for every new building to be equipped with a rainwater harvesting plant. But this bylaw was not being enforced. Mahender Kamal, a senior officer in the planning office of Jalandhar, admitted that they had covered twenty schools in Patiala and a few in Jalandhar in 2009, but the department presently lacked funds to undertake such projects. His boss, Tarlok Singh, conceded that despite the existence of this bylaw its implementation was "nominal" as "only commercial buildings are installing such plants."[60] This was the case in other urban centers as well. With the exception of Kerala, the prospect of rainwater harvesting on a mass scale elsewhere in the countryside was as yet not on the horizon.

Besides improving irrigation facilities—a slow process—India badly needed a major biotechnological breakthrough in agriculture to cope with static or falling grain output, since its population was rising by an average of 1.7 percent a year.

New Biotechnological Leap Needed

The high-yield variety seeds of wheat and rice originated in the United States in the early 1960s. A generation later, America once again pioneered a new technology in agriculture, based on a more refined process of gene splicing in plants that led to gene transfer. It enabled the agricultural engineers to impart certain desirable genes to organisms or to suppress or remove undesirable genes. Their early trials showed reduced frost damage in the treated plants. Later, this same technique was applied to potatoes.[61]

The next step was to produce genetically modified (GM) seeds by adding new traits to the plant, such as resistance to certain pests, diseases, or environmental conditions, or the ability to produce a particular nutrient or pharmaceutical agent. Both food and nonfood GM seeds have been developed. GM food crops have proved controversial because the long-term effect on humans of the toxins they carry has not been fully determined.

The first GM crop was approved for sale in the United States in 1994. It was a tomato that showed a longer shelf life. The following year the *bacillus thuringiensis* (Bt) potato became the first pesticide-producing crop to be approved by the U.S. Food and Drug Administration. Bt crops are GM plants that kill insects using a toxic protein from the Bt soil bacterium. Other foods followed, including maize, squash, and soybeans. In the nonfood category, Bt cotton seed produced by Monsanto Company in 1996 was a breakthrough of paramount interest worldwide.[62]

In 2011, India became the largest cultivator of Bt cotton, jumping from ten thousand hectares for experimental purposes to 10.6 million hectares, covering 88 percent of the record 12.1 million hectares under cotton cultivation.[63] This commodity was the most important raw material for India's Rs 1,500 billion ($30 billion) textile industry, which contributed nearly 20 percent of the country's total industrial output and employed more than 15 million people.[64]

When sufficient water was available for planted Bt cotton seeds either through rain or manmade irrigation, and these plants were treated with proper doses of fertilizer and pesticide, the crop was capable of increasing the cultivator's profit by 75 percent. Before the arrival of the Bt variety, even the traditional seeds benefited from the use of fertilizer and pesticide, not to mention the water extracted from tube wells for irrigation. As a result of these advances, the average cotton yield per hectare in India more than doubled, from 225 kilograms in 1991 to 519 kilograms in 2011.[65]

As for food, eggplant—called *brinjal* in India—has been in the news since 2005, when Mahyco coopted two Indian agricultural universities to develop Bt brinjal that would reduce the need of pesticides by deterring pests. In early October 2009, after studying the results of their experiments, an experts committee recommended the commercialization of Bt brinjal to the Genetic Engineering Approval Committee of the Ministry of Environment and Forests.[66] Soon after, permission was granted. But three months later, the environment minister, Jairam Ramesh, put a moratorium on the release of the transgenic brinjal hybrid, Bt brinjal, "until we arrive at a political, scientific and societal consensus."[67] But it was not until February 2012 that Ramesh revealed the full background to his decision, in an interview with CNN-IBN. "The Rural Development Minister told me, 'There was opposition from state governments. There was no scientific consensus on the need for Bt brinjal; scientists were divided. . . . The full protocol of tests had not been completed. Unlike Bt cotton, Bt brinjal is something you eat every day. Safety and reliability tests had not been completed. There had been no independent regulatory mechanism which could instill confidence in the public."[68]

Following a petition by environmental activist Aruna Rodrigues—made under the Public Interest Litigation provision[69]—before the Supreme Court, the court appointed a technical experts committee in May 2012 to advise on the open field trials for GM food crops. In its report issued that October, it recommended a ten-year moratorium on all Bt food-crop trials. This was in line with a report by a parliamentary committee on the cultivation of GM food crops in August. The technical committee's report also recommended overhauling the regulatory authorities that oversaw GM trials and reviewing regulations to ensure that GM crops posed no risk to human health or the environment. It stressed the need for specially designated and certified field-trial sites, and added that sufficient mechanisms must be established for monitoring the field trials before any could resume.[70]

Suman Sahai, of the advocacy organization Gene Campaign, pointed out a major lacuna in the approach of the current regulatory protocol. "In failing to consider the impact of a GM crop, for instance, on organic farming, the Indian regulatory system completely ignores the interests of farmers who would lose their markets if contamination with the GM product were to take place," she observed.[71]

The Role of Advocacy Groups

In Vidarbha, the farmers' advocacy group VJAS, founded by Kishor Tiwari, maintained an up-to-date blog, promptly disseminating all the news about the plight of the peasants in the region. Tiwari kept tabs on the farmers' suicides, a task made easy because of the ubiquity of cell phones in India, even in rural areas. The speed with which he shared these depressing news items kept the subject in the public eye throughout India.

He believed that he had a divine mission to accomplish. This was made explicit by the note in Hindi he prominently displayed on the windshield of his car: "God has sent this man to the poor." Sharing the back seat of his car as it was steered by his driver, he told a visiting journalist, "The same liberalization that is driving India's growth is breaking the farmers' backs."[72]

This has been the thesis of the leaders of the All India Kisan Sabha (AIKS, or All India Peasants' Council), the country's oldest peasant organization, dating back to 1936. After the Communist Party of India was legalized by the British government in 1942 in the wake of the Soviet Union joining the Allies in World War II, the AIKS became its front organization. When the Communist Party split in 1964, each of the resulting two parties claimed the AIKS as its own peasants' body. Its strength varied from state to state. By and large, it had tried to advance the interests of the middle-size farmers and neglected the interests of the landless and poor peasants.

When Indira Gandhi's government lost its majority in parliament in 1969, the members of the two Communist parties lent it support. Pressured by them, her administration passed such pro-poor measures as the nationalization of fourteen leading banks. The new law required government-run banks to provide 40 percent of their credit to "priority sectors: such as agriculture, small-scale industry, and small businesses." With the nationalization of six more banks in 1980, the branches of the public sector banks increased tenfold, to 64,000, by 2003, with half of them in rural areas, focused on agriculture.[73] Yet that amounted to extending banking facilities to only one in twenty villages.

In 2004, the Congress-led coalition of Manmohan Singh had to rely on the votes of the Communist-led Left Front MPs. They were instrumental in pressuring the government to pass the National Rural Employment Guarantee Act in 2005, which to some extent alleviated poverty in the countryside. But the credit for it went not to the Communists, who fared rather badly in later polls, but to the Congress Party, which was returned to the Lok Sabha as the largest group in 2009.

Between the solo campaign by Tiwari and a group decision by Left Front MPs in parliament, there was space for medium-size NGOs to help the downtrodden villagers. That was where the People's Science Institute, founded by Ravi Chopra in Dehradun, fit in. A graduate of an Indian Institute of Technology from Mumbai, Chopra obtained his doctorate in material science from Stevens Institute of Technology in New Jersey in 1973. He returned home and assembled a team of dedicated scientists and social workers to form the People's Science Institute to devise original schemes to combat environmental damage, droughts, and other disasters. To identify with the underprivileged he wished to help, Chopra switched to wearing the north Indian dress of a long shirt and loose pajamas, and grew a beard. The People's Science Institute managed to integrate traditional practices with the latest technology to design a watershed system that could act as an alternative to big dams. It helped village panchayats to draft self-sustaining development plans. It also tried to popularize rainwater harvesting in rural areas. Chopra's own house had a forty-kiloliter tank on the roof to collect rainwater.

He caught the attention of the national media in 1982 as the coauthor of the citizens' report on the state of India's environment. He also published a paper on the country's water needs in the twenty-first century. As a result, the Indian government appointed him to the Working Group on Perspective Planning, National Commission for Integrated Water Resource Development. Since then, he has remained in touch with top policymakers, politicians, and senior civil servants in Delhi. Chopra is therefore familiar with their strategic thinking. "The Indian government has no interest in making agriculture efficient," he told me. "It very much likes the rural migrants to provide cheap labor to thriving states like Gujarat or local cities for construction and other work."[74] As it happened, six months earlier, Prime Minister Manmohan Singh had made the same point but placed it in a different context. "The only way we can raise our heads above poverty is for more people to be taken out of agriculture," he stressed.[75]

5

Slums on the Rise

It was a windy February day in Delhi. The breeze whistling through the half-stuck window of our taxi turned fetid as we got off the historic Grand Trunk Road and turned into the sprawling capital's northeast district, which adjoins the impoverished, densely populated state of Uttar Pradesh. The unpleasant breeze seemed to announce our new destination: the slum of New Seelampur. The logic of qualifying a slum as "new" escaped me. It was only later that I discovered the reason for its name—to distinguish it from the much earlier, authorized Seelampur Colony, popularly known as Seelampur. The source of the malodorous air, however, was anything but new. It was a stagnant pond of sewage surrounded by rubbish and detritus, the numerous plastic and polythene objects shining in the pale sun, some of which had been set alight, the resulting weak, acrid smoke competing lamely with the foul exhalation of the simmering dark blue liquid.

From Flat Land to a Slum of 55,000

It required much physical effort on my part to reach the threshold of Sajid Farouk's tiny, single-room "health clinic," bordered by a channel of exposed sewage, home to countless malignant germs, with methane gas gurgling to the surface. I was helped by my companion, Omair Anas, a PhD student. A short, dark, squat man with a salt-and-pepper beard, Farouk, in his mid-forties, looked spruce in his blue cotton pants and a white shirt. He was a self-taught paramedic, known locally as a *hakim* (Urdu: physician). He treated a little boy with a running sore by applying a balm and bandaging it, charging him five rupees (10¢).

Farouk was born in Sanjarpur village in the Azamgarh district of Uttar Pradesh. "There was very little land to go around in our large family," he explained. "I was too poor to afford a wife. So I thought of trying my luck in Delhi. I arrived in 1997 only to find the city being very expensive. I ended up here because of the earlier migrants from Uttar Pradesh. The rent was low. In those days, there were only *jhuggi jhopris* [Hindi: makeshift huts] here, nothing made of red bricks."[1]

His carpenter friend, Abdul Haq, who had been reading a newspaper while lying on the upper berth of a two-berth wooden bed next to our plastic chairs, propped himself up on his right elbow and sat up. He put aside *Dawat* (Urdu: Feast), an Urdu newspaper, to reveal a man in his early thirties with a neatly trimmed mustache on a fair-skinned face "I was born locally," he said. "Thirty years ago, this was a plain field, government-owned. A few people from Uttar Pradesh put up jhuggi jhopris. The numbers started increasing rapidly about ten years ago here and in Seelampur, mostly villagers from Uttar Pradesh and some from Bihar."

Indeed, this happened at such a rate that this northeastern district of Delhi became the most densely populated in India, according to the 2011 census: home to 2.24 million people in an area of sixty square kilometers (twenty-three square miles).[2] "The migrants were mostly landless laborers in their villages," continued Haq. "They could not survive in the shrinking agrarian sector. They heard about jobs in Delhi, mainly building work, at Rs 150 [$3] a day."

Property developers in India's urban areas were operating in a sector that started booming from 2001 on. Taking its cue from the U.S. Federal Reserve's slashing of interest rates after the September 11, 2001, terrorist attacks, the Bharatiya Janata Party–led government in Delhi followed suit. Lower interest rates encouraged young middle-class professionals to switch from the traditional "save and buy" route to house ownership to the "buy now, pay later" path. Another factor that boosted demand for residences was the growth of smaller, nuclear families due to the gradual dissolution of the traditional extended family model in the predominant Hindu society. Research in 2006 showed that the average age of the owner of a new house had plunged from forty-five to thirty-two during the previous decade. The commercial property market was equally buoyant, with shopping malls, hotels, and showrooms springing up in cities and major towns. The expansion in office space was well illustrated by the 150 million square feet of newly built-up area required by the burgeoning outsourcing and information technology sector during 2006–10. Altogether, the revenue of the real-estate sector exploded from $10.1 billion in 2005 to $66.8 billion in 2010.[3]

Cement factories operated at full tilt to satisfy the construction industry's demand, which grew annually at 8 percent during 2001–11. The total cement output at the end of 2011 reached a record 320 million–plus metric tons a year.[4] Brick kilns could not cope with demand. No wonder then that the construction sector, accounting for 8 percent of the GDP, ranked second only behind agriculture.

Yet there was a much wider scope for the expansion of this industry. According to the National Sample Survey 63rd Round (July 2006–June 2007), 55 percent of urban residents lived, slept, cooked, and washed in an area of 5.5 square meters (fifty-nine square feet) per person. This happened to be the minimum specified living area for prisoners in America, according to Randeep Ramesh of *The Guardian*.[5]

For now, though, the construction contractors' growing prosperity did not trickle down to those who did the actual building. In Delhi, for instance, they paid their laborers well below the statutory minimum daily wage of Rs 190 ($3.80). At the very least, these underpaid workers could complain to their representative in Delhi's Legislative Assembly, I said to Farouk and Haq as we sat talking in New Seelampur.

"Ahmad Mateen [our representative] has more important things to do," Farouk responded. "He has helped us as a community. It was only when he intervened, we got proper electricity connections. Before that we used to steal it from the main supply line. Also we got the communal water taps at about the same time. But water comes only for a few hours a day." Haq piped up. "Still, it was a bargain. For getting that done, we gave him our votes. Most of the ten thousand families here did. That is how he has bagged the Assembly seat twice after his first win in 1998."

It was just before the 2003 Assembly elections that the slum dwellers were allowed to build proper brick structures. Each family was allocated a total perimeter of twenty meters (sixty-two feet). Most families partitioned the small space into two parts: one for cooking and daily activities, the other as the storeroom doubling as the bedroom. Five to six members of the typical family shared this cramped space. They dug a deep hole in the ground to serve as a latrine.

Sadly, the authorities failed to construct the sewage system. Individuals, lacking proper skills, built a brick-lined drain. As a result, the sewage did not flow down a slope. In the absence of a drain cover, the waste stagnated then spilled over into the street. The end result: a stomach-churning stink emanating from a revolting sight.

Despite the cramped indoor settings and the unhygienic outdoors, the general mood of the residents in New Seelampur seemed upbeat. There were many smiling faces, particularly among the young. A wedding was in the offing. Though the ceremony was to be held in the evening, the temporary shed on the edge of the settlement, erected on upright poles supporting a canvas roof, had become a source of Bollywood songs relayed from loudspeakers. Young boys gyrated with happy abandon while girls in colorful clothes of orange, red, purple, blue, and green, with an occasional flash of silver-thread embroidery, watched wide-eyed at a distance.

In the built-up part of the settlement, however, it was taxing for Omair and I to squeeze our way through the narrow, rutted, people-choked byways. So we sauntered along the main street. At the butcher's, the hanging meat was masked by an impregnable sheath of black flies. Hamid Baksh, the long-faced, toothless owner of a flyblown vegetable shop, selling tomatoes, onions, potatoes, cabbages, and peas, had arrived many years ago from a village near Meerut. His shop in the street exceeded the space he had been allocated for his family. A backless wooden bench by the side of the store served as a meeting point for slum dwellers to exchange gossip and watch color TV on a set placed behind Baksh's bent back. "The rent for cable TV is Rs 50 [$1] a month," he told us. "My daily turnover is Rs 120 [$2.40], and I make Rs 50 [$1] gross profit."

Among those who assembled at his shop was Abid Reza. Dressed in well-laundered khaki pants, striped shirt, and polished shoes, this clean-shaven, chubby-faced, fair-skinned forty-year-old man with a graying mustache stood out. "I come from a village near Rampur in Uttar Pradesh," he said. "After much trial and error I managed to find a job as a peon-messenger with a graphic design company in Seelampur Colony. It is called HM Graphics and specializes in outdoor advertising. Their clients include Unilever, General Motors, HDFC Bank, and Heinz. My salary is Rs 7,000 [$140] per month, and it is a six-day week. I have a bank account and a credit card." Yet he had no plans to leave the slum to follow the ten families who over the past fifteen years had moved to a decently habitable place.

Slum India Profiled

As the commercial capital of India, Mumbai, home to the Reserve Bank of India and the local and national stock exchanges, was at the forefront of financial globalization. The subsequent spurt in expensive private residential and commercial property development made the land and the built-up structures in India's most populous city among the most expensive on the planet.

In an upscale residential neighborhood of South Mumbai, land on Altamont Road was worth Rs 1.25 million ($25,000) per square meter in 2008. It was there, on a plot of 4,532 square meters, that a twenty-seven-story cantilevered structure—named after the mythical Atlantic Ocean island Antilia, featured in Iberian and Lusaphone folk legend, and valued at $1 billion—was unveiled in October 2010. It was the new "house" of Mukesh Ambani, the fifty-three-year-old, bull-necked, jowly-faced chairman and CEO of Reliance Industries Ltd., the country's second most valued company and the second largest by revenue after the Tata Group. Its first six floors, large enough to accommodate 160 cars, were meant primarily for visitors. Above that rose a cinema and a ballroom capped by a series of floating gardens, topped by a multistory health center, a swimming pool, and a floor of guest apartments—all of these serving as a base for the several stories that accommodated the five members of the Ambani family. Atop the Ambanis' core residence were three helipads. It required a staff of six hundred to maintain this new residence of Mukesh Ambani, whose net worth was then put at $29 billion.[6]

"The person who lives in there [Antilia] should be concerned about what he sees around him and [ask] can he make a difference," remarked Ratan Tata, worth $1 billion in assets, in an interview with *The Times* of London. "If he is not, then it is sad."[7] Indeed, after passing by the New Wonder of Mumbai, the Booker Prize–winning novelist and social activist Arundhati Roy wrote: "Is it a house or a home? A temple to the new India, or a warehouse for its ghosts?"[8]

Mumbai also has the distinction of attracting almost half a million rural migrants annually since 2001.[9] Some of the villagers walked to the outlying settlements of Mumbai with their family's milch cow in tow. Unable to find or afford suitable animal fodder, the migrant household let the animal free to roam and forage rubbish dumps to survive. It is common to see cows on the loose in cities like Mumbai, often standing pat in the middle of the road, immune to the noise and speed of the vehicles trying to bypass her.

The population of metropolitan Mumbai, however, increased only by 8.7 percent during 2001–11 because, as a peninsula attached to the mainland, it had limited habitable space. So the migrants ended up swelling the city's suburbs. Despite the rising wealth of the metropolis, the percentage of the slum dwellers in the city's population remained obstinately at 50 percent.[10]

Given the unhygienic conditions in which they survived and the absence of affordable healthcare, the life expectancy of a slum dweller was well below that of his counterpart living outside slums. Collectively, the life span of the typical resident of this "City of Dreams" was seven years less than the national average of sixty-six in 2010.[11]

The definition of a slum varies. The United Nations' agency UN-Habitat has defined a slum household as "a group of individuals living under the same roof that lack one or more of the following conditions: access to safe water; sanitation; secure tenure; durability of housing; and sufficient living area." The Indian government defines a slum area as a cluster of households lacking facilities of drinking water, drainage, and latrine. Using the cluster size of sixty households and limiting their survey to settlements with twenty-thousand-plus people, the census authorities in 2001 put India's slum population at 52.4 million, out of 278 million urbanites living in 5,480 cities and towns. Later this figure was revised upward to 61.8 million, or 22 percent of the total urban head count.[12] But, according to the United Nations, there were 158.4 million slum dwellers in India, more than half of the total urban population.[13] The final figures of the 2011 Indian census were expected to put the nationwide number of slum dwellers at over 93 million, a 50 percent increase in a decade. According to the World Bank, during the decade of 2000–2010 the growth in the urban population as a whole was 26 percent.[14]

In terms of sheer size of a city's slum population, Delhi was second to Mumbai. Its 3.16 million slum dwellers, as estimated in 2011, represented an increase of two-fifths since 2001.[15] This was so even when the capital was the second-richest city in India, a position it attained in part due to the dollops of cash that the central government showered on it. Its annual per capita income of Rs 176,000 ($3,520) was three times the national average.[16]

Yet Delhi was unable to buck the national trend wherein the unregulated and rising influx of rural migrants into urban settlements had led to a steady deterioration in water supply, education, healthcare, and round-the-clock electricity. Whereas Delhi's power supply was integrated into the national grid and divided into regions, the responsibility for providing clean, potable water to citizens rested with the local authorities. They had failed.

Even the middle-class neighborhoods suffered. The experience of Ritu Prasher, a resident of an apartment block in the Janata Colony—as narrated to Somini Sengupta of the *New York Times*—was typical. Since public taps discharged only reluctant trickles of water—partly because 40 percent was lost en route through leaky pipes—Prasher had to get up at 6:30 a.m. to queue for a private water tanker delivering muddy brown liquid. A melee invariably ensued the moment the private tanker arrived. To overcome the water deficit, the residents of middle-class colonies such as Janata had resorted to drilling deep tube wells. But so many tube wells had been drilled in greater Delhi over the past quarter century that the groundwater level had fallen sharply, and many of these wells had started delivering saline water, unfit for drinking or cooking.[17]

A similar trend prevailed in Bangalore, which also underscored an unmistakable linkage between globalization and accelerated urbanization. As the bastion of the information technology industry, it recorded the highest leap in population—65 percent—during 2001–11. Within a decade, Bangalore grew from the sixth-largest Indian city to the third-largest, after Mumbai and Delhi. Its slum population grew from 23 percent to 33 percent of the total.[18]

During that period, Ahmedabad, the largest city of Gujarat, ruled by Chief Minister Narendra Modi—a vigorous executor of neoliberal policy—since 2001, experienced the second-highest jump in population, 58 percent. That catapulted Ahmedabad from number seven among India's cities to number five. And the increase in the city's slum dwellers pushed their proportion in the estimated population of 5.25 million to 40 percent in 2010.[19]

Among other provincial cities where the rise in population between the latest decennial censuses stood out was Dehradun. A third of its total population, a shade lower than 450,000, lived in slums. The reasons were both domestic and global. In order to have a substantial presence abroad, ONGC Videsh Limited, a subsidiary of the Dehradun-based Oil and Natural Gas Corporation specializing in foreign operations, accelerated its efforts to acquire and exploit oil and gas reserves abroad from 2001 on. It succeeded. During 2002–10, ONGC Videsh Limited's annual oil output from its wells in fourteen countries climbed from 0.25 million metric tons to 9.45 million metric tons.[20] The subsequent growth in the Oil and Natural Gas Corporation's permanent staff raised demand for residential property in the city. Another factor causing the rise in the local population was the naming of Dehradun as the capital of the newly created state of Uttaranchal (later renamed Uttarakhand) in November 2000.

Landless peasants from rural Bihar started pouring in. With 79 percent of its population in 2001 living below the poverty line—as measured by the Multidimensional Poverty Index—Bihar was even poorer than the neighboring Uttar Pradesh, adjoining Uttarakhand.[21] Among Dehradun's existing slums that experienced rapid expansion was the one along the banks of Bindal, a seasonal tributary that was reduced to a drain during dry months. Of the city's 113 slums in 2000, ninety had grown near a drainage channel, and most of the remainder along railway lines.[22] These included both "notified" and "non-notified" categories, the former having been officially recognized and the latter not. The overarching failure of the local and state authorities was illustrated by the data collected on slums by the National Sample Survey Organization between July 2008 and June 2009. India had 49,000 slums, 24 percent of which were next to drains and 12 percent along railway lines.[23] Any slum clearance program periodically implemented by the local government applied only to a small section of the "non-notified" slums, as it lacked the resources to tackle the problem on a wider scale.

Bindal Bridge Slum

Though the official title of the waterway passing through Dehradun was the Bindal River, it was in reality a seasonal tributary that flowed into the Song River in the southeast. It came to life only during the months of monsoon. For the rest of the year, it became an open drain. Its unclaimed dry bed started attracting rural migrants, mainly from Bihar, from the mid-1980s on. Their number shot up after 2001. A decade later the jhuggi jhopris along the tributary's banks accommodated twenty thousand people—about three thousand families.

On a bright sunny day in early spring, the tributary was down to a blue-black ribbon of stagnant muck. The communal water tap planted on the margin of this shallow channel stood out because of the languid line of girls with plastic containers and white buckets painted sky blue all over except the space spelling ASIAN PAINTS. In the background was a haphazard row of ramshackle, hand-built, windowless shelters with decrepit doors, the structures held together by wooden planks, plastic sheets, tarpaulin, duct tape, plywood panels, empty sacks, and corrugated metal sheets. The linear slum was hemmed by sand bags and flat stone blocks in the front to keep the monsoon water at bay, and a robust fencing wall at the back to delineate it from the elegant, whitewashed, multistory homes of the wealthy.

During the day, when their husbands were away at construction sites, the wives and daughters spent a lot of time outside their shacks, cooking, looking after small children, washing utensils and clothes, and waiting at the shared water tap. Children mingled with one another and played with loitering pigs in dirty puddles.

I found Basanti Kurmi, the wife of Devidas Kurmi, scrubbing her five-year-old son with a wet rag. A dark, oval-faced woman with a round vermillion mark on her forehead and swept-back jet-black hair, she was wearing a bead necklace over a long-sleeved beige blouse and a dirty sari. Inside the four walls of wooden planks and loose bricks, topped with a corrugated metal sheet, some clothes hung precariously on nails. Other garments were strewn on a bunk bed. A straw mat was rolled up in a corner to be turned into a bed at night. Instead of a door, her shanty had a dirty rag hanging from a thick string tied around two rusty nails hammered into two vertical wooden planks on either side of the opening.

"The weather here is better than in Bihar," she remarked. "But monsoon is a problem. The river water rises up and flows fast. We have to guard our children closely to see that they don't fall into the water and drown. The rain falling on our metal roof is very noisy, like a horde of cows running on the roof. We cannot sleep at night." How was her family life? I asked hesitantly. She blushed as she reflected on my question. "My husband is a good man," she said. "He does not beat me like many others do to their wives when they get drunk."[24]

She had a friend in her neighbor Aarti, wife of Lakshman Ram. They and their husbands came from villages in the Gaya district of Bihar. Basanti looked after the toddler of the twenty-three-year-old Aarti during the day while the young mother went to the nearby tailoring and educational school run by the Aasra for Community Transformation, an NGO focused on improving the lot of the indigent. This open-plan facility, with some eighty students and tailoring equipment, was located below the shops along Omkar Plaza, next to the bridge.

Aarti was a slim, petite woman in a purple sari, with soulful eyes in an ascetic face and the vermillion mark on her forehead, the equivalent of a wedding ring for Western women. "We came from Gaya district seven years ago," she said. "My husband is a carpenter. He is now working in the houses they are building in the Prem Nagar Colony. At first we lived with my husband's maternal uncle, who had come to Dehradun earlier. But it was too crowded. So we built a hut on the riverbed. I do odd jobs for the Aasra school and get Rs 1,000 [$20] a month."

In contrast to Aarti, Gayatri, the wife of Bharat Ram, was large, dark, and curvaceous in a checkered sari and a tight blouse. But like Aarti, she was born in the impoverished Gaya district. Surprisingly, for a woman of twenty-nine, she was the mother of a fourteen-year-old son. "My husband knew someone from our village who worked in Dehradun. As he was a weakling, he could not do hard labor in the fields. Initially, he rented a slum hut for Rs 1,000 a month. But after I and the children arrived, we moved to a single room in a proper building. The rent is Rs 2,000 a month. I come to the tailoring class here. We have to bring our own cloth."[25]

With the upper-middle and upper classes in the city expanding, there was rising demand for maids, cleaners, cooks, and domestic servants. Older rural women, not encumbered with childrearing, and their young, unmarried daughters, provided the services needed. And a minority of the male villagers, intent on improving their lot, saved to learn how to drive, since most car owners in India hired chauffeurs to ferry them and their families.

As a longtime resident of Dehradun and a social activist, Ravi Chopra was familiar with the influx of villagers and the upsurge in the size and number of the city's slums. "When someone comes here from Bihar he gets inducted into the local Bihari community," Chopra explained. "As construction workers they get hired through labor contractors who take their commission. Their net daily wage is Rs 180 [$3.60], just above the minimum wage of Rs 150 [$3]. It reflects the high demand for construction. Initially, they send money home. Then some bring their families to live in a slum. It is the cheapest option for them, to build their own makeshift hut." But how does he acquire land? "Through the local mafia—with political and police connections. Somebody from that cabal will get the Bihari migrant a small plot on the riverbed to rent. As a tenant of the land, he has to pay three months' rent in advance." But that was not the end of the newcomer's dependence on the local fix-it don. "If the Bihari wants electric connection, or a voting card, or a ration card, the mafia man will arrange it for a fee."[26]

A ration card had the top priority for the rural migrant. India has a long history of rationing, dating back to the scarcity created by World War II. But back then, it only applied to urban areas. Food shortages in the mid-1960s led the Indian government to set up the Food Corporation of India, to procure and store food, and the Agricultural Prices Commission, to set prices for agricultural produce. These became part of the renamed public distribution system (PDS) for all of India. The PDS was administered by the Central Ministry of Consumer Affairs, Food and Public Distribution, and depended on the shipments from the Food Corporation's central pool. It aimed to stabilize prices, ration basic needs in case of a supply deficit, ensure availability of such commodities to the needy, and discourage hoarding and black marketing. The PDS was revamped in June 1992 to focus on the areas in need, and the task of delivering the goods was transferred to state authorities, which were put in charge of supervising fair price shops. The central government continued to be responsible for procurement, storage, and transportation of food grains.

Five years later, it introduced the concept of the Targeted Public Distribution System with a focus on the underprivileged. Households were divided into three categories, each identified by the color of their ration card: pink for "the poorest of the poor," called Antyodaya Anna Yojana (AAY; Hindi: Uplift of the Poorest Mini-Plan); yellow for "below the poverty line" (BPL); and green for "above the poverty line" (APL). The classification was to be done by state authorities. The primary commodities distributed included wheat, rice, sugar, and kerosene. However, it was not until December 2000 that the scheme was implemented.

The AAY cardholder was entitled to purchase thirty-five kilograms (seventy-seven pounds) of rice or wheat a month per person in the family at Rs 3 and Rs 2 per kilogram respectively. For the BPL families, the same amounts of rice and wheat were available at Rs 5.65 and Rs 4.15 per kilogram respectively. For the APL households, the purchase was subject to availability of stocks from the central pool, and the respective prices were about Rs 8 and Rs 6 for rice and wheat, the quality of both being rather standard.[27] Since the market price for a kilogram of rice varied between Rs 19 and Rs 38, and for wheat around Rs 13, the holder of a BPL ration card saved quite a lot on the food bill for his or her family.

A material subsidy of this sort went some way to mitigate the strain that a rural migrant felt by moving to a city. But it was not enough, given the arduous nature of his work and the filthy environment of his dilapidated homestead.

Home-Brewed Hooch Dulls Grim Reality

On arriving in a city, a rural peasant felt psychologically dislocated. In his village, he lived in a neighborhood among other members of his subcaste. He knew everybody else in the small community as well, even though he did not socialize with those who were outside his subcaste. Aside from the busy harvesting season, there was always time for leisurely gossip at the local open-air tea stall. He found the city unbearably impersonal. In the countryside, he had fresh air to breathe, not the polluted air of the congested, vehicle-choked urban roads or the putrid smell of the slum. Almost invariably, he made the adjustment to urban living through the intermediate step of sheltering himself in a cocoon of villagers from his native area.

Such had been the case with Lakshman Ram and Bharat Ram when they arrived in Dehradun. At the end of their first day as construction workers alongside other Biharis, their worksite was besieged by vendors of *desi* (Hindi: local) liquor, officially called *tharra*—the slang in English is "hooch." Poured neatly into quarter-liter pouches, it was priced Rs 5 (10¢) a unit. Lakshman and Bharat followed their coworkers' lead and bought a pouch or two. They found the first few sips pretty rough and the smell pungent, and that made them cough. But they needed to socialize with their comrades, so they continued. Eventually, they got hooked. Every day, they looked forward to a session of group drinking, enlivened with gossip, which released the tension of unremittingly hard labor. Their wives lamented their lapse. Increasingly, they resorted to snatching whatever cash they brought with them to the hovel. After all, they bore the ultimate responsibility for running the household and balancing the budget. A typical slum-dwelling family spent 60 percent of its budget on food and drink, 10 percent on rent, 15 percent on electricity and fuel, and the rest on footwear and clothing.[28]

Despite the efforts of those who ran the tailoring school near the Bindal Bridge and other contacts of mine in Dehradun, I failed to find a place where desi liquor was brewed. It was much later, in the slum of Nat Basti in central Jodhpur, that I finally tracked down the recipe for this hooch, which accounted for two-thirds of the alcohol consumed in India, according to *The Lancet*, the 190-year-old British medical journal.[29]

The recipe was disclosed to me by Ramesh Nat, a tall, wiry man with a thin mustache in his late twenties, wearing a well-ironed shirt and pants. "We fill large spherical earthen pots with rotten jaggery [unrefined brown sugar] and water, and add ammonium chloride to speed up fermentation. We bury the mixture underground for seven days. Then we transfer it to other containers and distill it. The yield of five liters of alcohol is then diluted with water to turn it into ten to twelve liters of tharra. The price is Rs 40 [80¢] per liter or Rs 10 [20¢] per quarter-liter." How was the business? "With all this building work in new colonies, the demand has gone up. People come to us to buy. We used to sell it for Rs 5 [10¢] a quarter-liter before."[30]

As a derivative of sugarcane, this rough, pungent drink is akin to unrefined rum, with alcohol by volume (ABV) of 40 to 50 percent. The cheapest legally produced rum sold for Rs 270 ($5.40) per liter, almost seven times the price of the moonshine version. By comparison, beer with ABV of 8 percent was considered insipid, but it still cost four times as much as tharra. Even so, every so often a distiller attempted to spice up his brew by adding some untried chemical that proved lethal, causing many deaths of the unsuspecting drinkers.

As a subcaste, the peripatetic Nats were entertainers who cheered villagers with their acrobatics, juggling, and singing. They brewed tharra for their own consumption. The advent of movies and television made their traditional calling redundant, so they started settling down in towns and cities. Their slum, Nat Basti (Hindi: Nat Settlement), was part of a bigger entity called Masuria Paharhi, established in the early 1970s. Its ten thousand inhabitants included Hindus of different castes, Dalits, and Muslims. A triangular saffron flag flew over the temple of the sacred Nagmichi Mata, revered by lower-caste Hindus, and there was a well-maintained mosque in front of the main tea stall. Located only two and a half miles from Jodhpur Railway Station, Masuria Paharhi was an integral part of the city.

One distinct feature of Masuria Paharhi was its haphazard brick buildings. Other than that, it had all the hallmarks of an urban slum: dust, puddles of dirty water like boils on a living body, wayward alleyways and pathways—the uneven surface of one resembling the terrain on a hill, broken bricks and other rubble piled up in heaps here and there. All human activity, except love-making, was on display. As in all other slums, privacy was an alien concept. What was refreshing, though, was the sight of a couple of youngsters, perched on string cots, studying. But this refreshed feeling vanished when the brewer told me that none of the Nat children went to school. The drab colors of men's clothes contrasted sharply with the floral frocks of girls and colorful salwar kameez of some women. Occasionally, a newly built shop brightened up the bleak environment. In scantily stocked shops the sign PHILIP LARSEN shone like a star in a murky sky.

I walked around the adjoining slum of Rajiv Gandhi Nagar with my university graduate auto-rickshaw driver, Ravindra Krishnawat. As elsewhere, there was a communal water tap, and the residents stole electricity from the overhead cables. To find a small car parked closely to the door of a neat house was a surprise. I met Sunil Kanodya, born into the subcaste of washer men. He was a short, skinny man in his mid-twenties. The dark reddish edges along the line of his teeth were a telltale sign of his habit of chewing tobacco. He was born in Saura, a village in Bihar's Gaya district, where his father, who had sired five sons and three daughters, owned five bighas (three acres) of land. As the youngest son, he had the least claim on the family land. He therefore pursued his education to the final year in a senior secondary school, but he did not opt for higher education. Instead, he traveled to Jodhpur to join a relative who told him about the jobs going in the building sector. Polishing marble slabs at worksites earned him Rs 200 ($4) a day.

The hills around Jodhpur were a rich source of marble, sandstone, and red stone. The demand for these stones had risen sharply all over India, since it was fashionable to furnish high-end residences and offices with marble floors and use sandstone and red stone as prestigious building materials. Jodhpur was sprinkled with signs for Navi Tiles, Baba Marble & Art Stone, Solanki Tiles, and JM Sandstone. While leaving the city on my way to Tinwari, I noticed huge mechanical saws slicing the surrounding hills into transportable layers, and smaller blocks of sandstone and red stone being carted away by camel carts to be shipped later by trucks to construction sites all over India.

What did the residents of the Masuria Paharhi think of the prosperity that had visited these traders in the area's natural resources, as evinced by the trendy Western clothing brands that fought for space alongside more local threads? To find out, accompanied by Krishnawat, I settled down on a wooden bench for a cup of black tea served in a thick, semi-opaque glass at the open-air tea stall opposite the mosque to chat with other customers. None of them wore jeans; their long pants were invariably cotton or cotton-polyester in beige, khaki, or blue. Nor did Van Heusen shirts leave them awestruck. The arrival of Western labels in apparel, an everyday illustration of globalization, meant nothing to them.

The slum dwellers had noticed the growing enrichment of businessmen and industrialists but attributed this to their good fate, *kismat* (in Urdu and Hindi). But, on the subject of politicians filling their own pockets, they all had a similar opinion because, as voters, they were approached by the candidates. "All the candidates say that we will improve your roads, clean up sewage, provide education for your children, get you free medicine, but in reality not much improvement takes place," said Abdul Ghani plaintively. "In the end, the same candidate does not come around the second time." Heavily built, unshaven, and wearing an open-neck shirt that showed the gray chest hair of a man in his late fifties, Ghani smoked *bidis*, made of unprocessed tobacco rolled in dry leaves. "Electoral candidates are supposed to fill our bellies, but we end up filling their bellies." He had come from his nearby ancestral village to Jodhpur thirteen years ago, and now earned his living as a taxi driver. "But my son is in the first year of his engineering degree course," he said with a wide smile.[31]

That was what made Masuria Paharhi stand apart from the Bindal Bridge and New Seelampur slums. It showed a glimmer of upward mobility. Also unlike the other two places, it had existed inside a city for decades. Yet they all had one thing in common: each of them was a quarry for the local police to shake down locals in order to fill their own pockets.

Hotbed of Illegality and Police Collusion

As elsewhere, upward social mobility in a slum was linked to education. New Seelampur's residents saw the opening of a primary school in 1991. Then, each year, the authorities added a grade, so that twelve years later it became a fully-fledged secondary school. "Now all small children go to school," said Sajid Farouk. "But the problem is that 80 percent drop out before the tenth grade." And very few among those who pass the final twelfth-grade examination enroll at a university. In all these years, the slum had produced only half a dozen university graduates, both men and women. "They are all arts graduates, nobody with a degree in engineering, medicine, or computer sciences," Farouk continued. "Unemployment among arts graduates is very high. To become a teacher in a town or city, you need an MA in arts plus a teacher-training diploma. Only in villages can you be a teacher with a BA. But who wants to return to a village when their parents left theirs?"

As a result, there was no role model for youngsters in New Seelampur. Some of the school dropouts got recruited by hardened criminals, which pushed up the local crime rate. "There are three major criminal activities here, and they pay far more than the Rs 150 [$3] a day for the building work," Farouk explained. "Stealing is one. Drugs distribution is another. Then there is gambling on the last digit of the closing wholesale cotton price on Mumbai's cotton exchange. We call it *satta* [Hindi: betting].[32] Some young fellows get recruited to become couriers for ganja and opium and other drugs. When one of them gets arrested, the big, rich dealer pulls strings, and he is released. That impresses the young fellows. They think the big dealer is truly influential, although it is a hefty bribe which does the trick. The satta gambling is illegal. So the police are bribed weekly, called *hafta* [Hindi: week], not to raid the bookies' dens."

It was the same in the Masuri Paharhi slum. "The police know what we do and where," confided Ramesh Nat, the brewer. "We pay them Rs 1,000 [$20] a week as protection money." This was a nationwide practice. Following the deaths of 140 tharra drinkers in Kolkata in December 2011, the source of the liquor was traced to an illegal distillery in Mograhat, thirty miles south of the city. Its residents pointed out that one shop openly selling this alcoholic drink was located opposite a police station.[33] In short, the police were in league with organized crime.

Yet in the overarching scheme of things in India, this racket was chicken feed compared to the corruption rampant in the political-business nexus that had garnered further power and influence with the advent of the New Economic Policy and globalization.

6

Sleaze Grows Exponentially

Among the many buildings constituting the administrative heart of New Delhi, the Sanchar Bhawan stands out. A three-story structure of polished stone interspersed with semi-opaque glass windows, with an entrance marked by two sturdy columns holding up the horizontal entablature with a flagpole, the Sanchar Bhawan combines elegance with modernity. It is the home of the Ministry of Communications and Information Technology, with one of its several divisions being the Department of Telecommunications. A well-maintained headquarters, the Sanchar Bhawan boasts functioning lifts and clutter-free hallways traversed by office peons carrying files and IT executives bearing sleek briefcases. Its quietude compares favorably with the nearby, barely visited National Philatelic Museum.

The Drama of January 10, 2008

But one afternoon in early January 2008, this usually placid building erupted with activity. Hordes of men were seen racing through the hallways, jostling and elbowing their way past each other, in pursuit of a crucial piece of paperwork, which, once obtained, they rushed with headlong toward a room where an ill-shaven clerk was leisurely processing applications. It was an exceptionally astonishing spectacle to see mature business executives stampede like unruly schoolchildren. What drove them was their unquenchable thirst for lucre. Just a few hours earlier they had spotted the ministry's press release on its website announcing a last-minute change of rules about a much-coveted prize, and if they were to have any hope of winning this prize, they had to present themselves at the Sanchar Bhawan that afternoon between 3:30 p.m. and 4:30 p.m., where the prize would be awarded on a first come, first served basis.

The prize was a license for electromagnetic waves—carriers of cell-phone service messages—to be allotted to cell-phone operators. Each portion of the spectrum was as valuable as a block of oil-bearing soil or seabed. Such a license would permit the operator to expand the bandwidth on second-generation (2G) telecom networks. For India's twenty-two telecom zones, the Department of Telecommunications had the authority to issue 281 zonal licenses.

The origins of the drama of January 10, 2008, could be traced back to 1994. As part of the New Economic Policy, the government of P.V. Narasimha Rao opened up telecom to the private sector, four years after the introduction of the first-generation (1G) advanced cell-phone system in America in 1990. The new arrangement specified revenue sharing between the government and the telecom operators, with the state receiving funds for allocating parts of the spectrum and a license fee. This arrangement raised the importance of the Department of Telecommunications as a revenue generator, which rubbed off on the Ministry of Communications.

It was not long after that Sukh Ram, the balding, square-faced communi-cations minister, became mired in corruption. In a raid on his residence in August 1995, the Central Bureau of Investigation, working directly under the prime minister, seized Rs 57.8 million ($1.8 million, at the 1995 exchange rate) that he had received as bribes and hoarded in pillowcases, trunks, and suitcases. The CBI also confiscated diaries containing bank accounts and names of individuals who had paid him. He was arrested the next month on the charge of owning assets disproportionate to his known sources of income.[1] Apparently, he had neither the foresight nor the wit to convert his ill-gotten black money into white money through a property purchase, or to spirit the money overseas through hawala, an informal money transfer system.

Five years later, during the rule of the first Bharatiya Janata Party–led gov-ernment, the Department of Telecommunications allocated the licenses for the 1G spectrum in India. Following the April–May 2004 parliamentary poll, a Congress-led cabinet assumed office, but only after coopting small regional parties to gain a majority in the popularly elected Lok Sabha (Hindi: People's Assembly). These groups included the Tamil Nadu–based Dravida Menne-tra Kazhgam (Tamil: Dravida Progressive Federation). One of its members,

Dayanidhi Maran, became the minister of communications, and another, Andimuthu Raja, became the minister of environment. In a cabinet reshuffle in 2007, Raja, a stocky, mustached, forty-seven-year-old lawyer from a small town in Tamil Nadu, with no background in technology or communications, replaced Maran.

In 2007, the government decided that it was high time to introduce the now fifteen-year-old second-generation cell phones in India. That necessitated a fresh allocation of 2G spectrum to the telecom companies. On September 25, the communications ministry issued a press release fixing October 1 as the deadline for 2G spectrum applications. Forty-six companies submitted 575 applications to the Department of Telecommunications. In November, Prime Minister Manmohan Singh and the finance minister instructed Raja to allocate the 2G spectrum licenses in a fair, transparent manner and to ensure that the license fee was increased from the 2001 figure for 1G spectrum.

On the morning of January 10, 2008, Raja decided unilaterally to consider only the applications received by his ministry by September 25, rather than October 1. He announced on the ministry's website that those pre–September 25 applicants who appeared in person between 3:30 and 4:30 p.m. that day would be issued licenses in accordance with the stated policy. Hence the mad scurry at the Sanchar Bhawan.

This event would snowball into a most egregious corruption scam, as the selling of the 2G spectrum at bargain-basement rates caused an estimated shortfall of Rs 400–500 billion ($8–10 billion) to the central exchequer. Compared to this enormous amount, the loss of Rs 17 million ($500,000) that resulted from the shady rewarding of a supplies contract by Sukh Ram in the mid-1990s was peanuts. Whereas the total bribes taken by Ram added up to less than Rs 50 million ($1.56 million), the backhanders allegedly received by Raja were estimated to exceed Rs 30 billion ($600 million).[2] The latest figure reflected the exponential growth in sleaze after 2001, when the privatization plans really took off.

The largest number of licenses (twenty-two), with a pricetag of Rs 16,610 million ($302 million), went to Unitech Wireless, a subsidiary of Unitech Group, which until then had focused on construction and lacked any telecom experience. It later sold 60 percent of its stake for Rs 62,000 million ($1.24 billion) to Telnor, a Norway-based company. Swan Telecom, the winner of fifteen licenses, did not meet eligibility criteria. Though Tata Teleservices received only three licenses, its successful entry into the 2G spectrum encouraged Japanese telecom giant NTT DoCoMo to pick up a 26 percent equity stake in Tata for Rs 130.7 billion ($2.4 billion) in November 2008.

Unsurprisingly, therefore, the later CBI investigation established that several rules were violated and that bribes were paid to favor certain firms that received the licenses at throwaway rates. The audit report of the comptroller and auditor general concluded that several licenses were issued to companies that were ineligible, or had suppressed relevant facts, or had no prior experience in telecoms.

And yet there was more. Further investigations laid bare the inroads that the relentlessly growing private corporations had made into shaping public policy at the level of the composition of the cabinet in Delhi. Deploying slick public relations executives, they had managed to plant stories with high-profile journalists in which backing for their parochial commercial interests was dressed up as "the national interest." This exposed lobbyists intervening in policymaking for industry regulation, the use of natural resources, and licensing of industries in power, natural gas, and aviation.

Graft of this scale and clout stood apart from nepotism and petty bribery, popularly called *baksheesh* (Hindi: gratuity), or speed money, in order to gain favor or special treatment. There was a long tradition of bribing civil servants and policemen to move a citizen's application from one desk to another, to certify that a family was below the poverty line, or to overlook a minor traffic transgression. Though this malpractice affected tens of millions of ordinary Indians, the amounts of cash involved were small. In independent India, a secondary level of graft had grown in the wake of the official schemes for low-cost housing and small businesses in the countryside. This led to collusion between the bureaucrats charged with the task of disbursing funds and their rural beneficiaries. But, given the modest aims of these programs, the size of backhanders was comparatively modest. Altogether, such underhand transactions had minimal impact on the political landscape at the state or national level.

What really impacted the nation's political economy was grand corruption involving large construction and supplies contractors, rigged licensing procedures, and fraud on a gigantic scale by private companies dealing with the government at different levels. Since elected officials operated through senior civil servants, the network consisted of businessmen, politicians, and top bureaucrats. These cozy relationships between business houses and the Congress Party had a long history.

Birth of the Business-Politician Nexus

The rapport between the Congress Party and the business community dates back to the early 1900s, when the rising Indian industrialist class supported the party in order to counter the influence of the British capital, an adjunct to the imperial government in London. The hostility of British captains of industry toward enterprising Indians with industrial aims was well captured by the curt refusal of Britain's steelmakers to advise Jamsetji Tata on establishing a steel mill in eastern India at the turn of the twentieth century.[3] The Congress Party–business affinity continued throughout the pre-independence era, when the party came to depend for its financial survival almost entirely on handouts from the leading Indian business houses.

After independence, these donations, some made in cash and others by check, became the chief source for the party's central election fund. This was the case during the first Lower House poll in 1951–52, and again in 1957. Later in 1957, when the new Companies Act of 1956 came into effect, designed to rationalize the working of companies, the public limited firms found themselves barred from making donations to political parties. But a later amendment to this law, which came into effect in 1961, allowed firms to pay up to 5 percent of their profits to political parties. In the 1962 general election, business houses hedged their bets by backing the pro–private sector Swatantra Party. Led by a few well-known politicians, the party lacked grassroots organization. But, following the 1964 death of Prime Minister Jawaharlal Nehru, the indomitable electoral asset of the Congress, the party's standing fell. Small, regional factions whose politics were to the right of the Congress Party emerged as rivals.

In the 1967 poll, company funds flowed generously into the coffers of these factions. Piqued by this and by the loss of power in many major states, the Congress government, led by Indira Gandhi, amended the law in 1968, banning contributions by companies to political parties. This drove the practice underground and benefited the Congress, which, being the ruling party in Delhi, could deliver an instant quid pro quo to businessmen making donations to it in black money.[4]

Nehru stayed away from the nitty-gritty of raising funds for his party, leaving the task to Sadashiv Kanoji Patil, a favorite of the industrialists in Mumbai, and Atulaya Ghosh, the doyen of Kolkata's business community. "The big business houses support the Congress with huge sums because they know that the party believes, in practice, in capitalistic development," said

Abhijit Sen, an industrialist in Kolkata, in 1970. "The Chamber of Commerce here would tell us before elections that Atulaya Ghosh would approach each of us for money; and he did. And we paid."[5]

On his part, Nehru made a point of choosing a finance minister, a key post in the cabinet—he appointed six of them—who was acceptable to the business community. His government revised the nation's industrial policy in 1956, after consulting with the Federation of Indian Chambers of Commerce and Industry. Both private business and the government were committed to the rapid industrialization of India, and they realized that this could be achieved only by building a solid base of basic industries. Since these industries required heavy capital investment with little or no return for many years, privately owned companies were financially unequipped to undertake this mammoth venture. That was why, with the consent and understanding of the private sector, the government's industrial policy reserved such basic industries as steel, metals, oil, and shipbuilding for the public sector.

However, Nehru had not expected that his only son-in-law, Feroze Gandhi, married to Indira, would turn into an investigative journalist and, as a Congress MP, expose the shady dealings of businessmen in the Lower House of parliament. Unlike his fellow Parsees, who invariably appeared in public in Western dress, this square-jawed, mustached man was always dressed in a homespun cotton long shirt, loose pajamas, and waistcoat, de rigueur for a Congress leader.

In December 1955, he laid bare the shenanigans of the Kolkata-based Ram Kishan Dalmia. He produced documentary evidence to prove that, as chairman of a bank and an insurance company, Dalmia had transferred their funds to acquire Bennett, Coleman & Company, a media group. Dalmia was arrested, found guilty of fraud, and sentenced to two years of imprisonment.[6] More important, this episode led to the passing of the Life Insurance Corporation of India Act in 1956, which nationalized all 245 private insurance companies by purchasing their shares and created the Life Insurance Corporation.

After being reelected to parliament in 1957 as a congressman, Gandhi exposed another underhand dealing. It revolved around a Kolkata-based businessman, Haridas Mundhra, who sold fictitious shares worth Rs 12 million ($2.4 million) to Life Insurance Corporation with the possible connivance of H.M. Patel, the principal secretary of Finance Minister T.T. Krishnamachari. Nehru, intent on preserving the clean image of his government like his well-laundered wardrobe, appointed an investigative commission led by

Justice Muhammadali Currim Chagla. He ruled that Mundhra had sold fake shares to Life Insurance Corporation. Nehru forced Krishnamachari to resign.[7] Mundhra was convicted of fraud and embezzlement and sentenced to twenty-two years in jail, a punishment that has not been meted out to subsequent embezzlers.

With the premature death of Feroze Gandhi in 1960, India lost its most valiant anticorruption fighter. But Nehru's lily-white image was tarnished when he dismissed the corruption charges against a Congress Party veteran in Punjab, Chief Minister Partap Singh Kairon—instantly recognizable by his long, unkempt, snow-white beard—and his family as "fantastic, frivolous and absurd." This led opposition Akali Party leaders to submit a memorandum to the president of India, Sarvepalli Radhakrishnan, listing twenty corruption charges against Kairon and his family, amounting to about Rs 10 million ($2.1 million). After a heated debate in parliament, the government appointed a commission of inquiry under Justice S.R. Das, a retired Supreme Court chief justice. Upholding several graft charges against Kairon, it concluded that such acts were "unbecoming of a person holding the high and responsible office of the chief minister of a state."[8] The commission submitted its report to Prime Minister Lal Bahadur Shastri in June 1964, a few weeks after Nehru's death. When Kairon refused to resign, Shastri released the report, thus forcing him to step down. But no further action was initiated against him or any of his family members.

Post-Nehru Era

Following Shastri's death in January 1966, Indira Gandhi became the prime minister. The fracturing of the Congress Party in 1969 saw Patil and Ghosh joining the conservative wing, which lost the subsequent faction fight for control of the party. With this, Indira Gandhi and her personal envoys became the recipients of the funds to shore up the party's central election chest. Power became concentrated in her hands.

The split in the party encouraged the corrupt leaders to join the Indira Gandhi camp, hoping their misdemeanors would be overlooked by her government. The case of four former Congress ministers in Bihar, including Ram Lakhan Singh Yadav, was typical. They were investigated by two commissions of inquiry and found guilty of corruption. Their houses were searched in September 1970 and April 1971 by the CBI, ostensibly with a view to starting court proceedings against them. But in the end nothing came of it. Indeed, soon after the last house search, Yadav emerged as a protégé of Gandhi and, with her active support, secured the leadership of the Congress group in the State Legislative Assembly, and became Bihar's chief minister.

On the eve of the midterm parliamentary poll in March 1971, the Gandhi-led Congress approached all prominent members of the business community, and, to quote K.K. Shah, then a minister in the central government, "There was no big businessman or industrialist who refused money to the ruling Congress." And the sums involved were higher than ever before. "These . . . [industrialist] owners of [major newspaper chains] are said to have given Mrs Gandhi roughly Rs 15 crores [$20 million] for election purposes," wrote Kuldip Nayar in his book *India: The Critical Years.*[9]

Besides making cash payments to a few top Congress leaders in Delhi, most of the big business houses instructed their sales agents in the country to help the local Congress candidate, in cash, and assured them that they would be reimbursed through proper "adjustments" in their commission on sales. They also asked their constituent firms at the local, state, and national levels to buy advertising space in hundreds of souvenirs and election news sheets to be published by the district Congress committees before the elections.[10]

At the state level, ministers were expected to tap their sources for "contributions" to the Congress election fund. For instance, the transport minister approached bus and trucking operators; the public works minister, construction and supplies contractors; the excise minister, licensees for the sale of alcoholic drinks; and the industries minister, local industrialists who depended on the state authorities for water and power supplies, protection of property, and harmonious labor relations.

During Indira Gandhi's premiership, nepotism and favoritism thrived. In 1971, the registration papers of Maruti Limited listed Sanjay Gandhi, the twenty-five-year-old younger son of Indira, as its managing director. Though he had no experience in car design or production, Maruti was given an exclusive license to manufacture a passenger vehicle. Nothing came of it, though. In June 1980, Sanjay crashed the airplane he was piloting at the Delhi Flying Club and died. A month earlier, he had been appointed general secretary of the Congress Party, following his election to the Lower House of parliament in January.

After Sanjay's death, his elder brother, Rajiv, an airline pilot with an Italian wife named Sonia, was inducted into Congress politics. He won the parliamentary seat held earlier by Sanjay. He was a rising star on the Indian political horizon. Among those who stood to gain by this sudden turn of events was Ottavio Quattrocchi (1939–2013), a young representative of the Italian oil corporation ENI and its petrochemical subsidiary Snamprogetti in Delhi since the early 1970s. After the introduction of Quattrocchi and his wife, Maria, to the Gandhis in 1974, close relations developed between the two couples and their children.[11]

During the next several years, Snamprogetti won contracts for building six fertilizer factories in India.[12] Intriguingly, a hugely profitable deal won by Quattrocchi in 1986 did not appear in the list of his successes. Unconnected with Snamprogetti, it was secured by a front company he had set up called A.E. Services Limited, connected to an account in a Swiss bank.

This was one of the mysteries unmasked by investigations into what became known as the Bofors scandal. Many shady facts came tumbling out from a cache of about 350 documents—payment instructions to banks, open and secret contracts, handwritten notes, minutes of meetings, and an explosive diary—leaked by a secret Swedish source to an Indian journalist, Chitra Subramaniam (later, Chitra Subramaniam Duella).

The Ticking of the Bofors Time Bomb

In March 1986, the Rajiv Gandhi government signed a $1.3 billion deal for the purchase of 410 field howitzers and a separate supply contract, worth almost twice as much, with AB Bofors, based in Karlskoga, 235 miles north of Stockholm, Sweden. It was the largest arms deal any Swedish company had ever signed and required hiring an extra nine hundred workers.

To secure these contracts against tough competition from a French rival, Bofors's managing director Martin Ardbo (1926–2004)—a slim, balding, oval-faced man—spent a lot of time in Delhi in 1985 to lobby and negotiate the terms of a possible deal. He was introduced to several middlemen who promised to swing the contract and agreed to receive their fees after it had been inked. Later, Ardbo told the chief Swedish police investigator, "If Bofors [had] ended the relationship with the agents, then they [Bofors] would not have got the contract."[13] More intriguing was the sudden arrival on the scene—toward the tail end of a drawn-out process—of Quattrocchi and his A.E. Services. In the interview that police chief Sten Lindstrom, the sole whistleblower, gave in April 2012, he revealed that before his death in 2004

Ardbo told him that he did not have a choice but to pay A.E. Services at the last minute.[14] Among other things, Lindstrom stated that Rajiv Gandhi did not receive any kickbacks. (Earlier, in 2004, a Delhi court had exonerated Rajiv Gandhi of any wrongdoing.)

This great swindle came unraveled when a news item was broadcast by the Swedish National Radio on April 16, 1987, alleging that Bofors had paid kickbacks to top Indian politicians and key defense officials in order to close the deal. Several senior journalists from India made a beeline to Stockholm and Karlskoga to dig deeper, but most of them got nowhere. The exception was a reporter for *The Hindu* who was based in Geneva, mainly to cover United Nations events—a sharp-witted, doe-eyed postgraduate of Stanford University, Chitra Subramaniam. She struck a chord with Lindstrom, a highly intelligent social democrat with a hang-dog expression.

Yet he waited for a year before deciding to hand over to Subramaniam the copious documentary evidence about kickbacks paid to Indian officials, middlemen, and Quattrocchi. The first documented details of the scam appeared in *The Hindu* in April 1988, followed by another in June. This was grist to the opposition's mill in India. It blew to smithereens Rajiv Gandhi's "view," expressed between April 1987 and January 1988, that neither "commissions" nor "middlemen" nor "Indians" were involved in the Bofors deal.[15]

In the wake of the exposure, Rajiv Gandhi and his aides changed tack, arguing that any payments made by Bofors to A.E. Services, Moresco-Pitco, and Tulip/Mont Blanc/Lotus were for the "services" they rendered to Bofors. The documentary evidence published in *The Hindu* in November 1988 showed that the only visible "service" they had performed was to provide "safe" clandestine recipient arrangements, thereby creating a cover for the illicit payoffs.[16]

By early 1989, the image of Rajiv Gandhi as Mr. Clean was blackened. He did what U.S. President Richard Nixon had done when the Watergate scandal broke in 1974: he devised an elaborate cover-up to sustain the myth that the Bofors payments were not commissions paid to acquire the much-coveted contract.[17] This scheme was detailed by B.M. Oza in his 1997 book *Bofors: The Ambassador's Evidence.* Oza was the Indian ambassador in Stockholm when the scam came to light in 1987.

But Rajiv Gandhi's ploy failed. In October, a month before the parliamentary election, *The Hindu* delivered the coup de grâce to his credibility. It published a facsimile of the secret part of the report by the Swedish National Audit Bureau that had been suppressed for more than two years by the Swedish government, in collusion with the government of Rajiv Gandhi. The Bureau concluded that the Bofors payments were "entirely proven commission payments to [the receiving] companies' accounts in Switzerland in relation to the Bofors FH-77 deal." It added that the Bureau's conviction that "these payments unquestionably relate to this business is based on the fact that this has been communicated in writing by AB Bofors to the Bank of Sweden." It then listed several payments made on May 22, 1986 (reference: Mont Blanc), July 3, 1986 (reference: Tulip), and July 8, 1986 (reference: Tulip).[18]

Altogether, Bofors paid out 3 percent of the $3.9 billion worth of contracts they had signed with the Rajiv Gandhi government. Of the $11.7 million in kickbacks, $7.3 million reportedly went to Quattrocchi, and the rest to the earlier agents and middlemen.[19]

By studiously trying to protect Quattrocchi, Rajiv Gandhi generated a strong impression that he was one of the recipients of the kickbacks. In the election campaign, the opposition groups, allied under the banner of the National Front, made hay of the Gandhis' close relations with Quattrocchi and Rajiv's efforts to cover up the sordid affair. The number of Congress MPs in the new Lower House plunged from 415 to 197, way behind the National Front's 275. It was bitterly ironic that the surviving son of the pioneering anti-graft campaigner Feroze Gandhi lost power for being seen as corrupt.

Whatever the impact of the Bofors scandal on the domestic scene, it signaled to foreign companies that an effective way to win major contracts in India was to hire well-connected middlemen to bribe Indian decisionmakers. In fact, this underhanded way of doing business in India accelerated in 1988, although its existence did not surface for some years, in the form of a scandal centered on the hawala dealings recorded in the diary of Surendra Kumar Jain. The hawala channel would become an important factor in the post-1991 liberalization era.

The Free Market Lifts the Sleaze Level

With the onset of the New Economic Policy, the Bombay Stock Exchange Sensitive Index—also known as BSE 30 Sensex—rocketed from 1,298 on July 5, 1991, to 4,285 on March 31, 1992. Financial commentators attributed this bonanza to the onset of fiscally sound business policies that were codified further in the free-market-friendly budget presented by Finance Minister Manmohan Singh.

But their analysis covered only half the story behind the precipitous rise of the BSE 30 Sensex, since the other half was subterranean at the time. It came to light on April 23, 1992. On that day, Sucheta Dalal, the financial editor of the *Times of India*, disclosed the details of how the Harshad S. Mehta Group, a financial brokerage, had stoked the market through fraud. Among Mumbai's financial brokers who traded on their own account, Harshad Mehta had a high profile. A robustly built man of thirty-eight, bespectacled, jowl-faced with a clipped mustache, he had earned the nickname "Big Bull," a moniker he savored as much as his mansion, "Madhuli," furnished with a mini-theater, a billiards room, a swimming pool, and a nine-hole golf course, as well as a garage for his fleet of imported luxury cars.[20]

A hardworking professional, Mehta had a full grasp not only of the regulatory regime of the financial sector but also its loopholes. He espied a major lacuna in intrabanking borrowing. It is a universal practice among banks to borrow from each other in order to maintain the government-imposed liquidity ratio (cash reserves to total assets) by using part of their assets as collateral. Government bonds or the shares of highly rated corporations are the most acceptable form of collateral. Banks are free to contact one another directly to sign such deals. Alternatively, in India, if a bank needed a loan for a short period of, say, fifteen days, it could approach a broker to find it a counterparty on mutually agreed terms. The safest collateral for a bank to borrow money is government securities registered with the public debt office of the Reserve Bank of India in its Securities General Ledger. Unlike nongovernmental securities, which are passed on physically between contracting parties, no such transfer takes place in the case of government securities. After the two banks have gone through the Reserve Bank's specified negotiated dealing system, the appropriate amendment is made in the Securities General Ledger, meaning that the lending bank has received the assets as collateral against which it is lending funds to the borrowing bank. The transacted sum is recorded in the receipt issued by the lender and is called the banker's receipt. The borrowing bank keeps the banker's receipt: it shows that the lender possesses the securities and will hold them until the borrower is ready to repurchase them at a slightly higher price, usually after fifteen days. The difference between the two prices is the fee that the lending party earns for parting with its money for a short, predetermined period.

This type of transaction is called a repro (repurchase) deal, or a Rapid Forward trade—that is, a transaction funded by selling a security held on a spot (ready) basis and repurchasing it on a forward basis. Depending on the demand, a lending bank could go through this exercise as many as twenty times in a year and make a tidy profit.

All this sounds straightforward. But it is quite possible to forge securities or create a bogus banker's receipt with no securities to back it up. A crooked broker could also find a way to get the check due to the account payee credited to his firm. Alternatively, avaricious bank executives could be bribed to issue checks without receiving securities or to obtain a copy of an amended entry in the Securities General Ledger. These are the tactics that cumulatively produced a monumental banking scam in an environment where the monitoring and surveillance systems in banks were very lax. Once Mehta, a master manipulator, had noted the loopholes in the financial system, he set out to exercise his extraordinary skills. He found bank executives prepared to issue banker's receipts that were either fake or lacked the backing of government securities. "Two small banks—the Bank of Karad (BOK) and the Metropolitan Co-operative Bank (MCB)—came in handy for this purpose," noted Dalal in her article. "These banks were willing to issue BRs as and when required, for a fee." Armed with bogus banker's receipts, Mehta passed them onto other, larger banks. The contagion spread. Fake banker's recceipts proliferated, and so too did forged securities.

The later revelations that emerged from the Reserve Bank's probe of the megafraud beggared belief. It found that that Bank of Karad, with equity of Rs 10 million ($570,000), had issued banker's receipts of Rs 10,000 million ($570 million), with Standard Chartered Bank accepting BRs of Rs 2,000 million ($114 million) from Mehta's brokerage firm. It caused a massive rise in the money supply. The committee also found that 60 percent of all stock-exchange trades were handled by brokers, and in 40 percent of all trades there was only a verbal understanding.[21]

This committee estimated the magnitude of the scam to be Rs 40.25 billion ($2.33 billion).[22] That is, Mehta and a few other unscrupulous brokers had drained the banking system of a colossal amount of money and injected it into the stock market, enriching themselves by artificially raising the value of the shares of the companies in which they had invested.

Mehta was the lead player. He focused on certain corporations included in the BSE 30 Sensex, and his aggressive buying led to these shares tripling in price between March 1991 and March 1992. During this period, shares of his favored ACC, a cement company, ballooned from Rs 500 to Rs 10,000. Overall, the total market capitalization of the listed shares in stock exchanges zoomed from 20 percent of the GDP to an eye-popping 50 percent of the GDP.[23]

When Mehta's racket was exposed on Thursday, April 23, 1992, the shell-shocked investors went into denial. It took three working days for the catastrophic revelation to sink in. On Tuesday, April 28, BSE 30 Sensex plunged 570 points (12.77 percent) to close at 3,870. Panic spread. The Securities and Exchange Board of India shut down the Sensex for the rest of the week. Further steep falls on May 6 and May 12 deflated the index to 3,086. In six weeks, Sensex shed 30 percent of its value, an alarming bear run.

Once the multibillion-rupee swindle was exposed, many banks, including the State Bank of India, National Housing Bank, and four foreign banks—Standard Charter, Citibank, Bank of America, and ANZ Grindlays—were left holding banker's receipts with a face value running into billions of rupees that were now worthless.

On June 5, the government arrested Harshad Mehta and his two brothers Ashwin and Sudhir. Their properties were taken into custody by the custodian appointed under the Torts Act.[24] After being held in custody for nearly four months, Harshad Mehta was released on bail. Following this debacle, the Securities and Exchange Board of India tightened up the trading and settlement procedures at the bourses. But these measures were far from foolproof, as another capricious operator, Ketan Parekh, would demonstrate eight years later.

The Mehta episode was a landmark in the history of sleaze in India. Thriving exclusively in the private sector, this scam broke new ground, courtesy of the New Economic Policy. Its scale put in the shade the earlier examples of corrupt practices among politicians and businessmen. The alliance between the two groups, however, remained firmly in place.

The Business-Politician Nexus, Continued

In June 1993 Mehta claimed that he had handed over Rs 10 million ($379,000) in two suitcases to Prime Minister P.V. Narasimha Rao at his official residence on the eve of an important parliamentary by-election in November 1991. Rao's denials appeared increasingly less convincing because of the contradictions in his own narrative of the episode and the furnishing of fabricated evidence to back his alibi.[25] This energized the opposition. Both right- and left-wing opposition parties came together to back a no-confidence motion against his government. On July 28, it survived, but just barely—by a vote of 265 to 251.

Meanwhile, the Central Bureau of Investigation moved at a snail's pace to prepare a charge sheet against Mehta. It was only in 1996 that it pressed fifteen charges of bank defraud against him and his associates. It took another year for the special court that had been set up to hear all the securities-scandal-related cases to approve prosecution on thirty-four charges of bank defraud.[26]

By then, other scams had surfaced. These followed the earlier pattern of collusion between businessmen, politicians, and top civil servants or senior executives of public sector undertakings. It transpired that, as the central food minister in 1993–94, Kalpnath Rai, a fat, flabby-faced Congress leader prone to making bombastic statements, had imported sugar at a price well above the international rate. It resulted in a loss of Rs 6.5 billion ($210 million) to the public treasury. He was arrested but later released on bail.[27]

At least the promised sugar arrived. This was not to be the case with a contract for urea, a white crystalline substance rich in nitrogen, a key element in producing fertilizers. The urea scam was a Byzantine episode that started in March 1995 and ended a year later. At its center was a young, wide-eyed man with a well-trimmed, drooping mustache, M. Sambasiva Rao, a relative of Narasimha Rao. He ran Sai Krishna Impex, a small trading company in Hyderabad. On learning that the government-owned National Fertilizer Limited was desperately trying to fill a shortfall of five hundred thousand metric tons of urea, he saw a lucrative business opportunity. He coopted P.V. Prabhakar Rao and Prakash Chandra Yadav, the respective sons of the prime minister and the fertilizer minister, Ram Lakhan Singh Yadav, in his scheme. Such filial links seem to have impressed D.S. Kanwar and C.S. Ramakrishnan, the executive director (marketing) and the managing director of National Fertilizer Limited.

Having failed to procure 300,000 metric tons of urea from foreign suppliers earlier in the year, Ramakrishnan persuaded his board of directors in mid-September 1995 to authorize him to approve contracts for the expeditous purchase of the chemical, in line with the "prescribed procedure."

Acting as an agent of National Fertilizer Limited, Agnaldo Pinto of Brasil Trading Limited, registered in London in May 1995, founded Karsan Danismanlik Turizm Sanayi Ticaret Limited in Ankara, ready to supply 200,000 metric tons of urea originating in former Soviet republics. To facilitate a possible deal, on October 30, Karsan Limited informed National

Fertilizer Limited that Sai Krishna Impex was its representative in India with its CEO Sambasiva Rao acting as its special agent. Sai Krishnan Impex made an offer to National Fertilizer Limited to deliver 200,000 metric tons of urea at $190 a metric ton.[28]

The standard procedure in such contracts is that the buyer pays the seller by a letter of credit for each shipment, after receiving the appropriate document describing the merchandise and the name of the receiver, called a bill of lading. Astonishingly, Ramakrishnan and Pinto set aside this protocol. Instead, they accepted Karsan's proposal of opting for a first-class insurance policy issued by Lloyds of London to cover the risk of nonperformance and nondelivery of the urea, with National Fertilizer Limited making the full payment of $38 million ($1 = Rs 35 at the time) on signing the contract. Ramakrishnan accepted the terms on November 1.[29]

A week later the contract was signed by Kanwar and Pinto for National Fertilizer Limited and by Tuncay Alankus for Karsan Limited. One article stated that neither party would be responsible for breach of contract caused by such circumstances as "inconvenient weather conditions" and local government decisions. National Fertilizer Limited's final payment to Karsan followed on November 14.

On February 28, 1996, the bombshell dropped. Karsan informed National Fertilizer Limited that they were unable to supply urea because of severe weather conditions in former Soviet republics. The swindle broke in June, as the newly elected government of the United Front alliance was settling in after their defeat of Narasimha Rao's Congress Party, which had been heavily tarred with accusations of graft. A preliminary investigation by the Indian Embassy in Ankara revealed that Karsan Limited operated from a room in a third-rate hotel in the capital. A simple translation of the company's name into English would have shown that the prospective buyer was being hoodwinked: Karsan Consultancy for Tourism Trade Limited.[30] The joke was on the Indian government. The contract was canceled in October 1996; the government failed to recover the money.

In Delhi, besides the Central Bureau of Investigation, the finance ministry's Enforcement Directorate, charged with enforcing the provisions of the Foreign Exchange Management Act, tried to get to the bottom of the fraud. Based on the CBI's investigation, two officials from National Fertilizer Limited, Sambasiva Rao, Prakash Chandra Yadav, and a few of their close associates were arrested in June and July 1996. They were released on bail when the CBI failed to produce charge sheets within the statutory ninety days.

At the end of two years of investigation, the CBI and the Enforcement Directorate established that Alankus of Karsan Limited had promised $4 million (Rs 140 million) to Sambasiva Rao and $3 million to Pinto as their commission on the contract. After receiving the full prepayment from National Fertilizer Limited, he remitted nearly Rs 110 million ($3.1 million) to Sambasiva Rao and his associates through the Dubai-based Edible Foodstuff Trading, with the assistance of Rajendra Bababni, a resident of that city.[31] The money was sent through a hawala channel.

By then, hawala channels had become an integral part of the global black economy.

The Inexorable Rise of Hawala

A derivative of the Arabic consonants H-W-L, meaning exchange, hawala as a means of transferring money has been in use since the Abbasid dynasty (750–1258 AD). But it started gaining more popularity in the Indian subcontinent in the mid-1970s, when the quadrupling of oil prices in 1973–74 boosted the economies of the oil-rich Gulf states, which tapped into the abundant labor markets of India and Pakistan. These expatriates found it cumbersome and slow to remit money to their families at home through the Indian or Pakistani banking systems. Therefore, they opted for the informal hawala system. The transfer fee was lower than Western Union's, and no identification was needed. Over the years, India, Pakistan, and the Gulf states developed a thriving hawala triangle.

The sender handed over cash to a hawala dealer for 2 percent commission (for international transfer), who gave him a code of one letter and four numbers. The sender conveyed the code to the recipient. The recipient called on the local agent of the foreign hawala dealer who had taken the cash from the sender, said the code, and received the money in local currency. Once this was done, and the two dealers had informed each other, both parties destroyed all codes or references and customer identification documents, except perhaps those required for the final settlement.

If X in Delhi wanted to send cash to Y in Wembley, Greater London, he handed over rupees to a Delhi-based hawala dealer. The Delhi dealer then contacted his counterparty in Wembley, the London dealer, to pay to Y the equivalent sum in British pounds, minus 2 percent. By so doing, the London dealer made a loan to the Delhi dealer. This could be settled through a reverse hawala transaction handled by the same brokers. If not, then the Delhi dealer would contact a hawala dealer in another country, with whom he maintained an open account. If that did not work out, then more dealers would be deployed to pay off the London dealer. Such a complex procedure required retail hawala dealers to work for wholesalers—the big players—who were part of an international network and knew one another.

What helped the hawala system strike roots in India quickly was that before the mid-1970s many affluent Indians had been exporting their ill-gotten cash to such tax havens as the British Virgin Islands, Bermuda, the Bahamas, the Isle of Man (United Kingdom), Mauritius, Singapore, and Switzerland. Latterly, the practice of buying and selling residential and commercial property in India with partial payment in cash had compelled the seller to seek out ways to hide his cash. He could do so by sending it through the hawala channel to a relative or an associate living in Britain, America, or in one of the Gulf states.

The stratospheric rise of Dubai as a leading international financial center, a booming property market, and a flourishing hawala hub made a significant impact on India. The extent of the hawala system's penetration into the Indian economy and politics came to surface in fits and starts. The discovery in May 1991 of a diary—code-named MR-71/91—maintained by industrialist Surendra Kumar Jain proved to be a watershed moment.

The Strange Tale of Document MR-71/91

A slight man with a skinny, tapered face, the jug-eared Surendra Kumar Jain was the CEO of Bhilai Engineering Corporation Ltd. in Bhilai, home to a large steel plant, with its executive office in Delhi. He was the key player in the hawala scam. His main transactions were noted and kept in a spiral notebook, code-named MR-71/91, by the company accountant Jaineendra Jain.

On May 3, 1991, while investigating the funding of Kashmiri militants, the Central Bureau of Investigation searched the premises of Surendra Kumar Jain, his brothers, and Jaineendra Jain, their accountant. They confiscated Rs 6 million ($170,000) in cash, some foreign currencies, two diaries, and two notebooks. The entries in diary MR-71/91 showed that between 1987 and April 1991, Surendra Jain had received Rs 640 million ($49 million) from foreign sources through the hawala system, and that he had disbursed this amount in 115 payments. The recipients were identified only by their initials. These turned out to be the initials of various high-ranking bureaucrats and top-flight politicians, both in and out of power.

On August 10, the Mumbai-based *Blitz* weekly splashed the scoop on its front page. But, for some mysterious reason, there was no follow-up. By March 1992, the CBI had pressed charges against two Kashmiri militants and consigned the Jain diaries to its archives. But the subject was revived when *Jansatta* (Hindi: People's Power), a Hindi daily, published most of the decoded names on August 24, 1993. When an official action did not follow, journalist Vineet Narain filed a petition with the Supreme Court under the Public Interest Litigation rule, authorized by Article 32 of the Constitution, on October 4, 1993.

Prodded by the Supreme Court, the CBI registered a case against the Jains on March 4, 1995. It also filed charge sheets against a host of leading politicians, some of whom had to resign from the Narasimha Rao cabinet on the eve of the April 1996 general election.[32]

It emerged, eventually, in January 1996, that half of the Rs 640 million ($18 million) paid out by Surendra Jain went to politicians in office and that the money came from foreign corporations in the steel and power generation business. According to CBI sources, the politicians included central power ministers Kalpnath Rai and Arif Muhammad Khan, and the total sum involved exceeded Rs 75 million ($2.1 million), with the French conglomerate Alstom SA acting as the final paymaster. Another major bribe channeled through the Jains was from the Soviet company Tyaza Premo, eager to win the contract to modernize the old government-run Durgapur Steel plant. Little wonder that the Kawas power project in Madhya Pradesh, which had been discussed endlessly, got a green light. And, between 1987 and 1991, the National Hydroelectric Power Corporation and the National Thermal Power Corporation cleared a record eleven projects.[33] Smaller amounts were paid to the leaders of the Congress Party and the BJP to fund their campaigns for the parliamentary polls in 1989 and 1991.

In its final judgment on December 18, 1997, the Supreme Court issued a set of directives, one of which recommended that the Central Vigilance Commission be given statutory status to oversee the CBI.

What was remarkable was that the Jain diaries episode brought together three interrelated issues: the growing tendency of foreign companies to bribe Indian politicians to win contracts; the role of Indian agents to act not only as middlemen for foreign interests but also to provide funds for internal hawala transactions; and the rapidly growing importance of the hawala trade, which would soon spill over into the informal domestic investment market. The annual interest on cash loans in this under-the-counter sector, determined by the rate of inflation, was 9.5 to 13 percent. The commission of the hawala dealer was 1 percent of each transaction. There was no collateral or security; the lender to a hawala dealer had just a promissory note on plain paper, and the maximum loaning period was three months. These deals were funded using discounted bank drafts and fake invoices.

Among those who relished the news about these shady deals being trumpeted in the media was Harshad Mehta. With so much sleaze floating around, his name lost much of the tarnish it had gathered some years earlier. He resurfaced as financial columnist for the *Times of India* and set up his own website in 1998. But this new life did not last long. In 1999 he made the false claim that his brokerage firm had lost or misplaced shares worth Rs 2.5 billion ($80 million). A CBI investigation established that the firm had laundered these shares by giving them to relatives and friends, who then injected them into the stock exchanges. He was jailed in November 1999. His bail application was due to be heard on January 4, 2002, but he died of heart attack on the last day of 2001.[34]

Before he died, Mehta had the satisfaction of seeing one of his former trainees, Ketan Parekh, run circles around the Securities and Exchange Board of India (SEBI). But, like him, he got caught when his insatiable avarice—coupled with hubris—led to the collapse of two banks.

Ketan Parekh, a Sharper Clone of Mehta

Ketan Parekh (b. 1963)—a tall, slim, attractive man, well coiffured, sporting designer sunglasses—was born into a family that ran Narbheram Harakchand Securities (NH Securities), a leading brokerage firm catering to institutional investors. He qualified as a chartered accountant. Molded professionally by Big Bull Mehta, he too learned to look for the chinks in the armor of the regulating authorities.

He found one at the Calcutta Stock Exchange (CSE). It had to do with the SEBI-imposed limit of Rs 200 million for a broker engaged in *badla* trading. An Indian innovation, badla trading was the term used when an investor bought shares on borrowed money—with the stock exchange acting as the intermediary—at an interest rate determined by the demand for a particular stock, with the maximum maturity of seventy days. In other words, the purchasing party had up to ten weeks within which it had to repay the loan, with interest. But, unlike the standard futures contract in the West, the broker—not the buyer or seller—was responsible for the maintenance of the marked-to-market margin. (The marked-to-market margin is imposed to cover any loss that a member incurs when a transaction is closed out at a price different from the one at which the transaction has been entered.) Parekh realized that the authorities at the CSE were lax in enforcing the limit of Rs 200 million on brokers' badla accounts. He then proceeded to set up a network of brokers in CSE to manipulate share prices—a tactic that had not been used before.

Like Mehta, Parekh and his cohorts deployed circular trading. Circular trading is the practice in which sell orders are entered by a broker who knows that offsetting buy orders—the same number of shares at the same time and at the same price—either have been or will be received. This boosts the trading volume of a share and attracts interest of genuine investors, who believe that a merger or acquisition is in the offing. And that in turn inflates the price of that stock. The benefit of the rise in share price goes to the brokers and the promoters of the targeted companies. Later, when the value of stocks inflated by Parekh's network in the Indian bourses inevitably deflated again, the banks that had lent the brokers funds against the collateral of their shares found themselves holding virtually worthless stocks.

A telling difference between the two scams was that in the early 1990s India's financial market was just entering a liberalizing phase, and the switchover from pit bidding to computerized trading was in its infancy. At the end of that decade, the Indian stock markets were linked with bourses around the globe in real time, and online trading was flourishing. Toward the end of the 1990s, freshly issued high-tech stocks were making the headlines in the United States. Given the globalization of the financial sector, the buoyancy of the American high-tech companies—largely listed on NASDAQ—rubbed off on their Indian counterparts. Parekh's penetrating mind identified a golden opportunity in the bubbling high-tech sector. He was bolstered by the bullish sentiment that followed the victory of the pro-business BJP in the general election of October 1999.

Parekh picked small high-tech companies. One was Visual Soft. Its share price shot up from Rs 625 to Rs 8,448 in a year. Another company was Sonata Software, whose shares leapt from Rs 90 to Rs 2,150. These successes gave Parekh an aura of the Mammon incarnate.

So far, unlike Mehta, the soft-spoken Parekh had maintained a compara-tively low profile. This changed when he threw a glitzy Millennium party on December 31, 1999, at his luxurious bungalow near the Mandwa beach, north of the Gateway of India sea terminal in South Mumbai. As a preamble, his guests, who included up-and-coming software magnates, fund managers, the Bollywood superstar Amitabh Bachchan, and the diamond merchant and fi-nancier Bharat Shah, assembled for a champagne reception at the Taj Mahal Hotel before boarding high-security catamarans to Mandwa.[35]

From that event onward, there was a mad rush of investors wishing to en-trust their money to Parekh, which he in turn used to boost stock prices. Using these highly valued shares as collateral, he started raising loans from a small Ahmedabad-based bank, Madhavpura Mercantile Cooperative Bank (MMCB). Over the coming months, MMCB became a critical element in Parekh's nefarious scheme. He constructed a pack of ten favored companies from the information, communication, and entertainment industries, eight of them high-tech, called K-10. These companies were Global Telesystems, Zee Telefilms, Himachal Futuristic Communications Limited, Silverline, Satyam Computer Services, Aftek Infosys, DSQ Software, Ranbaxy Laboratories, Pentamedia Graphics, and Visual Soft.[36] Their high-octane performance had a ripple effect on the BSE 30 Sensex. It surged past 6,000 on February 11, 2000.

In New York, the high-tech-heavy NASDAQ index crossed the record 5,000 on March 20, 2000, reaching 5,046, which proved to be the peak. The inevitable slump followed the crest. During the next two months, whereas NASDAQ declined by 35.9 percent, K-10 stocks crashed by a nerve-shattering 67 percent.[37] The plunging prices trapped Parekh in a double whammy: he had to keep on topping up the margins on his loans and simultaneously cover the losses on his investment.

In December 2000, when NASDAQ reached a nadir of 2,550, institutional investors worldwide rapidly dumped their high-tech stocks, including in India. Parekh and his brokerage firm faced an acute liquidity problem and lost piles of money. Parekh started milking MMCB. Desperate to shore up his share values, he took a Rs 1.4 billion ($33 million) pay order from MMCB. He then turned to Bank of India, where he had an account. It cashed the pay order with a discount and gave him Rs 1.37 billion ($30 million). This proved inadequate to plug the fast-expanding black hole in the K-10 shares. When this pay order was sent to the clearinghouse, it bounced. Since MMCB had issued the pay order without collateral, it collapsed when there was a run on the bank by the depositors.[38]

By February 2001, the shares held by Parekh's brokers at the CSE, which were originally worth Rs 12 billion ($263 million), had lost half of their value. By mid-March, the worth of Parekh's stocks plunged by a further half to Rs 3 billion ($65 million). With the Sensex going into a tailspin from January 2001 onward, falling to 3,097 in March, SEBI inspected the accounts of several brokers, including Parekh's Narbheram Harakchand Securities. The CBI arrested him on March 30 on charges of defrauding the Bank of India of about $30 million. The knock-on effect of this scam was spectacular. It wiped Rs 1,150 billion ($24.4 billion) from the value of stocks in bourses—a colossal amount in the Indian economy. Hundreds of individuals and businesses went bankrupt, and eight investors committed suicide.

After being released on bail following his first spell in police custody, Parekh was rearrested twice. One of his subsequent detentions was linked to the alleged misappropriation of funds from European Investment Ltd, a Mauritius-based company. The other centered around his suspected key role in the Rs 1.2 billion ($26.6 million) fraud at the CSE in March 2001.

Yet it was not until 2008 that Parekh was convicted. He was granted bail pending an appeal to the Supreme Court against his conviction.[39] Meanwhile, in December 2003, SEBI declared Parekh a rogue trader and banned him from trading in financial instruments for fourteen years under the Prohibition of Fraudulent and Unfair Trade Practices Relating to Securities Market Regulations of 2003.

However, the stockbrokers' contribution to corrupting the polity turned up elsewhere—specifically, in the swindle of fake stamp papers and revenue stamps that came to light in August 2000.

A Stockbroker Inspires the Counterfeit King

In terms of geographical sweep, the number of operatives involved, and the skill with which various parts of the complex counterfeiting enterprise had been assembled, this scam was unmatched. Official investigations revealed that the seed for this racket was planted when the master con man Abdul Karim Telgi (b. 1961) shared a prison cell in Mumbai with stockbroker Ram Ratan Soni in 1992. Despite their diverse backgrounds, Telgi and Soni shared a burning desire to become mega-rich. Among other things, Telgi learned from Soni that share transfers, being nonjudicial, though written out on government stamp papers, were exempt from registration with the Stamp Department, which concerned itself only with judicial documents.[40]

The stamp duty was introduced by the British via the Indian Stamp Act of 1899. The practice continued in independent India, though it was left to state governments either to follow the 1899 act or introduce an amended version. In either case, they continued to collect the duty. It turned into a substantial source of income for the state treasury.[41] For instance, in Maharashtra, more than 1.2 million documents required stamped paper for official registration during fiscal year 2001–2. The 1899 act also required a revenue stamp to be affixed on any receipt above Rs 5,000.[42]

Telgi was in police custody as a result of complaints against him of promising jobs in the Gulf monarchies for large fees but failing to deliver. He had set up a manpower consultancy in Mumbai after working in Saudi Arabia during 1987–89, following a two-year stint toiling in dead-end jobs in Mumbai. He had moved there armed with a commerce degree from a college near his hometown in Karnataka. Born into a lower-middle-class family, he had to struggle to pursue his education in the wake of his father's death when he was a child, which had fostered in him a vaulting ambition to mint money by fair means or foul. He was a con man, and like most tricksters he had a certain charm, which sat oddly with his hooked nose and protruding lower lip in a bloated face carried by an overweight torso resting on thin legs.

Once the cases against him and Soni failed to lead to conviction, the duo worked together to tap the loophole in the Bombay Stamp Act of 1958 about nonjudicial transactions, which included share transfers and insurance policies. To get started, Telgi managed to obtain a government-stamp vendor's license in Mumbai in March 1994. Initially, Ashih Chakraborthy and Mohammed Syed, coopted by Soni, supplied him bogus stamp papers.[43]

In June 1995, Telgi and Soni's selling of forged stamp papers was noticed by a law firm in Mumbai after it bought stamp papers worth Rs 1.66 million ($50,000) from them. Telgi lost his stamp vendor's license. Acting on the complaint that the law firm lodged at its local police station, the commanding officer assigned the investigation to Assistant Inspector Agatrao Baburao Sonvalkar in September. Sonvalkar was present at the Bombay High Court on December 1 when the judge rejected the anticipatory bail application by Telgi, who was in the chamber. Yet Sonvalkar, who was duty-bound to arrest him there and then, failed to do so.

Telgi disappeared instantly and remained at large for the next six years. In his final report, submitted in August 1996, Sonvalka described the case as "undetected." The puzzle was solved in February 2004, when Sonvalkar was booked under various sections of the Indian Penal Code and the Bombay Stamp Act.[44] The subsequent CBI investigation, published three months later, concluded that "by [his] acts of omission & commission, Sonvalkar aided and abetted accused Telgi knowingly and willfully."[45]

Between December 1995 and November 2001, Telgi succeeded in running his clandestine counterfeiting syndicate with impunity, assisted by his two brothers. He was successful for two reasons. First, he greased many palms. Second, the investigators had difficulty pinning him down legally, as he operated sixty-eight bank accounts between 1997 and 2001. A diary seized from his accountant contained details of payoffs to high-ranking police and administrative officials and several minor politicians. It was not until January 2006 that the case was finally settled by a special CBI court, which sentenced Telgi and Soni, respectively, to ten and seven years of imprisonment with hard labor.[46]

Telgi's shady business really took off in the late 1990s, in line with the feverish activity on the Indian bourses, as globalization and the New Economic Policy gathered pace, leading to a sharp rise in the demand for revenue stamps and nonjudicial stamp paper.[47] Like an accomplished criminal, he was methodical and meticulous. To obtain supplies of the nonjudicial stamp papers, sheets, chemicals, ink, and stamp paper rolls (for revenue stamps), he approached the same company that supplied the government's Indian Security Press in Nashik. Through his front man, the Nashik-based Jai Kishan Singh, he bribed three key employees of the Indian Security Press. Among other things, they provided him with the negative plates of the stamps. By gaining access to the terms of other bidders, Singh succeeded in purchasing for Telgi about a dozen printing machines, supposedly obsolete, at Indian Security Press auctions.[48]

Through his brothers and other family members, he created a network of salesmen who delivered the revenue stamp and nonjudicial stamp papers to clients at a discount. As Telgi's business boomed so did his investments. He reportedly acquired thirty-five properties in Maharashtra and Karnataka under different names. He invested in Bollywood movies through Sana Film Financial Corporation, fronted by Sana, his only (female) child.[49]

In a raid in Bangalore in August 2000, the police confiscated fake revenue stamps and stamp papers worth Rs 120 million ($2.67 million) as well as embossing and franking equipment. The arrested men revealed that they worked for Karim Telgi. This triggered Operation Telgi nationwide. During the next six months, scores of people were arrested in all the major states.

Telgi's arrest came in November 2001, when Bangalore City Police apprehended him in Ajmer, Rajasthan. By then he had been found to be HIV-positive. The prison authorities in Bangalore held him in an air-conditioned cell. Astonishingly, they also let him use a cell phone. He deployed it to run his counterfeiting syndicate unhindered. "I have just shifted my office from Mumbai," he quipped in July 2002. But, unknown to him, his conversations were recorded on fifty-six tapes and gave valuable leads to the investigators to catch the suspects.[50]

In October, he was transferred to Mumbai, his home base, to assist the investigations ordered by the state government, which had set up a special committee chaired by the deputy inspector-general of the Maharashtra State Reserve Police, Subodh Jaiswal. During his raid on Telgi's luxury apartment in South Mumbai, Jaiswal was shocked to see Telgi sharing chicken biryani and soft drinks with his brothers, supplied by the investigating cops. During his three-month interlude in Mumbai, Telgi did not spend a single day inside a police lockup.

Police across India unearthed equipment purchased at Indian Security Press auctions, including those for perforation, printing, and making watermarks. Other confiscated material included thousands of nonjudicial stamp paper sheets, stamp paper rolls with adhesive, and negative plates. The Home Ministry in Delhi estimated that Telgi's counterfeit activities had resulted in a loss of Rs 200 billion ($5 billion) to many state treasuries over the course of eight years. Yet what gave an energetic push to the drive against Telgi on the judicial front was the Public Interest Litigation petition to the Supreme Court by the anticorruption crusader Anna Hazare in June 2003. The Supreme Court ruled that the case be turned over to the CBI.

The special CBI court started handing out guilty verdicts against Telgi and his associates from January 2006 on. Telgi had proved to be such a larger-than-life character that a Bollywood producer was inspired to make a feature film based on his life. Following a court order, this 150-minute movie, titled *Mudrank* (Stamp), was shown to Telgi and his two lawyers, along with a police commander, inside the Yerwada Central Jail in Pune in April 2008. His attorneys argued that releasing the film would impact on the ongoing cases against Telgi.[51] The court agreed.

The cases against Telgi continued well into 2013, with the CBI court judge sentencing him to life imprisonment without remission in three separate cases in March 2012.[52] The movie *Mudrank* remained in the cans.

A major reason why Telgi's racket continued for as long as it did was that the state government in Mumbai lacked experts and the requisite technology to judge whether or not the stamps were genuine. It was only when the police in Pune called for help from a private detective agency that possessed specialist Reserve Bank of India–approved equipment that they discovered the absence of key microprinted features on the stamps produced by Telgi's outfit. That clinched the prosecution's case.[53]

To realize his dream of riches, Telgi created an elaborate infrastructure with the active help of his extended family while peddling a product with a history dating back to 1899. While the unprecedented upsurge in stock exchange trades, which benefited him enormously, stemmed from globalization and the New Economic Policy, he was untutored in the ways of corporate skullduggery. Accomplishing that required an expert sleight of hand in cooking the account books in a way that had not been done in the pre–information technology era. The distinction of blazing that trail went to the founder of Satyam Computer Services.

The Inverted Behavior of IT Giant Satyam, Meaning Truth

The Rs 78 billion ($1.5 billion) scam, which grabbed headlines with the resignation of Byrraju Ramalinga Raju, chairman of the Hyderabad-based Satyam Computer Services, on January 7, 2009, was world class in more ways than one. It was the mother of all scams in the private sector. The massive subterfuge involved insider trading, false bookkeeping, duplicitous inflating of the employees on the payroll, suborning statutory auditors, failure of Western credit-rating agencies to investigate the company's financial state, massive loans by major Indian and foreign banks, money laundering, and the appointing of a board of directors beholden to the chairman. In monetary terms, it dwarfed earlier swindles. And it was truly global, with its implications felt not just in India but in such diverse overseas institutions as the New York Stock Exchange; PricewaterhouseCoopers (PwC), one of the four leading accounting and auditing firms in the world;[54] the World Bank; and 185 corporations listed on the Fortune 500. It led inter alia to a delegation from the U.S. Securities and Exchange Commission being sent to Delhi to confer with the CBI.

The main culprit was Ramalinga Raju, born in 1954 in rural Andhra Pradesh. A brilliant student, he acquired an MBA from Ohio University at the age of twenty-three. Upon his return home, he started a textile mill, then switched to real estate. In 1987, along with his younger brother Rama Raju, he cofounded Satyam Computer Services. The firm went public in 1991. Later that year, Ramalinga Raju won his first offshore contract from an American tractor manufacturer. His outstanding business skills turned Satyam into a glittering success, with the Davos-based World Economic Forum describing it as one of India's rapidly growing entrepreneurial enterprises in 1997. The following year it entered into a joint venture with an affiliate of GE Industrial Systems.

Ramalinga Raju was among the early IT experts to spot outsourcing opportunities for the Y2K computer problem and exploit it to the hilt. In 2000, *Dataquest*, the oldest IT magazine in India, named this fish-lipped, mustached, bespectacled man of medium build, with a rich thatch of charcoal-black hair, its IT Man of the Year. Satyam's inclusion in Ketan Parekh's K-10 pack of white-hot stocks fueled the company's rise into the stratosphere. In May 2001, Satyam was listed on the New York Stock Exchange, a striking achievement for an Indian company.

But then came 9/11 and the concomitant drop in business confidence and stock market indexes. That affected Satyam, which had contracts with scores of U.S. corporations. Its sizzling business cooled; its revenue and profits dipped. Instead of accepting the rollercoaster pattern of the IT industry and its globalized structure, Ramalinga Raju conspired with managing director Rama Raju and chief finance officer Vadlamani Srinivas to buck the downward trend by doctoring the accounts in 2001–2. In the United States, business and stock markets picked up from the trough when the Federal Reserve Bank lowered interest rates to a record level. But, having fiddled the books, the trio found it hard to reverse direction and return to the straight and narrow path of honesty and ethical behavior. They followed their crooked but familiar course for the next seven years, reaping colossal gains for themselves. In his letter of resignation on January 7, 2009, Ramalinga Raju described how an effort to conceal a poor earnings performance in 2001 escalated: "It was like riding a tiger, not knowing how to get off without being eaten."[55]

The conspirators inserted fictitious invoices and fake bank statements to back these documents. They managed to do so by making sure that the company's internal systems were not integrated, thereby creating loopholes in its computerized accounting system. They booked fictitious fixed deposits and interests received from such prestigious banks as ICICI, HSBC, HDFC, PNB Paribas, and Citi. To complete the cycle of deceit, the plotters ensured that Satyam paid tax on nonexisting assets. This fraudulent practice was not noticed by the company's internal audit committee.[56]

Deception of this order should have been detected by auditors of such repute as PricewaterhouseCoopers. But it was not. The conspirators increased the fees for PwC three times in five years. By 2008 they were paying the auditing firm almost twice as much as Satyam's peers—Tata Consultancy Services, Infosys, and Wipro. PwC's senior partners, S. Gopalakrishna and Srinivas Talluri, set aside PwC's own independent auditing tools in favor of Satyam's in order to certify the manipulated figures. Worse, they did not check a single invoice or fixed bank deposit. Nor did they ask, How is it that a company with such robust finances was borrowing money from the banks against the collateral of shares?[57]

The inexorable ballooning of Satyam's revenue and profit fueled the dizzying ascent of its share prices. The three top officials lined their pockets by selling their holdings. The subsequent CBI investigation found that Ramalinga Raju and Rama Raju together had bought 1,065 properties worth a total of Rs 3,500 m ($750 million), including six thousand acres of land, housing plots, and constructed property. The finance ministry's Enforcement Directorate revealed money laundering by Ramalinga Raju and his family to the tune of Rs 10 billion ($200 million).[58]

Overall, the effort of the conspirators to delink their corporation—which was doing massive business in the United States—from the developments in the American financial markets was doomed. They managed to swim against the tide after 9/11. But the financial tsunami that engulfed the Western world after the spectacular collapse of Lehman Brothers investment bank on September 15, 2008, was far too overpowering to be contained by fiddling Satyam's computerized accounting system. On top of it all came the sensational terrorist attacks on downtown Mumbai on November 26. Market sentiment turned deeply bearish.

To stem the tide, Ramalinga Raju came up with the plan to acquire Maytas[59] Infra Private Limited for $300 million and Maytas Properties Private

Limited for $1.3 billion. His friendly board of directors endorsed the plan. On December 17, Ramalinga Raju announced the decision. The institutional investors objected vociferously. Why was a leading IT corporation buying construction companies? they demanded to know. As it was, Maytas Infra, founded in 1988 by Ramalinga Raju to undertake infrastructure projects, was later handed over to his elder son Teja Raju. Maytas Properties was established in 2005 by Raju Senior's younger son Rama Raju. It was a blatant example of nepotism. Satyam's share price nosedived by more than half. In his resignation letter, however, Ramalinga Raju would disingenuously describe this move as his last attempt to "fill fictitious assets with real ones."

The public fracas encouraged a former Satyam senior executive, Jose Abraham, who knew about the fraud that the top three officials had been perpetrating for years, to reveal what he knew in an e-mail on December 18 to the independent director Krishna Palepu, a professor at Harvard Business School. Palepu forwarded the message to the members of Satyam's auditing committee, then to the PwC senior partners and Ramalinga Raju himself.

On December 23, the World Bank terminated its contract with Satyam. The corporation's independent directors resigned. The drop in the share price became unstoppable. When Ramalinga Raju resigned as chairman fifteen days later it was not due to any pangs of conscience but to his stark realization that he had reached the end of the road. He had tried to bail out a fast-sinking boat with a bucket and had, predictably, failed. On January 7, 2009, Satyam's share price sank to an all-time low. Its latest market value—$500 million—was a puny 7 percent of the July figure, when the company claimed 53,000 employees instead of the 40,000 it actually had.[60]

The state police arrested Ramalinga Raju and his brother Rama Raju on charges of criminal breach of trust, cheating, criminal conspiracy, and forgery. The arrest of Vadlamani Srinivas followed a few days later.

This latest sleaze episode, which broke new ground, set alarm bells ringing in Delhi. It put India's booming IT industry—the main engine of the country's growth—in jeopardy. Keenly aware of the approaching general election in April–May, the Singh government moved with uncharacteristic speed to control the damage, even though the public sector was not involved in this imbroglio. The Ministry of Corporate Affairs immediately appointed its own directors, followed by the naming of a new CEO in February. And just a few weeks before the parliamentary poll, in a public auction, 46 percent stake in Satyam was bought by Tech Mahindra, part of the Mahindra & Mahindra conglomerate.

Big Business Infiltrates Public Policy Making

The nationwide poll returned the Congress Party to their role as the largest group in the Lower House. It needed a minimum of ten extra seats to secure a bare majority. As before, Manmohan Singh approached the leader of the eighteen-strong DMK faction to join his government. The DMK chief agreed, provided his group was given three ministries, including communications. The private telecom operators who had gained licenses from the communications minister Andimuthu Raja in 2008 were desperate to see him reappointed to the same post. According to the evidence that came to light later, they found a convenient go-between in the public relations firm Vaishnavi Corporate Communications Private Limited (VCC), with which many had accounts.[61]

VCC was founded in 1998 in Delhi by Nira Radia (also spelled Niira Radia), a self-made businesswoman. Her parents migrated from Nairobi, Kenya, to Britain in 1967, when she was eight years old. After graduating from Warwick University, she married Janda Radia, who aspired to become an affluent businessman. They worked together, but her husband lacked business acumen. After bearing three children with him, she struck out on her own.

She became an adviser to aircraft leasing companies such as ILFC, Singapore Airlines, and AAR. When the Narasimha Rao government opened the airline industry to private companies in 1992, several firms entered the market. With that, her attention turned to India, where her father, Narain Manan, had retired. In 1994, with the assistance of Manan, she found a job with Sahara Airlines. Since her marriage to Janda Radia had ended, she was freer to carve out a name for herself in business consultancy and public relations. She founded VCC. She was hired as an adviser to the Singapore Airlines–Tata Consortium formed in the wake of the disinvestment program of the government-owned Air India.

It was in that capacity that she met Ratan Tata. He was impressed by her professionalism. By 2003, she was handling public relations for fourteen leading Tata companies, including Tata Teleservices. Her association with India's most prestigious conglomerate opened many business doors for her firm. In 2007, Mukesh Ambani, the richest Indian at home, signed a contract with VCC to manage public relations for his giant conglomerate, Reliance Industries Limited.

By the end of that year, VCC had three hundred employees working in eleven cities and an annual turnover of Rs 3 billion ($60 million). The subsequent luxurious living of this high-flying woman, with her executive air, curvaceous figure, shoulder-length curly hair, and British passport, aroused envy, admiration, and suspicion in equal measure among her peers. After receiving tips about Radia's possible tax evasion and money laundering, the Income Tax department secured authorization from the home ministry to tap her phone lines for a period of sixty days at a time, starting on August 20 and October 19, 2008, and May 11, 2009. The end result was a collection of 5,851 recordings of thirty to forty minutes each, running into 82,665 pages of documents. Several agencies, including Internet service providers, were involved in making these recordings.[62]

In response to complaints filed in May 2009 against the Department of Telecommunications, the Central Vigilance Commission directed the CBI to investigate the irregularities in the allocation of 2G spectrum. Separately, the Delhi High Court ruled on July 1 that advancing the cutoff date for applications for 2G spectrum licenses from October 1 to September 25, 2007, by the minister, Raja, was illegal.

In October 2009, the CBI filed a First Information Report against "unknown officers of [the Department of Telecommunications] and unknown private persons/companies" under various provisions of the Indian Penal Code and the Prevention of Corruption Act. It then raided the department's offices. On November 16, it sought details from Nira Radia's tapped conversations to find out about the involvement of middlemen in the granting of 2G spectrum licenses to telecom companies.[63]

After the Income Tax Department handed over the Radia tapes to the CBI in May 2010, parts of the conversation between Radia and Minister Raja were leaked to the media. Popular interest in the case was aroused. In August, the Centre for Public Interest Litigation submitted a petition on the subject to the Supreme Court. The apex court took up the case within weeks. In mid-September, it asked the Indian government and Raja to reply within ten days to the petitions filed by the Centre, and others, alleging a loss of Rs 700 billion ($14 billion) to the public treasury in the granting of telecom licenses in 2008. On November 10, the comptroller and auditor general (CAG) submitted its report on the subject to the government, claiming a loss of Rs 1,760 billion ($35.2 billion).

On November 14, Raja resigned as communications minister, two days before the CAG's report on him was due to be published. The next day, Kapil Sibal, minister for human resources development, was given additional charge of communications ministry. CAG chief Vinod Rai noted in his report that Raja "flouted every canon of financial propriety, rules and procedures." His investigation showed that eighty-five of the 122 licenses went to companies that "suppressed facts, disclosed incomplete information, and submitted fictitious documents," and therefore did not comply with the requirements for licenses. He concluded that these licenses were, therefore, illegal.[64] On November 18, the Supreme Court criticized Prime Minister Singh for failing to respond to more than a year of requests to investigate the allegations. Six days later, the CBI informed the Supreme Court that it would examine closely the role of the corporate lobbyist Radia.

The next day, November 19, the seven-month-old Delhi-based *Open* magazine posted on their website excerpts of the audio recordings and transcripts of conversations between Radia and her high-powered friends between May 11 (two days before the last polling date in the 2009 general election) and July 10.[65] This was the critical moment for the formation of the new cabinet, and, working for her corporate tycoons, Radia pulled many strings to achieve what they wanted. That Radia was a friend of Raja helped enormously.

These conversations revealed two new, malevolent elements in the corruption saga: the cooption of high-profile print and TV journalists to do the bidding of Big Business, and the strong influence of industrial magnates on the composition of the federal cabinet and the shaping of public policy. By publishing these excerpts, the nascent weekly demonstrated how democracy was being subverted to serve the interests of those who already possessed massive economic clout. This single leak dramatically unearthed the innards of crony capitalism—the intimate modus operandi of top elected officials, the boundless avarice of business czars, and the contemptuous role of media stars.

Prominent among Radia's media ensemble were Vir Sanghvi, editorial director of the *Hindustan Times* and a columnist and TV host; Prabhu Chawla, editor of *India Today*, the country's largest-circulation news magazine in English; and Barkha Dutt, group editor of English news for NDTV, who also hosted a popular TV talk program called, in English, "We the People." They were heard promising to do political fixing for Radia's leading corporate clients.

"What kind of story do you want [for Mukesh Ambani]?" Sanghvi asked Radia. He then offered two options: a "fully scripted" TV interview and a "rehearsed" interview.[66] A standard, unrehearsed, spontaneous interview was not on the menu.

Further leaks from the earlier recordings provided a fuller picture of the network that Radia had cultivated since 2001. These conversations involved such business leaders as Ratan Tata, Mukesh Ambani, Anil Ambani, Sunil Mittal, other telecom barons, and the owners of private airlines; politicians of the Congress, BJP, and DMK; and bureaucrats-turned-lobbyists.[67]

The overall thrust of Radia's strategy was to influence policies on natural gas, civil aviation, and highways,[68] to rig cabinet appointments, and to plant stories with high-profile journalists in order to camouflage the business agenda of the leading conglomerates as acts of strategic national interest. By the autumn of 2010, however, the media were awash with another scandal, this one dealing with the sleaze surrounding contracts for the Commonwealth Games.

Common Wealth Funneled into Favored Pockets

It all started with glowing promises. In its bid for the quadrennial sports competition among the fifty-four nations of the former British Empire in 2002, India declared that it would "build state-of-the-art sporting and city infrastructure . . . create a suitable environment and opportunities for the involvement of the citizens in the Games; showcase the culture and heritage of India; project Delhi as a global destination and India as an economic power; and leave behind a lasting legacy."[69] That was how it won the contract in 2003 for the 19th Commonwealth Games, to be staged October 3–14, 2010.

Then, unsurprisingly, the project got entangled in endless red tape.[70] For four years, endless correspondence ensued between the Organizing Committee, the sports ministry, the urban development ministry of the federal government, the chief minister of Delhi, and other organizations. The number of agencies involved in the project mushroomed to twenty, with overlapping authority and responsibility, the Indian Olympic Association (IOA) being one of them. It was not until January 2010 that the federal cabinet decided to name Suresh Kalmadi (b. 1944), president of the IOA, as chairman of the Organizing Committee, and invested him with the ultimate decision-making authority.

A balding man with a thick beard and a sharp nose, Kalmadi had a checkered background. After leaving the Air Force in 1972, he joined the youth wing of the Congress Party. He was elected to the Upper House of the parliament between 1982 and 1996, when he bagged the IOA presidency. In 1985, Kalmadi founded Sai Service Station Private Limited in Pune, his home base, and went on to win dealerships in the sales and servicing of cars, auto-rickshaws, scooters, and motorcycles. His company became the authorized dealer for the popular Maruti Suzuki automobiles and for Bajaj Auto Limited's scooters and motorcycles in Mumbai, Pune, Kolhapur, Goa, Cochin, and Hyderabad. In 1996, Kalmadi was elected to the Lower House of the parliament from Pune; he was reelected to the position in 2004 and 2009. He became the general secretary of the Congress Parliamentary Party. All along, he remained the main driving force behind Sai Service Station, while his only son attended to the day-to-day operations of the company, which employed over 3,200 people.

Finding himself in charge of the generous budget for the Olympic Games, Kalmadi spotted an opportunity to increase his already impressive net worth. In his case, business and political power merged. This was a qualitative jump in the relationship between capital and government, which had already deepened from lobbying for tax breaks to the manipulation of licensing protocol, virtual hijacking of official policymaking, and draining of the public purse.

Reports of substandard workmanship on the sites for the Games reached the Central Vigilance Commission. In July 2010, it discovered forged safety certificates which revealed that twelve of the fifteen samples of concrete failed to meet the specified strength. The CVC's report was suppressed. It was only when advance teams of the participants started arriving from abroad in the third week of September that the incompetence was exposed.[71] Meanwhile, responding to a stream of media stories of bungling and bribes published in mid-August,[72] Prime Minister Singh promised that corrupt officials would be given "severe and exemplary" punishment after the Games.

The Games were plagued by missed deadlines, allegations of graft, illegal child labor, violation of Delhi's minimum wage rule, filthy accommodations for the athletes, and the collapse of a footbridge due to shoddy construction. In the run-up, many sponsors withdrew their support. All of this, plus the adverse publicity in the international media, created such a stink that the complacent federal cabinet in Delhi was finally jolted into action. It gave the Organizing Committee an interest-free loan of Rs 18.5 billion ($370 million) to complete the construction project on time. The committee went into overdrive, hiring extra hands by the tens of thousands. In the end, the Commonwealth Games cost the public exchequer Rs 106.5 billion ($2.13 billion)—ten times the original budget of Rs 10.5 billion ($210 million). The opening ceremony on October 3 went smoothly, and so did the closing event on October 14. India won the highest number of medals after Australia.

As promised, the government's investigative wheels turned. On May 20, 2011, the Central Bureau of Investigation filed the first charge sheet against Kalmadi in a special CBI court. It alleged that he was the main accused in awarding the timing-scoring-result system contract to Swiss Timing, based in Corgemont near Berne, Switzerland, for Rs 1.41 billion ($28 million) instead of the standard fee of Rs 460 million ($9.2 million).[73] Kalmadi was arrested and held behind bars until his release on bail in January 2012.

But at least the Indian authorities were in a position to arrest Kalmadi. That was not the case with Lalit Modi. Before the finance ministry's Enforcement Directorate could get his passport revoked, Modi flew to London after being removed as chairman of the Indian Premier League (cricket) in April 2010. Six months later, the authorities issued a "look out circular" for him at India's ports of entry.

Spurt in the Private Sector Sleaze

Lalit Kumar Modi (b. 1963) was born into an affluent business family whose patriarch, Gujarmal Modi, had founded the industrial town of Modinagar in western Uttar Pradesh. His father, Krishan Kumar, head of Modi Enterprises, who had inherited Godfrey Phillips India Limited, a joint venture with Philip Morris International, prospered as Godfrey Phillips became the country's second-largest producer of cigarettes.

Soon after graduating from Duke University in Durham, North Carolina, Lalit Modi was convicted on charges of drugs and assault. Following a plea bargain, he was placed under five-year probation in 1985. But, as a result of the intervention by his father's rich American friends, he was allowed to return to India on health grounds in 1986.

He started working for Godfrey Phillips India. While his parents looked for a suitable match for him, the twenty-eight-year-old, dark-skinned, hirsute Lalit, endowed with a fleshy mouth and deep-set eyes, fell in love with a family friend, the thirty-seven-year-old Minal Sagrani (née Aswani), a fair-skinned, svelte, high-browed divorcée with a child.[74] Both of his parents objected, but he stuck to his guns. His father eventually came around and gave his consent to the marriage, which took place in 1991. He promised his newly married son a maintenance allowance and appointed him a director of Godfrey Phillips India. Then he dispatched him to Mumbai to oversee a small factory of Modi Enterprises.

When the Indian government opened up the broadcasting sector to private companies in 1992, Lalit Modi perceived an opportunity to exploit a fresh avenue. In 1994, he became the India distributor of the sports broadcaster ESPN on a five-year contract. He spurred ESPN to start airing cricket matches. He went on to establish Modi Entertainment Network as part of Modi Enterprises and entered into a joint venture with the Walt Disney (Images) Company. The ten-year agreement gave Modi Entertainment Network the rights for marketing Disney programs in India. To Modi's dismay, neither of these ventures took off.

Through a mutual friend he was introduced to Vasundhara Raje, the leading light of the BJP in Rajasthan. When Raje became the chief minister after state elections in 2003, Modi's sagging fate showed signs of life. He moved his family to Jaipur and became an aide to Raje. Advised by him, Raje brought the Rajasthan Cricket Association under the jurisdiction of her government.

Modi was elected president of the Rajasthan Cricket Association in 2004, which entitled him to a seat on the Board of Control for Cricket in India, where he was appointed vice president the following year. He got deeply involved in the commercial side of cricket. Guided by his latterly developed business skills, the Board signed several lucrative deals, including selling telecasting rights to Zee TV and the Mumbai-based Nimbus Communications Ltd. in 2005–6.[75]

In 2007 Modi floated the idea of an Indian Premier League Twenty20 tournament, limiting each side to twenty overs, with eight top teams competing. The Board adopted the scheme and appointed Modi chairman and commissioner of the League. Under his leadership the Twenty20 tournament took off like a rocket. Before its inaugural in April 2008, the Board sold the eight franchises for Rs 32 billion ($723 million). Its contract with ESPN for global broadcasting rights of the Indian Premier League was worth Rs 44 billion ($1 billion), and the IPL media rights deal with Sony-WSG was worth Rs 55.4 billion ($1.26 billion). For the second season, in 2009, played in South Africa, the price tag rose to an astonishing Rs 110.7 billion ($2.46 billion).

Moving among Bollywood stars and megarich businessmen, Modi found his place in the sun. He adapted to an obscenely ostentatious lifestyle with gusto. He deployed his private Learjet like a taxi, spent holidays on the Italian Riviera, celebrated the New Year in Mexico in the home of the late Anglo-French billionaire James Goldsmith, rented a mansion in upscale Bel Air in Los Angeles, and befriended the founders of Blackstone, an asset management firm specializing in private equity and real estate. "I believe in free markets deciding everything," this silver-spooned beneficiary of nepotism famously declared in an interview with the Delhi-based *Tehelka* magazine.[76]

The first sign of a gathering storm came in March 2010, when income-tax officials raided his offices in Mumbai. By then, however, the plans for the third tournament were well advanced. Sports analysts estimated that the gala event had cost more than Rs 185.9 billion ($4.13 billion), an eye-popping record. But as soon as it ended on April 25, the directors of the Board of Control for Cricket in India removed Modi as chairman of the India Premier League.

The Board accused him of misappropriation of Rs 4.7 billion ($104 million),[77] and on October 14 the Mumbai police registered a case against him on that count. By then, however, he was out of the reach of the Indian authorities. He had fled to London soon after being elbowed out as IPL chairman, claiming that, despite recently hiring a posse of bodyguards, he faced "an elevated threat to his life in Mumbai."

This scam sullied the reputation of India's most popular sport. "The IPL is possibly the murkiest sporting league in the world," a senior Enforcement Directorate official told the Hong Kong–based *Asia Sentinel*. "Slush money from tax havens, foreign ownership through dubious means, *benami* transactions [in which properties are held in the name of another individual or company], fraud, money laundering on a massive scale, illegal betting, bribery in awarding TV rights has all been a part of the IPL package with the connivance of top officials. I won't be surprised if match-fixing too has been a part of the racket."[78]

Because several of Modi and Minal's relatives were fabulously rich nonresident Indians living in Britain and Nigeria, it was comparatively easy for the whole clan to move black money in and out of India. But that did not discourage Enforcement Directorate officials from probing into their international money transfers. Despite the periodic crackdowns on the hawala dealers, they had become a permanent feature of the financial sector in India. According to the Enforcement Directorate, in late 2010 more than five hundred hawala dealers were active in Delhi, with a similar number in Mumbai, followed by smaller contingents in Kolkata, Chennai, and Hyderabad. Altogether, they transferred Rs 10 billion ($217 million) daily, equal to what the central government collected in direct taxes in a day. Assisted by a couple of close relatives, a typical hawala dealer, operating clandestinely from a cramped office and using ever-changing cell-phone numbers, earned Rs 50 to 100 million ($1 to 2 million) a year, tax free, a sum that made many CEOs of multinational corporations in India green with envy.[79]

All the corrupt practices that were associated with crooked politicians were now leveled at Modi, the face of the meteorically successful IPL tournament: nepotism, awarding contracts for backhanders, and opacity in decision making. The official investigations pinpointed graft in the 2008 franchise auctions for the first tournament. It was in 2008 that Modi ensured the most profitable franchises went to relatives and friends of his and of his wife, Minal. The same preference was at work when it came to awarding contracts for the digital and mobile rights of the India Premier League.[80]

In ideological terms, those who had upheld the IPL as a gleaming example of the New India—its gigantic consumer clout, opulent conglomerates, superb marketing skills, and its headlong rush to monetize everything—were deeply disappointed. On the other hand, as a consequence of globalization and the two decades of the Big Bang economic liberalization at home, a culture of consumerism and avarice had taken hold among many middle-class Indians. The contagion of monetizing everything had spread widely. It had infected those areas of Indian life that had so far been untouched by sleaze.

The Monetizing Contagion

In mid-2012, NDTV, a leading TV network, sued the Nielsen Company in the New York Supreme Court, accusing its Indian joint venture with Kantar Media Research—called TAM Media Research Private Limited, based in Mumbai—of providing "false, fabricated and manipulated data" on TV ratings for nearly a decade. TAM's data was regarded as the definitive source of ratings, and it was used by advertisers and networks to price broadcasting time.

NDTV argued in its petition that TAM collected data only from 8,150 homes fitted with electronic monitoring devices. By contrast, the sample size in China, with a slightly larger population than India's, was 55,000. When NDTV advised TAM to increase its sample size to 30,000, the idea was dismissed for being too expensive. Yet when NDTV executives met two field employees of TAM in a Mumbai hotel in April 2012, they were told that if NDTV agreed to pay them $250 to $500 for each home that they got to watch NDTV's channels, they would raise the network's ratings. NDTV also video-recorded another sting operation, which it showed to a Neilson security executive during his visit to India. In its suit, NDTV claimed to have lost almost $1 billion (R55 billion) during the past decade because of TAM's unrepresentative ratings data.[81]

In Mumbai, some tutors had set up coaching classes to teach students how to cheat at exams by copying. "I was told it is a general lecture for important tips on how to write the exam and how to revise before the exam," a student told Hemali Chhapia of the *Times of India*. "But after some time, we were being told how to copy safely and escape if caught copying." Citing her tutor, she added, "You can either carry chits or in desperate situations even your text, in case your exam seat is a window seat." The handwritten notes on pieces of paper could be easily tucked away inside socks, rolled-up shirt-sleeves for male students, and inside bras worn by female examinees. If caught, the student was instructed to immediately swallow the paper, and they were told to practice swallowing at home before the final test. If a student was caught using a textbook by the supervisor, he should instantly throw it forward or out the window, added the private instructors.[82]

Far more seriously, graft afflicted the media in the form of "paid news." Companies started bribing reporters and editors for favorable news coverage. So too did politicians, followed by movie producers and distributors. Some of the biggest newspapers and TV channels practiced paid coverage, and corruption in the media was "pervasive, structured and highly organized," according to a study by the Press Council of India, a statutory body, published in 2010.[83] To the deep regret of upright journalists and citizens, this odious practice had become firmly established.

Unethical behavior spread to the polling agencies during the run-up to elections. In late February 2014, a sting operation by a Hindi news channel, News Express, showed that eleven of the thirteen polling agencies were willing to manipulate the results of the upcoming general election to suit the interests of a political party—for a bribe. One agency agreed to raise the margin of error from 3 to 5 percent to allow more seats for one party or the other. Going by the axiom that nothing succeeds like success, each party liked to be shown to have more electoral support than less and thus improve its actual performance on polling day. The Indian branch of the global market research company Ipsos agreed, for an under-the-counter fee, to provide two sets of figures—one genuine, based on the professional norms of the margin of error, with the number of fence-sitting seats excluded, and the other with the undecided seats allocated to the client. It was the second set of statistics, the set favoring the client, that was published. At the same time, the party's senior officials were privately informed of the lower figure.[84]

All along, the insatiable appetite for ever higher revenues and profits drove Big Business to corner as much of the nation's natural resources as cheaply as it could. As a consequence, the battle for grabbing the resource-rich land intensified. The latest of the megascams to surface—dubbed Coalgate—is best viewed and analyzed in that context.

Resource-Rich Land Up for Grabs

As in the earlier cases, Coalgate, the coal allocation swindle, had its roots in the introduction of the 1991 New Economic Policy. It virtually reversed the 1956 Industrial Policy, which had led to the formation of the state-owned National Coal Development Corporation, with the coalfields owned by the railways as its nucleus. The 1956 policy was viewed as the first step toward the planned development of the coal industry, but due to the continued failure of private colliery owners to invest sufficiently to meet the nation's burgeoning energy needs—as well as improve the deplorable working conditions in the mines—the Indira Gandhi government passed the Coal Mines (Taking Over of Management) Act in 1973. It nationalized collieries on May 1, 1973, and formed the Coal Mines Authority Limited, headquartered in Kolkata, which changed its name to Coal India Limited two years later. It became a holding company with several subsidiaries. Making an exception of the private steel companies, the Coal Mines (Nationalization) Amendment Act of 1976 allowed them to hold on to their coal leases.

Following the New Economic Policy, the Narasimha Rao government decided to open the power industry to the private sector. Recognizing the need for such firms to have captive coal mines, it formed a screening committee in 1993 by an administrative fiat, composed of serving and former officials from coal and railways ministries, along with representatives chosen by the cabinets of coal-bearing states.

What went unreported was the stepmotherly treatment that the central government adopted toward Coal India Limited. This policy would be revealed almost two decades later by Hansraj Ahir, an MP belonging to the BJP, who represented the coal-rich district of Chandrapur in eastern Maharashtra. "The state-owned Coal India Limited began shrinking due to government apathy and hundreds lost their jobs in Chandrapur," he told the *India Today* magazine in 2012. "There are twenty-seven coal mines in Chandrapur, and coal blocks were being given away for free."[85] Some of the new owners promptly sold their licenses to steel or power companies for large sums.

During its fourth year in office, in 2003, the BJP-led government coined the phrase "Power to all by 2012." But the task of fulfilling this promise fell to the Congress Party, which defeated the BJP in 2004. Defying the national trend, Ahir entered the parliament as the MP for Chandrapur. He was elected to the parliamentary committee on coal and steel. In that capacity, he found out that Coal India Limited's role had been downgraded all over the country, and that a nexus had grown between private companies and elected and appointed government officials in the coal-rich regions.

When Singh's Congress-led government concluded that Coal India Limited would be unable to supply coal to thermal power stations to produce an extra 100,000 megawatts by 2012, it decided in 2005 to allot more mines to private and government-owned companies to help them generate power for their own use. During 2006–9, it issued an additional seventy-five coal blocks to private players and seventy to public sector firms through its screening committee procedure. The guidelines for giving these licenses were altered in 2005 and 2006, and again in 2009. The later audit report by the comptroller and auditor general (CAG) would describe these criteria as "non-transparent."

In 2006, the Singh cabinet considered the alternative of allotting coal blocks by auction but rejected it because that would have required a new law and the consent of the governments of the coal-bearing states—a complicated affair. Later, the cabinet changed its mind. In October 2008, it introduced a bill titled the "Mines and Minerals (Development and Regulation) Act 1957 Amendment Bill," which provided for coal blocks to be sold through a system of auction by competitive bidding, effective September 2010.

As this procedure was acceptable to all the concerned parties, the subject should have been considered closed. But there was a certain unfinished, fishy affair, which Ahir, reelected in May 2009, wanted to probe. He drew the CVC's attention to the irregularities in the allotment of twelve coal blocks to private firms in 2009. He followed this up in November 2010 with a complaint to the CAG that coal from the captive blocks allocated to certain private companies was being illegally diverted to the open market instead of being used by the licensees.[86] This specific charge prodded the CAG to act.

On March 22, 2012, the *Times of India* splashed exclusive extracts from the first draft of the CAG report, titled "Performance Audit of Coal Block Allocations." What particularly gripped readers and the general public was the CAG's statistic for the astronomical "windfall gains" made by the companies by obtaining the coal block licenses cheaply. Windfall gain was the difference between the high market price of coal sold by Coal India Limited and the lower cost of coal extracted from captive blocks by the companies. The CAG came up with the jaw-dropping estimate of Rs 10,673 billion ($194 billion), which nearly equaled the total annual tax revenue of the federal government! (Five months later, it would cut this figure down to $34 billion.)

Coalfields did not have the glamour of IPL cricket tournaments, with lycra-clad cheerleaders in tight miniskirts, all-night post-match parties, colossal merchandising, and TV tie-ins. But, since coal-fueled stations produced 57 percent of the electricity, the mined commodity was associated in the popular psyche with power generation, or rather, with frequent outages due to the chronic shortfall in power supplies—a bane of urban life.

The opposition BJP grabbed this opportunity to paint the Congress-led government in the most unflattering colors. Among other things, this enabled the BJP to downplay a few corruption scandals of its own, especially one surrounding B.S. Yeddyurappa, the BJP chief minister of Karnataka from May 2008 to July 2011. Accused of profiting from the illegal iron-ore export from Karnataka, he was arrested in October 2011 and later released on bail. Based on the report by the Central Empowered Committee in April 2012, the Supreme Court ordered an official CBI enquiry into the case on May 11, to be completed within three months.[87] Though the cash amounts involved in the two cases were different, the BJP could not claim to be squeaky clean. Indeed, in October 2012, the CBI would charge Yeddyurappa and JSW Steel Limited with criminal conspiracy, forgery, and corruption.[88]

In the nationwide coal-block allocation issue, on May 31, 2012, the CVC ordered the CBI to investigate the allegations made earlier by Ahir. In the Lok Sabha, the raucous standoff between the government and the BJP, which demanded the immediate resignation of the Singh cabinet, paralyzed the month-long monsoon session.

Media reports asserted that MPs, ministers, and chief ministers of coal-producing states had successfully lobbied for coal blocks to be allocated to certain private firms. Among those who were named was Naveen Jindal, chairman and managing director of the half-century-old Jindal Steel & Power Limited. He was elected to parliament as a Congress Party candidate in 2004. He was allotted a coalfield in Orissa with reserves of 1,500 million metric tons in February 2009, well after Delhi's cutoff date for the allotment of coal blocks. In stark contrast, the government-owned Navratna Coal India Limited was turned down and told to seek coal blocks in Mozambique.[89]

When the CAG submitted its final report on August 17, what drew the most attention was its revised estimate of the windfall gains by the licensees.

It had shrunk to 18 percent of the earlier leaked figure—down to Rs 1,869 billion ($34 billion). The CAG's first estimate was based on the weight of the coal in situ, instead of the weight of the finished product, following a heavy loss in mass due to mining and washing.

Despite a thorough perusal of the minutes of the screening committees' meetings and other documents, the CAG failed to see any record of how each of the applicants had been evaluated and the final winner named. In the case of one coal block, only two of the 108 applicants gave detailed presentations to the screening committee, yet the committee recommended six names! Some private companies secured licenses for collieries that contained more coal than was needed for generating their own electricity. Many licensees sat on their blocks instead of exploiting them, thus defeating the overall purpose of allocating the licenses in order to increase power supplies.[90] Of the eighty-six coal blocks that were required to produce coal by 2010–11, "only 28 blocks (including 15 allocated to the private sector) started production as of 31 March 2011," noted the CAG's final document. Their aggregate output during the year was less than half of the official target.[91]

As before, a PIL was filed by one or more social activists with the Supreme Court challenging the legality of the protocol followed in awarding coal blocks. The first to move the apex court was an advocate named L.M. Sharma. In mid-September the Supreme Court bench dismissed the solicitor general's argument to reject the petition and ordered the coal ministry's secretary to file an affidavit within eight weeks that stated the guidelines used for allotting coal blocks.

The bench also wondered aloud why the names of politicians and their relatives had cropped up among the alleged illegal licensees of coal blocks in which the procedure of competitive bidding was not followed.[92] An answer to their query came a few days later in a *New York Times* article quoting an anonymous businessman in Central India who had been allotted coalfields. The *Times* reported that "relationships with politicians served as a 'master key' enabling industrialists to gain access to natural resources." As the businessman put it, "Whoever has a master key wants to eat up all of India. Whoever doesn't have a key is struggling to survive."[93]

The master key here was expected to provide access to the riches of the soil concentrated in the northcentral region of India, which had emerged as a bastion for Maoists—known locally as Naxalites or Naxals—with the district of Dantewada as one of their hubs.

7

Maoists in the
Mineral-Rich Heartland

The Road to Dantewada

In the absence of a satisfactory inn in Dantewada, a visitor has to settle for
reaching it from Jagdalpur, a far bigger urban center, fifty miles to its east.
The 190-mile road journey to Jagdalpur starts at the freshly built airport of
Raipur, the capital of Chhattisgarh (Hindi: Thirty-six Forts). A brief run
along a tree-covered avenue leads to a city of mismatched structures. Baby-
lon Hotels and Restaurants stands next to a garage marked Silverline Automobiles, with its mechanics in greasy uniforms lounging near the clinically
clean Marble Art, written in Hindi, displaying marble statues of Mahatma
Mohandas Gandhi and Jawaharlal Nehru.

Once you leave Raipur, the asphalt road becomes smooth and uncluttered,
except for occasional motorcycles driven by men wearing Bedouin-style headgear. In the surrounding plain, the dwellings range from huts of flimsy
material to brick houses. These are built inside compounds delineated by
walls of bamboo or plastered, baked bricks. Often the walls are overlaid
with gigantic advertisements in red, blue, and yellow. The dominance of
cement companies—ACC ("Build with confidence"), Jaypee Cement, and
Ambuja Cement—interspersed with signs for GK (TMI) Mortgage Company underscores the boost given to the construction industry in the wake of
the New Economic Policy. The approach to a village en route, hosting such
signs as Kashyap Cycle Store and Kalpana Ready Made Clothes, is signaled
by speed breakers of bent steel bars or stone-hardened asphalt.

After a three-hour drive, you begin to ascend. The distant hills are thickly forested. The highway becomes a ribbon between clearings and fields that are neither large nor particularly fertile. Sighting a tractor is a rarity. The clearings are dotted with electricity pylons and cell-phone transmission towers. The sudden appearance of a red-and-white Aircel billboard between these skeletal gray frames is a dramatic reminder of the communications revolution. Colors of human-made structures—green, blue, yellow, and white—merge with those of nature. Along the road you see an occasional Hindu temple, with its round pyramidal architecture, painted saffron. The area is the domain of Adivasis (Hindi: original inhabitants), most of whom live in villages in the interior, so there are very few people walking along the margins of the road. Occasionally, a lean Adivasi woman carrying a bundle of long, thin tree branches, used as cooking fuel, is seen trudging along.

Then the road turns into a series of ascending serpentine twists that can be maneuvered only in low gear. My Adivasi driver, Arjun Das, who was prone to speeding, slowed down. He stopped near the village of Koska, in the bend of a very sharp hairpin turn near a stone structure bearing a sign that read in Hindi MAA TELINA SATI (Mother Telina Sati). He left the car and disappeared into a semidark shrine huddled between two gigantic boulders to receive the female saint's blessings for safety on the road. For the slender, twenty-one-year-old Das, with the frame and looks of a boy in his mid-teens, this ritual was more reassuring than heeding the warnings in English—"Speed thrills but kills"—posted along the highway, which he could not read.

We resumed our run. Kanker, a town of thirty thousand, lies in the shadow of the forested terrain of the Gadiya Mountain, as if guarded by it. The terrain around Kanker makes the visitor realize that the almost half of Chhattisgarh is forest, rich in dark green *sal* (Latin: *shorea robusa*) and teak trees used for construction.[1] Kanker is only the second place on this journey where we have seen signs of police presence (they were also present at Pherasgaon)—a police station in a yellow brick building. The main street in Kanker contains a large mosque with a tall minaret and a huge sign proclaiming YA ALLAH in Arabic. Two miles from this landmark appears a signboard for the "Counter Terrorism College."[2]

Jagdalpur turned out to be home to nearly fifty churches. Here was an unmistakable sign of the deep devotion of the Adivasis who had converted to Christianity, since the group forms only one-seventh of Jagdalpur's 150,000 inhabitants.

The next day, on the way to Dantewada, the sighting of a camp of the para-military Central Reserve Police Force in the village of Karlo indicated that we were nearing the epicenter of the Naxalite insurgency. Yet upon our arrival at the boundary of Dantewada we were greeted by a simple concrete archway welcoming the visitor. It was the site of the temple to Maa Danteshwari,[3] much revered by Adivasis and non-Adivasi Hindus.

On the surface, Dantewada appears sleepy, a backwater town with a single street of shops and offices serving as its marketplace. Besides the clothing and shoe stores, tea stalls, modest eateries, groceries, a cycle shop, and a cell-phone outlet, there is a motorcycle sales facility. The sight of Levi Strauss Jeans for Rs 599 ($11) is a reminder of the globalization of a brand name. And two signs in Urdu point out the presence of a Muslim minority in the settlement. There is the inevitable urban debris in the street on both sides.

The town's activity is centered around the bus stand in a square connected by two small bylanes to the main street. The mix of shops and offices here give Dantewada a semblance of modernity: DISH TV; AISECT-IGNU-Track Computers, Hardware and Software; C-Planet Computer; a well-scrubbed cafeteria; and a shop offering photocopying, subscriber trunk dialing, and a public call office.

Given the devotion that Das had for goddesses and female saints, he shot off to seek the blessing of Maa Danteshwari after depositing me at the office of the *Bastar Impact*, a Hindi daily, in the main street. Maa Danteshwari is revered as an incarnation of *shakti* (Hindi: strength, specifically female power) in Hindu mythology. She was the patron goddess of the Hindu ruler of the princely state of Bastar (Hindi: Magic) during British rule.[4] Her temple, located on the town's outskirts, is an impressive whitewashed structure behind a large arch carrying the temple's name. Even though she is seated on a raised platform and decked profusely from neck to toe in multilayered satin of various hues, with a heap of garlands covering her torso down to her groin, the jet-black idol of Maa Danteshwari projects intense ferocity. To look closely at her black face—elliptically round white shapes representing her eyes, a tight mouth, and a pierced nostril holding a rounded fish ornament—is to invite fear.

Symbolically, though, this image of power summed up the mortal struggle then in train in Dantewada district between Naxalites and the security forces. Here was a hub of the Naxalite insurgency in the region, with not a single cop or a paramilitary trooper in sight. It was a puzzle that I was resolved to crack.

Vinod Singh, a fair-skinned, robustly built man of medium height in his early forties, came to my rescue. He greeted me in the cramped office of the *Bastar Impact*. "Nowadays, even on incident-free days, policemen do not leave their stations wearing uniform," he told me in Hindi. "When they leave in vehicles they change their registration numbers, and they do not use lights at night. Sometimes the CRPF [Central Reserve Police Force] patrol our streets at night in their vehicles; but that is all." I sipped black tea while he refreshed himself with a cup of sweet, milky brew.

"Naxalites have been active along the Andhra Pradesh border since 1980," Singh continued. "They infiltrated small villages and began questioning the role of the patwaris, land recording officials. They defied the patwaris and insisted on land deeds for tribals, a popular move. In 1994 they blew up a police vehicle in this area. The tribals were impressed by the challenge they threw at the government and got away with it with impunity. That built up support for them."

Singh reeled off the names of villages in Dantewada district under Naxalite control: Takilode, Satva, Dharma, Belnar, Poosal, Neerum, Pidiakot, Pollevaya, Palla, Kodanka, Parkeli, Markapal, Oorsapara, and Oothia. These settlements were part of the nearly 60 percent of the district administered by Naxalites. He drew a sketch with Dantewada as the nucleus. "Ten kilometers to the east, there is a CRPF company on the edge of the Naxalite area, at Kuakond," he said. "Next, fifteen kilometers to the north, is another Naxalite stronghold, and beyond that is a CRPF company at Katekiyan. And fifteen kilometers to the west is a Naxalite area and to its southward edge is a CRPF company at Barsur. Lastly, ten kilometers to the south is a guerrilla territory and at its southern edge there are three CRPF camps at Mirtur, Kuper, and Komaloor." By cutting off access roads and digging ditches at the freshly created gaps in the roads, Naxalites had barred vehicle-borne security forces from entering these settlements. "So any forays by the security forces into these areas have to be on foot, which makes them vulnerable to ambushes by armed Naxalites."[5]

It had taken the Naxalites three decades to reach this stage.

Naxalbari: The Spark

Naxalites believed in overthrowing the established order through armed struggle. Their initial targets were large landlords, usurious moneylenders, venal forest officers, and oppressive police commanders. The only place where they could establish a secure base was among the Adivasis living in the inaccessible forested hills in the contiguous parts of West Bengal, southern Bihar (which later became Jharkhand), and Orissa. Their movement started when, led by the militant members of the Communist Party of India (Marxist), landless peasants occupied plots they did not own and confiscated rice stocks in the Naxalbari area of West Bengal, adjoining Nepal and East Pakistan, during March–May 1967. Their leader was forty-nine-year-old Charu Mazumdar, a bespectacled man with a thin, horsy face, a big nose, and a thatch of black hair on a large head. He advocated seizing political power through protracted armed struggle based on guerrilla warfare. This strategy required gaining a foothold in rural and remote areas, upgrading them to guerrilla zones, then to guerrilla bases—embryonic liberation zones—before encircling and overtaking cities.[6]

In West Bengal, their first violent act was to attack a police station in Naxalbari on May 23, 1967. The state government in Kolkata dispatched a large contingent of its police force to the trouble spot. The militants scattered to the areas inhabited largely by Adivasis in the tristate area of West Bengal–Bihar–Orissa. The next territory to raise the banner of armed struggle was the tribal-inhabited village of Srikalulum in northeastern Andhra Pradesh, along the coast. Mazumdar visited Srikalulum in March 1969.

The following month, the Communist Party of India (Marxist-Leninist), or CPI (ML), was formed clandestinely. It focused on organizing landless and wretchedly poor peasants. But its initial stress on the peasantry's economic demands soon gave way to violent attacks on exploitative landlords and moneylenders. When the anticipated revolutionary fire did not ignite in villages, Mazumdar instructed party activists in 1970 to resort to exploding bombs in Greater Kolkata without having set up strong rural bases around the city. Therefore the party's seven hundred "action squads" ended up carrying out individual "annihilations."[7]

Once the party shifted its focus to the state capital, it became easier for intelligence agents to infiltrate it. Indira Gandhi's central administration intervened, much strengthened after the Congress Party's impressive electoral victory in March 1971. In coordination with the state government, it deployed three army divisions against the Naxalites under Operation Steeplechase. The soldiers sealed off an area in Greater Kolkata while the state police carried out house-to-house searches. By the end of the year, nearly 1,800 Naxalite activists were killed, and thousands of CPI (ML) members and sympathizers were jailed. Of the party's twenty-two original members of its Central Committee, nineteen were arrested or killed, or died.[8]

Because of CPI (ML)'s association with China and the Chinese Communist Party, which opposed the transformation of East Pakistan into the independent nation of Bangladesh—a scenario enjoying almost universal backing of the people in West Bengal—it lost the last remnant of support after the establishment of Bangladesh in December 1971. On July 16, 1972, Mazumdar was arrested at his hideout in Kolkata. Twelve days later, he had a fatal heart attack, according to prison officers.[9] With his demise, those colleagues of his who had left the CPI (ML) because of their disagreement with his strategy went on to form different Naxalite factions.

One group, which believed in armed revolution but had not joined the CPI (ML), was called Dakshin Desh (Hindi: Southern Land).[10] It was headed by Kanai Chatterjee, who stressed that mass mobilization was an essential requisite for engaging in armed struggle. It was active in the Burdwan district of West Bengal, an area covered in thick forest, where Dalits and Adivasis formed substantial sections of the population. In 1975 it changed its name to Maoist Communist Centre of India, generally known as MCC. It formed political militia squads who toured villages to mobilize landless and indigent peasants. They seized grain stocks and firearms, and assassinated those they considered police informers. The MCC extended its activities to eastern Bihar. Its politburo would go on to form the People's Liberation Guerrilla Army.[11]

In the south, the Telangana region of Andhra Pradesh, with a long history of militant peasantry, proved to be an incubator for the newly named CPI (ML) People's War, commonly called the People's War Group, in 1977. Its leadership urged their student followers to go to villages. The landlocked Telangana shares borders with Maharashtra, southern Madhya Pradesh (later Chhattisgarh), and Orissa.[12]

People's War Group activists' analysis of the countryside showed that land distribution was grossly skewed and that in Telangana, containing nearly half of the state's forests, the impoverished Adivasi inhabitants were also exploited by the forest department's officials and contractors. Initially, the local tribals were wary of the Telugu-speaking urban students. The newcomers learned Gondi, the predominant language of Adivasis, but that was not enough.[13] What really improved their acceptance was their advice to Adivasis to boil their drinking water, which reduced infant mortality by half. It made the Adivasis listen to what the radical activists had to say on more weighty subjects, such as the miserly Rs 0.03 that forest contractors paid them for a bundle of seventy tendu leaves they collected.[14] These leaves are used for wrapping tobacco to make bidis. Forest officials also curbed the Adivasis' legal right to other forest produce, from tamarind to bamboo.

In 1980, two People's War Group squads of twelve people each entered the Dandakaranya (Sanskrit: Forest of Punishment) region, which, besides northern Andhra Pradesh, includes parts of eastern Maharashtra, southern Madhya Pradesh (later, Chhattisgarh), and southern Orissa. Shaped like a quadrilateral pressed down in the middle, and delineated by the Eastern Ghats in the east and the Abujhmad (Gondi: Unknown Highlands) Hills in the west, it is spread over 35,600 square miles. It measures two hundred miles from north to south and about the same distance east to west. Within a generation, it would become a bastion of Naxalites, the Indian Maoists.

In 1984, the party's politburo formed a Forest Liaison Committee in Dandakaranya to coordinate the movement. That in turn led to the establishment of the Dandakaranya Adivasi Kisan Mazdoor Sangh (Hindi: Peasants-Workers Union).[15] It launched its "land to the tiller" campaign in response to the exploitation of Adivasi peasants by forest department officials and contractors, as well as their own tribal chiefs. Forestry bureaucrats subjected them to illegal and extralegal exactions, and the traditional chiefs, who owned large tracts of land, demanded free labor from them. As a result of tending the chief's plots first, a typical Adivasi could attend to his own patch only during the last weeks of petering monsoon. That meant harvesting only one crop a year.[16]

When, led by the party's cadres, poor Adivasis refused to work the tribal chiefs' lands, the latter called on the Madhya Pradesh government to intervene, which it did. Colluding with the tribal chiefs, its police force killed dozens of party activists. It was at this point that the group's politburo decided to offer—in its own words—"defensive violence" to counter the violence that the government had unleashed in order to reverse the gains the underprivileged had managed to make. To arm themselves, the party's cadres at first resorted to snatching weapons from law-enforcement agents, then they graduated to encircling police stations in the forested interior and disarming their occupants. This type of action was the building block for creating guerrilla zones.

On the political-administrative front, the Dandakaranya Adivasi Peasants-Workers Union had started to replace the traditional chieftains and the official panchayat system, with villagers referring their problems to the union.

This heralded a gradual transfer of power. Fearing for their physical safety, patwaris stopped visiting villages to collect land revenue in the expanding guerrilla zone.

In 1995, the People's War Group's All India Special Conference endorsed the leadership's decision to build a "Gram Rajya Committee" (Hindi: Village Rule Committee), a body elected by all villagers above the age of eighteen, with the main aim of developing agriculture. With that goal in mind, party cadres started a program of constructing irrigation tanks in villages. They encouraged a cooperative movement. Three or four families would agree to plow the land. For constructing houses or other buildings, teams of eleven members were formed. The cooperative system helped develop a communal feeling.

The party also engaged in the cultural and social lives of the community. Its cultural wing, Chetna Natya Manch (Hindi: Awakening Dramatic Arts Front), visited villages to conduct dance, drama, poetry, and musical work-shops. The Manch's cultural activities inspired young people to join the party. The songs such as "Land to the Tiller," "Oh, Brave Lady," and "Our Flag Is Red" pressed the right emotional buttons in the audience. The lyrics were often inspirational or rhetorical—as in Subbarao Panigrahi's "Our Flag Is Red" (originally in Telugu):

> Our flag is red
> With the blood of toilers.
> Our march is driven
> By the dreams of the martyrs.

Or in Cherabanda Raju's poem (original in Telugu):

> Gearing the fallows,
> Plowing the fields,
> With our sweat as streams,
> We harvested the crop.
> Whose was the grain?
> Whose was the gruel?[17]

The Chetna Natya Manch started publishing a bimonthly, multilingual magazine, *Jhankar* (Hindi: Creative), in August 1994. The languages of its articles—Gondi, Hindi, Marathi, Bengali, and Telugu—showed the areas where the People's War Group was active.

In the late 1980s, the MCC, now chiefly active in Bihar, claimed five hundred cadres and ten thousand members. In its enclaves, it conducted a parallel judicial system of people's courts. It had set up mass organizations among peasants and students, and it had an armed wing called the Red Defense Force. Given its strength among low-caste Hindus and Dalits, its armed wing clashed with the militias defending upper-caste interests.[18]

In Andhra Pradesh, with the rise of the regional Telugu Desam Party as an alternative to the Congress Party in the 1980s, the People's War Group played one against the other at the time of panchayat polls. While it remained committed to boycotting elections because of the absence of any party genuinely interested in fighting for the exploited masses, the party used its influence in rural areas to secure the release of its imprisoned members and an easing of police pressure.

The introduction of a vigorous neoliberal agenda by P.V. Narasimha Rao's government in 1991 encouraged the leaders of the three major Naxalite factions—the People's War Group, the MCC, and the CPI (ML) Party Unity, active in Bihar—to coordinate their struggles. In September 1993, they banded together their senior cadres to form the All India People's Resistance Forum.

The Slow Burn

From 1993 on, a correlation developed between the liberalizing of the official mineral policy and the rise in the influence of the Naxalite factions, which opposed the New Economic Policy and globalization. The main base of Naxalites was in Adivasi territory. According to a report by the expert group appointed by the Central Ministry of Rural Development, these areas were "the storehouse of mineral wealth"—100 percent of uranium, 92 percent of coal, 92 percent of bauxite (aluminum ore), 85 percent of copper, 78 percent of iron ore, and 65 percent of dolomite—in the country.[19]

The Indian constitution allocates mineral rights to the states, which receive all the royalties that result from mining them. But the regulation of the mining and minerals sector is undertaken by the central government. In 1994, the Narasimha Rao administration amended the 1957 act to allow private domestic and foreign investors to explore mines and extract minerals—except coal, as it is a hydrocarbon energy mineral—on a case-by-case basis. The Naxalite People's Resistance Forum responded by holding a protest rally in Hyderabad that attracted one hundred thousand participants. But it made no difference to Delhi's policies. In 1997, the United Front alliance government introduced an automatic approval route for foreign direct investment (FDI) of up to 50 percent equity in mining.

By amending the 1957 law in December 1999, the BJP-led government authorized state authorities to acquire land for mining (a right until then vested with the central government according to the amended 1984 law) and to make rules about mines and minerals in their territory. It also permitted 100 percent FDI for the processing of mines and minerals—except coal—with effect from February 2000.[20] Through these changes, the BJP made itself the prime target of the Naxalite factions.

In November 2000, part of southern Madhya Pradesh was hived off and turned into Chhattisgarh (population: 21 million), and southern Bihar was reconstituted as Jharkhand (population: 27 million, with a quarter composed of Adivasis, and forests covering about a third of its area). In Chhattisgarh, 37 percent of the inhabitants were Scheduled Tribes and another 23 percent were Scheduled Castes.[21] All of the nation's tin, much of its coal, and one-fifth of its iron ore—about 2.336 billion tons, averaging 68 percent purity—concentrated in the five districts of the old princely state of Bastar. It also had bauxite and limestone (to produce cement). Roughly a third of Jharkhand's population was Adivasis. Nationwide, Adivasis were at the bottom of the socioeconomic pyramid. At 59 percent, their literacy rate was well below the national average of 73 percent, according to the 2011 census, which used the official term of Scheduled Tribes for Adivasis.[22]

The following year, 2001, the People's War Group conference resolved to set up bases within guerrilla zones as a prelude to forming the people's army, backed by popular support and inside a suitable terrain. It started founding Revolutionary People's Committees, each representing five hundred to three thousand village households. It formed a dozen such bodies in each district as a nucleus for a guerrilla base, including the transformation of the 1,545-square-mile Abujhmad area north of Indravati River into the Central Guerilla Base.[23] It extended its activities into the 460-square-mile Saranda (literally, "seven hundred hills") forest. This mineral-rich area in Jharkhand, adjoining Orissa (population: 37 million, one-fifth of which were Adivasis; and two-fifths of its territory covered by forests), would become the second most important Naxalite stronghold, after the Dandakaranya forest. The party's politburo would later integrate previously autonomous units in parts of Andhra Pradesh, Bihar, Chhattisgarh, Jharkhand, Orissa, and West Bengal into the People's Guerrilla Army.

The introduction of foreign multinational corporations (MNCs) into the mining industry raised the level of conflict between the state and the Naxalite factions. After 2002, foreign corporations such as BHP Billiton of Australia, ArcelorMittal of Luxembourg, Posco of South Korea, Rio Tinto of Britain and Australia, Texas Power Generation Company, and Vedanta Resources of Britain, as well as the indigenous companies like Essar Steel, Jindal Steel and Power, and Tata Steel, focused on India's east-central zone to secure mineral rights.[24]

The governments in these states acquired mineral-rich land through compulsory purchase orders authorized by the colonial-era Land Acquisition Act of 1894.[25] This process proved controversial. The acquisition law was to be invoked only when the land was for such public purposes as building a road, railway track, hospital, school, or administrative building. But now, state governments started acquiring land and selling it to private companies, after paying the landowners derisory compensation.

When the BJP came to power in Chhattisgarh in May 2004, private mining companies enjoyed a bonanza, while the Naxalites' animosity toward the party intensified. The state government started signing scores of memorandums of understanding (MOUs) with domestic and foreign MNCs.[26] While it accorded favorable terms to MNCs, the government paid meager compensation to the tribal landholders. Violating their promise to the state authorities to provide jobs to the displaced Adivasis, the MNCs either ignored them altogether or engaged them as "contract laborers" on daily wages without job security, and not as full-fledged employees entitled to certain rights. Such was the case in other resource-rich states as well. Discontent among Adivasis grew, yet they failed to find any mainstream political party to speak up for them.

Among those who monitored the situation in Chhattisgarh was the Jagdalpur-based Pavan Dubey, a tall, muscular, mustached, forty-five-year-old journalist. "Neither the Congress nor the BJP pays attention to the tribals. If there is a health clinic in an Adivasi village, there is no doctor or nurse. If there is a school, there is no teacher. After getting elected to the State Legislative Assembly, these party leaders do not visit their rural constituencies. They make promises which they do not keep. So, in desperation, the Adivasis turned to Naxalites."[27]

Such negligence by major political parties enabled the People's War Group to enhance its popularity. Its leaders were encouraged to break new ground. Around nine p.m. on February 6, 2004, some 150 of its armed guerrillas, traveling in two cargo trucks, two Jeeps, and five motorcycles, arrived at the bus station of Koraput, capital of the tribal-majority Koraput district, under the legal jurisdiction of Orissa but forming an integral part of the Dandakaranya forest. They ordered the shopkeepers to draw down their shutters and go home. They split in three groups, with one driving off to the district armory, another to the two police stations, and the third group to the local prison.

During the next six hours, they ransacked the armory and the police stations, raided the camp of the Orissa State Armed Police battalion, and exploded a landmine at the camp of the CRPF. They left fifteen security personnel dead. According to the official account, their weapons haul included more than a thousand machine guns, sub-machine guns, and rifles, as well as hundreds of bombs and grenades. The military-style precision with which the guerrillas executed their operation shook the local and state authorities. "Police have been placed on high alert," announced B.B. Mishra, deputy inspector-general of police. "The situation is grim."[28]

This incident opened a new chapter in the chronicle of the Naxalite movement. It signaled the start of low-intensity warfare between the movement and the state. It also paved the way for the two main Naxalite factions—the People's War Group and the MCC—to merge.

The Flame: Communist Party of India (Maoist)

In a clandestine meeting on September 21, 2004, the politburos of the two factions agreed to form the Communist Party of India (Maoist), with fifty-four-year-old Muppala Lakshmana Rao, aka Ganapathi, as its general secretary. Below the newly formed politburo was the thirty-two-member Central Committee. The unification decision was made public on October 14, 2004.[29]

A lean, bespectacled man with graying hair, Ganapathi measured a little over five and a half feet. He was born into a landholding family in Beerpur village, near Karimnagar in northern Andhra Pradesh, part of the state of Telangana formed in June 2014. After obtaining undergraduate degrees in science and education, he worked as a teacher in Karimnagar. He quit the job after a few years to pursue postgraduate studies at the newly opened Kakatiya University in Warangal. There he came under the influence of CPI (ML) leader Kondapalli Seetharamaiah. Following the party's call to its members to go to villages, he left his family to work with rural Adivasis in the Telangana sector of the Dandakaranya forest. He rose through the ranks of the People's War Group.

The program adopted by the newly founded party, however, was in essence a rehash of the document adopted by the CPI (ML) in 1969. It described India as "a semi-colonial, semi-feudal country with uneven development." It stated that the major contradiction between "feudalism and the broad masses" could be resolved only through "an armed agrarian revolution"—that is, a "protracted people's war," just as in China. The strategy to follow was "to liberate rural areas first and then, having expanded the base areas—the center of democratic power in rural areas—advance toward countrywide victory through encircling and capturing cities."

A major addition was the party's declaration that it opposed privatization, economic liberalization, and globalization. Making a specific mention of "Adivasis or tribes," the official program stated, "they have been neglected socially, culturally and politically." The emergence of a unified party gave momentum to the Adivasis' resolve to resist the corporate takeover of their forestlands. That in turn provided them with a strong link between their ethnic identity and their economic exploitation.[30]

Given a much larger area of activity, the party's politburo divided its Central Committee, charged with deciding the general strategy, into regional bureaus, each of which was divided further into zonal committees, charged with deciding tactics, with the latter divided further into divisions, which supervised the front organizations for peasants and workers, women, and youth, as well as Revolutionary Peasants' Committees and Women's Liberation Front—popularly known as *sanghams* or *sanghatana*, collective or union. After merging the armed militias of the two Naxalite factions, the Central Committee named the unified force the People's Liberation Guerrilla Army (PLGA). It functioned under the party's Central Military Commission, which was headed by Jagdish. According to the central Home Ministry, by the end of 2004, the attacks by Naxalite-Maoists on the police, paramilitaries, and malevolent forest officers totaled 1,533.

Determined to shore up the mining industry, the Indian authorities made the united party their primary target. They banned it under the Unlawful Activities (Prevention) Amendment Act of 2004. Anti-Maoist operations in

Andhra Pradesh escalated in October 2004 and continued throughout 2005. The party suffered a loss of 1,800 cadres.[31]

Later, the hawks in Delhi would hold up the Andhra Pradesh model for eradicating the Maoist movement, stressing the role played by the specially trained police, called Greyhounds. This argument overlooked the fact that the massive expansion of the police force coincided with a wide extension of the intelligence network, which the state government was able to achieve during the ceasefire that preceded its peace talks with the People's War Group / CPI (Maoist), and which it had conducted in bad faith. At the same time, it undertook extensive development projects in the tribal areas where the government had been absent until then.

On its part, in August 2005 the Chhattisgarh government inaugurated the Counter Terrorism and Jungle Warfare College in Kanker, located in a terrain similar to where Maoists were embedded. Directed by retired brigadier Basant Ponwar, it had a staff of nearly three hundred. Ponwar had run the Indian Army's jungle warfare school in the insurgent-infested Mizoram, a small northeastern state populated by the universally Christian ethnic Mizos. Besides the standard shooting and firing ranges, the college had facilities for rock climbing, slithering, rappelling, and unarmed combat, as well as a natural obstacle course and an endurance track. Guided by the motto "Fight a guerrilla like a guerrilla," its six-month course put students through a rigorous regime to train them to undertake sustained offensives in counterinsurgency and counterterrorism operations in forests and urban areas.[32]

Colluding with Tata Steel and Essar Steel, which reportedly provided much of the funding, the state government supported the rise of the armed anti-Naxalite tribal militia called Salwa Judum (Gondi: Purification Hunt). It was founded by the Adivasi leader of the Congress Party in the state legislature, Mahendra Karma, a dark, stocky, square-faced, fifty-five-year-old man with a receding hairline. During the second half of 2005, the five-thousand-strong Salwa Judum, working alongside the CRPF and police, terrorized Adivasis, setting alight villages suspected of being Maoist. Over the next three years, they torched 644 settlements and displaced 350,000 people.[33] Nearly 300,000 dispersed deep into the forest or fled to Andhra Pradesh.

However, Maoists were not just passive observers to this onslaught. "At one meeting of the Salwa Judum in Dantewada district the Naxalites created a melee and killed about ten Salwa militias," said Vinod Singh. "That made people wary of supporting Salwa Judum or attending their meetings in that area."[34]

Maoist cadres helped to rehabilitate the displaced while stressing that their expulsion was a prelude to depopulating the forest and turning over the Adivasi land to the mining corporations. They referred to the economic gains Adivasis had made under their leadership—the payment for the collectors of tendu leaves had risen thirty-five fold, from Rs 0.03 per bundle. As laborers they often earned more than the statutory minimum wage. Party workers urged Adivasis to join the People's Militia to fight Salwa Judum. They got a favorable response—the strength of the People's Militia and the People's Liberation Guerrilla Army grew.

Outside this region, the Operation Jailbreak that its Central Military Commission carried out with meticulous planning and execution in Jehanabad, Bihar, on November 13, 2005, was remarkable on several counts. Jehanabad, a small town only thirty-five miles from the state capital, Patna, was in the plains, with no hills or forest in the area. The Central Military Commission inducted experienced guerrillas from Jharkhand and Orissa for the operation, and the contingent that executed the offensive included a medical unit, trained to rescue the injured and dead militants. Finally, besides confronting the security force, the armed Maoists assassinated two leaders of the landlords' militia, Ranveer Sena (Hindi: Desert-Conquering Army), who had terrorized Dalits and low-caste Hindus with murder and arson since the late 1980s. Unlike in the tribal region, the conflict in the caste-ridden Bihar was between lower castes and Dalits on one side and the landowning upper castes on the other.

Around 8:30 p.m. on November 13, 2005, about two hundred PLGA guerrillas[35] converged on Jehanabad on motorcycles. They called on the residents to stay indoors and cut off the power lines. Using a public address system, they stressed that their raid was directed against "the oppressive police and government." Simultaneous assaults on the police lines, the district administrator's office, and the jail ensued. There was only a skeleton police force in the town, as most of their colleagues had been deployed in another part of Bihar to oversee the third phase of the state election. After an hour-long gun battle, the police officers surrendered. Once the jail fell to the insurgents, they released all 340 prisoners, including 140 Maoists, headed by their leader Ajay Kanu, a Central Committee member. They left with a haul of two hundred rifles.[36]

This daring offensive by armed Maoists in the Hindi-speaking heartland of India shocked the state and central governments. In an unprecedented move, Delhi rushed two companies of the elite National Security Guard commandos to Bihar and equipped them with helicopters. In the absence of actionable intelligence, however, the authorities made scant progress in apprehending the raiders.

In general, though, the Maoist leadership continued to be selective in its targets. To equip its guerrillas and members of the People's Militia with adequate supplies of explosives to produce many hundreds of booby traps,[37] small pressure bombs, and improvised explosive devices (IEDs)—also called land mines—it targeted the warehouse for munitions used by the National Mineral Development Corporation at Kirandul, twenty-five miles from Dantewada. The storage depot was part of the vast Bailadila (Gondi: Bull's Hump) mining complex. Soon after midnight on February 9, 2006, a large contingent of Maoist guerrillas cut the power supply to the complex and engaged the sixteen-strong team of the Central Industrial Security Force. In a brief firefight, they killed half of them and gagged the rest. A large force of the People's Militia poured into the compound and emptied the depot of fourteen tons of explosives, along with detonators and fuses used to blast the mountainside and loosen iron ore.[38]

In public, the deeply embarrassed central government, which owned the National Mineral Development Corporation, downplayed this pathbreaking event. But its home minister, Shivraj Patil, was sufficiently rattled to table a status paper on Naxalites before the parliament five weeks later.

More Mining, More Maoism

Overall, after 2005, the pace of allocating large swathes of land to mining corporations by the state authorities accelerated. According to Rajendra Sail, a social activist and ecumenical leader,[39] of the 105 memos of understanding that the Chhattisgarh government signed between 2005 and 2009, all but one were about mineral-based industries and the preliminary mining steps of reconnaissance, forest clearance, and prospecting.[40] It was left to the signatories whether or not to make these documents public. By and large, they did not, arguing that the documents contained "commercial secrets," thereby ignoring the larger public interest in the deals. This lack of transparency turned the documents into the subject of fervid speculation about unseemly concessions given to the mining interests.

In Jarkhand, between 2002 and 2007, the government inked forty-four mining MOUs with Tata Steel, ArcelorMittal, Essar Steel, and Jindal Steel and Power for megaindustrial ventures worth Rs 1,983.6 billion ($39.6 billion), giving them ownership of 45,000 hectares (115,000 acres) and involving the eviction of one million people, according to Xaviar Dias, coordinator of Bindrai Institute of Research Study and Action, a tribal rights group.[41]

This development swelled the ranks of the CPI (Maoist), which alarmed Prime Minister Singh. Addressing the states' chief ministers in December 2007 he said, "Left wing extremism is possibly the single biggest security challenge to the Indian state." But Shivraj Patil, his home minister, continued to maintain that Naxalites were "our children gone astray." He referred to his ministry's 2006–7 report, which mentioned Naxalite violence in areas covered by 395 police stations, out of the nationwide total of 12,476, or a mere 3 percent.[42]

Singh and Patil were viewing the Naxalite violence from differing perspectives. Patil had a very narrow interpretation, focused on law and order. By contrast, Singh seemed to take a more sweeping view of the Maoists' rebellion. His assessment took into account their ideology and strategy and their impact on the official policy of exploiting mineral resources to underwrite a robust economic growth of India for decades to come. He noted the difference between the insurgency by Maoists and those in Kashmir and in the northeastern region on the fringes of the mainland. Whereas the latter were rooted in minority religion or ethnic identity and had limited appeal, the Maoist movement had the potential of gaining the support of vast numbers of the underprivileged in rural India. Second, Maoists challenged the very foundation on which India's social system rested. Their most subversive aim was to counteract the awe and fear inspired in ordinary people by the security personnel—the most effective coercive arm of the state—by creating a parallel armed force backed by a popular militia. Singh would have noted with grave concern that as a result of the Maoists' targeting of lawmen in Orissa, 40 percent of police jobs there remained unfilled.[43] The corruption-free governance system that the Maoists had established in their areas—based on triennial elections and manned by cadres leading Spartan lives—provided a practical alternative to India's corrupt and inept administrative-political system. Finally, by resisting the growing presence of Indian mining corporations and the introduction of foreign multinational corporations in their areas of influence, Maoists were slowing the neoliberal economic development of the country to which Singh was ardently committed.

Meanwhile, mining companies continued to multiply their profits. The state governments collected a royalty of 60¢ per metric ton of iron ore from the mining corporations, even when the mineral's price had rocketed to $200 per metric ton in the international market. By comparison, the going royalty rate in Australia was more than $3. They also gave generous tax holidays to these firms. In return, the beneficiaries made lavish donations to the major national and regional political parties to help fund their hugely expensive electoral campaigns. Part of these contributions ended up in the pockets of ministers. The most publicized case was that of Madhu Koda, chief minister of Jharkhand from September 2006 to August 2008. He was arrested in November 2009 and charged with receiving bribes to allocate mining rights, money laundering, and illegal investments. He allegedly amassed a fortune equivalent to a quarter of the state's annual tax revenue.[44]

These events fueled the Adivasis' discontent. The escalating tensions were noted inter alia by the authors of the Approach Paper for the Eleventh Five Year Plan (2007–12). "Our practices regarding rehabilitation of those displaced from their land because of development projects are seriously deficient and are responsible for a growing perception of exclusion and marginalization," they stated in their report. "The costs of displacement borne by our tribal population have been unduly high, and compensation has been tardy and inadequate, leading to serious unrest in many tribal regions. This discontent is likely to grow exponentially if the benefits from enforced land acquisition are seen accruing to private interests, or even to the state, at the cost of those displaced. To prevent even greater conflict . . . it is necessary to frame a transparent set of policy rules that address compensation, and make the affected persons beneficiaries of the projects, and to give these rules a legal format."[45]

But such recommendations fell on deaf ears in the portals of power, providing further traction to Maoists, whose leaders upgraded some of their guerrilla zones into liberated areas. "Maoists cut off access roads to villages where they were based, and set up their People's Government, called [in Hindi] *Janatana Sarkar*," said Vinod Singh. "They tell the tribals, 'You have no health service, no schools, no development; your Gondi language is not recognized. Now the government has come to take your land away. It is taking out your minerals with no benefit accruing to you.' Slowly, the tribals understood that Maoists were there to protect their rights." In response, the government did some development work, short of providing electricity to the villages in the district. "It introduced the public distribution system[46] to distribute subsidized food. It thought that that would finish off the militants. But it did not. So the state authorities in Chhattisgarh formed the

Salwa Judum. The central government dispatched two battalions of the Naga tribes from northeast India. Like the police and the CRPF before them, they found that killing Maoists was a high-risk job. The guerrillas blew up their vehicles with homemade land mines. So the Nagas were withdrawn. And when the Home Ministry in Delhi sent the CRPF, Maoists resorted to killing its personnel. Now every so often the police and CRPF make a foray into a liberated zone but do not stay. In return, Maoists attack police and CRPF camps."[47]

The Singh government changed tack and took ameliorative action. The result was the passing of the Scheduled Tribes and Other Traditional Forest Dwellers (Recognition of Forest Rights) in 2006, known popularly as the Forest Rights Act. It conferred forest rights on tribal and non-tribal forest dwellers. But its effectiveness was marred by excessive red tape. It went into effect only in 2008. The Forest Rights Committee had to be formed to accept and process claims. Illiterate Adivasis found they had to fill in forms they did not understand and rely on the corrupt forest department to survey their land.

Fixing fair value for land proved contentious, with the advocates of the Adivasi cause arguing that it should take into account the fact that the land in question had not only sustained the owners so far but was also the sole guarantee for the survival of the coming generations. The price could vary from Rs 375,000 ($7,500) to Rs 2.5 million ($50,000) a hectare. The Forest Rights Committee dismissed the basis for generous compensation, while the agents of the mining corporations warned the tribals that if they rejected an offer, the money would be given to others.

Government's Mantra of "Holistic Approach"

The Forest Rights Act was presented as part of a "holistic approach" to the Naxalite challenge that the central government claimed to have adopted when they tabled Patil's status paper on the subject in March 2006. It stated that the Naxalite movement, operating in the administrative and political vacuum engendered by it, was spreading geographically and that its violence was intensifying. The number of Naxalite attacks had increased from 1,533 in 2004 to 1,594 in eleven states in 2005, with fatalities rising from 556 to 669, including 153 police personnel, up from 100 in the previous year. Espousing the demands of the marginalized sections of society, the Naxalite movement offered them an alternative system of governance that would free them from the clutches of the "exploiter" classes through the use of force.

The document described an official policy geared toward addressing "this menace simultaneously on political security, development and public perception management fronts in a holistic manner." It drew a strict red line. "There will be no peace dialogue by the affected states with the Naxalite groups unless the latter agree to give up violence and arms." It recommended Andhra Pradesh's surrender and a rehabilitation policy for Naxalites.[48] It offered funds to the affected states to modernize their police forces with improved weaponry, telecommunications systems, and mobility, and to fortify police stations in the Naxalite-influenced areas. It referred to the exemption that the Delhi government had given them from paying the cost of the deployment of the Central Armed Police Forces (CAPFs)[49] for three years, starting in 2004. It urged them to pay greater attention to developmental projects and job creation in the affected territories, with special focus on building roads, communications, and power, as well as schools and health clinics.[50]

But the Home Ministry itself had failed the test of applying the "holistic" approach in practice. Its status paper had been almost wholly devoted to the law-and-order aspect of the Naxalite insurgency. A similar pattern was on display when the ministry announced the formation of the special Naxal Management Division in October 2006. Dominated by senior police officers and security experts, the new division described its principal role as assisting state governments to create "operational infrastructure and logistics required to combat LWE [Left-Wing Extremism], with Maoists as the lead players." Crucially, it mentioned "media and public perception management." Nonetheless, the latest document gave flesh and blood to the abstractions in the status paper. The central government volunteered to contribute four-fifths of the Rs 20 million ($400,000) each for building or reinforcing the four hundred fortified police stations in the Left-Wing Extremism–affected districts, with the state government covering the rest.

Delhi spelled out a whole raft of fresh commitments. These included accelerating the modernization of state police forces; reimbursing the states for security-related expenditures; providing helicopters for anti-Naxalite operations; assisting in the training of state police through the Defense Ministry, the Central Police Organizations, and the Bureau of Police Research and Development; sharing intelligence; facilitating interstate coordination; and founding counterinsurgency and antiterrorism schools for state police.

In a bid to manipulate media and popular perception of Naxalites, the Naxal Management Division asserted that the Maoist insurgency doctrine glorified "violence as the primary means to overwhelm the existing socio-economic and political structures." In its initial phase, the PLGA had resorted to guerrilla warfare with the goal of "creating a vacuum at the grass-roots level of the existing governance structures" by killing petty civil servants, policemen, and members of panchayats. These acts were accompanied by strident propaganda against "the purported and real inadequacies of the existing state structure." Maoists had also set up many front organizations to facilitate mass mobilization in semi-urban and urban areas through "ostensibly democratic means," stated the Naxal Management Division. These organizations were often led by well-meaning intellectuals, who took up such issues as human rights violations by the security forces and made "fantastic claims" that got coverage in the mainstream media.

The rhetorical assertion by the government that the Naxalite insurgency was not simply a matter of law and order was at odds with its policies. In the critical section titled "Review and Monitoring Mechanisms," only one of the five listed items referred exclusively to "An Empowered Group of Officers, headed by the Member-Secretary Planning Commission, with officers from the development Ministries and the Planning Commission to oversee effective implementation of development schemes in the Left Wing Extremism–affected States."[51]

In its ongoing drive to shape public opinion, the Home Ministry placed advertisements in all national and regional newspapers that read "Naxals are nothing but cold-blooded murderers," illustrated with pictures of corpses of the people allegedly killed by them.[52] From then on, this ministry, as well as assorted security experts, maintained that Maoists no longer had a political ideology and were no more than a party of murderous extortionists who aimed to destabilize India and impede its economic development—the standard narrative dished out by governments worldwide when facing serious insurgency.

Counterpoint

On the opposite side, periodic, well-planned "swarming attacks" on police armories by the People's Liberation Guerrilla Army, backed by the People's Militia, continued. Between the first assault of this kind in February 2004 and early 2008, there were fifty such raids. The fear of Maoist attacks discouraged potential recruits to the police force.[53] As a result, the Left-Wing Extremism–affected states came to rely increasingly on the paramilitary contingents dispatched by Delhi. For instance, Chhattisgarh hosted nineteen Central Reserve Police Force battalions by 2007. The central government also sent senior police officers to the United States and Israel for training in counterinsurgency.

On February 15, 2008, PLGA guerrillas carried out an offensive in the tribal-majority Nayagarh in Orissa on an unprecedented scale. According to the official account, about 360 armed Maoist cadres—arriving in buses, cargo trucks, Jeeps, and motorcycles from two different directions—launched simultaneous raids on the district armory, the police training school armory, and the police stations of Nayagarh town (population: approximately sixty thousand), as well as three police outposts in the district. They did so after cutting off power supply and communications lines, and blocking all entries into the town. In their gun battles, they killed fifteen policemen. The insurgents reportedly decamped in five hijacked trucks and a bus, loaded down with 1,200 arms, including 900 rifles, 3 light machine guns, 20 AK-47s, and 70 self-loading rifles, as well as 100,000 bullets, from the armories and police stations.[54]

During their two-week clandestine trip to a Maoist-controlled zone in the Dandakaranya forest in January 2010, Gautam Navlakha, an Indian human-rights activist with the People's Union for Democratic Rights, and Jan Myrdal, a Swedish author and columnist, mentioned the Nayagarh episode during their interview with Ganapathi. The Maoist leader explained, "Military action was only one part of the operation. It was preceded by eight-to nine-month-long political work in the area. That is why it was code-named Operation Ropeway, enabling the Party to leap from Rayagada to other areas, close to the state capital of Bhubaneshwar. For months, party members infiltrated Nayagarh and worked among the people, recruiting some of them, and setting up a base. The political mobilization was more important than the military aspect of looting the police armory."

The bottom line was that the politburo viewed every military operation as helping to expand the Party's political reach. "Militarily, the action was considered less successful," continued Ganapathi. "Our reconnaissance overestimated the number of weapons in the armory. Instead of 1,200 weapons and 100,000 rounds of ammunition, there were no more than 400 to 500 weapons and 50,000 rounds of ammunition. Also, the raid was to have been carried out in the middle of night with the guerrillas escaping unseen. Instead, since the operation was completed in the early hours of the morning, the residents of Nayagarh, who had gathered outside the armory, saw the direction the fleeing guerrillas took. Due to the inadequate number of guerrillas they could carry only 300-plus weapons and 50,000 rounds of ammunition."[55]

There were significant differences in the two narratives. The official version inflated the number of the attackers as well as the targets they assaulted, thus implicitly rationalizing the security forces' failure to repel the attack. It also exaggerated the number of arms and ammunition seized by the Maoists. The tone of Ganapathi's version was far from triumphant. Indeed, it contained self-criticism. His version incidentally provided evidence that, after each raid, the planners analyzed the actual performance to learn from the experience and make their future projects more efficient. As for the figures, Ganapathi's statements about the size of the guerrilla force (an "inadequate number") and the arms haul were more reliable than those announced by the government. Finally, the Maoist leader articulated a fundamental tenet: that armed operations were subservient to the overarching political aims. This contradicted the official propaganda about the party.

"We cannot afford to strike at will and be reckless," a party spokesman told Navlakha and Myrdal. "We generally avoid engaging the enemy unless we are prepared. Also we believe in focusing on such attacks that can get us weapons." He added that the party always owned up to their actions, even if they went "bad" for it. "We are in a period of strategic defense."[56] This dovetailed with the statement of a top bureaucrat at the Home Ministry, Gopal K. Pillai, in March 2010. "Maoists are not fully prepared to face the onslaught of the state machinery," he said. "So they would rather go very slowly."[57]

Globalizing Indian Corporations' Mineral Rush

As explained in chapter 2, the main commercial advantage that Tata Steel had over the far bigger Corus Plc—operating steel plants in Britain, France, and Holland—was its access to reliable, domestic sources of iron ore at low prices. Once it acquired Corus in 2007, Tata launched a concerted drive to enlarge its ownership of the iron-ore-rich land in Chhattisgarh, Jharkhand, and Orissa, and Tata Steel acquired vast tracts in Lohandiguda in Jagdalpur district and Jindal Steel and Power in Bhansi in Dantewada district. A similar push was made by Essar Steel after its purchase of Canada's second-largest steelmaker, Algoma Steel, for $1.6 billion.

These domestic steel giants, along with foreign multinationals—ArcelorMittal, De Beers of South Africa, Rio Tinto, and others—pressured the Indian government to liberalize its mining policy further by introducing seamless transfer from reconnaissance to prospecting and finally to mining, and by amending the strict provisions of the Environmental Protection Act of 1986.

The result was the revised National Mineral Policy, published in April 2008. It emphasized the need for "scientific prospecting and state-of the-art technology." It recommended relaxing the regulatory mechanism to "make it more conducive to investment and technology flows." At the same time, it proposed "a framework for sustainable development" and paid lip service to the protection of the interests of the "host and indigenous (tribal) population . . . through comprehensive relief and rehabilitation." But this had to be done in the wider context of the "efficiency" of the sector (meaning higher profits for the mining companies) and enhanced sources of revenue for the states. By making environmental regulations voluntary under the rubric of a "Sustainable Development Framework," the revised policy privatized environmental and social regulations in mining through the back door.[58] In short, it aimed to promote privately owned, large-scale, mechanized mines, and if they were controlled by the multinational corporations, domestic or foreign, so much the better. Among other things, it encouraged Lakshmi Mittal of ArcelorMittal to press ahead with his plans to invest Rs 1,000 billion ($24 billion) to extract iron ore in Jharkhand and Orissa as raw material for two steel mills to produce 24 million metric tons of the end-product.

In mid-May 2008, the Adivasis gave their verdict on the National Mineral Policy. More than five thousand Adivasi from twenty-five settlements gathered in the Faraspal village of Dantewada district to object to the mining of iron ore from the Bailadila mountain range. They claimed that the government had granted mining leases in this area to ninety-six industrial houses, besides Tata Steel and Essar Steel. Adivasi leaders demanded that the mountain—twenty-five miles long and six miles wide, containing over 2,300 million metric tons of iron ore—should not be leased to private companies for mining, since they were insensitive to the environment and tribal culture.[59] Though the rally and the march were organized by the Adivasi Mahasabha (Hindi: Great Assembly), a front organization of the legal

Communist Party of India, its demand was ignored by the state and central governments.

So too was a report titled "Development Challenges in Extremist Affected Areas," submitted to the Planning Commission in April 2008.

> An official database of persons displaced/affected by [development] projects is not available. However, some unofficial studies, particularly by Dr. Walter Fernandes, peg this figure at around 60 million for the period from 1947 to 2004, involving 25 million hectares which includes 7 million hectares of forest and 6 million hectares of other Common Property Resources. Whereas the tribals constitute 8.08 percent of country's population, they are 40 percent of the total displaced/affected persons by the projects. . . . Only a third of the displaced persons of planned development have been resettled.[60]

On the nature of the Naxalite movement, the authors of this report differed from the official assessment and policy. "Though its professed long term ideology is capturing state power by force, in its day-to-day manifestation it is to be looked upon as basically a fight for social justice, equality, protection and local development," they observed. "The two have to be seen together without overplaying the former." They also took issue with the 2006 status paper of the Indian government. "Clause 4 (v) of the Status Paper states that 'there will be no peace dialogue by the affected States with the Naxal groups unless the latter agree to give up violence and arms'. This is incomprehensible and is inconsistent with the Government's stand vis-à-vis other militant groups in the country."[61]

While mouthing its mantra of "holistic approach" to curb the Naxalite rebellion, the state and central governments failed to overcome their egregious failures on the development and ameliorative fronts while accelerating their plans to parcel out resource-rich land to Indian and foreign multinationals. Therefore, as before, Chhattisgarh and Jharkhand, endowed with vast amounts of natural resources, accounted for two-thirds of the Maoist violence in the country in 2008. The party's activities in the neighboring districts of Orissa, containing untapped minerals, increased as well.

Following the sixty-hour-long attacks in Mumbai by terrorists from Pakistan on November 26, 2008, the inept Patil resigned as home minister. Prime Minister Singh replaced him with sixty-three-year-old Palaniappan Chidambaram, known to be competent. Born into a rich family in Tamil Nadu, he had capped his undergraduate degrees in science and law with an MBA from Harvard Business School. Later, as a lawyer, he represented in court the London-based Vedanta Resources, engaged in India's aluminum industry, and the notorious Houston-based Enron International, which went bankrupt in 2001.

As home minister he prioritized "wiping out the Naxalite menace." He discovered that in the past there had been lack of coordination between the central and state authorities to decimate Naxalites. So in February 2009 he consulted the affected states on forging a common strategy. In the parliamentary poll of May 2009 he was reappointed home minister (and served in this position until a cabinet reshuffle in July 2012 returned him to the Finance Ministry).[62] Coordination between the national and state capitals to eliminate the Maoist threat improved. But the anticipated success eluded the authorities. Indeed, Maoists attacks on the police, paramilitary troopers, and venal forest officers rose to a record 2,240 in 2009, with Chhattisgarh and Jharkhand being the most affected.

In September 2009, addressing the states' police chiefs in Delhi, Prime Minister Singh deplored the lack of progress in curbing the Maoist rebellion. He conceded that Maoists had growing appeal among a large section of Indian society, including tribal communities, the rural poor, as well as sections of the intelligentsia and the youth. "Dealing with left-wing extremism requires a nuanced strategy—a holistic approach," he added. "It cannot be treated simply as a law and order problem."[63]

The Police on the Ground

State police and the Center's armed paramilitaries had little time or inclination for nuance. Overall, the police force in India functioned as an oppressive instrument of the state—a legacy of the British imperialist rule in the subcontinent—and not as a benevolent agency to serve the community. Even in normal times in cities, police acted as corrupt racketeers working hand in glove with crime syndicates at best, and as extortionists at worst, refusing to register complaints without a bribe. Charged with wiping out the Naxalite contagion in rural areas, they, as well as Central Reserve Police Force troopers, routinely tortured suspects and frequently resorted to extrajudicial killings, attributing them to fake "encounters" with the militants.

During combat with the Maoists, the state police and CRPF most feared improvised explosive devices (IEDs). An IED would be hidden under a road surface and detonated with a remote control to immobilize the security forces. After inserting nails, ball bearings, nuts, and bolts into several kilograms of explosives packed into a bucket, the guerrillas covered the device with poly-thene to keep it dry then buried it in the road, with its wires leading to a battery in a hideout, and used a camera flash-gun to connect the wires. To ensure that the IED exploded at the right moment, they hung a piece of cloth from a tree branch to signal the approach of an enemy vehicle. When the cloth shook becuase of the sound of the engine, they connected the wires, and the IED exploded to lethal effect.

By breaking up access roads, or blocking them with felled tees, Maoists kept the security forces away from the tribal settlements that they controlled. If a convoy of vehicles carrying police and paramilitaries managed to cir-cumvent these obstacles, it faced the prospect of encountering the deadly IEDs. If they survived these challenges, the vehicle-borne security forces had to disembark to engage the enemy in an absolutely unfamiliar terrain. When faced with a superior force, the armed rebels invoked Chairman Mao Zedong's guideline about guerrilla warfare: maintain mobility in a familiar terrain, and thus keep the enemy, unfamiliar with the terrain, guessing about your latest position. Small wonder, the security forces' forays into the guerrilla zones had to be brief. In the Saranda forest region, for instance, they normally engaged the armed insurgents for about half an hour or so, then withdrew.

Their successive failures to hold the ground and set up camps inside the Maoist-ruled enclaves went down badly with their political masters. Added pressure brought to surface the simmering grievances that police command-ers had been nursing for some years. "Our policemen have to cope with the jungle, the hills, the lakes and the waterfalls when they go on Naxalite op-erations," said an unnamed police commander in Jharkhand to Mark Tully, an India-based British journalist, in 2010. "They are on duty for twenty-four hours. There are no living arrangements, so many policemen get malaria and other diseases from insects and lack of clean drinking water. There are also food problems; they don't get food on time. Many are left in the jungle or in the hills for six months at a time. Some bulletproof cars came, which could be pierced by the bullet of a Lee-Enfield rifle, and some wireless equipment was bought which was useless. It had to be thrown away. It could not be re-paired."[64] A police officer of a higher rank in Jharkhand—who later spoke to Tully—faulted the strategy of pressing the security forces into a fight, when the media was better informed than the Intelligence Bureau in Delhi.[65]

The fate of those posted at the fortified outposts in a Maoist-controlled area was unenviable. "It is an open jail for us," lamented Ajay Bhushari, the commanding officer in the village of Laheri in Gadchiroli district, adjoining Abujhmad. "Either we are sitting here or we are on patrol. There is nothing else."[66] But the federal government had provided extra funds to the affected states to increase the size of their police forces and improve their equipment, so that is what they did.

The basic problem was the failure of the security forces' officers to comprehend the issues that fueled the Maoist insurgency: grossly skewed ownership of land, large-scale evictions of Adivasis, lack of access to forest products (in violation of the national law), and above all the corrupt nexus between the police, local contractors, and politicians who were committed to implementing "development" on the back of broken promises, deprivation, and disempowerment of the tribal people. A blatant example of the unholy alliance between corrupt officials and loggers was the impunity with which the latter continued to violate the 1995 Supreme Court ruling outlawing deforestation.

This fundamental lack of understanding pervaded in the highest ranks of the state police and the CRPF. Having conceded that about one-fifth of Jharkhand had "a good presence" of Maoists, Raj Kumar Mallick, the police inspector general in charge of anti-Maoist operations, claimed that a mere 1 to 2 percent of Adivasis liked the Maoists, and that the source of their support was "fear of the gun." He estimated the strength of the Maoist armed squads and the PLGA at a mere two thousand people, yet three anti-Maoist operations launched by him, along with CRPF troopers, during the second half of 2010 had failed to flush out the militants.[67]

Operation Green Hunt

Having advocated "a nuanced approach" in September 2009, Prime Minister Singh gave the go-ahead to the Home Ministry's belligerent anti-Maoist campaign, code-named Operation Green Hunt, a month later.[68] The objective of the planned "massive and coordinated operations" by the central and state governments was to expel the Naxalites from more populous areas into the forests and hills, and ring-fence them as a prelude to wiping them out.

But Home Minister Chidambaram claimed that no such operation or code name existed. His statement was echoed by top officials in the state capitals. This was a deliberate ploy used to control information that might leak to

Maoist leaders. More seriously, this stance was adopted because, without saying so publicly, government leaders intended the anti-Maoist offensive to be a long-term, open-ended confrontation—not a sharp, quick operation. In a way, the government unveiled its own "long march" to counter the rebels' much-vaunted long march. Meanwhile, officials were content to describe the forthcoming upsurge in the security forces' activities as "police action" to restore civil administration in the districts where it had ceased to exist.

The anti-Maoist offensive, which started in the Gadchiroli district of eastern Maharashtra, abutting Andhra Pradesh and Chhattisgarh on two sides, was modeled on the offensives that the authorities had so far conducted in the small states along foreign borders in northeastern India and in Kashmir. The security forces were equipped with weaponry ranging from self-loading rifles with night-vision capability to helicopter gunships. The strategy was to seal off a certain area of the forest and carry out a combing operation with the cooperation of young, armed Adivasis, appointed earlier as Special Police Officers, and engage in "encounters" with the Maoist guerrillas. As a preamble, the Chhattisgarh government started harassing human rights organizations, and even demolished a nonviolent Gandhian ashram. Burning down Adivasi settlements that were considered Maoist strongholds became an integral part of the strategy.

The police forces of the selected states totaled 100,000 officers (one hundred battalions) and were backed by 75,000 heavily armed officers from the Central Armed Police Forces—two-thirds of whom were from the CRPF. They were assisted by the military, which deployed its helicopters for aerial surveillance and to ferry security forces in and out of the combat zone. In the five districts of the Bastar region in Chhattisgarh, the size of the security forces expanded from 45,000 before Operation Green Hunt to 60,000 in 2010, and then to 80,000 the following year.[69]

To justify the deployment of a force of this order, the governments exaggerated the size of the territory under Maoist control or influence. Even a single assault registered as "Naxalite/Maoist" by a police station in one of India's 625 districts was considered enough to describe the territory as "affected" by Naxalites. This gave a grossly inflated figure of 223 affected districts, occupying two-fifths of the country. It was left to state governments to grade a Naxalite-affected district as "strongly affected" (where security forces were unable to enter or set up camps) or "marginally affected" (where front organizations of the Maoist party could hold public meetings), with the rest categorized as "moderately affected." Whatever the degree of Maoist influence, an affected district entitled its state administration to claim a grant from Delhi to counter the threat. Therefore, state capitals had a vested interest in exaggerating the total. In reality, though, according to Navlakha, less than one-tenth of India's districts were affected by Maoists to varying degrees: "very strongly" in ten districts, "moderately" in another twenty-four, and "marginally" in another twenty-five, to the point of being able to hold big rallies sponsored by their front organizations.[70] The authorities mounted counterinsurgency Operation Green Hunt in thirty-four districts, focusing first on the ten most strongly affected.

The security forces started regulating inward and outward movement of residents in these districts. Every inhabitant was required to carry an identity card signed by the police superintendent. Weekly markets were moved to local security camps. Those picking up their rations had to register and provide a list of family members who needed rations, one week at a time, to ensure they did not purchase extra provisions for Maoists. Despite this, and their vastly increased numbers and firepower, the security forces faced an arduous task to uproot Maoists from their bases. The principal reason why this assignment was so formidable was how the Maoists administered their liberated enclaves.

Life in a Maoist Zone

Of the 15,450 square miles controlled by Maoists, incorporating about four thousand villages, a contiguous area of 11,600 square miles in the Dandakaranya forest region—with a population of 2 to 2.5 million—was administered by the People's Government, known locally as the Janatana Sarkar.[71] The second-largest contiguous area was in the Saranda forest in Orissa.

In the Maoist-controlled rural India, an elected Revolutionary Peoples' Committee (RPC) ruled three to five villages, containing 1,500 to 3,000 households. Each elected RPC had a standing committee of the president, the vice president, the financial head, and the defense head.[72] Fifteen such committees constituted one Area RPC (ARPC), with three to five ARPCs forming one Division. By 2010 the Janatana Sarkar had redistributed 300,000 acres of land, giving six acres each to a family and another three acres for homestead. Hence the typical statement by an Adivasi in a liberated zone: "Before the Naxalites I had nothing. Now I have six acres."[73] In an agrarian society, land ownership means more than the principal means of livelihood, since it also confers a social status above that of the landless. Investing the previously landless with land ownership was the ultimate source of the Maoist strength in rural India.

An armed squad of eight to twelve party cadres, called a *dalam*, visited a village and stayed for two days in plastic tents outside the settlement, but never twice in the same spot. (Sometimes PLGA personnel rotated as armed party cadres.) Among other things they supervised the front organizations. In their outposts, they displayed pictures of Chairman Mao Zedong, Charu Mazumdar, and Kanai Chatterjee, leader of the MCC. They followed strictly Mao's dictum that guerrillas must never take anything from villagers, so they traveled with their own supplies. When they bought them at the weekly market they shared the carrying of provisions.

They rose at five a.m. After morning tea, they did physical exercise for half an hour, and then maneuvered their guns vertically and horizontally. After breakfast of *khichri* (rice and linseeds) mixed with peanuts, and more tea, they went to the village and performed different tasks, from helping peasants with plowing to digging irrigation ditches and tanks and giving simple medicines to the sick. They discouraged drinking but did not interfere with the brewing of traditional alcoholic drinks from *mahua* (*madhuca longifolia*) flowers. They did not smoke and actively discouraged smoking.[74]

The party ran mobile schools lasting two to four weeks. The teacher-student ratio was 1:10. The curriculum included basic math, history, government, and primary instruction in healthcare, with focus on malaria, the most common disease. The educational system tried to undermine the unscientific tribal beliefs about the universe and evolution by focusing on daily events and offering scientific evidence. In addition, the party ran a Basic Communist Training School, where a selected group of twenty-five to thirty pupils in their early teens went through a six-month crash course in the basic tenets of Marxism-Leninism and Maoism, Hindi, English, math, and social science, as well as lessons on computers and the handling of different weapons. The Education Department had transcribed Gondi, a spoken language, in the Devnagri script used for Hindi. Where possible, it conducted adult literacy classes. If there were government schools in the Maoist enclaves, the party kept them intact. It allowed the teachers to go to the district capital to collect their salaries.

To improve the lot of Adivasi women, the party founded the Krantikari Adivasi Mahila Sanghatana (Hindi: Adivasi Women's Revolutionary Union), which was committed to bringing about gender equality. By tradition, tribal women were excluded from sharing landed property, and married women were barred from moving from one village to another. But the Agriculture Department of the Janatana Sarkar issued title deeds for land in the name of the family instead of the male householder. Women constituted two-fifths of the party's membership. They were to be seen not only in the administrative arm of the Janatana Sarkar, which ruled according to a written constitution, but also in the People's Militia and the People's Liberation Guerrilla Army. Many PLGA platoons were commanded by women. And men and women shared equally such tasks as cooking and collecting firewood and water.

Historically, the PLGA expanded in parallel with the rise of the civil administration, with a single division backed by one PLGA company of 100 to 125 personnel. The first such arrangement was devised in March 2007. The next step was to form zonal governments, to be backed up by a battalion (600 to 1,000 strong). That happened in August 2009, two months before the government launched Operation Green Hunt.[75] The total strength of the PLGA nationwide was estimated at 10,000 to 12,000 people. They were armed with 20,000 rifles, a few hundred AK-47s, a few scores of two-inch mortars, an unknown number of grenade launchers, and caches of explosives. They were backed by the approximately 80,000-strong People's Militia, who were the eyes and ears of the movement and the PLGA. Two out of five militia members were women.[76]

The unsalaried but uniformed guerrillas received food, clothing, and other basic items for personal use. Each guerrilla was given three changes of uniform, toilet soap, toothpaste, washing soap, gunpowder, and a bow and arrows. They either moved in squads (five to seven people) or in platoon-size groups (twenty to twenty-five people). If a guerrilla was injured or killed, the Janatana Sarkar looked after his or her family. They each traveled with a backpack stuffed with weapons, ammunition, rations, books, notebooks, and other kit, weighing forty-five to fifty-five pounds. Their literary collection invariably included Mao Zedong's "little red book" in Hindi. The political education of PLGA volunteers consisted of basic Marxism, means and modes of production, and the role of labor in production. They also read avidly the magazines published by the Janatana Sarkar. Each of the Janatana Sarkar's eight divisions published its own magazine in Gondi or Koyam. Their titles ranged from *Rebellion*, *Earthquake*, and *Thunder* to *Sun* and *Fireplace*.[77] They also read out-of-date newspapers and magazines in Hindi. Their two main meals consisted of rice with lentils and vegetables. Chicken or fish was served once a week.[78]

For ammunition, People's Militia members used the gunpowder pellets that the tribal men deployed for hunting boars. They were also trained to produce small pressure bombs and booby traps. The Militia, consisting of a wide network, was part of the Maoists' intelligence apparatus. Within it there were party cells of two or three members.

There was one radio for three PLGA personnel. Every company was equipped with solar panels to power lights, computers, and TV sets. TV programs and debates were downloaded from YouTube and copied and circulated among companies. Lights helped guerrillas to read books, which were downloaded from the Internet when they had access to it. For news broadcasts they turned to the BBC News in Hindi. They monitored local radio news for negative reporting. For entertainment, they tuned into a radio program that aired Bollywood songs in Hindi requested by Indian soldiers. If and when they watched TV, they stuck strictly to news.

When a senior party member visited a camp he brought along a laptop that was used to show movies, according to Navlakha, whose report "Days and Nights in the Heartland of Rebellion" contains a multifaceted description of a Maoist-administered enclave. The DVD collection included Bimal Roy's *Do Bigha Zamin* (Hindi: Two Bighas of Land; 1953), a heartrending tale of a Bengali peasant's struggle to hang on to his patch of agricultural land; Gillo Pontecorvo's *The Battle of Algiers* (1965), a thrilling yet realistic reconstruction of the successful armed struggle of nationalist Algerians against imperialist France; *The Long March: The Red Army Story*, a two-and-a-half-hour documentary in Chinese with English subtitles; and Harry Dunham's *China Strikes Back* (1937), a twenty-three-minute documentary of the Chinese response to Japan's aggression, with the Red Army advancing through a village outside the liberated zone of Yenan, and including scenes from the liberated areas. Someone sitting next to the laptop gave a summary in Hindi of what was being said in the film. Among contemporary Bollywood movies, Ketan Mehta's *Mangal Pandey* (2005) and Rakeysh Omprakash Mehra's *Rang de Basanti* (Hindi: Colors of Spring; 2006) were favorites.[79]

As part of its propaganda, the party periodically distributed leaflets and pamphlets either appealing to the unemployed youth to join the PLGA or to the security forces to refrain from killing, looting, raping, and making illegal arrests of ordinary peasants and workers in order to turn over the region's mineral wealth to Indian and foreign multinationals. The authors of these pamphlets argued that it was in the context of such instances of gross injustice that Maoist guerrillas used land mines and attacked the police and paramilitaries.

The Judicial Department of the Janatana Sarkar settled disputes on the basis of "class line and mass line." In land disputes between family members, it followed the principle of equality between brothers and sisters, thus deviating from the Adivasi tradition of giving a bigger share to the eldest brother and depriving women of property rights. In the event of a dispute or minor crime, the Justice Department called a meeting of the whole village. Each side presented its case, then there was a vote and the majority decided the verdict. Those accused of serious crimes were tried by judges, with the verdict issued according to a majority vote. The guilty were then sent to labor camps where they were reformed through political education. Capital punishment was applied only for "counterrevolutionary crimes," the principal one being assisting security forces to stage an ambush that resulted in deaths. It was imposed only on hardened informers who had failed to heed repeated warnings. Capital punishment had to be endorsed by the zonal Janatana Sarkar.

To run the Janatana Sarkar required funding. One source was contributions from sympathizers, made in the form of voluntary labor when they donated one day's earnings to the party every year. Another source was the tax that the party levied on the mining corporations. This was mostly collected from those contractors who supplied goods and services to these companies.[80] Another source was the levy that Maoists specified for all those engaged in the construction and maintenance of infrastructure: 5 to 10 percent of the cost of road building, and 5 percent of railway work. Each coal truck paid Rs 1,000 for safe passage.[81] In 2010, between 50 to 60 percent of the coal-rich area in Jharkhand was in the Naxalite belt.[82] Jarkhand had the distinction of being a state where almost half of the raw materials were extracted illegally.[83]

Those mining corporations that refused to pay suffered costly sabotage. This was the fate of the processing plant of Essar Steel in Chhattisgarh when, in May 2009, Maoists blew up its 170-mile underground pipeline used to transport slurry saturated with iron ore from the Bailadila complex to Visakhapatnam port, passing through the Naxalite stronghold of Malkangiri district in Orissa. The underground pipeline, built in 2005, was marked by five-foot poles with yellow circular orbits painted with an emergency phone number and the logo of Essar. Its use reduced the cost of transporting one metric ton of ore from Rs 550 ($11) to Rs 80 ($1.60). Between 2005 and 2009, Maoists blasted the pipeline fifteen times.

In May 2009, they damaged Essar's plant at Chitrakonda, where the corporation pumped water from Sileru River to flush the pipeline. Gudsa Usendi, spokesperson for the Maoist Dandakaranya Special Zonal Committee, explained that they blasted the pipeline because it was draining natural resources. By the time Essar had repaired the pipeline in December 2010, it claimed to have lost Rs 18 billion ($360 million).[84] It was estimated that 70 percent of India's iron ore was in the Maoist-infiltrated areas then.[85] "Once or twice a year Naxalites blow up the long conveyors transporting the area's iron ore," said Vinod Singh in Dantewada. "This is done to show that they are around. It helps them to raise funds."[86]

Along with its Operation Green Hunt, the Indian government launched a propaganda campaign. It published inflated statistics about the threat that Maoists posed to the security forces and the vast amount of cash they extorted. This figure varied between Rs 1.4 billion ($280 million) and Rs 2 billion ($400 million) a year collected through "drugs and extortion." These figures were then treated as hard fact in the mainstream media by journalists and security experts.[87] According to the Indian intelligence sources, Naxalites charged duty from interstate transporting and bus companies and collected levies from construction contractors and tendu-leaf traders, as well as mining and metallurgical corporations.[88]

A party spokesman considered even Rs 1.4 billion ($280 million) an inflated figure. "If we had so much we would be able to do much more," he told Navlakha and Myrdal in January 2010. Most of the cash was collected in the form of "royalty" on the tendu leaves, bamboo, tamarind, and other forest produce, he explained. The party taxed some of the companies or contractors operating in the guerrilla zones. The estimates by nonpartisan experts on the Maoist movement ran around two-fifths to half of the sums provided by the government.

The information collected by Navlakha about the budget of a Maoist enclave administered by an ARPC with three-thousand-plus households belied the claims made by the officials. For 2009, the income, including a grant of Rs 500,000 ($10,000) by the Janatana Sarkar to maintain the PLGA, was Rs 1,001,000 ($20,000); the expenditure was Rs 822,185 ($16,400). The tax on contractors brought in Rs 360,000 ($7,200), and donations through work days and one day's wage amounted to Rs 250,000 ($5,000). On the expenditure side, agriculture consumed Rs 140,250 ($2,800); healthcare, Rs 100,000 ($2,000); education, Rs 10,000 ($200); trade, Rs 60,000 ($1,200); and public relations, Rs 5,000 ($100).[89]

As part of his drive to mold public opinion in the government's favor, Home Minister Palaniappan Chidambaram mounted a peace initiative. He offered that if Naxalite leaders decided to "abjure violence," then within seventy-two hours he would be ready to talk to them. He stressed that he was softening the earlier demand of the government to "abjure violence and arms." But his gesture was ill-considered.[90] Given the inaccessible areas in which guerrillas operated, and the complicated means the politburo deployed to communicate with the rank and file, the time frame of three days was grossly unrealistic.

In the final analysis, however, the core of conflict between the two sides was the future of the vital mining industry and the neoliberal economic development model that successive governments in Delhi had followed since 1991.

The Crux of the Conflict

The CPI (Maoist) was vehemently opposed to the granting of mining leases to multinational corporations, whether indigenous or foreign—all the more so when they were exporting minerals instead of shoring up domestic industries. It also advocated strict regulation and restrictions, and greater emphasis on preserving the ecosystem. The party was not against industrialization per se, but it was uncompromisingly opposed to big industries and business houses. It favored giving priority to processing forest produce—such as tamarind, bamboo, and wood—into high-value products, thus eliminating the parasitical nontribal contractors and middlemen who had been gaining the most out of forest produce.

"The tribals are convinced that [government] development is introduced to quash resistance and to take away land for mining," explained Jagesh, chief of the northern regional command of the CPI (Maoist) in Chhattisgarh, to a BBC correspondent during his clandestine visit to a guerrilla zone. "We have managed to impart this education."[91]

In an interview to the Delhi-based *Tehelka* magazine on the first anniversary of the Mumbai attacks, Home Minister Chidambaram presented the official viewpoint. "Mineral wealth is wealth that must be harvested and used for the people," he said. "Do you want the tribals to remain hunters and gatherers? Are we trying to preserve them in some sort of anthropological museum? Yes, we can allow the minerals to remain in the ground for another

10,000 years, but will that bring development to these people? We can respect the fact that they worship the Niyamgirhi hill, but will that put shoes on their feet or their children in school? Will that solve the fact they are severely malnutritioned and have no access to health care?"[92]

Chidambaram's interviewer, Shoma Chaudhury, pointed out, "History had very few examples to show the local communities benefited from mining." Chidambaram retorted by referring to Neyveli in Tamil Nadu and Jamshedpur in Jharkhand, with the latter's history dating back to 1907. But in India, 60 percent of the top fifty mineral-producing districts were among the 150 most backward in terms of human and social indicators, according to the National Sample Survey Office of the Indian government's Ministry of Statistics. The resource-rich West Singhbhum district in Jharkhand, where two out of three inhabitants were Adivasi, was a case in point. It was the state's most mined district of the past few decades and accounted for almost its entire iron ore output. Yet nearly half of its population lived below the official poverty line.[93]

An insight into how business was done in resource-rich Chhattisgarh was provided by Pavan Dubey, a veteran journalist. "MOUs between the state government and large companies are signed in the name of industrialization, but their contents are kept secret," he said. "There is no transparency in the present system. The National Mineral Development Corporation, set up in 1958 in Hyderabad, began exploring the Bailadila mountain range in the 1960s, and started mining iron ore at Bacheli in 1968. At this site, 70 percent of the employees are Adivasis, but mostly unskilled labor. This mining facility and the one at Kirandul have not helped the surrounding tribal area to develop economically or socially. Those who benefit from iron mining and refining are the outsiders, the nontribals. Only in the past two or three years the idea of the corporate social responsibility[94] has come up."[95]

The iron mines are at the highest peak of Bailadila, around the village of Akash Nagar (Hindi: Sky Town) at the end of a fifteen-mile ascending road of stomach-churning hairpins from the Bacheli Township, built behind high compound walls twenty miles from Dantewada. It is at Akash Nagar that the mountainside is loosened by controlled explosions, and iron ore shipped out by conveyor belts, largely to Visakhapatnam port, for export to Japan.

Halfway to the Bacheli Township from Dantewada, I noticed a small feeder road broken up by a deep ditch, an unmistakable sign that beyond the trench was a guerrilla zone of Maoists. The signboard outside the township read

OPENED IN 1977. When my driver Das and I got past the lightly guarded entrance gate, we saw a small shopping center that included a computer shop and an open-air vegetable stall run by an Adivasi woman. Quite near was the fenced playground for children and young students. This township of fifteen thousand had two schools and a hospital. "We don't have any good hospital in a radius of 400 kms [250 miles]," said Ravi Sekhar Rao, chief administrator of the National Mineral Development Corporation Apollo Hospital. "So, in case of emergency, patients either have to go to Raipur or Hyderabad. That's why we always keep ourselves prepared with all necessary facilities."[96] But these facilities were for the residents of the township where Adivasis, being mostly manual laborers, were an insignificant minority.

The current situation in the mining sector was described to Chidambaram by the journalist Chaudhury of *Tehelka* magazine thus: "Our mining is not need-based. It is market based. Tribals are being evacuated from ancestral land without being made stakeholders in these projects. No CSR clauses are being worked into mining leases." She then asked the minister, "What do *you* think is the blueprint for more equitable and sustainable mining?"

Chidambaram replied, "Every single concern you have mentioned is already accommodated under the present law. No one can mine unless a mining plan is approved by a competent authority. How much you can mine, how you'll restore the land, how much you'll be taxed, all these things are stipulated and worked out. There's nothing wrong with the mining plan itself. *The point is we don't enforce what we lay down.* People get away with impunity by cheating or bribing or violating the plan because the executive is weak."[97] (The emphasis is mine.)

It was not that the executive in general was weak. On the ground, the executive, either knowingly or otherwise, worked against the law or bent it to favor mining interests. The following example was typical. In 2005, the BJP government in Chhattisgarh signed an MOU with Tata Steel for a steel plant in the Lohandiguda area of Jagdalpur district to produce 5.5 million metric tons of steel a year. It required the acquisition of two thousand hectares of land by Tata Steel, 30 percent of which was owned by 1,700 Adivasis, the rest by the state government. As required by the law, Tata Steel and the District Collector organized a public hearing on the environmental impact assessment in October 2009. The company official pledged to invest 10 percent of the total budget of Rs 195 billion ($3.9 billion) into environmental protection and conservation, without offering any outline of the restoration plan. In October 2010, the District Collector called a public hearing at his headquarters in Jagdalpur to sound out the 3,200 householders in the ten villages to be affected by the project. He later announced that it received overwhelming approval.

But the villagers, interviewed by a correspondent of the Chennai-based *Frontline* magazine, claimed that both meetings were stage-managed. Those attending were contractors, real estate agents and their employees, and others from Jagdalpur, while the Adivasi villagers were pressured to stay away. In retaliation, in November 2010, they held a rival meeting in the settlement of Badanje. They rejected the project unanimously. They mailed the minutes of the meeting to the Minister for Environment and Forests in Delhi. They got no response. Instead, they experienced police harassment in the form of false accusations leveled at about one hundred protesting Adivasis, with some of them ending up in jail.

In March 2012, the central government gave the final go-ahead to Tata Steel by approving the forest clearance. But District Collector Anbalagan Ponnusamy failed to inform the Adivasi landholders who stood to lose their fertile agricultural land. It was left to Purnima Tripathi of *Frontline* to convey to them the depressing news in April.[98] Meanwhile, Operation Green Hunt was not progressing as Chidambaram had anticipated.

Hawks and Doves in Delhi

While Chhattisgarh, Andhra Pradesh, and Maharashtra cooperated with Delhi in its onslaught against Maoists, the non-Congress governments in Jharkhand and West Bengal dragged their feet. Chidambaram lost patience. He resorted to using the media to compel these states to fall in line. "Even though we are putting in pressure in Chhattisgarh, Jharkhand has now become a loose end and hence Naxalites easily enter the state when they are under attack," a Home Ministry source told the Press Trust of India in February 2010. "The same goes for West Bengal."[99]

This tactic worked. On March 10, the Jharkhand government joined Operation Green Hunt. Following the general pattern, the security forces set up camps in schools. They supervised local weekly markets to ensure nobody bought more than their weekly needs, in order to deprive the Maoist cadres of their provisions. The security forces' strategy of encircling rural settlements to carry out combing operations meant that many local Adivasis were unable to collect the forest produce on which their livelihood depended.[100]

Three weeks later, seven thousand Adivasis, led by the Kanda Reddy Un-nayan Sangha (Hindi: Kanda Reddy Uplifting Union), staged a protest march and rally against Operation Green Hunt outside the district headquarters in Malkangiri. Their petition stated that the tribal people were the worst affected by the anti-Maoist campaign, as they were prevented from entering the forest to gather produce. They demanded clean drinking water and healthcare for the villagers. Collector R. Vineel Krishna promised to consider the petition.[101] This was a routine response; it meant nothing in practice.

What mattered were the words of Chidambaram. "We are determined to uproot Naxals," he declared on April 5, 2010. "Only because we were toler-ant over the past ten to twelve years we've got this big task now. The Centre is firm, the Prime Minister Manmohan Singh and [Congress President] Sonia Gandhi are firm." He went on to assert that, "There is no place for naxalism and terrorism in India. . . . Till we have the last drop of blood in our body, we will aggressively fight against terrorism and Naxalism and assure you that we would bring them totally under control in two or three years."[102]

Chidambaram's first statement failed to acknowledge the vast change in the political economy of India wrought by the New Economic Policy and glo-balization in which, as the finance minister during 2004–8, he had played a prominent role. He was unashamedly pro-business. It was the commitment of the successive governments in Delhi to the neoliberal orthodoxy that had led local and foreign multinational corporations to rush to extract minerals in the largely Adivasi-inhabited areas, thus fanning the Maoist movement, which was fiercely antagonistic toward this development model.

His second statement contradicted what the most senior bureaucrat in his ministry, Gopal K. Pillai, had told a symposium in Delhi a month earlier. Even though the joint anti-Naxal operations were ongoing, he conceded that "the Naxals have not suffered any significant reverses so far, and the govern-ment would need seven to eight years to have full control over the areas which were lost to the Maoists."[103]

In response to Chidambaram's iron-fist policy, the Maoist Central Com-mittee launched its Tactical Counter Offensive Campaigns. These operations reached an apex on April 6, 2010. On that day, a CRPF company on patrol in a grassy area near Chintalnar village in Dantewada district faced gunfire from Maoist insurgents. As its members fell to the ground to fire back, they triggered booby traps hidden in the grass.[104] As a result of this Maoist ploy and the subsequent firefight that ensued, seventy-six troopers lay dead and another fifty were injured. It was the Maoists' bloodiest assault on the security forces so far. Chidambaram described the event as a dramatic illustration of Maoists' "brutality and savagery." The government honored the dead paramilitaries as if they were army soldiers dying in a conventional war.[105] Gopal, a top Maoist leader, called the attack "a direct consequence" of the government's Operation Green Hunt offensive, which, in his estimation, had resulted in the deaths of 129 Adivasis between June 2009 and April 5, 2010.

The Maoist operations continued. On May 17, a land mine planted by the rebels blew up a bus on a highway, killing forty-four people, including twenty-five Special Police Officers. Toward the end of June, the insurgents killed twenty-six CRPF troopers in the Narayanpur district of Chhattisgarh.

While Maoist politburo leader Kishenji (aka Mallojula Koteswara Rao) called on the authorities to stop Operation Green Hunt, the Indian government warned in May 2010 that intellectuals and academics disseminating "Maoist propaganda" could face up to ten years in jail. Human rights groups denounced this warning, arguing that it stifled debate.

These events intensified the internal debate between hawks and doves at the highest level of the Delhi government. To satisfy the dovish camp, Chidambaram made a public overture of talks with Maoist leaders if they renounced violence. Both sides used Swami Agnivesh (aka Shyam Vepa Rao), a seventy-one-year-old social activist from Chhattisgarh, as a trusted intermediary. But Azad (aka Cherukuri Rajkumar), the Maoist party's politburo member charged with fixing the date for a ceasefire, became a victim of extrajudicial killing by security and intelligence operatives around July 1 while on his way by train to Nagpur to meet other party leaders to finalize the ceasefire date.[106]

Azad's assassination convinced the doves in the ruling Congress Party that Chidambaram was too much of a hawk. The party's general secretary, Digvijay Singh, publicly criticized him for being "rigid" and "intellectually arrogant," and for pursuing a police-centric policy while failing to address the "root causes" of the Maoist insurgency. When challenged, this senior Congress official asserted that his views were shared by many in the party. This contradicted Chidambaram's earlier claim that his strategy had the backing of Congress president Sonia Gandhi. He hit back, saying that Digvijay Singh had his job to do and that he, Chidambaram, was fulfilling his responsibilities as home minister "in the best possible manner."[107]

While maintaining a defiant stance in public, Chidambaram reviewed what had been achieved by Operation Green Hunt, and at what cost, and decided to modify his stance without announcing it. As a consequence, the Home

Ministry changed its strategy of "clear, hold and develop" to emphasizing development works under the Integrated Action Plan, opting for "intelligence-based operations with minimal collateral damage," according to Ajai Sahni of the South Asia Terrorism Portal. This led to a curtailment of anti-Maoist offensives.[108]

There were perhaps differences among Maoist central committee members as to how to cope with the onslaught unleashed under Operation Green Hunt, but the public was not privy to them. During his interview with Navlakha and Myrdal in January 2010, however, Ganapathi summed up the party's general strategy thus: "If we are able to protect our core, no matter how many reverses we may encounter, we will be in a position to sprout elsewhere."[109] Indeed, that is what the People's War Group had done in the past.

When Chidambaram ratcheted up the anti-Maoist campaign, the party leaders decided to lie low, and ordered its cadres to scatter, with most of them entering the adjoining West Bengali territory.

A Fork in the Road

Ultimately, both camps scaled down their conflict. In 2011, the number of fatalities among the security personnel in Chhattisgarh dropped to 67 from 153 in 2010, and Maoists' deaths slipped from 102 to 70. This led director general of police Anil Navaney to claim that the Maoist activity in the state had been "contained."[110]

Such a conclusion was at odds with what Suvojit Bagchi of the BBC discovered during his tour of southern Chhattisgarh toward the end of 2011. Citing police sources, he reported that Maoists had gained new recruits to the PLGA from the local population. "In Bastar district, in the south of Chhattisgarh, the Maoists recently launched a new division of the party called Mahasamund, named after a district on Bastar's eastern fringe and thus connecting Bastar with the Maoist-affected districts in neighboring Orissa."[111]

He quoted one police officer saying that Maoists controlled 40 percent of southern Chhattisgarh, while police held sway in another 40 percent. "The fighting is going on for control of the remaining 20 percent." The reason why Maoist military ambushes had declined was due to each side paring down its operations in the territories not under its control. During his extended tour, which involved visiting the Maoists' "liberated zone" beyond Indravati River, he did not see any police camp or personnel. "'We don't enter their areas, they don't come to ours,' said one paramilitary trooper in Dantewada district."[112]

Security forces were hampered by lack of intelligence. The commander of several police stations complained that they received "very little information" about Maoist movement from the village-level police constable, called *kotwal*. "The kotwals' families live in the villages and are exposed to the Maoists," he explained. "So they refuse to divulge information." On the other side, hundreds of youths from among Adivasis, dreading eviction and police atrocities in the guise of development, joined Maoist ranks and were absorbed into the People's Militia or deployed as plainclothes informers. Along with collecting intelligence, they assisted the PLGA in combat by slowing down the security forces on their way to confront the insurgents. The authorities had failed to infiltrate or disrupt the ranks of these plainclothes Adivasi youths.[113]

Earlier, in July, Maoists dug ditches at hundred-meter intervals on the fifteen-mile, land-mine-resistant road from Bijapur to Gangalur in Dantewada district.[114] In September, they attacked and set ablaze a CRPF camp eleven miles from the district headquarters of Bijapur.

When the government started equipping its security forces with mine-resistant patrol vehicles, Maoist guerrillas increased the amount of explosives they packed in their IEDs. This led CRPF director general Vijay Kumar to concede in October 2011 that the new patrol vehicles had become "coffins on wheels" in Naxal-controlled tracts. He ordered that all CRPF should patrol on foot, which led to fewer and slower patrols.[115]

On the afternoon of May 25, 2013, Maoists ambushed a convoy of twenty-five vehicles carrying two hundred Congress Party leaders, workers, and government security personnel who were engaged in the pre-election campaign in the Darbha Valley of Chhattisgarh's Sukma district. The rebels blocked the convoy with felled trees and blasted it with an IED. A ninety-minute firefight ensued between them and the armed police, who eventually ran out of ammunition. The commander of the 150-strong guerrilla group, which included women, ordered the Congress leaders to surrender. A team of armed guerrillas then sought out Mahendra Karma and the State Congress chief Nand Kumar Patel and killed them. The episode left twenty-seven people dead, including twelve Congress functionaries and eight security personnel.[116] It created a crisis in the state, ruled by the BJP since 2004, with Congress lawmakers demanding the state government's dismissal by the president in Delhi. This occurred at a time when, according to retired brigadier

Ponwar, the CPI (Maoist) had 20,000 armed cadres and another 50,000 personnel in its People's Militia. The membership of its various front organizations was almost 100,000.[117]

Outside Chhattisgarh, though, the security forces achieved better results, partly because their ranks had been bolstered by the deployment of the battalions of the CAPF in Orissa at Chidambaram's behest, and partly because of improved intelligence. But he was not satisfied with the Orissa government's performance. In late 2011, he criticized it for failing to "contain the Maoist menace." He was most likely disappointed by the small number of suspected Maoists killed—twenty-three—with only three in the last ten months of the year. Most security specialists took a diametrically opposite view. They concluded that the latest statistics indicated that the Maoist leadership in Orissa was paralyzed. They noted that improved intelligence had led to the arrest of four prominent Maoist leaders, with one of them carrying a reward upon capture of Rs 1 million ($20,000) and another Rs 400,000 ($8,000).[118]

Coordinating its plans with Delhi, the Jharkhand government, along with its counterpart in Orissa, launched the five-week-long Operation Anaconda on July 31, 2011, in the dense Saranda forest area of West Singhbhum district, to flush out the Maoists whose eastern zonal bureau was based there. Shortly after, the Jharkhand Human Rights Movement called on the official National Human Rights Commission to investigate charges leveled against the security forces of wanton violence, including torture and murder, arson, and theft. Though prevented by the state police from visiting certain villages, the National Human Rights Commission's team confirmed the allegations.[119] In the course of their ongoing scorched-earth tactics, the security forces burned down the existing land records, thus defeating the purpose of the Forest Rights Act.[120]

Nationwide, such offensives as Operation Anaconda raised the overall deaths attributed to the Maoist rebellion. Almost two hundred Maoists lost their lives in 2011, as did 128 security personnel. This in turn led to a policy review by CPI (Maoist) leaders. An indication came in July 2012 when the Dandakaranya Special Zonal Committee stated that "a change must occur in our work methods in accordance with the material conditions, level of the movement and our tasks. . . . [We must] guard against losing manpower by amending flaws that have crept into the organization."[121] The leadership decided to regroup its forces, invigorate its recruitment drive for the PLGA, devise an alternative communications system to stem the leakage of information, accentuate propaganda through front organizations, and escalate public activities and protest.

For its part, the central government resolved to link security with development by making the Saranda forest an attractive model. In April 2012, its Ministry of Rural Development announced a Rs 2.63 billion ($520 million) development plan—funded in part by the mining corporations under their corporate social responsibility programs, without divulging the breakdown between state and corporate funds—for the 36,000 Adivasis living in fifty-six forest villages. It looked impressive. The seventeen corporations that had secured mining leases in the forest, which contained almost 2 billion metric tons of iron ore, included ArcelorMittal, Tata Steel, and Jindal Steel and Power. In the past, those companies that had participated in the corporate social responsibility scheme had done so with a token contribution. For instance, in 2009–10, the National Mineral Development Corporation scooped up profits of Rs 34.48 billion ($690 million) but spent only 2.5 percent of that amount on its social responsibility projects.[122]

A breakdown of the development project in the Saranda forest region, however, showed that 62 percent of the budget would be spent on building offices and sturdy cement roads to be used by the heavy trucks of the mining and metallurgical companies, in violation of the state's rule allowing only unpaved paths inside the forest. And, true to their previous pattern of bending the law, the government and corporations colluded to achieve a predetermined result. For instance, the public hearing for ArcelorMittal's proposed mining project was held fifteen miles away from the mining site, as were the hearings for Rungta Mines and Electrosteel, a Chinese company. Jaunga Banda, a part-time miner, was among the few from his settlement to attend a meeting. "I could not comprehend what was going on," he complained. "I just hope that they leave some forests for our graves."[123]

"In the context of Saranda, this [accusation of collusion between the state and business] applies to both Anaconda and Anaconda II anti-Maoist security operations," noted Sudeep Chakravarti, author of *Red Sun: Travels in Naxalite Country*. "Moreover, it goes against norms of business ethics and corporate social responsibility, besides norms of constitutional governance.[124]

The overly ambitious Saranda Action Plan was based on the assumption that the forest had been cleared of the Maoist rebels. This was not the case. An admission to this effect came from the government, indirectly, when it launched the two-month-long Operation Anaconda II in the forest in December 2012. In retaliation, Maoist guerrillas conducted an eight-hour firefight with two hundred CRPF troopers in another jungle in the state, killing seven and critically injuring twelve in January 2013.[125]

Notably, the number of major incidents—involving three or more fatalities—attributed to the Maoist insurgency plunged to twenty-two in 2012, as against forty-seven in the previous year. "Available data suggests that the Maoists have been able to limit the loss of cadres in 2012 to the 2008–09 level—the stage prior to the escalation provoked by the Center's disastrous 'clear, hold and develop' campaigns in the Maoist heartland," observed Fakir Mohan Pradhan, an Indian security expert, in March 2013. "Their hold over other States in the 'Red Corridor' areas—Jharkhand, Chhattisgarh, Bihar, Orissa and Maharashtra—however, remains firm."[126]

The main reason for the strength of the CPI (Maoist) influence lies with the tenacity with which its cadres, leading simple lives, have fought for the rights of the indigent and underprivileged and the manner in which, inside their zones, they have assisted the inhabitants to improve their lives through land ownership, education, better agricultural practices, and a simplified judicial system in a corruption-free administrative system.

While studiously staying out of an electoral system that, in their opinion, lacked any party battling for the poor, Maoists made use of their influence in rural areas to pit one political party against another and thus exploit the contradictions that, according to their thesis, exist between bourgeois parties. This is what the People's War Group did in the early 1980s in Andhra Pradesh. More recently, Maoists played this card in Jharkhand. In the local council polls in Orissa in 2012, the CPI (Maoist) displayed posters in the areas of its influence urging voters to consult its members before voting. In Koraput district, it backed the candidates of its front organization, Chasi Mulia Adivasi Sangh. Most of them won.[127]

The CPI (Maoist) welcomed the Delhi government's decision in February 2014 to carve out ten northwestern districts of Andhra Pradesh to form the state of Telangana. The party had been among the pioneers of the movement for a separate Telangana. This region of Andhra Pradesh has a history of radical peasant organizations. The Andhra Pradesh Reorganization Act was signed by the president and published in the government gazette on March 1, 2014. The new state was formed on June 2, after the general election.

As before, Maoist leaders urged their followers to boycott the 2014 Lok Sabha poll. On the eve of two rallies to be addressed by Narendra Modi in Sasram and Gaya in southern Bihar in late March 2014, more than one hundred Maoists blew up two cell-phone towers. They left behind live bombs and handwritten notes exhorting people to boycott the elections.[128]

Modi Ascendant, Back to the Big Stick

In its comment on the formation of the BJP-led National Democratic Alliance (NDA) government in Delhi, the CPI (Maoist) predicted that the Modi government would prove to be "an existential threat to the armed agrarian revolutionary war, religious minorities and oppressed nationalities and Dalits and other oppressed communities," and that "the neo-liberal policies implemented by the UPA [United People's Alliance} government [of Manmohan Singh] will now be even more aggressively executed by the NDA government led by Modi."[129]

Within weeks, the Modi administration relaxed environmental and other regulatory rules to expedite clearances for mining and other industrial projects. It diluted the provisions of the Forest Conservation Act of 1980, the Environment Protection Act of 1986, and the Forest Rights Act of 2006, but it did so with minimum publicity. Only the business press took note.

Environmental and forest clearances were delinked to allow work on such projects as highways along non-forest land without waiting for approvals for the passage through a forest. The provision that the certification by local village councils must be settled before a project could be implemented was excised from the Forest Rights Act. The new rules vested clearance authority with the District Collector, who was mandated to complete this exercise within sixty days, irrespective of the number of project-affected villages or the complication of the process. In addition, prospecting for minerals in forests was exempted from acquiring the consent of local village councils or settling tribal rights. In coal, the Environment Ministry exempted the expansion of collieries from public hearings. Mining projects on less than one hundred hectares of land were exempted from inspections by ministry officials.[130] In July, the Modi government changed the criteria used to define forests as violate or inviolate, diluting them so as to allow mining over a greater part of India's forests.[131]

Since most of the mining and prospecting for minerals was in the Maoist-affected areas, tensions between the security forces and Maoists were set to escalate. Official policy toward Maoists began to harden. Modi's appointment of Ajit Kumar Doval, the retired chief of the Intelligence Bureau, as the National Security Adviser was a clear indication of this hardening. Doval was a superhawk, as far as Maoists were concerned. "[Maoists] have started the war; it will be finished by us," he wrote in his column for the Vivekananda International Foundation, a think tank founded by him after his retirement in 2005 and affiliated with the ultranationalist Rashtriya Swayamsevak Sangh. "Left wing extremists are enemies of the nation. . . . There is no room to treat them anything other than being enemies of the state who have to be fought, vanquished and neutralized."[132]

Unbeknownst to him, his words echoed what UPA Home Minister Chidambaram had said four years earlier. "We are determined to uproot Naxals," he said. "We will aggressively fight against terrorism and Naxalism and . . . bring them totally under control in two or three years."[133] Tellingly, after noting the failure of his strategy to "clear, hold and develop" the Maoist-affected areas, Chidambaram opted to "clear and develop simultaneously." Now his BJP successor Rajnath Singh decided to revert to the failed policy of clear first and then develop.[134] It was a classic example of the newly elected officials rediscovering the wheel.

In addition to reducing the once mighty Congress Party to a rump in the Lok Sabha, the BJP-led alliance had crushed the freshly arrived political entity called the Aam Admi Party (Hindi: Common Man's Party). Led by Arvind Kejriwal, a social activist, it had received a tacit endorsement by Anna Hazare, a veteran anticorruption campaigner, in late 2012.

8

Innovations and Distortions
of Indian Democracy

"April is the cruelest month"—the opening line of T.S. Eliot's classic poem "The Waste Land"—applies more to Delhi than it ever did to London, where the American-born poet spent most of his adult life. In the Indian capital, summer starts in April, with the average temperature rising from 90°F to 102°F as the month progresses. But in April 2011, the air in Delhi became infused with extra heat, of the political kind. It was generated by a dramatic gesture by a social activist from a village in Maharashtra, born Kisan Baburao Hazare but known as Anna (Marathi: elder brother) Hazare.

A man of medium build, with fat, crumpling cheeks, jug ears, and deep-set eyes behind spectacles, he was always dressed in a long shirt and loose pajamas of white handspun cloth, with his graying patch of hair covered by a folded, flat-cloth headgear called a Gandhi cap.

Amid much advance publicity, Hazare started the day on April 5 by walking along a stone path to the walled enclosure that houses the memorial to Mahatma Mohandas K. Gandhi, built on the spot where he was cremated near the banks of the Yamuna River following his assassination on January 30, 1948. It is a square, black marble platform with a metal enclosure that covers an eternal flame. His homage to Mahatma Gandhi was appropriate for two salient reasons. Like the iconic leader, Hazare had repeatedly resorted to indefinite fasts to apply "moral pressure" on those who had failed to concede his demands for social or political reform. And, subscribing to the Gandhian idea of creating self-contained villages, he had done pioneering work to improve the appalling conditions of his native village of Ralegan Siddhi in

Maharashtra—an enterprise that had won him India's third-highest civilian award, the Padma Bhushan (Hindi: Lotus Ornament), in 1992.

After his visit to Mahatma Gandhi's memorial, Hazare boarded an open-air Jeep to the India Gate, the capital's landmark along the road leading to the circular, red stone building of the Parliament. He disembarked and, cheered by onlookers, walked to the vast ground next to the open-air five-acre Jantar Mantar observatory at the end of Parliament Street. Sheltering under a huge white marquee on a well-cushioned platform, he started his fast unto death to demand a greater public role in the anticorruption Lokpal Bill (Hindi: People's Protector)—the Ombudsman Bill. Such legislation was first drafted in 1968, when Indira Gandhi ruled as leader of a minority Congress Party in parliament, supported by Communist MPs who were foremost in demanding it.[1] The bill was tabled before the Lower House but lapsed with the dissolution of the House in March 1971. Seven subsequent attempts also lapsed, and one was withdrawn. It was only when the stench from a string of high-profile cases of epic-scale sleaze became unbearable that the Manmohan Singh government produced its draft in 2010.

But the anticorruption campaigners, including the NGO India Against Corruption (IAC), slammed the draft bill as "a complete eyewash." They argued that the bill envisaged demolishing whatever safeguards existed under the guise of the current anticorruption systems, and sought to insulate corrupt politicians from any action against them. A five-member committee of the IAC, consisting of a former Supreme Court judge and two Supreme Court lawyers, prepared an alternative Jan Lokpal Bill (Hindi: People's Ombudsman Bill). It proposed that the Lokpal/Ombudsman's office should subsume the present Central Vigilance Commission (CVC), so that political leaders, including the prime minister and bureaucrats as as well as the judiciary, came under its jurisdiction. Also the Lokpal should be given police powers.

Nervously aware that Hazare had tapped into rising popular anger against sleaze, leaders of the ruling Congress Party appealed to him to call off the protest, since a cabinet minister was already examining the IAC's draft. He ignored the plea. It had taken him three and a half decades to achieve such influence.

The Fasting Lobbyist versus Machiavellian Politicos

Born in 1940 into a poor village household in Maharashtra, Kisan Hazare was adopted by his childless aunt who lived in Mumbai. There he went to school, only to drop out midway through his secondary education. He sold flowers in the street to pay for his upkeep and eventually became the owner of a small flower shop in central Mumbai. When the army lowered its recruitment standards in the wake of the Sino-Indian War in 1962, he got a chance to enroll in the military. He signed a twelve-year contract in 1963 and served as a driver. He saw combat on India's West Pakistan border during the war between the two neighbors in 1965 and survived a lethal attack by the enemy. He took to reading books by Mahatma Gandhi and Swami Vivekananad, a Hindu social reformer.[2]

After his honorable discharge from the army, he returned to his ancestral village of Ralegan Siddhi, located fifty-five miles from Pune, in the shadow of a mountainous terrain. Its population of less than two thousand people was mired in abject poverty and survived by distilling illicit liquor. His long years in the army had turned him into a disciplined citizen, and his military service earned him the adulation of fellow villagers. In the community, he combined his advocacy of prohibition, family planning, and voluntary labor for communal good with a ban on felling trees. He persuaded villagers to construct an embankment and associated works to store water and allow it to percolate, improving the ground water level for better irrigation. Later, the settlement installed solar power for street lighting, and biogas facilities and a windmill for other energy needs. The transformation of Ralegan Siddhi from an indigent village to a self-sufficient entity was something Mahatma Gandhi had visualized in the preindependent era for rural India. It won Hazare the kudos of the Indian government and a much-coveted award of Padma Shri. (Mr./Mrs. Lotus) in 1990.[3]

He then turned his attention to the problems that afflicted the state of Maharashtra. He found that the Right to Information Act passed by the state assembly in 2000 did not enable citizens to demand transparency in governance. He led a movement to strengthen it. As a result, the subsequent legislation, which came into effect in August 2003, made information sharing an obligation of the state government.

Corruption in public life was a running story in the media. When his demand to investigate the bribery charges against four ministers in the state government were ignored, he undertook a fast unto death on August 9, 2003, to pressure Chief Minister Sushilkumar Shinde to take action. His self-imposed ordeal ended nine days later when Shinde capitulated and appointed an inquiry commission headed by a retired Supreme Court judge. This won Hazare an Integrity Award from Transparency International.

(The inquiry commission would find three of the four ministers guilty of taking bribes.)

His next target was red tape. His campaign led to the passing of the Prevention of Delay in Discharge of Official Duties Act of 2006, which stipulated disciplinary action against bureaucrats who moved files too slowly and a monitoring program for those involved in corrupt practices. In reality, however, this remained only a law on paper.

Once the Right to Information (RTI) Act was passed by the central government in 2005, Hazare deployed it to shed light on bribe-taking by politicians and bureaucrats. At the first national RTI Convention, held in Delhi in October 2006, he met other leading RTI activists. They decided informally to pool their individual anticorruption efforts under the aegis of India Against Corruption (IAC). The IAC gained traction as a "people's movement" when, in 2010, following the Commonwealth Games scandal in October, a lawyer-founder of the IAC, Shanti Bhushan, filed a writ petition on behalf of the IAC against the scam. Next, the IAC focused on the Lokpal Bill under consideration by the parliament, with its leading legal lights producing the alternative Jan Lokpal Bill.

Given the massive media publicity accorded to Hazare's indefinite hunger strike in early April 2011, and tens of thousands of people across two hundred cities and towns who fasted in sympathy, Singh's cabinet watched the development with trepidation. On his part, Hazare kept his crusade strictly apolitical by banning political dignitaries from his dais. As a result, success came to him sooner than even his ardent fans had hoped. On April 8, the government agreed to form a ten-member joint drafting panel, with members divided equally between government appointees and nominees from "civil society." The five cabinet ministers, led by finance minister Pranab Mukherjee, were balanced by Anna Hazare; N. Santosh Hegde, a former Supreme Court judge; Shanti Bhushan; Arvind Keiriwal, a social activist; and Prashant Bhushan, a Supreme Court lawyer.

On April 9, Hazare broke his fast by accepting a glass of juice from a girl. A mass celebration followed. His admirers, waving the national emblem and singing and dancing to the rhythmic beating of drums, transformed the ground near Jantar Mantar into a carnival site. Appearing on the dais along with his eminent nonpolitical aides, including Swami Ramdev and Swami Agnivesh, he addressed a nationwide audience. He named August 15, India's Independence Day, as the deadline for the passage of a stiff anticorruption law. "We have a lot of struggle ahead of us in drafting the new legislation," he said. "We have shown the world in just five days that we are united for the cause of the nation."[4] It was significant to note that Swami Agnivesh, who had acted as the intermediary between the central government and Maoists in the past, appealed to the rebels: "Shun violence and adopt Gandhian methods to fight injustice."[5]

But Agnivesh's statement was based on the assumption that Hazare's demand had been met. This was not the case, as the subsequent events would show. The Hazare camp's celebration was to prove premature.

Tricks of the Parliamentary Trade

At the joint drafting committee meeting on May 30, the two sides clashed on the question of the Lokpal's jurisdiction over the prime minister, Supreme Court and High Court judges, and members of parliament. The central ministers were opposed to this measure, whereas the civil society nominees were in favor, arguing that this provision was included in the 2005 United Nations Convention against Corruption to which India was a signatory.[6] As chairman of the joint drafting committee, Mukherjee widened the debate by seeking the views of state chief ministers, as well as leaders of all political parties, on this and other contentious issues, such as whether or not the Central Bureau of Investigation (CBI) should be an independent body like the Election Commission of India (ECI).

The constitutional status of the CBI became a pivotal issue. The investigation and prosecution of corruption cases were carried out by the Central Vigilance Commission (CVC), the CBI, and the Anti-Corruption Bureaus of States.[7] They did so under the Prevention of Corruption Act of 1988 and the Indian Penal Code of 1860. The CVC was a statutory body that dealt with corruption cases in government departments. The CBI functioned under the CVC, but its director general reported directly to the prime minister. The CVC referred cases either to the Central Vigilance Officer in a government department or to the CBI. The CVC or the Central Viligance Officer recommended the action to be taken against a public servant, but the decision to take any action against that official rested with the departmental chief. Crucially, the investigating agency in Delhi or a state capital could initiate prosecution only after it had obtained the prior sanction of the central or state government. This meant that the ultimate decision for the CBI over whether to proceed with prosecution rested with the prime minister, an elected politician prone to taking into account political factors. The cases under the Prevention of Corruption Act of 1988 were tried by special judges appointed by the central or state government.

Tension between the two groups on the joint panel intensified when the Delhi police forcibly evicted Swami Ramdev and his acolytes from Ramlila Park on Sunday, June 5, to end their hunger strike against black money and corruption. In response, Hazare and his IAC colleagues boycotted the joint drafting panel meeting the next day. Later, they decided to end their boycott only if future meetings were televised. This proposal was rejected by Mukherjee. And, after promising to forward the draft bills of the government and the IAC to the full cabinet, he submitted only the amended official document to fellow ministers.

In early August, the government tabled a weak Lokpal Bill for debate before the Lower House. The bill exempted the prime minister, MPs, high-level judges, and lower-level civil servants. It covered only the central government.

When the Lokpal Act failed to appear on the statute books by August 15, Hazare announced his decision to commence his fast until death the next day. The Delhi police arrested him, saying that he had violated his agreement to fast for only three days. When he refused bail, the magistrate sent him to jail for a week. This led to protest marches across the country. The opposition leaders condemned his detention, and both houses of parliament adjourned. When informed that he was free, Hazare refused to leave the prison and continued his hunger strike behind bars. The government temporized and permitted him to fast for fifteen days. Upon his release, he continued his hunger strike at Ramlila Park, demanding that the government pass the Lokpal Bill in the current parliamentary session, ending on September 8.

His critics condemned Hazare's pressure tactics. The National Campaign for People's Right to Information took issue with his setting of the deadline for the passage of the bill, arguing that it undercut the very basis of democracy, which operated by "holding wide-ranging consultations and discussions, allowing for dissent and evolving a consensus. . . . [Hazare] has the right to protest and dissent. But nobody can claim it as an absolute right and deny the right of dissent to others."[8]

But public disgust at the ever-expanding sleaze had reached such a pitch that criticism of Hazare got short shrift in the media and popular thinking. Unnerved, Congress leaders engaged an intermediary to talk to Hazare and find "points of consensus." At the government's behest, the parliament referred Hazare's demands for the proposed legislation—which included a citizen's charter, the inclusion of lower-level civil servants, and the creation of state-level Lokpals, called Lokayuktas (Ombudsmen)—to the parliament's Standing Committee. The next day, Hazare ended his fast.[9] His close aides—now identified by the media as Team Anna—were relieved and joyous.

Besides Hazare's proposals, the Standing Committee considered some thirteen thousand suggestions that poured into its office from ordinary citizens and countless NGOs. After spending almost four months sifting through this pile, it submitted its recommendations to the government. The end result was the renamed Lokpal and Lokayuktas Bill (Ombudsman and Anticorruption Ombudsman Bill). It was considered weak by Communists and other leftist factions in the Lower House. It retained the executive's control of the CBI and vested the power to appoint the Lokpal with a Selection Board in which the government had a majority. The opposition groups, including the BJP, walked out in protest on December 27, which enabled the ruling Congress Party to claim that the legislation had received unanimous backing. The subsequent debate in the Upper House was cut short due to lack of time.

In the parliamentary chambers, the opposition BJP was vociferous in slamming the Congress-led government for dragging its feet. But, in this regard, the record of its rising star, Narendra Modi, the chief minister of Gujarat, was infamous. After the resignation of Justice S.M. Soni as the Lokayukta in 2003, the Modi government made "half-hearted attempts"—in the words of Justice B.S. Chauhan of the Supreme Court—to fill the post for nine years.[10] When Gujarat's governor, Kamala Beniwal, appointed retired Justice R.A. Mehta as the Lokayukta in August 2011, on the recommendation of the state's Chief Justice, Modi contended that Mehta had "anti-government bias" and moved the High Court to have him removed. But the High Court upheld Mehta's appointment in January 2012.[11]

In May 2012, debate resumed in Delhi on an amended bill that empowered state governments to appoint their own ombudsmen. Suddenly, the leader of a minor faction proposed that the draft should be referred to a Select Committee for reconsideration. The subsequent Select Committee included members of all political parties. Angered by this foot-dragging, Team Anna addressed a letter to the Select Committee Chairman Satyavrat Chaturvedi, a Congress Party leader, stating that his committee was the third to be established in the past year. "The Bill has been sent to committees 11 times [since 1968]," added the team's missive. "How is this Select Committee different from the earlier Standing Committees?" they asked. "As this Select

Committee has members from all parties, we feel that they have to answer these questions first." To underline its apolitical credentials, Team Anna seized the opportunity to bracket the opposition with the ruling coalition, thus showing that the whole political class—right, left, and center—was against the introduction of effective Lokpal and Lokayuktas. "Nobody knows who is in the ruling dispensation and who is in opposition as both speak in similar voices," remarked its spokesman, Arvind Kejriwal.[12] Such strictures left the political establishment unmoved. Its pussyfooting continued, so that even by the summer of 2013 the Lokpal and Lokayuktas Bill had not been adopted by the bicameral Parliament.

The narrative of this long-running saga provided a telling illustration of the innovations and distortions of democracy in action in India. Team Anna's statements echoed what Maoists had been saying for a long while. At their core, there was no difference between political parties, and politicians of all hues were united in safeguarding the privileges that the political class enjoyed—including the power resting with the executive to authorize an investigation into charges of bribe-taking by politicians. The insistence on exempting the prime minister and all MPs from the purview of the proposed Lokpal provided ironclad evidence to support this argument.

While sharing the Maoists' overarching assessment of the political establishment in general, Team Anna and its followers believed fervently that the system could be changed for the better through peaceful tactics. They believed that the democratic process was flexible enough to respond to extraparliamentary, nonviolent pressures. That demarcated the Indian system from the practices of Western nations, where fasting unto death by even a widely revered apolitical figure had no chance of resonating with the public. The proponents of reform through peaceful, grassroots pressure could hold up the trophy of the adoption of the Right to Information Act, first at the state level, and then nationally.

Right to Information Act and Its Unexpected Martyrs

In retrospect, the adoption and enforcement of the Right to Information Act could be seen as giving the Lokpal Bill a much-needed push in the legislative system. The roots of the law lay in the Mazdoor Kisan Shakti Sangathan (Hindi: Workers' and Peasants' Strength Union; MKSS). The MKSS was formed in 1990 by Aruna and Bunker Roy, the founders of the Social

Work and Research Center in the central Rajasthani village of Tilonia, to improve the lot of the area's rural communities. The trigger to establish the MKSS was the local feudal landlord's usurpation of the communal land in Tilonia and the filching of the funds by the contractors charged with building roads and irrigation channels. They did so by creating ghost workers and underpaying their illiterate employees. The MKSS, a nonpolitical body, demanded access to the financial accounts of the contractors and the government department. This went unheeded at first, but, led by the highly educated and articulate Roys, the MKSS succeeded in getting the authorities to hold a public hearing in December 1994 on the awarding of the contracts and payments made to the workers.[13]

This unprecedented exercise underlined the significance of information to ordinary citizens and also enlightened them as to why officials and contractors were so adamant about keeping the records under wraps. The MKSS thus fired the first successful shot in the battle for the public's right to information. The event made headline news in the national media. This event, in turn, led to the establishment of the National Campaign for People's Right to Information in 1996 to campaign for an effective right to information law at the state and central levels. Within four years, three states, including Rajasthan, enacted Right to Information (RTI) laws. This created pressure on the BJP-led central government to do likewise.

The resulting Freedom of Information (FoI) Bill of 2000, which eventually became law in 2002, contained too many exemptions, including requests that would involve "disproportionate diversion of the resources of a public authority."[14] Also, there were no penalties for failing to respond to an application for information. As such, the FoI Act made minimal impact.

During its campaign for the general election in 2004, the Congress Party described the FoI Act as anemic and promised that, if returned to power, it would pass a more robust law. When the party failed to win an outright majority in the Lower House, the Communist-led Left Front offered to support its minority government if, among other things, it would fulfill its promise to enact a strong RTI legislation. Congress Party leaders agreed. The resulting strengthened RTI act went into effect in October 2005. It gave citizens and NGOs the right to demand "written answers" from the Kafkaesque and often venal Indian bureaucracy and other state institutions. The bureaucracy had become sclerotic because there was no reward or punishment for performance in a civil service post; it was a job for life regardless of how the employee performed.

Since 2005, individuals and NGOs have wielded this tool with varying degrees of success. Over time, the number of applications under the new RTI Act stabilized around 270 a day. Given the country's thirty-six administrative units—twenty-eight states, seven union territories, and one central government—the score was eight per day per administrative unit. This meant that RTI awareness had barely reached the rural population. Villagers' chances of resorting to this right virtually disappeared when, for instance, the Uttar Pradesh government hiked the fee for each query to Rs 500 ($10) from the original Rs 10 (20¢) stipulated in the central RTI Act, with Chhattisgarh following suit in 2012.[15]

The RTI Act's users generally fell into one of three categories: officials of an NGO, specializing in a particular subject; individuals who intermittently focused on specific causes, such as the number of days their elected lawmakers attended the legislature; and citizens who became professional inquirers and called themselves RTI activists.

The reluctance of the opaque bureaucracy to share information was well illustrated by the experience of Amitabh Thakur, a graduate of the Indian Institute of Technology, Kanpur, who, after serving as a commissioned police officer, pursued a doctorate in management at the Indian Institute of Management, Lucknow. When he sought details of the annual confidential report on him for 2004–5 from the home department of Uttar Pradesh, he received no response. Finally, he had to appeal to the higher authorities. "That's when we realized that if we, as government officials, find it so difficult to extract information, it must be twice as difficult for the masses," observed his wife, Nutan Thakur, who held a doctorate in Hindi literature.[16] In March 2010, long before the 2G spectrum scam broke, the couple filed an RTI application seeking clarification on the appointment of Andimuthu Raja as communications minister. Ten months on, they had received no reply from the Central Vigilance Commission.[17] "Everyday, RTI applications are rejected for a variety of reasons because parts of the Act are still open to interpretation," Nutan Thakur said. Undeterred, they founded the National RTI Forum, a registered trust with over 150 activists on board. It built up a considerable following on social networking sites.[18]

As for citizens of lesser standing, the relentless efforts of RTI activists to promote transparency and accountability in the working of myriad public institutions exposed them to harassment, physical attacks, and even murder. Those trying to garner information about panchayats (village councils) were often ostracized. As individuals living in the same areas as the suspected but powerful wrongdoers, who were keen to conceal their misdeeds, they were vulnerable as residents of villages. Those who got beaten up regularly by hired goons ran into the dozens. And each year half a dozen of them got killed.

Among those killed was thirty-five-year-old Shashidhar Mishra, a street vendor with a secondary-school education, in the town of Baroni in Bihar, as reported by Jason Burke of *The Observer.* He was murdered by hitmen using muffled guns on February 14, 2010. A conscientious citizen, he targeted a dairy owned by the municipality where animals were mistreated. Then he focused on the unlicensed stalls set up on public land outside the railway station. His exposure of the illegal use of communal property led to their demolition. Next, he sought information about land deals by local councillors. His probes revealed that the town's market, largely constructed by a local businessman, was on government land. At the end of 2009, he showed that the contracts for resurfacing the roads were deliberately nontransparent. He then inquired about the fate of the vehicles the police impounded. On February 9, he applied for the list of contractors charged with constructing a road in the market and for the municipality's 2009 accounts. By the time this information arrived in May—showing that the municipality had paid Rs 5.20 million ($120,000) for fictitious work—Mishra was long dead. An electricity outage plunged his street into darkness for a few minutes, just enough time for the professional killers to do the nefarious deed. The timing of these events suggested collusion with high-ranking officials.[19]

Lalit Mehta—a thirty-six-year-old, broad-shouldered father of two, with a pleasant, mustached visage—had the distinction of being the first RTI martyr. He was attacked while riding a motorcycle on a highway in the Palamau district of Jharkhand on May 14, 2008. He was beaten to death, and his corpse was found in a field.[20] A leading member of the Right to Food campaign, he used the RTI route to investigate corruption in the implementation of the central government's National Rural Employment Guarantee (NREG) scheme to provide jobs to villagers willing to build public works. The NREG had a provision for the auditing of accounts by select members of the community, called a social audit. Its preeminent advocate was Jean Drèze, a Delhi-based development economist and social activist, and a former member of the National Advisory Council, chaired by Sonia Gandhi.[21] The police chief in Palamau failed to note that Mehta was killed just one day after Dreze arrived in the district, leading a team of NREG volunteers from Delhi. Instead, the Palamau officer emphasized that since the motorcycle and the cash that Mehta was carrying were missing, it was a case of armed robbery. But the subsequent public protest in the capital city of Ranchi and pressure put on the central rural development minister in Delhi compelled Jharkhand's chief minister Madhu Koda to act. On June 16, after conceding the failure of the state's criminal investigation department and Palamau's district administration to name the murderers, Koda recommended an inquiry by the Central Bureau of Investigation.[22]

Six days later, local Maoists intervened. "We know the killers of Lalit Mehta and they will be brought to justice," read the Maoist leaflet. "We will make the perpetrators of heinous crimes such as murder pay with their lives. We have started the process for this and it will soon culminate in strong and decisive action." The flyer named the local contractors allegedly involved in pilfering NREG funds who, it alleged, had conspired to kill Mehta.[23] The Maoists' pledge to avenge the killing of a nonviolent social activist shook the political and administrative establishments in Ranchi and Delhi. It should have also jolted the CBI to fast-track its investigation. But it did not.

Instead, it left the Maoists to deliver on their promise. On January 5, 2009, the police recovered the corpse of Raju Singh, the prime accused in Mehta's murder, with an accompanying handwritten pamphlet. It stated that Maoist cadres had shot him dead as the murderer of Lalit Mehta and as an armed robber. "Now there is nothing to inquire into the Lalit Mehta case," said the district police chief, Udayan Singh. This was not strictly true. The same news item stated, "Now, the police are investigating the link between Mehta, Dreze and Maoists."[24]

The Mehta-Dreze-Maoists chain should have been extended to include Sonia Gandhi, chairperson of the ruling United Progressive Alliance (UPA). For, following Mehta's murder, she had stated that it "was engineered by vested interests that were apprehensive of Lalit's exposing their corrupt practices."[25]

The Groundbreaking NREG Scheme and Its Pitfalls

Enacted in August 2005, the National Rural Employment Guarantee Act (called the Mahatma Gandhi National Rural Employment Guarantee Act after October 2, 2009) went into effect in February 2006 in two hundred districts. Later it was extended to most of the remaining districts of India.

This sop to the village poor needed to be seen as a balancing act to the reduction in the corporation tax. In 2001, under the BJP-led government, the rate was 39.55 percent; five years later, under the Congress-led administration, it stood at 33.66 percent.[26] Predictably, dispatches by the United States Embassy in Delhi, published later by WikiLeaks, were scathing about the NREG scheme. "At worst, the jobs plan is political patronage run amok and horrid economic policy," one cable opined.[27]

The NREG scheme guaranteed employment for one hundred days in a year to adult members of any rural household ready to work on small-scale village infrastructure projects as unskilled laborers at Rs 100 ($2) a day. The funds were supplied by Delhi, but the program was implemented by the state governments through village councils (panchayats), with the elected *sarpanch* (mayor) and the appointed gram sevak (Hindi: village servant) handling the cash. The sarpanch was also authorized to decide what to build, after consulting his constituents. To abort, or at least curtail, the chances of fraud, the act had a provision for a social audit that empowered villagers to act as watchdogs.

But, as had happened in the implementation of the mining law requiring public hearings, in most states these social audits were either perfunctory or manipulated by the sarpanch and the secretary in league with the contractors. With Delhi earmarking Rs 400 billion ($8 billion) a year for the NREG program, rich pickings awaited dishonest contractors, politicians, and bureaucrats. The execution of the NREG program turned into an ongoing battle between the central government, keen to keep it clean, and the nexus of sarpanchs, contractors, and bureaucrats.

When rural laborers complained that sarpanchs were docking payment and demanding cash in return for job cards, the Delhi administration decided in 2008 to remit money directly to workers' bank accounts. This led to inordinate delay in payments because of the red tape in the public sector banks. On the other hand, the number of villagers with bank accounts soared to almost 100 million by the end of the decade.

In 2009, a crackdown in Karauli, eighty-eight miles from the state capital of Jaipur, revealed that a quarter of the two hundred thousand job cards were bogus. A random visit by *Wall Street Journal* reporters in April 2011 to a dam-building site in the Kaladevi subdistrict showed that a third of the sixty workers on the muster roll were absent. In violation of the law, the site lacked a medical kit, resting area, and childcare facilities. This was also the case in Rajasthan, which, composing 6 percent of the national population, received

20 percent of the Rs 450 billion ($9 billion) that the central government allocated to the NREG for the fiscal year ending on March 31, 2011.[28]

On the other end of the spectrum was Andhra Pradesh (population: 76 million), where, facing the Maoist challenge in the mid-2000s, the government was compelled to clean up its governance. Here, villagers examined records for fraud, then held public hearings, naming the corrupt officials. The results were posted online. As a result, in the first five years of the NREG program, social audits had detected fraud of Rs 900 million ($20 million), with 4,600 officials facing criminal or administrative charges.[29]

Unsurprisingly, those milking the NREG scheme resisted social audits. Often sarpanchs refused to part with their documents. If that failed, higher-ranking corrupt politicians openly intervened. For instance, at a public audit in Nagarkurnool, seventy-five miles from Hyderabad, a senior Congress Party member pushed his way onto the platform next to the official supervising the audit. He attempted to hijack the procedure and frequently intervened to defend local contractors and sarpanchs. When B. Sardharkar Reddy, a contractor in a nearby village, was accused of falsifying measurements on a project, he contested the auditors' technical prowess to take such measurements. "These people are not qualified," he declared. "If it is a 10 percent deviation, what is the big deal?" Ruckus followed. Finally, the case was referred to a technical expert.[30]

A *New York Times* report from rural Andhra Pradesh in late 2010 provided further details. Those auditing the accounts were mainly young men who had been trained for the task. Among them was Zamiruddin, a twenty-four-year-old auditor from another village in the same Ranga Reddy district as Nagarkurnool. Flipping through a muster roll dating back eight months, he spotted a list of ghost workers. "These names are in different handwriting than the ones above," he explained. "That is the first problem." Also, all the laborers had signed their names rather than some of them pressing their thumbprints, which should have been the case because of the substantial illiteracy among rural workers. Lastly, the documents reported 100 percent attendance, with Rs 6,400 ($130) paid for five days of mulching. Both of these figures were fraudulent. He then visited the village of Manthati and interviewed those whose names were high on the list. None of them recalled seeing the workers whose names were listed below theirs in a different handwriting. Altogether, Zamiruddin established that Rs 139,000 ($3,000) had been paid to ghost laborers. At the public hearing, the field assistant who maintained the roster was suspended, and the fraudulent wages were ordered to be recovered from him.[31]

Overall, in 2010, the NREG program provided a much needed safety net for about 50 million households, thus helping the laborers and their 200 million dependents. Significantly, one-third of those enrolled in the scheme, at least on paper, were women who would otherwise be doing nothing more than unpaid housework. With the daily wage tied to the cost of living (and running at Rs 125 in 2011), the payment had proved a higher wage than other unskilled rural jobs. The scheme had furnished landless workers with a bargaining tool to demand better payment for their labor in other activities. It had also encouraged them to continue living in their native settlements, thus slowing down, at least marginally, rural migration to urban centers.

In February 2012, on the sixth anniversary of the launching of this scheme, Sonia Gandhi said, "We have achieved successes in MGNREGA in [the] last six years, but there are still many challenges before us."[32] Since she played an important role in transforming the idea of creating jobs for rural Indians into a national law, she had a vested interest in its evolution. To achieve this end, she had deployed her influence as chairperson of the National Advisory Council.

National Advisory Council: An Innovation

After the victory of the Congress Party under her leadership in May 2004, Sonia Gandhi advised Prime Minister Manmohan Singh to appoint a National Advisory Council (NAC) to supervise the enforcement of the National Common Minimum Program that her party signed with smaller factions, including the Communist-led Left Front, to gain a majority in the Lower House. He did so and appointed Gandhi as the salaried chairperson of a fifteen-member NAC consisting of nonpolitical specialists and social activists. It was meant to be "the conscience" of the Congress-led administration. As a pressure group, it successfully pushed for the RTI Act and the NREG Act, which were part of the National Common Minimum Program. It also promoted the Forest Rights Act to give land titles to traditional forest dwellers.

The opposition in parliament argued that there was no constitutional provision for the NAC to function as part of the government. It also pointed out that a sitting MP was barred from holding "an office of profit," a term that applied to the NAC chairperson. As a result, Gandhi resigned as the head of NAC and as an MP in March 2006. She contested the subsequent by-election and regained her parliamentary seat. Soon the parliament passed the Office of Profit Bill, which exempted the post of NAC chairperson and fifty-five other positions from the office of profit category. But, the term of the NAC ended in March 2008.[33]

Following the return of the Congress Party as the largest group in the Lower House in May 2009, the idea of reviving the NAC cropped up. Prime Minister Singh did so in March 2010 and appointed Sonia Gandhi as its chairperson. Earlier, she had been reelected chairperson of the ruling Congress-led UPA coalition. The government now officially presented the NAC as its interface with civil society. The NAC's proponents hailed it as an innovation of Indian democracy, since no such body existed anywhere else in the democratic world.

Its fifteen members included scientists, economists, former civil servants, educationalists, NGO leaders, businesspersons, and social activists with experience delivering services to a community. It narrowed its focus on such socioeconomic issues as poverty elimination, land reform and land rights, sustainable management of natural resources, establishing a security net for disadvantaged groups, and improving the lot of Dalits and tribal people. It appointed specialist subcommittees to prepare draft legislation for more pressing needs, such as food security. At the same time some of the NAC's recommendations were publicly described by Prime Minister Singh as impractical or beyond the financial means of his government. Since NGOs and social activists had easier access to NAC members than to government ministers or even MPs, the NAC could claim that its existence helped embed democracy firmly within the government structure by acting as a conduit for conveying ideas and proposals to policymakers.

At critical moments, Sonia Gandhi intervened on behalf of the aggrieved in direct opposition to the stance of Prime Minister Singh. For instance, in September 2010, she stressed that while land was required to build industry, "the land acquisition must be done in a manner that does not result in the loss of large tracts of fertile and productive agricultural land so indispensable to grow food grains and feed people." She added, "If farmers are deprived of their land-based livelihood, they must be provided with adequate compensation and alternative occupations."[34] She also stated that environmental concerns could not be summarily dismissed. Her words contradicted those that the prime minister had uttered three days earlier. "The only way we can raise our heads above poverty is for more people to be taken out of agriculture," he said. "There has to be a balance. You cannot protect environment by perpetuating poverty." Such divergence of views at the heart of an administration would in normal circumstances paralyze it.[35] But such was not the case in India. The government muddled through, trying to balance its tilt toward industrialists with a periodic sop to the needy.

It could be argued that, functioning outside the cabinet, Sonia Gandhi was not burdened with the onerous task of squaring the circle by attempting to serve the interests of both the predatory capitalists and the exploited peasants. Such tactics were deployed to deal with the insistent demand for the food security legislation.[36]

Food Security: A Twelve-Year Battle

The protracted debate on the subject had its origins in the writ petition in the Supreme Court that the Rajasthan unit of the People's Union for Civil Liberties (PUCL) filed in April 2001. The petition was based on Article 47, which states: "The state shall regard the raising of the level of nutrition and the standard of living of its people and the improvement of public health as among its primary duties." It demanded that India's food stocks be used to alleviate hunger and malnutrition. It argued that the constitutional ground of the "right to food" stemmed from Article 21, which guaranteed the fundamental right to life. The Supreme Court upheld its case.

This proved to be the seed out of which sprouted the Right to Food campaign in which a growing number of trade unions, NGOs, social activists, and grassroots organizations participated. They received periodic impetus as the Supreme Court issued a series of interim orders. In May 2002, it appointed Dr. Naresh C. Saxena its commissioner, charged with monitoring the implementation of its orders relating to the right to food. He was authorized to investigate any violations of the court's orders and demand redress, and was required to submit periodic reports to the court on the subject. Another important interim order required the central government to ensure across-the-board application of such welfare programs as midday meals for schoolchildren.[37]

After the enforcement of the NREG Act, the attention of the NGOs and civil society organizations committed to improving the lot of the underprivileged turned to food security. They argued that while the Indian economy had expanded at an average annual rate of 9 percent since 2006, its hunger and malnutrition levels were worse than those of sub-Saharan Africa. In response, the Congress Party promised a food security law in its 2009 election manifesto. Soon after the general election in April–May, Sonia Gandhi forwarded a model bill to Prime Minister Singh that approached the issue in an integrated way. It stressed nutrition—not just food grains—to fill empty stomachs and proposed providing access to food through community kitchens. Initially, Singh argued that selling food to hundreds of millions of Indians at giveaway prices would discourage farmers from growing food and raise wages, stoking higher inflation. But he later temporized. He referred the matter to a group of ministers for consideration. This panel produced a draft bill in March 2010 that narrowed the definition of food security to a legal right to buy a certain amount of food grains at subsidized prices.

It was not until September 2011 that the full cabinet debated and finalized the National Food Security Bill (NFSB) and released the draft for public comment. This occurred against the backdrop of a spectacular fall in the Singh government's popular standing due to a string of megascandals and an inflation rate of nearly 10 percent. Three months later, the government tabled the bill before the parliament.

With the pro-business Palaniappan Chidambaram returning to the Finance Ministry in August 2012, the industrialists' lobby took heart. This lobby disapproved of the NFSB without being overly critical. It took advantage of the fall in the rate of economic expansion during that year—caused primarily by the failure of infrastructure to keep pace with the rise in GDP—to press the case of domestic and foreign multinational corporations who wished to raise the ceiling for foreign direct investment (FDI) in certain sectors. It succeeded.

In mid-September, Delhi eased FDI norms in multibrand retail, civil aviation, and broadcasting, after Singh and Chidambaram had secured the go-ahead from Sonia Gandhi. It permitted multibrand foreign retailers such as Wal-Mart and Tesco to open stores in India and acquire 51 percent ownership, and allowed foreign airlines and broadcasters to raise their stake in their respective sectors in India to 49 percent. Chandrajit Banerjee, director general of the Confederation of Indian Industry, described the official decision as "a tremendous boost not only to the sectors in question but also a huge mood lifter. Global and domestic perceptions [will] also change." Industrialist Banerjee's prediction would prove to be more hope than achievement.

On the other side, Doraiswamy Raja, an MP and the national secretary of the Communist Party of India (CPI), pointed out, "In retail, 40 million people [8 percent of the labor force] are involved. If you include family members also, it will affect 160 million people. It will also adversely affect the small and marginal farmer."[38] Having made a brazenly pro-business policy decision, the government came under renewed pressure by grassroots organizations, as well as Sonia Gandhi, to make a balancing move to help fill the empty stomachs of the poor.

By the time the NFSB went through the committee stage and was ready for the final reading and vote on May 6, 2013, the growth of the economy had slowed to 4.5 percent. This provided the corporate sector with an economic argument to oppose the law. It estimated that the new scheme would require the central government to procure 61 million tons of food at the cost of Rs 1,247 billion ($21 billion), which would further increase the budget deficit. It warned that if the country failed to achieve the promised 5.2 percent growth in 2014, the credit-rating agencies could downgrade its investment standing to junk status, which would make it harder and costlier for companies to raise loans for investment.[39]

But with the next parliamentary poll only a year away, Congress leaders could not politically afford to let a bill with a massive vote-winning potential to lapse. After all, the final draft covered 810 million people, vastly expanding the existing food subsidy scheme, which covered some 180 million who received subsidized food grain through licensed fair price shops. The figures in the newly proposed NFSB included three-quarters of the rural population (630 million) and half of all urbanites (180 million). These households were to be entitled to buy five kilograms of food grain per person each month for Rs 3, Rs 2, and Rs 1 per kilogram for rice, wheat, and coarse grains, respectively. "The government has passed [the NFSB] with great reluctance and obviously corporate India is not very happy," said Biraj Patnaik, adviser to the Commissioners of the Supreme Court in the Right to Food case.[40]

In parliament, the opposition groups claimed that the government had introduced this bill with the upcoming general election in mind. It disrupted the proceedings to the extent that the speaker had to adjourn the house sine die on May 8. The cabinet hit back by unanimously approving the issuance of the Food Security Ordinance on July 3. Once the state governments prepared the beneficiary list, the program would be implemented. However, the ordinance had to be passed by both houses of the parliament by January

2014.[41] With a nationwide election due in a few months, it would have been foolhardy for any political party to oppose transforming this pro-poor ordinance into an act of parliament.

It is a common and accepted practice in parliamentary democracies for the ruling party to offer economic and other concessions to voters on the eve of a general election. What is not accepted legally or otherwise in such countries is corrupt practices in electioneering, including bribing leaders of vote banks and spending sums on the campaign that are several times the legal limit. While backing the legislation aimed at eradicating graft in the bureaucracy, none of the party leaders, including Sonia Gandhi, had targeted blatant electoral corruption. She had instead focused on the constitutionally granted discretionary powers of central and state ministers.

Discretionary Powers

Noting the anticorruption wave that had swept the country, Sonia Gandhi decided to go with it. She spoke up as Congress president. In her address to party activists in January 2011, she emphasized avoiding extravagance. "Simplicity, restraint and austerity must be our chosen way," she stressed. "We cannot order this as law. But in a country where poverty is still widespread, let us at least have more sensibility to avoid vulgar display of wealth and waste." She wrote a letter to federal ministers and state chief ministers to request they give up some of their discretionary powers, particularly in land allotment issues.[42] The constitution authorized these ministers to use their discretion to favor an applicant or a contractor when deciding the delivery of certain services or allocation of land or other resources.

Responding to Sonia Gandhi's call, Singh appointed a nine-member Group of Ministers to pursue the matter. At first the Group favored a blanket abolition of discretionary powers of all federal ministers. But once it received feedback from eighty-four ministries and departments, the Group moderated its stance. Thirty-seven of these ministries and departments reported that they already lacked such powers. The remaining forty-five had limited discretion, most of it nonfinancial, such as allocating seats for the Hajj pilgrimage. "In a majority of the cases, the discretionary powers are in fact exercised by ministers in performance of their bona fide duties," such as appointments to boards and corporations, the Group's report concluded in March 2012. Nonetheless, the Group instructed all central ministries to establish guidelines on the disbursal of favors through ministers' discretionary powers and post these online.[43] But it failed to appoint any monitors to ensure compliance.

The "nonfinancial" adjective could not be applied to the generously funded defense ministry, with its annual budget of Rs 1,800 billion ($36 billion), which included funds for purchasing expensive advanced weaponry domestically and abroad. So it was widely noted and approved when defense minister Arackaparambil K. Antony gave up his discretionary power to name the winner of a particular arms deal in August 2012. The need for using discretionary power arose because there were almost always deviations between the technical parameters stated in the initial request for a proposal and the final product. Once these deviations were spelled out, it was the defense minister who until then had the final authority to let the deal be signed or to cancel an ongoing procurement contract.[44] He transferred this authority to the eleven-person Defense Acquisition Council, which was chaired by him and included the ministry's highest civil servant and the chiefs of the three armed services.

The core of the discretionary powers of state ministers, on the other hand, was their privileged access to land and natural resources—the value of which had exploded in the aftermath of the New Economic Policy (NEP)—since the ownership of land rested with the states.[45] As a consequence, the NEP reinforced the earlier business-politics nexus, which revolved principally around the funding of election campaigns.

Rampant Electoral Corruption

Electoral corruption stemmed from the link between unaccounted cash and the political establishment, and the egregious violation of the legal caps placed on election expenses by the independent Election Commission of India. There was no incentive for the political parties to alter the system, since they were its largest beneficiaries.

A dramatic example of the blatant role that money played in the parliamentary system was provided in March 2011 by WikiLeaks' publication of secret cables sent by United States diplomats to the U.S. State Department. In July 2008, the Singh government was desperate to defeat the no-confidence motion placed against it when the Communist-led Left Front's MPs withdrew their support in protest over the civil nuclear cooperation agreement between India and the United States.

The WikiLeaks report showed that five days before the vote, Nachiketa Kapur, a political aide to a senior Congress politician, Satish Sharma, showed a U.S. diplomat two chests full of cash—a portion of the Rs 500 to 600 million that the Congress Party had accumulated to buy the support of MPs for the confidence vote. Out of this treasury, four MPs of a regional party had been paid Rs 100 million ($2 million) each for their vote. "Money was not an issue at all . . . the crucial thing was to ensure that those who took the money would vote for the government," Kapur reportedly said. A second party official told the U.S. diplomat that formerly a minister "could only offer small planes as bribes," but "now he can pay for votes with jets."[46] Kapur shared this scandalous information with an employee of the U.S. Embassy on behalf of the Indian government in order to reassure the George W. Bush administration in advance that the controversial civil nuclear cooperation agreement between Delhi and Washington would be passed by the Lower House of the parliament. In the event, the Singh government survived the no-confidence vote by 275 votes to 256 votes, with ten MPs abstaining.

Frederick J. Kaplan, head of the U.S. Consulate in Chennai, along with his colleagues, conducted interviews with Indian politicians of high rank and their aides in Tamil Nadu and Andhra Pradesh. These interviews were summarized in Kaplan's secret cable to the State Department on May 13, 2009, which were part of the WikiLeaks that *The Hindu* newspaper published in a series of articles by Sarah Hiddleston. Karti Chidambaram of the Congress Party, M. Patturajan, a close ally of a federal minister, and MP Asaduddin Owaisi spoke freely to consulate officials about how their party operatives funneled money to voters during the election campaign. "Bribes from political parties to voters, in the form of cash, goods, or services, are a regular feature of elections in South India," noted Kaplan. "The money to pay the bribes comes from the proceeds of fundraising, which often crosses into political corruption." No matter where he and his colleagues went, "journalists, politicians, and voters spoke of the bribes as a commonly accepted fact of the election process."[47]

During visits to slums in Chennai and Hyderabad, they were told by a DMK (Tamil: Dravidian Progressive Federation) political strategist that "slums are critical to a campaign because their population density and poverty allow them to be more 'easily mobilized' by bribes." Representatives of an NGO working in a Chennai slum said, "the two main political parties in Tamil Nadu—the DMK and the AIADMK (All India Anna DMK)—regularly bribe voters." They described the procedure: "Weeks before, the elections agents of the parties come to the neighborhood with cash carried in rice sacks. They have copies of the voter lists and they distribute the money based on who is on the list." The agents arrived in the middle of the night, "between two and four in the morning, when the Election Commission is asleep." (It is worth noting that Andimuthu Raja, the central minister at the core of the 2G spectrum scam, was a DMK leader.)[48]

Kaplan explained how the DMK in Thirumangalam distributed cash bribes to voters for the State Assembly election. Every person on the voting roll received cash in envelopes inserted in their morning newspapers, along with the DMK voting slip, which instructed the recipient for whom they should vote. In this way, the DMK turned every voter into a bribe-taker. S. Kannan, a mid-level Congress Party official in Madurai, complained that "the [DMK's] 5,000 rupees [$110] per voter in Thirumangalam changed everything," noting that previous bribes to voters had topped out at Rs 500 [$11].

In Hyderabad, Owaisi operated differently. "If they [voters] want a well, I give them the money, but make sure they use it for the well," he said. He paid Rs 35,000 ($700) to cover the marriage of an orphaned girl. Owaisi contrasted his practice of funding projects for communal benefit with the tactics of the Congress and Telugu Desam Parties, which gave money to individual voters. When the U.S. diplomats asked Owaisi if donations for digging wells or paying for marriages were illegal, he replied, "Of course, but that's the great thing about our democracy."[49]

What were the sources of the money that candidates dispensed? As described in chapter 6,[50] the ruling Congress Party tapped businesspersons and industrialists for funds in cash to finance its election campaigns; other parties followed suit.

Research by the Association for Democratic Reforms showed that in 2010 the average wealth of an MP in the Lower House of Parliament was Rs 53 million ($1.06 million), which was 250 times the average wealth for an adult Indian. In other words, they were richer than 99.97 percent of adults in India, a country where 95 percent owned assets worth less than Rs 500,000 ($10,000).[51] Between the general elections of 2004 and 2009, the number of MPs with assets exceeding Rs 10 million ($200,000) almost doubled—accounting for nearly three-fifths of the 543-strong legislature—and so too did their average *declared* assets. These figures were derived from the affidavits that all the candidates had to submit with their nomination papers, as mandated by the federal ECI, an autonomous agency, charged with administering all electoral processes at the state and federal levels.

But the accuracy of such a declaration was suspect because the candidates were not required to give information about the sources of their income. After the 2004 Lok Sabha poll, the ECI sent a copy of affidavits submitted by the candidates to the Central Board of Direct Taxes to check whether the declared assets were acquired through known sources of income. In September 2008—according to Ruchika Singh, a scholar at the think tank the Hindu Centre for Politics and Public Policy—the Central Board informed the ECI that there were 103 cases where the statements given in affidavits did not match the income tax returns and 195 cases where income tax returns were not filed even though substantial assets were declared.[52]

According to the submitted affidavits, seven out of ten Congress MPs had a net worth of Rs 10 million or more, as did half of BJP members. The average assets of the sitting MPs who contested the poll in 2009 almost trebled during their five-year tenure. What seemed to help MPs enrich themselves, irrespective of being part of the ruling party or not, was their privilege to spend at their discretion Rs 20 million ($400,000) a year on development of their constituencies, according to the Member of Parliament Local Area Development scheme launched in 1993. In 2011, the ceiling for this scheme was raised to Rs 50 million.[53] By favoring a particular infrastructure project over others, an MP could set the scene for enriching himself or herself by receiving kickbacks from businesspeople who secured the building or maintenance contracts through an intermediary.

A pristine believer in democracy would have described these practices as serious distortions, which were increasingly giving the Indian model an odious aura among its honest citizens and foreign wellwishers.

Down to Villages

The extent to which these malpractices had seeped down to the village level was alarming, as I discovered in my field research in the rural area around the city of Jodhpur. The case of the 2010 sarpanch (mayor) election for the panchayat of Sangariya Block near Jodhpur was illustrative. The panchayat covered the settlements of Sangariya, Bhakarasni, Kuri Bhagtasni, and Tanawara. Its electorate was 16,500 strong. Candidates had to be residents of the settlements, and they could only enter the race as individuals—not as party members, who were permitted to use the party symbol allocated to them by the Election Commission of India. Of the dozen candidates, only five were serious contenders.

According to the candidate who lost the election by twenty-one votes, the winner, Lakshman Rao Chaudhary—a broad-shouldered professional land trader of medium height, often dressed in a dhoti, long shirt, and turban— lavished about Rs 1.5 million ($30,000) on electioneering. The defeated contestant admitted spending a little over half that amount. The legal cap, set by the State Election Commission, was Rs 40,000 ($800), about Rs 2.50 (5¢) per voter.[54]

Chaudhary, a native of Tanawara, started campaigning two months before the poll by hiring a team of canvassers who ate and drank at his expense. Almost two weeks before the poll, he reportedly opened a free kitchen for all. Together these gestures cost him an estimated Rs 800,000 to 900,000 ($16,000 to $18,000). The bill for the fuel for the vehicles he used—cars, Jeeps, and people carriers—was Rs 200,000 ($4,000). To clinch his victory, two days before the polling day, he probably bought the votes of those likely to favor his most serious rival by bribing the heads of subcastes who controlled vote banks. This reportedly set him back by another Rs 250,000 ($5,000). For those outside this network, he paid Rs 1,000 per voter directly to the head of the household, an exercise with a price tag of Rs 100,000 ($2,000). Posters, banners, leaflets, stationery, and other miscellaneous items cost him Rs 100,000 ($2,000).[55] Little wonder that the voter turnout was an unprecedented 80 percent.

The only way Chaudhary, with the meager annual sarpanch's salary of Rs 36,000 ($720), could recoup his massive expenditure and make a profit on his investment was by using his official powers to extract bribes. He had plenty of avenues for that, but he needed the cooperation of the gram sevak, who was charged with processing applications for land or house transfer, maintaining office records, writing minutes of meetings, and auditing accounts. The other state official the sarpanch had to deal with was the patwari, who kept the ownership records for land and houses.

The sarpanch's signature was required for the building and maintenance of infrastructure in his area—roads, sewers, water supply, power, schools, and health clinics. Any land or house transfer was legal only after he had signed it and affixed the official seal. There was a widely known bribe of Rs 2,000 ($40) for the sarpanch to authorize water or electricity connection, with 10 percent of it going to the gram sevak. Then there were the kickbacks on the infrastructure contracts. But the main source of graft was from land transfers, for which a small part of the sarpanch's bribe was funneled to the gram sevak. Land transfers were on the rise because of the proximity of the four villages to the fast-expanding Jodhpur, where agricultural land was being turned into residential and commercial property. The sarpanch's reported kickbacks for legalizing such transfers were 20 percent for the deals below Rs 100,000 ($2,000), 10 percent for transactions worth up to Rs 10 million ($200,000), and 5 percent for any sum above that figure. The estimate of his aggregate graft was put at a minimum of Rs 10 million ($200,000) during his five-year tenure.[56]

State and National Levels

With the average constituency for a seat in the State Assembly having 250,000 voters, a successful candidate ended up spending Rs 10 to 20 million ($200,000 to $400,000), and the average of the total amount spent by all the contestants often totaled Rs 25 million ($500,000). If that member of the legislative assembly belonged to the ruling party, he would then use his influence to see that Company A got a lucrative government contract instead of Company B or C. After his favored firm had signed the contract, its chief executive would pay the legislator in cash through a third party, and thus the legislator would begin to recoup his expenses.

An average parliamentary constituency, composed of several state assembly constituencies, covered 2.23 million people and 1.5 million electors. For the 2009 Lok Sabha election, the expenses cap varied between Rs 3.5 and 4 million. According to the Association for Democratic Reforms, or ADR, the candidates often underreported or disguised these expenses. Almost all of the 6,753 candidates for the 543 seats in the Lok Sabha declared that their outlay on the campaign was 45 to 55 percent of the legal cap.[57] Earlier, Atal Bihari Vajpayee, a former BJP prime minister, had lamented the fact that "Indian politicians start their legislative careers with a lie—the false spending returns they submit."[58] During the run-up to the 2014 parliamentary poll, Gopinath Munde, the BJP's deputy leader in the Lok Sabha, said, "When I first contested the elections to the Maharashtra Assembly in 1980, my expense was Rs 9,000, of which Rs 7,000 was borne by the party. But my expenditure in the last elections was Rs 8 crore [Rs 80 million]."[59]

As it was, there were massive loopholes in the law. There were no limits on the expenses that a political party could incur on its candidates' behalf. And, astonishingly, friends and associates of a candidate could spend unlimited amounts on behalf of him or her without the latter's consent.[60]

There was indisputable evidence that the roots of widespread corruption lay in the elections, the centerpiece of the democratic system in India. That the electoral process was in need of reform was recognized by the government under Prime Minister Vishwanath Partap Singh, leader of the Janata Dal (Hindi: People's Union), a progressive faction, in 1990. It appointed a commission to recommend reform. But his premiership lasted only a year. Since then, the size of electoral graft has ballooned, and six more government-commissioned reports on the subject have collected dust. All the same, the ritual continues. A news story published in March 2013 stated that the Law Commission was "working on the issue of electoral reforms."[61]

Surprisingly, only a few NGOs have focused on this fundamental issue. The Campaign for Electoral Reform in India has a one-point agenda: to see the present first-past-the-post system replaced by proportional representation. The Association for Democratic Reforms, founded in 1999 by some professors of the Indian Institute of Management, Ahmedabad, succeeded in 2003 in getting the Supreme Court to rule that candidates for public office must disclose their criminal record, assets and liabilities, and educational qualifications in a sworn affidavit as part of filing a nomination form. According to the affidavits signed by the members of the Lok Sabha elected in 2014, 35 percent of the 281 BJP parliamentarians had a criminal record, versus 18 percent of the forty-four Congress MPs.[62]

Political Parties Shield Accounts

In July 2004, T.S. Krishnamurthy, the chief election commissioner, addressed a letter to Prime Minister Singh on the subject of political parties' accounts. According to the Representation of the People Act of 1951, political parties must submit a "contribution report" every year to the Election Commission of India listing contributions above Rs 20,000 received from any individual or company.[63] Krishnamurthy recommended that they must be required to publish these annually for scrutiny by the general public and noted that the present rules required them to maintain such accounts, properly audited. Nothing came of it.[64]

But, using the Right to Information (RTI) Act, the ADR wrote to the Central Information Commission (CIC) in February 2007 to suggest that the income tax returns of political parties must be made public. The CIC asked all the parties recognized by the ECI to respond. The All India Congress Committee (AICC), supervised by Sonia Gandhi, bristled. "The applicant/appellant is a busybody having malafide intent and that they are seeking the information for ulterior motives," the AICC replied. "The documents [in question] are personal information of the political parties and also contain commercial confidential data, the disclosure of which is barred under Section 8(1) (d) and (j) of the Right to Information Act." The BJP also objected to the disclosure of the "confidential" information, citing the exemption granted by Section 8(1) (j) of the RTI Act. Of the remaining twenty-two political parties, only the CPI and Communist Party of India (Marxist) said that they had "no objection" to making public their income tax returns.[65]

The ADR responded to these reactions. It argued that since political parties were working in public domain and using public funds, the information about their financial condition was in the public interest. The Central Information Commission upheld its appeal in April 2008. It directed the public authorities holding such information to pass it on to the ADR within six weeks. The CIC noted that while political parties were, in essence, NGOs, they exercised governmental power through direct or indirect influence, and that brought them within the ambit of the RTI Act, requiring as much transparency of them as of state institutions.[66]

An analysis made by ADR of the documents submitted by the national parties between April 2004 and March 2012 showed contributors' identities were not included on the contribution forms for 75 percent of the funds received by the parties either because these donors contributed less than Rs 20,000 or because they deliberately withheld information. The principal reason was that the donors were passing on black money. "Where does a political party get its funds from?" asked industrialist Rahul Bajaj, worth $3.4 billion, in his address to the Confederation of Indian Industries conference in Mumbai in 2010. "Come on, I've been in Parliament for four years. It's not [by] checks, it's not by small members. All money comes in through black money. Black money doesn't come from heaven."[67]

The identified contributors donated Rs 3.79 billion ($75.8 million) between April 2004 and March 2012. Of these donations, seven-eighths of the cash came from corporate and business houses, with the BJP receiving Rs 1.925 billion (38.8 million), amounting to 85 percent of its voluntary contributions, and the Congress receiving Rs 1.723 billion, amounting to 92 percent of its voluntary contributions. The General Electoral Trust of the Aditya Birla Group was the top donor to the Congress (Rs 364 million) and the BJP (Rs 266 million).[68]

A determined effort to get black money out of electoral politics would involve aligning the provisions in the Representation of People Act of 1951 with all the laws dealing with money: the Income Tax Act, the Wealth Tax Act, the Companies Act, the Foreign Exchange Management Act, the Prevention of Money Laundering Act, the Banking Regulations Act, and Cooperative Society laws and audit standards. A far simpler and more basic approach would be to pass a law on political parties, such as the one that already exists in forty countries.

The earliest such law was enacted in 1967 by the government of the Federal Republic of Germany (aka West Germany). It provided a legal definition of a political party and outlined the internal democratic structure it had to maintain, the procedure it had to follow to nominate candidates for elections, and how it should maintain its finances and its presentation to the public—as well as outlining the government's implementation of bans on unconstitutional parties.[69] (After the reunification of East and West Germany in 1990, this law became applicable to reunited Germany.) This is the model that Indian lawmakers should follow to rid the country of its worsening electoral corruption.

Staggering Expenses During the 2014 Lok Sabha Election

For the 2014 election, the ECI raised the expenditure ceiling from Rs 2.5–3.5 million for smaller states to Rs 5.4 million, and from Rs 4 million to Rs 7 million for larger states.[70] The Associated Chambers of Commerce and Industry of India estimated that a majority of the 8,251 candidates would end up spending Rs 50 to 70 million each, giving a boost of Rs 60 billion to the GDP.[71] This figure turned out to be an underestimate. The BJP spent an estimated Rs 50 billion on advertising in all media, according to a report in the *Hindustan Times*.[72] By comparison, the estimate for the budget of the Congress to refurbish the image of Rahul Gandhi was put at Rs 7 billion.[73] Among the BJP's corporate donors, the Adani Group stood out if only because of Modi's use of the conglomerate's aircraft for his whirlwind electioneering.[74]

The Adani Group was founded in Ahmedabad in 1988 and became a publicly traded entity six years later. But its exponential rise came only after Modi became the chief minister of Gujarat in October 2001. Between 2002 and March 2014, the group's revenue increased twelvefold, to $9.4 billion. By then, the Mundra port, built in the Adani Port and Special Economic Zone (APSEZ) and owned and operated by the group's flagship, Adani Enterprises, which also operated India's largest thermal power plant and was the country's largest coal importer, had emerged as the largest private port as measured by the cargo volume it handled.

The evidence for the group's pro-Modi leanings was provided by the ADR. Its research showed that between April 2004 and March 2012 the Adani Group donated $721,000 to the BJP, 1.7 times the amount it contributed to the Congress Party. In January 2014, Gujarat High Court ordered the closure of twelve out of twenty-one APSEZ-based industrial facilities because they had failed to obtain environmental clearance from the central government. On appeal, the Supreme Court allowed the facilities to function but not expand, and ordered the ministry to decide on permits. The troubles at APSEZ did not quell the enthusiasm of investors for Adani Enterprises. With the prospect of Modi's victory rising, Adani Enterprises stocks surged an unparalleled 23 percent, with its share price doubling from its February 2014 value, compared with the rise of only 20 percent in the infrastructure index.[75] The company had come a long way from the days when the Environment Ministry fined it Rs 2 billion ($40 million) for damaging mangroves, creeks, and the local environment in September 2013, an event that had caused a 6.4 percent dip in its share price.[76] In early 2014, however, the investors bet the right way. Modi became the prime minister on May 26, and on July 15 his environmental minister, Prakash Javadekar, granted the Adani company the necessary clearance. It was part of the Modi government's decision to relax the environmental standards of the Environment Protection Act of 1986, a law that was passed in response to the horrific accident at a Union Carbide chemical plant in Bhopal in December 1984 that led to the deaths of nearly 3,800 people.

The fact that the BJP had a majority in the Lok Sabha on its own, which it had never enjoyed before, enabled Modi—given to an authoritative style of governance—to centralize power. He did so with alacrity. Even Rajnath Singh, a senior BJP leader who served as home minister, was not allowed to make minor decisions unilaterally.[77]

With Modi exercising supreme authority in Delhi, the sky was the limit for such business houses as the Adani Group and similar conglomerates. Their largesse to the BJP was expected to increase, which made the passage of any law mandating that political parties publish annual audited accounts an even more remote possibility. Any pressure for such legislation could only come from NGOs. As it was, a staggering number of NGOs had sprouted in the wake of the New Economic Policy. They performed myriad functions, with a minority among them agitating against neoliberal policies and globalization.

Multiple Roles of NGOs

In India, all nonprofit organizations were classified as NGOs. These organizations were required to register under the Societies Registration Act of 1860, or its subsequent variants in individual states. In addition, there was a long list of other pertinent laws. It included the Religious Endowment Act of 1863, the Indian Trust Act of 1882, the Charitable and Religious Trust Act of 1920, the Mussalman Wakf Act of 1923, the Public Trust Act of 1950, the Wakf Act of 1954, and the Public Wakfs (Extension of Limitation) Act of 1959, as well as Section 25 of the Indian Companies Act of 1956. A study conducted by a government-appointed committee showed that in 2010 there were 3.3 million NGOs in India. This worked out to three NGOs for a typical village with an average population of 1,200![78] Even more remarkable was that between 1990 and 2009 the number of NGOs had increased sixfold. They were funded by domestic sources, ranging from the government to individuals, or by foreign NGOs, foundations, or trusts, in which case they had to register with the Home Ministry in Delhi, as required by the Foreign Contribution Regulation Act.

What mattered most, in view of the rising tensions in the Indian polity after the New Economic Policy, was the role played by the NGOs grappling with socioeconomic and civil rights issues. There, broadly speaking, NGOs focused on one or more of the following specific areas: preserving the ecosystem by opposing the construction of large dams or industries causing large-scale pollution; providing education and vocational training; improving healthcare and basic sanitation; providing or improving housing; promoting cultural activities; safeguarding civil and human rights; monitoring such national laws as the ban on child labor; improving the lot of slumdwellers or Adivasis; fighting for the underprivileged; and assisting other NGOs.[79] In

Dehradun district alone, there were 7,469 NGOs in 2010. Their annual budget ranged between Rs 2.5 million ($50,000) to Rs 20 million ($400,000).[80]

Nationally, the People's Union for Civil Liberties and the People's Union for Democratic Rights had been working for decades to safeguard civil and human rights as guaranteed by the Indian constitution. At local or state level, Aasraa Trust in Dehradun specialized in educating slum children and offering vocational training to slum-dwelling women. In contrast, PAHAR (People's Association for Himalayan Area Research), based in Nainital, Uttarakhand, raised awareness of the fragile Himalayan environment and brought together scientists, social activists, and local residents to save the Himalayas. Formed in 2000, the SAMARPAN Society focused on providing healthcare to adolescents and urban poor in Uttarakhand. It was funded initially by the United States Agency for International Development (USAID) and later also by the central government's National Rural Health Mission. The Rural Litigation and Entitlement Kendra, based in Dehradun, was committed to fighting for the underprivileged within the judicial system and campaigning for fresh legislation wherever necessary protections did not exist. It focused on the nomadic communities in Uttar Pradesh and Himachal Pradesh, and provided them with elementary education and healthcare.

Sensing the disgust that an increasing number of citizens felt at the exponential growth in graft and the declining standards of such public services as healthcare and education, some state governments resorted to outsourcing the delivery of these services to NGOs. They figured that since NGO employees were socially committed and not corrupt, the quality and delivery of these services would improve. In Uttarakhand, for example, the state's health department started outsourcing to NGOs the operations of the rural and urban health centers and mobile medical units.[81] Some viewed this as an innovative feature of India's democracy, while others considered it a further application of the neoliberal agenda, geared to reducing the role of state. NGOs that received this type of contract from the government were invariably nonpolitical.

At the other end stood the National Alliance of People's Movements (NAPM), a network of NGOs that specialized in focusing on the voiceless and shining a light on their plight—a stance that led it to resist the NEP and globalization, but through nonviolent means. The NAPM alliance evolved gradually with a meeting of like-minded activists in Bhopal in December 1992. They were the prime movers of an anti-NEP mass rally in Delhi three months later. The rally was followed by a series of conclaves in major cities to forge a common ideology and program. This culminated in a national conference in September 1995 in Mumbai on the topic of the NEP and the displacement of the underprivileged. These delegates were bound together by their opposition to the eviction of people from their homes, agricultural plots, forests, water sources, and their means of livelihood by dams, forest enclosures, mining enterprises, steel and aluminum works, soft drink plants, and Special Economic Zones, where companies were exempted from tax and labor laws—a process that accelerated in the NEP era. They favored communal control over land and natural resources.

At the Mumbai conference, the organizers sought the active cooperation of like-minded lawyers, artists, and journalists. They then toured fourteen states as a preamble to holding a national convention. The tour ended at Sewagram Ashram in Wardha, Maharashtra, the main base of Mahatma Mohandas Gandhi, to stress the alliance's commitment to nonviolence. At the convention in Mumbai in December 1996, representatives of ninety NGOs participated and adopted an ideological charter and a program. Sanjay Mangala Gopal was elected the National Coordinator.

"We oppose the uncontrolled powers of global and national capital," stated the NAPM's ideological charter. "The present process of globalization is artificial and unsustainable. . . . We oppose the profit-oriented New Economic Policy with its attendant liberalization, privatization and globalization, because it marginalizes and even excludes a majority of people and exhausts the resources of the nation for the sake of accumulation of profit in the private hands of a minority at the national as well as international level. . . . We oppose the integration of [Indian] agriculture into the world market." The charter favored a "people-oriented," sustainable development model but failed to offer a blueprint.[82] Its membership was limited to domestically financed NGOs, with foreign-funded bodies relegated to associate membership. It reiterated its commitment to nonviolent direct action. It affirmed its boycott of electoral politics in the belief that all political parties were implementing the NEP at the state or central level. Its representatives participated in the protests at the World Trade Organization ministerial conference in Seattle in November 1999. During the next decade its network expanded to more than two hundred NGOs in fifteen different socioeconomic fields, ranging from dam building and mining projects to slums and child labor. It organized such peaceful direct action as rallies, marches, demonstrations, and strikes.

The NAPM succeeded in some campaigns and failed in others. It supported the peaceful agitation by its constituent, Narmada Bachao Andolan (Hindi: Save Narmada Movement), against the construction of a series of dams in the valley of the Narmada River flowing through Madhya Pradesh, Maharashtra, and Gujarat. Though it helped to generate a national debate on the issue, and the subsequent controversy led the World Bank to withdraw its offer of a loan of $450 million, it lost the battle at the Supreme Court in October 2000. The court ruled by two votes to one that the building of the Sardar Sarovar dam on the Narmada could go ahead.[83]

In May 2003, when the panchayat of Pudussery in Kerala revoked the water-use license of the Pepsi factory, arguing that it had depleted the ground-water to the extent of causing scarcity, the NAPM's Medha Patkar endorsed the move. Gopal, the national coordinator, reported, "People from villages in Varanasi in Uttar Pradesh in the north, and Thane in Maharashtra in the west, have also asked us to initiate agitations against the lavish use of scarce water resources by multinational soft-drink companies."[84]

The NAPM became a storehouse of popular experience that it deployed to mobilize those who had in the past been either dormant or passive, at best, to inject their concerns into the national discourse. In July 2006, Patkar and other NAPM activists arrived in the village of Medhiganj, Uttar Pradesh, to back the local struggle against a Coca-Cola bottling plant that was overutilizing the settlement's water supply. Hundreds of villagers gathered around the platform set up near the plant gates. In her speech, Patkar narrated the experience of the residents of Plachimada village in Kerala, who had also been battling a Coca-Cola factory with some success, and she listed the lessons of that agitation.[85]

Earlier that year, the NAPM was a major player in securing the reversal of the decision of the West Bengal government, led by the CPI (Marxist), to establish a fifteen-thousand-acre APSEZ on fertile agricultural land for an Indonesian multinational corporation. Later in 2006, the National Commission for Dalit Human Rights, a leading network of Dalit movements, officially joined the NAPM. But the NAPM's attempt to mobilize all its constituents to launch a concerted, nationwide attack on the NEP, starting with a huge mass rally in Delhi in March 2007, failed. Though activists from sixteen states turned up for the meeting, its size was unimpressive.[86]

Overall, though, the NAPM's activities had created political space for discussion and debate outside the political establishment. And on important domestic events, it offered comment and analysis that the media often took up and reported. For instance, while commenting on the Maoist ambush on a Congress Party convoy in the Darbha Valley on May 25, 2013, it referred to an earlier episode on the night of May 17–18, when a firefight between the security forces and Maoists guerrillas had led to the deaths of eight Adivasis near another village in the same valley. "If life of those in power and leadership are important [then] so are the lives of common Adivasis who are being tortured, jailed and killed by security forces and Maoists," it said. "In the Darbha Valley where the attack by Maoists has killed Congress leaders, the State administration had violated all existing laws and procedures to facilitate land grab for Tata Steel."[87]

Since the NAPM was wedded to nonviolence, it continued to function freely. So did all other NGOs, most of them with a single-issue agenda. As a rule, they pressed their case at first by recording it on the grievance sections of websites maintained by the central administration and many state governments. If nothing came of it, they then sought meetings with local legislators, members of parliament, and ministers. If that failed, and if they had the wherewithal, they hired a competent lawyer to file a Public Interest Litigation with the high court in a state capital, in accordance with Article 226 of the Constitution.[88] But these courts were creaking under heavy backlog. In the spring of 2013, there were nearly five hundred thousand cases pending in high courts. But, if a high court decided that a particular PIL petition was weighty and urgent, it could fast-track it. If the NGO's attempt failed or it lost the case, then it had the option of approaching the Supreme Court, according to Article 32 of the Constitution.[89] At this court, the backlog of cases was a mere fifty thousand.[90] In both instances, the petitioner had to establish prima facie that the fundamental rights of citizens were at stake and that the subject was of public interest.

Public Interest Litigation: The Prime Innovation

Public Interest Litigation rested on the basic principle of letting an individual or group file a petition on behalf of others. It was Supreme Court judge V.R. Krishna Iyer, former minister in the Communist government of Kerala, who introduced this concept in 1976 when he ruled that the Mumbai Kamgar Sabha, Bombay (Hindi: Mumbai Workers' Council) could be the appellant for the workers of M/S Abdulbhai Faizullabhai & Ors. "Public interest is promoted by a spacious construction of *locus standi* in our socio-economic circumstances and conceptual latitudinarianism permits taking liberties with individualization of the right to invoke the higher courts where the remedy is shared by a considerable number, particularly when they are weaker," he stated.[91] Later, the Supreme Court would assume the power to initiate litigation itself if it concluded that the aggrieved party lacked the means to do so or felt intimidated.

After the Emergency imposed by Prime Minister Indira Gandhi from June 1975 to January 1977, when all civil and human rights of citizens were suspended, there was a strong sentiment in the nation to find a way of circumscribing future excesses by the executive. It was in this social environment that Supreme Court advocate Kapila Hingorani drew the attention of the Court to the deplorable plight of prisoners awaiting trial, which had been exposed in a series of newspaper articles. Prisoner Sunil Batra wrote a letter to Justice Krishna Iyer referring to widespread torture of fellow inmates by their jailers. A social activist drew the Court's attention to the slave-like conditions of bonded workers in quarries. Several cases of this nature followed. In the course of dealing with these petitions, the Supreme Court formed a new set of citizens' rights and state's obligations, and new methods of accountability.

In 1982, Justice Prafullachandra Natwarlal Bhagwati described public interest litigation as "a strategic arm of the legal aid movement which is intended to bring justice within the reach of the poor masses who constitute the low visibility area of humanity [and] is a totally different kind of litigation from the ordinary traditional litigation."[92] Soon after being promoted to chief justice in July 1985, Bhagwati placed PIL within the context of Article 32 of the Constitution, which accords the citizen the right to move the Supreme Court to bring about the enforcement of his or her fundamental rights listed in the Constitution. This move vastly enlarged jurisdiction of the Supreme Court, giving it the power to remedy the actions or omissions of the executive branch, while in the process acting as monitor of the investigating and prosecuting agencies of the government.

Declaring that the principle of judicial independence meant noninterference by the executive or the legislature in the appointment of its judges, in 1993 the Supreme Court divested the president of India of the power to nominate Supreme Court judges in consultation with the cabinet. That authority was transferred to the Chief Justice and a collegium of the four most senior judges. They advised the president, who did the formal appointing. Since, according to Article II of the U.S. Constitution, the president has the power to appoint justices of the Supreme Court, subject only to confirmation by the Senate,[93] judicial independence is more firmly guaranteed in India than in the United States.

With rising inequality and a higher rate of capital accumulation in the wake of the NEP, the number of PILs on corruption rose. The failure of the Congress Party government of P.V. Narasimha Rao to follow up the leads of underhand payments made by Surendra Kumar Jain, as noted in his diaries, led journalist Vineet Narain to file a PIL with the Supreme Court in October 1993. It was the intervention by this court that goaded the CBI to file a case against Surendra Jain and his brother in March 1995.[94]

When dealing with cases not linked to graft, the Supreme Court's wish to demonstrate its impartiality led it to rule in favor of the government's massive infrastructure projects. Such was the case when it dealt with the objections raised by NGOs against a series of dams in the Narmada Valley. In October 2000, it concluded that the long-term benefits accruing to the inhabitants of the region from this enterprise outweighed the near-term loss of homes and land to those displaced by the project.

In April 2011, it upheld the PIL filed by the People's Union for Civil Liberties for food to be regarded as part of the fundamental right to life. Its subsequent interim orders to the central government gave a push to the Right to Food campaign by NGOs. Yet it took twelve years for food security legislation to materialize, and that too only in the form of an ordinance with a maximum life of six months.

The Supreme Court required a PIL application by Anna Hazare in June 2003 to compel the state governments of Maharashtra and Karnataka to turn over the case against the master con man Abdul Karim Telgi to the CBI, which in turn energized the wheels of justice at the lower level.[95]

In the broadcasting field, the Bombay High Court gained front-page headlines in August 2006 when it directed broadcasters to give an undertaking that they would abide by the Cable Television Network (Regulation) Act of 1995 as well as its orders within twenty-four hours in view of widespread public interest.

Both the Delhi High Court and the Supreme Court won plaudits from the public with their rulings on the 2G spectrum scam in 2009–10, centered round the misdeeds of communications minister Andimuthu Raja. The High Court ruled on July 1, 2009, that Raja's decision to advance the cutoff date for applications for 2G spectrum licenses from October 1 to September 25 was illegal. The scam came to light fully only in stages, after the Centre for Public Interest Litigation made a PIL application to the Supreme Court in August 2010, which the court accepted within weeks. When Ratan Tata tried through legal means to limit the publishing of the audiotape records that would confirm the nefarious backdoor dealings, the Centre sought the active intervention of the Supreme Court to lift the cloak of secrecy that concealed from public gaze the subversion of official policy for the benefit of private company interests. In short, it appealed to the court to publish the entire collection of the Radia tapes in its possession. The court granted the plea. This gave the general public an unvarnished view of the unholy alliance between politicians, businesspeople, lobbyists, and senior journalists—searing evidence of the distortions of the world's largest democracy.[96]

In the Coalgate scandal that broke in 2012, it was once again a PIL, this one filed by advocate L.M. Sharma, that exposed the skullduggery in the allocation of coal blocks through a Byzantine procedure that skirted competitive bidding to favor politicians and their kith and kin.[97]

Such a dismal record of his government should have caused Prime Minister Singh much soul searching at the very least. His prestige hit rock bottom when the Supreme Court publicly criticized him on November 18, 2010, for failing to respond to more than a year of requests to investigate the allegations against minister Raja. Almost three months later, Singh got a chance to express his views in his inaugural speech to the Commonwealth Lawyers conference in Hyderabad. He referred to "a series of landmark decisions of our Supreme Court," where "our judges have also widened and deepened their scope and reach as law givers." Conceding that "the judicial process" was "the guarantor of justice to litigants and an upholder of the constitutional ideals of our nation," he stressed that "the basic structure of the constitution is not subordinated to political impulses of the moment or to the will of transient majorities." He added, "While the power of judicial review must be used to enforce accountability, it must never be used to erode the legitimate role assigned to the other branches of government."[98] In plain English, Singh was complaining about the intrusion of the Supreme Court into the policy and administrative spheres of the state's executive organ.

His complaint was misplaced. As a rule, the Supreme Court and lower courts do not delve into administrative matters. But when dealing with PILs, the Supreme Court and the High Courts are required to rule whether or not an administrative decision is in the public interest and if it is fair and just. It can do so only by examining official documents and instructing the government to submit an affidavit.

The Changing Social Ambience

Taking a panoramic view, there are two basic questions to pose. Have the interventions of the Supreme Court encouraged the process of embedding the democratic system in India or hindered it? And what was the socio-economic background to the decisions made by the Court?

By periodically ordering the executive to right the wrong it has done, the Supreme Court has kept alive the hope of those who feel victimized or oppressed or those who loathe the nefarious, corrupt practices of the rich and the influential that the present social system has fostered. In the final analysis, though, Supreme Court judges have served, in essence, as the knowing or inadvertent agents of maintaining the status quo, content to tweak the system here and there.

Since 1993, the Supreme Court had delivered verdicts in a rapidly changing social environment. When the NEP was introduced in 1991, only one out of two Indians was literate. Two decades later, three out of four were counted as literate, a 50 percent improvement.[99] During that period, the sources of information and comment available to ordinary citizens multiplied. For example, until 1991, the Ministry of Information and Broadcasting (MIB) had a monopoly on radio and TV communication, with their respective channels—All India Radio (aka Akashvani, Hindi: Sky Speech) and Door Darshan (Hindi: Distant Vision)—underwritten by the Indian Telegraph Act of 1885. In early 1991, when the eleven-year-old Atlanta-based Cable News Network (CNN) satellite TV channel wanted to make its coverage of the Gulf War available in India, the government allowed it to access satellite uplinks. This provided an opening to other cable networks.

In late 1993, a dispute between the Cricket Association of Bengal and the MIB regarding the worldwide telecasting of a cricket tournament by the New York–based TransWorld International was hastily resolved by the imposition of a compromise devised by the Calcutta High Court. TransWorld broadcast the matches, but neither the MIB nor the Cricket Association was satisfied with the outcome. They appealed to the Supreme Court.[100]

In February 1995, the three-judge bench of the Supreme Court ruled that the right to "impart and receive information" was implicit in the right to freedom of speech and expression guaranteed by Article 19 (1) (a) of the Constitution and recommended that the Indian government end the state monopoly on broadcasting as well as satellite uplinks. In a separate ruling, Justice B.P. Jeevan Reddy ruled that the Indian Telegraph Act of 1885 was "wholly inadequate and unsuited for" electronic media and that the Parliament should enact new laws for this means of communication.[101] With the introduction of the Prasar Bharati (Hindi: Indian Broadcasting) Act in 1997, the operation of Door Darshan and All India Radio was passed onto Prasar Bharati, a nominally autonomous body whose chairperson was appointed by the president. Since it was dependent on the government treasury for its financial survival, it was regarded as a public broadcasting service. It was invariably given priority treatment by all high officials of India, including the latest, pro–private sector prime minister, Modi.

By 2012, there were 150 million TV sets in India and 823 TV channels offering news, sports, entertainment, and religion.[102] A single Door Darshan channel mushroomed into twenty-one outlets, with DD National, a terrestrial channel reaching 92 percent of all homes in the country, outstripping all other channels. Overall, about one hundred channels aired news and commentary in sixteen Indian languages, including English. Four-fifths of these news stations were twenty-four-hour channels. Heavily dependent on advertising revenue in a very competitive market, TV channels pitched content to the lowest common denominator to raise their audience figures. All the same, there was greater choice for viewers than ever before.

Videsh Sanchar Nigam Limited, a public sector company, became the first service provider of the Internet in India on August 15, 1995. In 2001, the number of Internet connections reached 7 million, or 0.7 percent of the population. That statistic jumped to 110 million ten years later, or 9.1 percent of the population, rising to 15 percent two years later. But most of these connections were in urban centers.[103] A similar division prevailed in the cellphone sector.

The rise in cell-phone subscriptions, which started in August 1995, has been phenomenal. It zoomed from under 37 million in 2001 to over 924 million in 2014.[104] This had a positive impact on economic expansion. It was estimated that an extra 10 percent penetration of cell phones in India led to an increase of 0.44 percent growth in the GDP.[105]

"The total telecom density of the country [in 2012] is about 71 percent but only 33 percent of rural India, which has 70 percent of the country's population," noted a report by Telecom India in 2012.[106] A study by the Indian

Council for Research on International Economic Relations in 2008 showed that the states with 10 percent higher cell-phone penetration produced 1.2 percent higher annual economic expansion that those with a lower cell-phone density.[107] Little wonder that the rural population had received a miniscule share of the wealth generated by the post-NEP boom.

Even within that portion, there was much variation between regions and between those settlements near expanding cities and those far removed from the bustling urban centers.

9

Perspectives from the Grassroots

Some of the factors that shaped the perspectives of the villagers I met were fixed and others variable. The distance of a rural settlement from a large town or city was a constant, and so was the subcaste into which Hindu Indians were born and which confined them to a particular neighborhood in their native settlement. The extent of villagers' education changed with time; so too did the irrigation facilities for their crops and the availability of electricity and drinking water for their homes. Equally, their social and political consciousness was affected by changes in communication wrought by advances in technology and the dissemination of information. These observations stemmed from my field research of Johri Gaon and Rasulpur in Uttarakhand, Kuri Bhagtasni in Rajasthan, Sisola in Uttar Pradesh, and Kekra Ravoli in Chhattisgarh.

Johri Gaon

The year 2000 has a special place in the history of Johri Gaon (Hindi: Johri Village). It was in that year that the state of Uttaranchal (renamed Uttarakhand in 2007) was carved out of northwestern Uttar Pradesh, with Dehradun as its capital. The exaltation of that city rubbed off on this settlement located five miles from its northern boundary.

As the capital city of a state with a population of 8.5 million people, famed for its salubrious climate, Dehradun attracted businesspeople and contractors from Delhi as well as retired company executives and army officers from the warmer parts of northern India. This influx raised property values. Finding the inflated house prices in Dehradun too steep or the affordable residences unsuitable, the newly arrived cast their eyes on Johri Gaon, then a settlement of 1,500 people living in modest cottages dotted between agricultural fields and clumps of lush green woodlands. Its inhabitants were served by a few poorly stocked shops.

Land prices zoomed after 2000. "When I was a boy one bigha [750 square meters] cost Rs 1,000 [$20]," recalled the stocky, forty-one-year-old civil servant Yogesh Bist, as he chewed betel-nut paan that had turned his teeth red. "Now a single bigha costs Rs 5 to 6 million [$100,000 to $120,000]."[1]

Local landholders found the offers for their plots too tempting to resist. The resulting transactions put a lot of cash into the pockets of the villagers. They spent their new wealth in a variety of ways, depending on their educational background and the advice they managed to garner from those with basic financial expertise. Most of them upgraded their cottages to brick-and-mortar two-story buildings, sometimes aping the architectural style of the upscale neighborhoods of New Delhi. "When I was a boy there were many huts and houses of mud," recalled Bisht. "Now all houses are made of baked bricks. We also have piped water. In old days, a rich person owned a cycle. Now some rich families have two cars." In addition, there were the spacious and architecturally distinct houses of the well-off urbanite immigrants, many of them with gardens, basements, and rooftop rain-harvesting tanks.

For the remaining agricultural land, the tools of production changed. "There are tractors for plowing now," added Bisht. "Very few oxen plows are left." The landless villagers who were made redundant by the tractors traveled to Dehradun to find menial work or to learn to drive trucks or taxis.

As for the surplus cash left after the improvement in housing, the uneducated among the former landholders lavished funds on expensive weddings and feasts, or on booze. The rest invested in businesses, ranging from shops selling consumer goods to hardware stores catering to the ongoing construction projects.

The transformation of this nondescript settlement of 1,500 souls into a semi-urban suburb within a decade was well captured by the story of Baru Pal, a lean, dark, middle-aged man with a light stoop. He owned three bighas of land and worked as a truck driver to eke out a living for his family of five. In 2000, as the demand for new houses for urban outsiders rose, he started to sell his land in stages. The boom in local construction led him to become a supplier of building materials—gravel, sand, cement, bricks, wood, and paints—which he stored on the half bigha of land he retained for himself. As part of his expanding business, he acquired a dump truck, a water carrier, and an outsize auto-rickshaw. He also forged contacts with carpenters, plumbers, and electricians.

Catering for the recently settled urbanites, the enterprising villagers provided goods and services that citizens in a freshly globalizing world were getting used to—from canned foods to beauty parlors to Internet cafés. The enterprising and highly educated Bhatt family, ensconced in a large mansion, had branched out of selling construction materials to running a travel agency and an Internet café, as well as selling and servicing computers and hardware.

Along the same street, below the sign RAINA BEAUTY PARLOUR appeared the following text: "(Only for Ladies); Mobile 9557683226; Bridal Makeup; Party Make-up; Skin and Hair Treatment; Hair SPA; Trained by VLCC Beautician; Expert in Make up in hair and skin." The beautician was Sheetal Jhapa, a bright-eyed, ebullient, twenty-five-year-old with a smiling face and sleek black hair, in jeans and a flowery blouse. "VLLC stands for the Vandana Luther Curve Club in Dehradun," she explained. "They also make a skin whitening cream, a fairness cream." The traditional Indian aspiration to be fair-skinned has been accentuated by widespread exposure to Western movies available on cable TV.

She talked to me in the shadow of a cell-phone transmission tower of Bharat Sanchar Nigam Limited, erected in 2006. Cell phones were ubiquitous. "These companies charge by the pulse, which is thirty seconds," explained Avdesh Kaushall, a tall, skinny man with sunken cheeks and missing teeth who ran a general provisions store in the main street. "The monthly charges vary between Rs 100 to 300 [$2 to $6]. Mobiles are good because that way you know what is happening where. It is good for business; that is why I use it in the shop. At home I have a landline phone." His shop displayed signs of Vodafone and Airtel logos, for which he received no payment from the companies.[2]

Cell-phone company logos could be seen even in villages that lacked electricity: cumulatively these accounted for nearly half of the rural population of the nation.[3] Though street lighting and electricity came to Johri Gaon in 1990, electrification of homes proceeded slowly during that decade. Later, the pace picked up. But, as of 2010, not all residences were electrified.[4]

Johri Gaon had the distinction of having a primary school as far back as 1963, according to Sumanta Banerjee, a veteran journalist and writer who lived in Delhi until 2001. "Now there are three schools providing education up to higher secondary stage [eighteen-year-olds], and the youngsters in the village are almost all literate," Banerjee told me. "Besides, there is an *anganvadi* [Hindi: around a courtyard], a government-sponsored village institution-cum-crèche run by female teachers and paramedics to look after children and the health of local women." But the village lacked a health clinic. It had only one practicing doctor. "His minimum fee is Rs 50 to 100 [$1 to $2]," said Jhapa. "In Dehradun you pay Rs 150 to 200 [$3 to $4], the average wage of a day laborer. And for emergency treatment, you pay Rs 300 [$6]."

Overall, Johri Gaon reflected the upbeat mood prevalent in Dehradun, which had witnessed the opening of six shopping malls in as many years. In several ways, the village was being urbanized. Yet it suffered from the fate typical of rural India, which was at the receiving end of the traditional ineptitude and corruption of the bureaucracy. It was glaringly manifest in the ramshackle state of roads. "In our village, roads are neglected for years," complained Banerjee. "On the eve of State Assembly elections, the candidate of the ruling party gets the public works department to repair roads. This impresses the public and gets the candidate votes. Roads look fine. But the contractor had done a cosmetic job, using substandard materials and shoddy workmanship. Come monsoon, and the roads collapse. The one to our village from the city remains flooded during the rainy season. So we have to wait for the next election when the candidates listen to our complaints and get our village roads repaired."

Periodic elections keep the flickering flame of hope alive. "The candidates deliver 30 percent of the promises they make when they win," stated Binode Nautiyal, a muscular man in cotton trousers with a weather-beaten face, who had been eavesdropping on the conversation at Kaushall's store. "If one candidate does not deliver, then we go for another. If he fails, then we try the third. I used to vote Congress, but I was impressed by Atal Bihari Vajpayee as the prime minister. So now I vote BJP [Bharatiya Janata Party]."[5] It later transpired that, in this village of two thousand people, the voter turnout for the panchayat as well as State Legislative Assembly was high, between 80 to 85 percent.

Since its founding, Uttarakhand has been ruled alternatively by the Congress Party (2002–7, and 2012 onward) and the BJP (2000–2002 and 2007–12), with both of them committed to furthering the New Economic Policy. The situation in Rajasthan since 1990 has been similar, with the Congress Party and the BJP alternating terms in the state capital of Jaipur.

Basking in the Urbanizing Sun

Predictably, the prime beneficiaries of urbanization, accelerated by the NEP, have been the villages surrounding cities and large towns. If a particular settlement also found itself included in a national highway-building project, then its chances of being urbanized soared. Such was the case with Kuri Bhagtasni (aka Kudi Bhagtasni). Most of the householders in Kuri Bhagtasni were peasants, with the remainder being carpenters and potters. The village was situated ten miles from the center of Jodhpur, the headquarters of the Jodhpur Development Authority (JDA), established by the state government to ensure a planned expansion of the city.

In 1989, the JDA decided to acquire, in stages, 2,500 bighas in Jodhpur's surrounding rural areas for "public purposes" under the Land Acquisition Act of 1894. Five years into this project, it targeted Kuri Bhagtasni. It started paying Rs 35,000 ($700) per bigha of the rural land, handing over checks to sellers. In the mid-1990s, with the Ambala-Pali National Highway 65 passing by the settlement, land prices soared. In 1999, the JDA decided to sell a third of its acquired land to Ansal Housing and Construction Limited, a big player in property development. It did so at Rs 125,000 ($2,500) per bigha; the JDA made a handsome profit, according to the interviews I did with the villagers.

Attracted by Kuri Bhagtasni's location along the National Highway 65, some large handicraft factories in Jodhpur moved to the area around it. The value of land increased further, with the government rating it at Rs 200,000 ($4,000) per bigha. Ansal offered two to two-and-a-half times as much. But there was a catch. It paid the vendor two-thirds of the price in cash and only a third by check. Other realtors did the same. The local landholders had no objection to this arrangement. In agriculture, there was no tax either on income or on capital gains derived from sale of land. But this method enabled the purchaser to transform his black money into white money.

For the land buyer or builder, the income earned from selling his property to others or from developing it was white money. In both cases, he profited enormously. He either divided the property into small plots and sold these individually to predominantly urban buyers at a hefty mark-up, for payment by check, or he built a housing colony and sold individual homes for large sums, also paid for by check.

"An accelerated sale of agricultural land started from 2005 onwards," recalled Khinv Raj, a sturdy, bearded, twenty-seven-year-old PhD student at a university in Delhi. "Real estate agents arrived with sacks full of cash—all of it black money—to buy land in and around my home village of Kuri Bhagtasni. Those who had large plots—around thirty bighas or so—got more than Rs 10 million [$200,000]. In 2007, one of our neighbors received Rs 8 million [$160,000] cash in one sack plus a check for Rs 4 million [$80,000]. He needed help to count the money. I volunteered. We worked through the night. Once that was done, he took the sack to the local security guard, armed with a gun, for safekeeping. Later, he divided the cash among his two brothers and their families. His two sons, working in a factory prior to this deal, quit their jobs. They now had enough money in their bank accounts to sit at home."

By 2010, therefore, there was no agricultural land left next to Kuri Bhagtasni. Those landless peasants who used to work the land found jobs in handicraft factories or in Jodhpur, as I discovered during my visit to Kuri Bhagtasni. I met a dozen villagers at the newly renovated house of Hanuman Ram Jangid. The house had marble floors, piped water, a porcelain washbasin, and a flat-screen color TV. Older men were dressed in white dhotis, long white shirts with a breast pocket, and large colored turbans. Some of them wore tiny hooped earrings or studs. The younger ones were clad in cotton-and-polyester pants and white shirts. After a general discussion, a consensus about the state of the village emerged. The arrival of electricity had been beneficial, and so had the availability of piped water. (The Jangid house also had a storage tank.) The opening of a cell-phone repair shop had been a boon. The assembled noted too that the daily wage of Rs 300 for work on a building site in Jodhpur, which some villagers had taken up, was two-and-a-half times the amount paid under the National Rural Employment Guarantee scheme.

The slim, neatly dressed Bhagat Lal handed me a glossy brochure that read "Ashiana Amarbagh, Jodhpur."[6] Earlier, I had seen vast billboards in Jodhpur advertising this company's housing colony with an alluring image of a villa accompanied by the text: "Ansal Ashiana Amarbagh. Landline 0291.272.1286. Village Kuri Bhagtasni, Pali Road, Jodhpur 342001." Armed with the brochure, I crossed the National Highway 65 to find a few modest trading posts—a tea stall, a cell-phone outlet, a cycle repair shop—installed on the fringe of the fenced complex, with a sentry box at the gate. A very wide strip containing thirty two-story villas, complete with a garage, led to a vast trapezoid-shaped colony measuring fifty bighas. It contained almost 370 villas with open terraces. The residents could count on around-the-clock power and running water. With a three-bedroom residence worth Rs 3.3 million ($66,000), the value of the Ashiana Amarbagh stood at Rs 1,200 million ($24.4 million).[7]

The artist's rendering of the gated community in the brochure was telling. None of the six women in the color drawing was wearing a sari or salwar kameez. They were all slim, with short hair or ponytails, and wearing jeans. Of the three men, the one drawn most prominently was dressed in a business suit and carried a slick briefcase. This brought home to me what Raj had told me earlier: "My fellow villagers are intimidated by the overbearing presence of the rich in the Ashiana Amarbagh Colony, erected in front of their 'invisible' settlement."

The benefit of the surge in land values varied widely for the farmers in Kuri Bhagtasni and the surrounding villages of Bhakarasni, Sangariya, and Mogra. "Most of those who sold land to Ansal were illiterate or semiliterate, low-caste peasants," said Raj. "They had never seen so much cash in their lives. There was nobody around to advise them how to invest their money to get steady interest or dividends. Only one in twenty made proper use of cash as investment. Others spent it on new gadgets, expensive mobiles, Jeeps, and cars. Many young villagers sat at home and turned alcoholic. And once the cash was exhausted the former landholder became a laborer on a construction site for Rs 300 [$6] a day."[8] Raj's statement matched the conclusion I had drawn on this subject from my conversations with the assembled villagers in Kuri Bhagtasni.

All told, inhabitants of Kuri Bhagtasni as well as other nearby villages had benefited by the economic transformation of their settlements, but, as individuals and companies, the outsiders had gained many times more. Once again, this illustrated the skewed nature of the NEP-fed boom in India. And, as elsewhere in the country—the mining region being the most blatant—the companies that had profited massively from exploiting the local resources had shown total disregard for the welfare of the native community. None of these villages had yet acquired a hospital. An educational facility in Kuri Bhagtasni had remained unchanged over the past decades. "In 1993, I passed my fifth grade [at the age of eleven] from the Government Primary School of Kuri Bhagtasni," recalled Raj. "After that I had to go to the neighboring village of Sangariya, four kilometers [two-and-a-half miles] away, which had a school up to the tenth grade. Every day I walked eight kilometers [five miles]. Even today, the school in my village is only up to the fifth grade." During my visit I called on the headmistress, who put the number of pupils at thirty-eight. While the pupils pursuing further studies still trudged daily to Sangariya, the ones living in the Ashiana Amarbagh Colony were picked up by the buses of the privately run, English-speaking St. Anne's School in Jodhpur.

Such a situation existed in Kuri Bhagtasni, which hosted a prominent Congress functionary, Hanuman Ram Jangid. In his contest for the sarpanch of the Sangariya panchayat, he narrowly lost to his BJP rival, Lakshman Rao Chaudhary. The result of this poll was reflective of the state of the two national parties in Rajasthan. And this made the public at large set much store in periodic elections.

Proximity to a city—a repository of political and economic power—was an important factor in generating a popular feeling among the rural inhabitants that, though economically lagging behind urbanites, they were not powerless. An altogether different mood prevailed in the villages far removed from the thriving urban centers. Such was the case with Rasulpur and its twin village Rasulpur Tongia, fifty miles south of Dehradun on the edge of a forest.

Rasulpur

If an inhabitant of Rasulpur wished to visit Dehradun, he had to trek three miles along a stony pathway to Bandarjoot to catch a bus. The journey to the capital on a dilapidated road lasted three grueling hours. This artery became flooded during monsoons, so the village periodically lost its link with Dehradun via Bandarjoot. The only alternative was to ride a bus in the opposite direction to the Hindu pilgrimage city of Haridwar, then do a U-turn to Dehradun—an expensive and time-consuming exercise.

No wonder the settlements of Rasulpur and Rasulpur Tongia felt neglected. Yet their problems were typical of the villages outside the charmed circle of prospering cities. When the only functioning tube well in these villages broke down due to its faulty motor, months passed before the water department in Dehradun acted to remedy the desperate situation.

Of the two primary schools, the older one consisted of a single room with fifty pupils of varied ages taught by a single teacher. The later addition boasted two classrooms constructed on a brick-and-cement platform with three teachers and 125 students. The uneven, dusty playground in front of the built-up area was used as an open-air classroom for the youngest children, sitting cross-legged, taught by an unqualified female teacher who received her salary only intermittently. Since the male teachers did not live in the twin settlement, they were immune from any pressure from the pupils' parents to perform their job diligently. Of the four open-air toilets with rickety doors, only two seemed usable. On the positive side, it was claimed that all kids up to the age of nine attended school—a welcome development in a place where male literacy was 50 percent, and female literacy 30 percent.

Next door stood a three-classroom junior secondary school (sixth to eighth grade) for twelve- to fourteen-year-olds. "What appears as a junior secondary school in a finished and painted building with a kitchen and toilets in the records of the government's education ministry is in reality this," said my host from Dehradun. "This" was a skeleton—a half-finished structure with bare bricks, no plaster, without a kitchen or toilet, or even furniture in its classrooms. It had ninety pupils but only one teacher, the thirty-year-old Amit Kumar, who, I was told, looked permanently harassed. There was no way of finding out then, because he lived outside the village, arriving daily by a motorcycle, and—more to the point—he was not there on that day in early March 2011. The school was padlocked.

Nonetheless, many villagers, including some of the school's pupils, gathered around our Jeep. They were all male, invariably wearing cotton pants, checkered shirts, and ill-fitting shoes or open sandals. Remarkably, nobody was seen in jeans, an unmistakable sign of sartorial globalization. Speculation about the missing teacher followed. "He is getting married," quipped a wide-eyed student wrapped up in a striped shawl. Giggles stirred the cold air. Others speculated that he was visiting the education ministry in Dehradun to collect his monthly salary, believed to be Rs 25,000 ($500). That was the more likely scenario.[9]

There was no primary health clinic in Rasulpur or Rasulpur Tongia. Sewage and waste disposal were absent. Puddles of sewage were scattered all over the twin settlements. All the same, there were some improvements. "Electricity came to public buildings in 1979," recalled Prem Singh Pawar, the sarpanch of the local panchayat. "But it was only in 2003 that it was extended to street lighting. But most houses are not yet connected. What we do is hook up." The term "hook up" was a euphemism for stealing electricity by connecting a lead from the overhead cable to a house. "We hook up in the evening and disconnect in the morning."

The villagers hooked up in order to watch TV after sunset. Their sets received only three terrestrial channels, the most popular being the public broadcaster Door Darshan, which offered an ample fare of game shows, drama serials (such as *Balika Vadhu*, the story of a child bride married to an older man), and Bollywood movies. Younger watchers preferred televised sports events. Very few villagers, if any, could afford to pay to access cable TV channels.

Television was the sole source of news for this rural community. Nobody was known to read newspapers in Hindi, although the names of such popular dailies as *Ujala* (Hindi: Eternal Light) and *Dainak Jagran* (Hindi: Daily Awakening) were familiar to the sarpanch, Pawar. But the only way he could have these papers delivered to him would have been by way of a bus to Bandarjoot from the nearest town of Biharigarh. It was not surprising, therefore, that the queries about the Right to Information Act and the Public Interest Litigation left Pawar looking puzzled. "Such provisions have little meaning or application for a village of the Rasulpur type," remarked Bharat Sharma, an official of the Friends of Doon, a nongovernmental organization that sought to improve villagers' living conditions. "Here people are totally busy with earning their daily bread. They have no time for or interest in the procedures which do not directly affect their daily lives, and which can be time-consuming."[10]

As a rule, elections elicited interest, more so when these were local. Yet the basic rules about this centerpiece of democracy, such as expense caps for electioneering, were unknown. "When I asked Pawar about the legal limit for the election campaign for the panchayat sarpanch, he replied Rs 25,000 [$500], then lowered the figure to Rs 20,000 [$400], and finally arrived at 15,000 [$300]," said Sharma. "Actually, he did not want to share this information in public with so many villagers present. Most of them know that the actual amounts spent by the candidates are much higher than the approved one."[11]

When it came to State Legislative Assembly polls, villagers' interest and participation declined. The general consensus was that the winning candidate delivered only about 25 percent of what he had promised. Moreover, after the election, the successful lawmaker never visited their village. The most downbeat statement came from Ajab Singh, a robustly built fifty-one-year-old man who owned three bighas of land and a poultry farm. "Electoral candidates get away with not keeping their promises because we voters are largely illiterate." His wife, Momo, was illiterate, but he had four years of schooling. He possessed the only computer in the twin-village settlement—sadly, out of order—and his house was equipped with a TV satellite dish, a rarity in the area.

During the run-up to the May 2014 Lok Sabha election, he received an SMS on his cell phone urging him to vote for the lotus, the electoral symbol of the BJP, whose candidate was Ramesh Pokhriyal Nishank, a former chief minister of Uttarakhand. No such message came from the office of the Congress candidate, Renuka Rawat, a lawyer and the wife of the current chief minister of the state, Harish Rawat. They were the main contestants for the parliamentary constituency of Haridwar, which had returned the Congress candidate to the Lok Sabha in the 2009 general election. Now, reflecting the national trend, Nishank defeated Rawat by 592,320 votes to 414,498.[12]

By all accounts, the voter turnout in Rasulpur–Rasulpur Tongia was a record high. Prem Singh Pawar canvassed for the BJP. "As a BJP official, I promoted Narendra Modi as the prime minister," he said. "My focus was on person-to-person canvassing. And I also addressed small meetings of fellow villagers." Little wonder that the BJP's landslide victory left Pawar smiling effusively. "Now that the BJP leader is in power, I am very happy." Will Modi make a difference? "Certainly," replied Pawar. "He will take India to new heights if he is not obstructed." But Om Pal Singh, the sarpanch of the nearby Daluwala Kalan village, was skeptical. "Nothing will be different," he said. "Modi will carry out the old schemes with new names."

Equally, there was disagreement on the impact that the Modi government would have on the corrupt ways of bureaucrats. "Now that all government departments are online, there will be less corruption," explained Pawar. "Online transactions will reduce villagers' face-to-face meetings with officials and the chances of bribe-taking." (However, it was the Congress government in Uttarakhand that had introduced and expanded online communication with civil servants.) "It seems there will be less corruption," said Ajab Singh. "But it is very hard to end it at the low end of bureaucracy. For us villagers, the two officials who matter most are the Village Development Officer and the patwari [land records keeper]. They are the source of corrupt activities."[13]

To assess the long-term demographic trend in Rasulpur, I inquired if poor living conditions in the settlement had driven some inhabitants to nearby towns. "Yes," replied Pawar. "In the past twenty years, about fifty families have left to open a shop in town or take up a salaried job." This was the extent of their social mobility.

When I asked the group of youths gathered near the secondary school their aspirations in life, I received the following responses: "I want to own a shop"; "I want a government job"; "First I want to get a job and save, then open my shop"; and "I want to study up to the highest secondary education grade, then become a teacher." This was a revealing snapshot of the dreams of youngsters growing up in rural India, which constitutes one-eighth of the global population of 7 billion people. Their living standards were so low, and their view of the horizon was so constricted, that their idea of prosperity did not exceed a modest job with an assured check at the end of the month.

Sisola

The fertile Gangetic plain is the heart of the heavily populated northern region of India. A fifteen-mile drive along a tarred road from the Uttar Pradesh city of Meerut (population: 1.3 million) leads to the village of Sisola, in the midst of green fields of sugarcane, mustard, and wheat.

Salahuddin, who shepherded me around, was a thirty-seven-year-old father of four in a beige bush shirt with matching pants. As the owner of fifty bighas (seventeen acres) of land and a tractor, he was affluent by the standards of rural India. "Five years ago, I extended my pucca house of baked bricks and cement," he beamed. "In my house I have a washing machine, also a large metal silo to store food grains. Also a fridge. But electric supply is a problem, [we have it] only for twelve hours a day, alternating every two weeks." His well-being was symptomatic of how the NEP had favored those who were already better off than those at the bottom of the heap. Yet his rising prosperity did not lead to fast-track treatment in government offices. "If you want to get anything done, your best approach is to give a bribe," he said with a shrug.

Outside Salahuddin's neatly painted house, a few cows and water buffaloes chewed their cud, discharging their excrement on the ground, a feast for flies and other insects. Mangy dogs wandered around or snoozed in winter sunshine. During Salahuddin's lifetime, the village population had soared from two thousand to five thousand, whereas the arable land owned by villagers had remained static. That was the primary reason for the presence of immigrants from this area in the slums of Delhi and Gurgaon.[14] Sisola had its share of those who struggled to survive, particularly when a breadwinner had a large family to support. The skinny, unshaven, oval-faced Abdul Hashim, age fifty, was a day laborer. His wage of Rs 150 ($3) a day was insufficient to properly feed five mouths.

A stop-over at the modest shop of the seventy-five-year-old Khurshid Ali, who was sporting a long white beard and selling sweets, matchboxes, and notebooks, drew a small group of villagers. It turned out that most of the adults voted in elections. At the same time, they nursed cynical views about the practitioners of politics. "Before the election, politicians come with folded hands, saying, 'I will do this and that,'" said Ali, mimicking the typical politico. "But once he gets elected he refuses to see you. His assistant says that he is away in [state capital] Lucknow or that he is asleep." Those around us nodded their agreement. In Uttar Pradesh, besides the Congress Party and the BJP, there were two other major contenders for power: the Samajwadi Party and the Bahujan Samaj Party, with strong roots among different Hindu castes and Dalits. Led by a charisamtic Dalit woman, Mayawati Kumari, the Bahujan Samaj Party had swept the polls in 2007. Five years later, the Samajwadi Party, with a strong base among mid-level Hindus, displaced them from the seats of power.

There was another subject mentioned by Khurshid Ali where the assembled group was of one opinion: the importance of education. "All of my children and grandchildren are getting educated," said Ali loftily. "One of my sons is now at university."[15]

Despite all the villagers' criticism and cynicism about politicians, the rivalry generated by elections had its benefits for Sisola. On the eve of the last State Assembly elections, the village's dusty paths were paved with baked bricks and cement, with open drains on both sides. But, as was often the case with public works in rural settlements, the channels were not cleared regularly. As a result, uncollected, simmering junk spilled over and rotted, creating a hazard to public health. Squalor was a common feature of even flourishing villages in India's hinterland. By contrast, the Adivasi settlements were almost invariably clean.

Kekra Ravoli

The hamlets of Bagram Lala and Kekra Ravoli in the Dhamtari district of Chhattisgarh, situated seven miles apart, were easily approached by a metaled road from Kanker, the headquarters of the Counter Terrorism and Jungle Warfare College, thirty-two miles away. They were typical of Adivasi settlements.

A visit to these hamlets led to a revision of the commonly held belief that squalor was the inevitable consequence of grinding penury. The inhabitants of Bagram Lala and Kekra Ravoli were mired in indigence, yet the streets were well swept, with none of the debris that is the hallmark of Indian villages and city slums. The houses, whitewashed or painted in primary colors, had low, slanted roofs covered with rounded tiles, which were supported by sturdy wooden beams fashioned from the trees of the surrounding forest. Since independence, Adivasis were allowed to fell trees or hack off branches for fuel and to build houses and shops.

Entering the house of Bhurao Gorih in Kekra Ravoli required bending on my part to get through the well-carved wooden door. Gorih was the headman of the hamlet of 350 people, all but fifty of whom were Adivasi. His residence consisted of a small interior courtyard and a veranda, with a separate kitchen, a living room, and a bedroom. An unshaven, beady-eyed man of forty-seven, wearing a navy blue *lungi* and checkered shirt, Gorih was born in Bagram Lala, where he attended school up to the eighth grade, the highest level available. His wife, Kusim, wearing a sari printed with flowers and herbs, hovered in the background as I interviewed him in Hindi.

"In our hamlet, a school opened only in 2000," he said. "It is now up to the eighth grade, and there are seventy to eighty pupils. The teachers are non-Adivasi, and they come from outside. We got electricity only in 2005. Not many houses are connected as yet. There are only four TVs, so the neighbors gather to watch. Nobody reads print newspapers." I mentioned the hand pump I had seen near his house. "Yes, that is an improvement," he averred. "Before, we got water from the river one kilometer away."

The hamlet favored the Congress Party, and the local representative in the State Assembly was a Congressman. But the area could not immunize itself from the rise of the Maoist party. "The nearest police station is at Nagri, thirty kilometers [twenty miles] to the north," Gorih explained. "When we call them, they arrive by Jeep in civilian clothes because they are afraid of being attacked by the Naxalites. They wear uniform only at the police station, not outside."[16]

Since 2007, the local police had received reinforcement from the Central Reserve Police Force (CRPF). "There is a CRPF camp at Nagri, and also at a place forty kilometers [twenty-five miles] to our west and another thirty kilometers [twenty miles] to the east," Gorih said. "At the time of state and national elections, about a dozen CRPF troopers are posted at each polling station."

Overall, though, the Naxalite presence had not subsided. "Even though we Adivasis have been tilling our lands for many generations here, they gave us title deeds only in 2008 because of the Naxalite movement. Also, because of the Naxalites the moneylenders have disappeared. They used to charge exorbitant interest." In short, the local tribals had reaped benefits from the Naxalite movement in the area, even though they were not part of it. Indeed, they ignored the Naxalites' call to boycott the parliamentary election in April 2009. The voter turnout in the hamlet was 80 percent.

Meanwhile, the state government continued to take actions that alienated large sections of the tribal population. For instance, in mid-2008, it declared the Sitanandi Wildlife Sanctuary a tiger sanctuary and decided to extend it by taking over the surrounding forty-four settlements, home to seven thousand Adivasis. "The government did not consult the local Adivasis," lamented Gorih. "When we are removed from our homes and land, the government does not provide us with alternative accommodation or land. It gives very poor compensation, like half a rupee [1¢] for a mango tree." The affected tribals around the wildlife sanctuary staged a protest rally in Nagri in November 2008, but it had no impact. This led the disaffected villagers to turn to the Maoists for help. The militants decided to hold a rally in Risgaon in the spring of 2009.[17]

The subsequent events were narrated differently by Gorih and the mainstream media. "On the weekly market day in Risgaon, sixteen CRPF troopers were shot dead by unknown gunmen," said Gorih. "That area is near the Orissa border, with a lot of Naxalites. So immediately the government said that the Naxalites had murdered the policemen. They arrested many, including some panchayat presidents. These murders made local Adivasis happy, though they did not express their feelings. But they decided not to leave their villages, and instead kept up the protest." According to the Express News Service, Maoist guerrillas ambushed a vehicle-borne forty-one-member police force in the Mandagiri hills between Risgaon and Madapoti villages, attacking them with improvised explosive devices (IEDs) and engaging them in a firefight. They killed thirteen policemen and injured sixteen more.[18] Almost certainly, this was the version of events that was aired on Door Darshan terrestrial TV channel, which reaches outlying villages. Yet Adivasis trusted more the accounts they heard from fellow tribals than the official news.

This underlined the extremely challenging task that awaited the Indian political establishment: to eradicate the Maoist influence now deeply embedded in a region containing vast amounts of coal and vital minerals and metals. The official view was that the government had no option but to exploit these resources expeditiously after conducting nominal consultation with the affected communities—in line with the loosely enforced law—and that this was the necessary first step to achieving and maintaining a high growth rate as a means to reduce poverty in the nation at large. This belief was held by the leaders of both the Congress Party and the BJP, with BJP Prime Minister Modi intent on overriding the opinions and interests of the local population altogether for the benefit of Indian and foreign multinational corporations. Given this, the Maoist insurgency in the east-central zone of India is likely to continue.

10

Overview and Conclusions

The electoral politics in a poor country such as India precludes the chance of a political party openly espousing the cause of landowners and capitalists and expecting to win. To meet the monumental task of enabling the indigent masses to rise above the official poverty line through sustained industrialization and productivity gains in agriculture, political parties resort to proposing quick-fix measures—a process known in the Hindi lexicon as *jugaad*, improvised arrangement—or, in plain English, "muddling through."

My study of the Congress Party's history and its style of operation since Indian independence—conducted as part of my book *Inside India Today*, published in 1976—highlighted the exacting challenge it faced: how to present itself as the party of the poor to win the popular vote while pursuing policies that primarily benefited the upper-middle and upper classes who dominated its leadership.

A remark by Prime Minister Indira Gandhi during an exclusive interview with a prominent Indian journalist and author in 1969 was enlightening. "We spoke of socialism because that was what went down well with the masses," she said.[1] She refined this candid statement later. "My [Congress] party adopted a particular way to socialism in which both capitalists and noncapitalists can coexist," she told a correspondent of the *Hindustan Standard* in March 1971.[2] Such thinking led her to adopt the catchphrase "Remove poverty!" as her slogan in the 1973 general election. It worked beyond her fondest dreams.

After her assassination in 1984, the term "socialism" lost much of its luster. Her successor, Rajiv Gandhi, paid lip service to the concept as he initiated a program of privatization. His death by suicide bomber in May 1991 marked the end of the pretense. With the introduction of the New Economic Policy two months later, devised and implemented by Finance Minister Manmohan Singh, a firm believer in the neoliberal model, the retreat of socialism—as it was once visualized by Indira Gandhi's social-democrat father, Prime Minister Jawaharlal Nehru—was complete.

Globally, the 1990s witnessed a revolution in information and telecom technologies, and a dramatic decline in global telecom charges. The arrival of the Internet and affordable cell phones impacted not only personal and social relations but also business and politics. Domestically, the loosening of government's monopoly in broadcasting, which started with allowing the Atlanta-based Cable News Network (CNN) satellite channel to air its programs in India beginning in early 1991, opened the airwaves to other cable networks. This development worked against the Congress Party, which had ruled India since independence, except during 1977–80. By implication, it aided the rising right-of-center Bharatiya Janata Party (BJP), which was busily trying to bolster its popularity by mounting an anti-Muslim campaign. The Supreme Court's ruling to end the government's monopoly in broadcasting in 1995 opened the TV and radio industry to the private sector. Indian voters became exposed to multiple sources of news and comment in the electronic media.

To distinguish itself from the Congress Party, the BJP stressed swadeshi, or self-reliance, which chimed with its earlier, complementary call for Hinduization—popularly called Hindutva—in the cultural field. In the 1998 general election, the BJP emerged as the largest group and formed a coalition government that lasted only a year. It was only after the 1999 parliamentary poll that the BJP was able to form a stable coalition cabinet. It underscored its commitment to the New Economic Policy and to globalization by further cutting tariffs, lowering barriers to foreign direct investment, and redefining swadeshi as "competing effectively in the global economy." This stance was not surprising. It had evolved out of the Jan Sangh, a party that enjoyed much support among upper-caste Hindu traders and business-people. It also adopted the Special Economic Zones policy in 2000, declaring such areas to be foreign territory for the purposes of trade, duties, and tariffs. Earlier, the Foreign Exchange Management Act of 1999 had allowed freer movement of capital in and out of India. To expedite privatization, the BJP-led coalition established the Ministry of Disinvestment. Annual GDP expansion broke out of the 5 to 6 percent band in 2003. The BJP coined a beguiling phrase: "India Shining!" Confident of winning a fresh mandate from voters, the party advanced the general election by several months, to April–May 2004.

Its leaders had not foreseen the opposition Congress Party, led by a freshly confident Sonia Gandhi, adopting the leftist parties' criticism that the distribution of the extra wealth generated by the boom was grossly skewed. She presented the Congress as the party of *aam aadmi* (Hindi: common man), and she asked rhetorically, "For whom is India shining?" Certainly not for the average citizen. The ploy worked, as it had for her mother-in-law, Indira Gandhi. The size of the BJP group in the Lower House shrank by almost half, to 137 members. The strength of the Congress Party rose from 114 to 141. It led a coalition government under the moniker United Progressive Alliance (UPA), which enjoyed the backing of the fifty-nine-member Communist-led Left Front, which forewent cabinet posts. The UPA administration passed such pro-poor laws as the National Rural Employment Guarantee Act.

Yet when it came to making public its income tax returns in 2007–8, Sonia Gandhi's party was as adamantly opposed as the BJP. Both major national parties had a good reason to hide their finances from public scrutiny. Their funding came from large corporations and rich donors who had benefited inordinately from their neoliberal development model.

Fighting elections had become grossly expensive, with helicopter rentals and TV advertising pushing up the cost enormously. An average parliamentary constituency in 2004 had 1.23 million votes (this figure rose to 1.3 million five years later), often spread over hundreds of villages. With the legal limit for electioneering in a constituency set at Rs 2.5 million ($50,000), the average expense per voter came to Rs 2 (4¢), a puny amount.

In stark contrast, it was estimated that in 2009 each individual candidate and his or her political party would spend Rs 80,000 million ($1.6 billion). Of this sum, their parties would provide about a fifth—Rs 16,500 million ($350 million)—while the candidates and their friends and associates would spend Rs 53,500 million ($1.25 billion), including Rs 25,000 million ($500 million) in cash bribes to voters. Of the amount to be spent by all political parties, the Congress and the BJP combined would account for almost 60 percent of the total.[3] Little wonder that 70 percent of the 203 Congress MPs in the Lower House owned assets worth Rs 10 million or more, as did half of the 118 BJP members.[4]

In the pre-NEP period, when the Congress Party exercised power most of the time, Big Business used its links with the party behind the scenes. Discretion was the order of the day. But as privatization and deregulation gathered pace, the size of the private sector grew sharply both in industry and such services as telecom, construction, and transportation. Rapid capital accumulation also occurred through the privatization of natural resources and land at the expense of the native communities that were evicted wholesale from the mineral-bearing territories.

In that context, privileged access to natural resources and land that could be granted by the ministers of state governments under their discretionary powers acquired paramountcy. Economic liberalization recast these discretionary powers and reinforced the business-politics nexus, more powerful than ever before. Industrial and business barons became bolder. Some of them enrolled as party members and got elected as MPs. The blatant examples of this development were Suresh Kalmadi at the center of the Commonwealth Games scam in 2010 and Naveen Jindal in the Coalgate scandal two years later.[5] Tellingly, whereas the country's GDP growth faded from 10.2 percent in 2010 to 6.5 percent the following year, the annual earnings of Jindal soared from Rs 583 million ($11.7 million) to Rs 674 million ($13.5 million).[6]

The publication of the Nira Radia audio tapes in December 2010 shone a light on the malevolent collusion that had developed between politicians, business tycoons, senior bureaucrats, and leading journalists. The indisputable evidence provided by these tapes showed how the principles of transparency, accountability, public interest, and democratic policymaking had been torpedoed by a cabal of men and women using their economic and public opinion–molding powers.

The Root Cause of the National Malady

The roots of manipulation and corruption in the administrative and economic decision making lay in the vast amounts of money that politicians spent on getting elected, which originated in the illicit gains made by them, their close associates, and sponsoring political parties. There was correlation between these galloping costs at all levels, from the village panchayat to the national parliament, and the exponential growth in sleaze, which was related to the acceleration in deregulation and privatization. Exterminating this seminal virus required political parties to publish their audited accounts annually and selecting candidates for public office in a transparent manner.

In 2010, the Association for Democratic Reforms and Right to Information activist Subhash Agarwal petitioned the Central Information Commission (CIC) to declare political parties as "public authorities," thus bringing them in the ambit of the Right to Information Act. In response, the parties stated that they gave electoral expense details to the Election Commission, which was free to post them on its website (but it never did). They also stated that they filed income tax returns (which were not made public). The ADR responded that keeping financing and donors secret could raise suspicions of quid pro quo and that citizens were entitled to know whether or not large donations to the parties made them captive to special interests. It pointed out that political parties received direct or indirect state funding as follows: they were exempted from paying income tax and service tax when selling their coupons to raise funds; they were given government accommodation in Delhi and state capitals; and they were allocated free time on Door Darshan TV and All India Radio. In June 2013, the CIC declared that since six national parties received direct and indirect government financial assistance they were "public authorities." These parties were the Congress, BJP, Bahujan Samaj Party, Communist Party of India, Communist Party of India (Marxist), and the Nationalist Congress Party.[7]

Except for the Communist Party of India, which had merely four MPs in the Lower House, all the other parties rejected the CIC ruling. This response clearly marked them as the political establishment exercising, or aspiring to exercise, executive power, which in India is allied with legislative authority. Along with large and medium-size companies, these parties formed the core of the social system, which was overlaid with the judiciary, whose higher ranks were entitled to intervene to protect citizens' fundamental rights listed in the constitution. These political organizations were bound together by their commitment to pursue the economic development paradigm defined, essentially, by free-market orthodoxy. While conceding that the net outcome of this model had been to better the lot of those who were already well-off, while providing marginal succor to the vast majority, the advocates of neoliberalism took comfort in the expansion of the urban middle classes who mattered most in day-to-day politics.

This solid core of vested interest had to deal with an amorphous universe of nongovernmental organizations (NGOs). Their varied functions included monitoring the executive, safeguarding human and civil rights, and working for the welfare of the underprivileged on a small or medium scale. Basically, these groups operated in three different modes. One group of NGOs received government contracts and funds to perform certain services normally delivered by a public authority. Another depended on funding by private individuals, foundations, or companies to undertake social welfare projects or to work to preserve ecosystems or safeguard human rights. The third group received funds from both the government and the private sector. A small, privately financed minority among NGOs specialized in challenging nonviolently those official actions that were seen to benefit a few at the expense of many. Finally, there was the layer of outliers, the Maoists, dedicated to overthrowing the system through decades-long armed conflict.

Low-Intensity Warfare

The initial Naxalite activity, which started in the late 1960s, withered against the iron-fist response of the government and the blunder of its leader, Charu Mazumdar, in resorting to "guerrilla actions" in Kolkata. The situation changed radically as the NEP and globalization gathered momentum in the early 2000s. The rising opposition to this development led the two leading Naxalite factions, which had focused on rural communities, to merge and form the Communist Party of India (Maoist) in 2003. By then, their cadres had acquired a good footing among Adivasis, the most neglected and exploited section of the Indian society, inhabiting forests that happened to contain most of the nation's mineral wealth. Encouraged by the government, domestic and foreign multinational corporations targeted these resources for exploitation. With that, the contradiction sharpened between globalized capital, backed by the Indian authorities, and the Adivasis who possessed mineral-rich land. The result was low-intensity warfare between Maoists and the security forces.

But it was not the first time that the central and state governments faced such a challenge. As early as the mid-1950s, there was an armed rebellion by ethnic Nagas in the northeastern state of Assam. Delhi deployed the military to crush the insurgency and passed the Armed Forces (Special Powers) Act in 1958 to give it legal immunity for its actions in the areas it declared "disturbed." As more ethnic groups took to arms for independence or autonomy in the region, the central government extended the Act from Assam to Arunachal Pradesh, Manipur, Meghalaya, Mizoram, Nagaland, and Tripura. Despite these draconian measures, which were coupled with development funds and bribes to tribal leaders, and the comparatively small size of the disaffected populations, it took a few decades to pacify this corner of India. The example of insurgency in Mizoram, with a population of less than a million in 2011, was illustrative. "It took thirteen years to end the insurgency in Mizoram," said retired brigadier Basant Ponwar, who was the commander of the Counter Terrorism and Jungle Warfare School in Vairengte, Mizoram.[8] The draconian act was extended to Jammu and Kashmir in 1990 under the title Armed Forces (Jammu and Kashmir) Special Powers Act. It was not until the end of the decade that Delhi was able to curb the insurgency there, after deploying up to five hundred thousand soldiers and armed policemen.

In both instances, the insurgencies were far removed from the heartland of India, both geographically and ethnically. The rebellious tribals in the northeast were Christian and, being East Asian, racially distinct from the predominantly Hindu Indians. And though Kashmiris were racially the same as North Indians, they were almost wholly Muslim, and they lived in the northwestern corner of India. Thus geographical location and ethnic-racial differences militated against the rebels gaining any identification with mainstream Indians.

The situation was quite different when it came to the Adivasi rebels mobilized on the basis of class, not ethnicity or religion, in the heartland of India. As one of the Scheduled Tribes listed in the Indian constitution, Adivasis were counted as Hindus in the national census, even though their religious beliefs and practices differed from Hindus'. While Adivasis had many mother tongues, most of them understood and spoke Hindi, particularly if they attended school and were exposed to Bollywood movies and songs. This meant that the base that Maoists had established among them in the Hindi-speaking states of Chhattisgarh and Jharkhand had the potential of spreading to the rest of the Hindi belt where they had already acquired a foothold in southern Bihar—a state where 80 percent lived below the poverty line as established by the multidimensional poverty index. Since Maoists' appeal transcended religion and ethnicity, they had the potential of attracting vast numbers of the underprivileged in rural areas largely untouched by the New Economy.

The most worrisome aspect of the Maoist movement to the authorities was that, in their areas of control or influence, they had succeeded in drastically reducing the awe and fear in which ordinary citizens held the security personnel by creating a parallel armed force backed by a popular militia. Besides countering the regular forces of the government, it protected a corruption-free administrative governance system, based on triennial elections, set up by the party leaders.

These threatening political implications figured as prominently in the minds of India's policy makers as did the economic challenge that the Maoists posed by resisting mining projects in the central-eastern region. The Maoists were not against industrialization in principle. They were opposed first and foremost to foreign multinational corporations, second to domestic multinational corporations, and offered the least resistance to public-sector undertakings. They also favored developing industries related to forest produce. But, despite repeated promises, their leaders had failed to publish a coherent policy document on mining and on forest produce.

"People before Profit": A Worthy Concept, but Too Idealistic

In the legal sociopolitical sphere, the National Alliance of People's Movements—a network of NGOs focused on improving the lot of the most marginalized—shared with the Maoists an opposition to globalization, privatization, and liberalization, but while abjuring violence. What placed them in the same column was their common slogan of "people before profit" and their stiff resistance to the displacement of people in order to develop the economy. Implementing this agenda required discarding the free-market, neoliberal development model that the Indian political establishment had embraced since 1991.

"People before profit" was an overarching, seductive concept. Its specific application in present-day India boiled down to consulting the people who faced displacement and/or loss of their means of livelihood by a proposed development project. On paper, this provision already existed in the law. But, as the evidence marshaled in chapters 7 and 8 clearly demonstrates, such legal requirements were either circumvented or manipulated with the active assistance of politicians and senior bureaucrats to benefit predatory multinational corporations. If and when any compensation was offered to those facing eviction, it was often grossly unfair and derisory. It was chiefly up to the NGOs affiliated to the National Alliance to monitor the situation, mobilize resistance, and inject public opinion into the equation.

As matters stand in the mid-2010s, no matter which of the two main national parties leads the coalition government in Delhi, the current pattern of advancing neoliberal tenets will continue. If so, these tenets will provide fuel for the antagonistic camp. In that divide, Maoists will act as the vanguard of resistance to globalization and deregulation. But their area of operation will remain limited mainly to dense forests and hills.

Though numerically strong, the poor and marginal peasants and landless laborers are unable to wield the power or influence commensurate with their size. Being largely illiterate or semiliterate, they rarely throw up an articulate and well-read leader who decides to continue living in his native village. Their only opportunity to exercise any influence comes at the time of elections. But fighting an election, even for the presidency of a panchayat, has become so expensive that the winner can seldom resist the temptation to take bribes at the expense of the well-being of his community.

There is little prospect of the Maoist movement spreading to large towns and cities. There, official intelligence agencies successfully curbed the Maoist leaders' attempt to extend their party's influence to urban centers during 2004–7. And, despite the incompetent and venal bureaucracy and police, there is a general sense of well-being and hope among urbanites, more so in some parts of India than others due to the uneven development of the country. As such, the reasons for the earlier failure of the Maoist party to penetrate urban areas have not altered.

Basically, the role of Maoists and the National Alliance will remain reactive. So far, they have proved to be a corrective to the relentless pressure that Western governments and multinational corporations continue to apply on India. Yet the Congress-led cabinet in Delhi succumbed to these pressures in September 2012 when it allowed the likes of the colossus Wal-Mart Stores Inc. and Tesco Plc to open retail branches in the country. Domestically, this would benefit those medium- and large-size farmers whose produce is available for pickup by trucks plying on metaled roads, and improve the service and quality of goods to the minority who live in urban areas.

After this achievement, Western capitals and multinational corporations will intensify their effort to gain entry into the vital financial services of India. Their success in this sector would expose the country to grave risk. By maintaining control of banking, with 75 percent public ownership, the Indian government is able to ensure prudent behavior by bankers in general. It was this fact that saved the country from the worst effects of the banking crash in the West in 2008–9. The National Alliance and the Maoists, along with trade unions, will continue to provide the ballast for popular resistance to allowing foreign firms into banking, insurance, and accountancy.

"Globalization by a democratically elected government, as experienced in India, runs the risk of going stop and start, and even reversing," writes Nayan Chanda, an India-born journalist and author based in America. "The slow and uneven redistribution that capitalist economic growth inevitably generates can turn impatient citizens against openness [to world markets]."[9]

It is hard to visualize a proactive role played by the National Alliance or Maoists in economic policymaking. Neither of them is in a position to produce a blueprint of an alternative development paradigm. Such a plan would require the resources of a massively funded, left-of-center think tank, which has yet even to be conceived, let alone launched. Merely stating that development should be sustainable, that governments should opt for small dams rather than large ones, and that they should not contribute to climate warming or pollution does not add up to a coherent alternative to the development model being implemented now. However, what can and should be done is to divert government resources to revive and rejuvenate rural India. That will be possible only if there is greater political consciousness and activism among the majority of villagers.

Meanwhile, the predominantly urban middle classes will continue to garner the lion's share of the growth in GDP, and inequality between the haves and have-nots will keep on expanding, as it has been in the advanced economies of the West. In the United States, for instance, the ratio of the average CEO's earnings to the average worker's earnings spiraled from 60 to 1 in 1991 to 354 to 1 in 2012.[10]

India's adoption of the New Economic Policy and its willing exposure to globalization endeared it to the United States. The two-way trade in goods and services between the two countries zoomed from $5.2 billion in 1991 to $86 billion in 2011.[11] During the same period, the number of Indian immigrants (aka Asian Indians) in the United States nearly quadrupled to 3.2 million, making the community the third-largest Indian diaspora in the world, after Nepal and Myanmar.[12] A similar upsurge occurred in the number of Indian students enrolled in American universities. Their number crossed the one hundred thousand mark in 2012.

The Prospering Indian Diaspora in America

A postgraduate degree in business administration or computer science from a prestigious American university eased the way for ambitious, talented

Indians to settle in the United States, and many gravitated toward the up-and-coming information technology (IT) industry. Over time, the diaspora threw up a batch of successful stars in business and high-tech innovation.

The credit for pioneering the outsourcing business goes to Narendra Patni, an MBA of the MIT Sloan School of Management in Cambridge, Massachusetts. In 1972, he started encoding data on paper and magnetic tape in India at low cost and transmitting it by telephone for printing in America. Two decades later, this process was adopted by the Mumbai-based Consultancy Services for the IT services it offered. Other companies followed their lead.

Overall, the Indian diaspora in Silicon Valley became a key resource for both the United States and India. It made irreplaceable contributions to America's high-tech industry and exported to the homeland much of the energy, creativity, and experience gained in the United States. In the scientific-technological field of the computing business, the contributions of Suhas Patil, Kumar Malavalli, and Sabeer Bhatia were remarkable.

Among those who combined deep technical knowledge with extraordinary entrepreneurial flair, Vinod Khosla stood out. He was the moving spirit behind the founding of The Indus Entrepreneurs, a nonprofit organization, in San Jose soon after the launching of the New Economic Policy in India. It aimed to foster entrepreneurship globally through mentoring, networking, and education, with special focus on the Indian subcontinent. During the next two decades, it acquired 15,000 members, including 2,500 charter members, with its largest overseas contingent based in India. Other similar examples included Ashok Trivedi, Sunil Wadhwani, and Phaneesh Murthy. Reflecting the stratospheric valuation of high-tech shares, followed by a tailspin crash in 2000, the fortunes of these high flyers varied wildly. By and large, they showed sufficient resilience to survive and stage comebacks that were modest by the standards of their earlier achievements. As elsewhere, for each of these success stories there were many failures that went largely unrecorded.

There were outstanding achievers in traditional businesses as well. In 1994, Rajat Gupta became the first India-born executive to head the New York–based McKinsey & Company, a multinational consultancy company. Later, Ajay Banga made his mark as president and CEO of MasterCard, followed by Indra Nooyi, who became the CEO of PepsiCo in 2006. By highlighting the vast potential that India's economy held in the wake of the NEP, they succeeded in getting their respective boards to invest there earlier rather than later, thus gaining an advantage over later arrivals.

In 2007, the acquisition of the Atlanta-based aluminum corporation Novelis Inc. by the Mumbai-based Hindalco Limited made a splash in North America. The driving spirit in this instance was Kumar Manglam Birla, an MBA from the London School of Business and a fourth-generation member of the Birla industrial family. He had to juggle to raise a loan of $2.8 billion from three leading Western banks, half of it in the form of a bond with the steep interest rate of over 7 percent. When the chilly winds of the 2008–9 Great Recession in the West froze Hindalco's credit lines from Western financial institutions, Birla offered Hindalco shares at a discount to the present shareholders to save his company the humiliation of default.

Habil F. Khorakiwala, a native of Mumbai, provided a contrasting case. After obtaining a master's degree in pharmaceutical science from Purdue University in the United States, he singlehandedly built up Wockhardt from a modest firm producing cough syrups to a multinational pharmaceutical corporation. By coordinating manufacturing and distribution facilities in India, Britain, and America, he acquired a powerful edge over the British and American competitors in the manufacturing sector in the same way that Tata Consultancy Services and other major Indian IT corporations had done in the services sector.

More striking examples of this strategy became apparent with the entry of leading Indian companies into the economy of Britain, which had ruled the Indian subcontinent for almost two centuries until 1947.

Historic Indo-British Economic Relations Reversed

Before the New Economic Policy, the presence of an India-based company in Britain was limited to the Tata Group, whose steel company had maintained an office in Manchester (later in London) since 1907. It was seven decades later that Tata Consultancy Services, an IT company, opened a branch in London. Its clientele expanded dramatically from the mid-1990s onward because of the rising fear of local computer systems crashing on January 1, 2000.

Its subsequent phenomenal success stemmed from the fact that three-quarters of its work was done in a low-cost country like India, and only a quarter at the site of the Western client. In contrast, the proportion was re-versed for its Western competitors. This approach also enabled smaller Indian IT firms to establish themselves in Britain. By 2012, there were about seven hundred Indian companies operating in the United Kingdom, employing ninety-thousand-plus people. This allowed them access to 500 million con-sumers in the European Union. One out of ten Indian firms was listed on the London Stock Exchange or the Alternative Investment Market. In 2007, India became the second-largest inward investor in the United Kingdom.

In 2006, Lakshmi Mittal, a self-made Indian steel tycoon, acquired Luxemburg-based Arcelor SA, the world's second-largest steel producer, in a bitter takeover bid for a price tag of $34 billion. He managed to meet his onerous financial requirements by borrowing heavily from the West-ern banks, which, in the final analysis, formed the bedrock of business globalization.

Western banks again played a pivotal role when Tata Steel won its bid to purchase the London-based, Anglo-Dutch Corus Group, which had an out-put four times Tata's own in 2007. Tata Steel's move was rooted in economics. Enjoying self-sufficiency in iron ore, its cost of production—at $160 per ton of steel—was second lowest in the world. It upped the offer made by the rival Brazilian corporation Companhia Siderúrgica Nacional. In the heat of the moment, Ratan Tata, chairman of the Tata Group, paid too much. Tata Steel managed to borrow a lot of capital from Western banks, which, barred from purchasing Indian financial enterprises, were seeking opportunities to fund Indian corporations' takeovers of foreign businesses. But, because of the credit crash in the West in 2008–9, Tata Steel had to supplement loans from Western banks with capital raised at home. The Tata Group's financial prob-lem became acute after Tata Motors bought Jaguar and Land Rover brands from Ford Motor Company in Britain in 2008. The timing was inauspicious. However, when Tata Motors could not refinance its debts due to the credit freeze in the West, it avoided default by issuing new shares to its existing shareholders at a discount to the market price.

These examples showed that, in the globalized capital market, the Indian corporations had the option of turning to the investors at home when the Western financial institutions could not come to their rescue. In compari-son, Western companies did not have this choice, because their investors at home were subject to the same pressures they were.

Once the Western economies improved somewhat, the Mumbai-based Essar Energy made a mark by raising £1.3 billion ($1.95 billion) at the London

Stock Exchange in 2010, the biggest premium listing it had seen for an international company since December 2007. It bought Britain's second-largest oil refinery at Stanlow near Liverpool from Royal Dutch Shell and gained entry into FTSE 100, the index of the one hundred most capitalized companies listed on the London Stock Exchange.

While corporations such as Essar Energy and Tata Motors made headline news in the Western and Indian media, small and medium-size Indian firms operating in Britain and North America remained below the popular radar. This was particularly true of those firms among the 180 that had invested in Britain's IT sector.

Irrespective of the size of an Indian company, the key to its success lay with localization. It needed to understand the business culture of a Western country. This could be achieved by setting up a joint venture with a British or American company and/or making sure to have a team that included both local Westerners and Indian expatriates.

All in all, the Indians who have settled in the United Kingdom or the United States since the New Economic Policy are on an upward trajectory. As a community, the Asian Indians in Silicon Valley—where the median household income is almost 50 percent higher than the national average—are the richest group of Indians at home or abroad, with an average income of $132,000 in 2010.[13] The prosperity of the Indian diaspora in America and Britain runs parallel to what is happening to the upper-middle and upper classes in India. At the same time, they are immune from any tensions or crises that Indians at home are likely to face in the future, which is not expected to be as rosy as the first decade of the twenty-first century.

Challenges of Lower Economic Growth

During the remainder of the current decade, the GDP growth rate in India is likely to stabilize around 5 percent. There are three main reasons for this slack. Expansion in the infrastructure has failed to keep pace with the rest of the economy. And the two major factors that contributed to the spike in the economy during the first decade of the century have reached a plateau. One was the extraordinary growth in the booming information and communications technology industry. The other was the explosive rise in the use of cell phones, which contributed almost half a percent growth to the GDP for every 10 percent penetration.[14]

The second major reason is ever-increasing inequality, which fuels graft, dampens small-scale enterprise, and raises social tensions. The third reason is underinvestment in education, public health, and sanitation by the state and central governments. A well-educated, healthy population raises labor productivity, which lifts living standards. Whereas increased investment in infrastructure can yield beneficial results over the short term, such results from enhanced allocation of funds to education and health will materialize only after a long period. In short, there is no quick fix for deficiencies in these vital areas.

Reduced GDP expansion rate will result in a smaller economic pie to be shared in the context of widening inequality. This will happen against the background of an increasing number of better-educated Indians, including those living in villages, gaining access to instant information and commentary via the Internet. The increasingly aware and literate masses will demand a bigger slice of the national income than what they have received so far.

So there will be plenty to keep the likes of the National Alliance of People's Movements busy. Any success it achieves through peaceful protest or the rulings of the Supreme Court will help lower the tensions between the haves and the have-nots, which in turn will reduce the chance of the Maoist ranks swelling.

As for the governments in Delhi and the state capitals, they will meet the challenge as they have before—with short-term palliatives of subsidies, loan waivers, and minor improvements to the threadbare social safety net. In sum, the template of the past, dating back to the early days of the Congress Party rule, is likely to extend into the future in the context of wider disparities between the highest and the lowest income earners.

Epilogue

On arrival in Delhi I found the city gripped by election fever. It was mid-January 2015, and Narendra Modi had been the prime minister for eight months. The interest in the poll for the Legislative Assembly of the Union Territory of Delhi, the capital of India, was far wider than in any of the other six Union territories.

Walking the streets of Delhi, you would have thought it was a rerun of the earlier Lok Sabha election. It was hard to miss Modi's image. His trimmed white beard, rimless spectacles, trademark tight collared shirt, and waistcoat dominated the multicolor posters pasted everywhere. On the other side of the poster, in a corner, appeared a much smaller photograph of the BJP's chief ministerial candidate in Delhi, Kiran Bedi. A short-haired, moon-faced woman of sixty-four, she had had a long career in law enforcement, winding up as deputy commissioner of police before her resignation in 2007 to write books and become an active anticorruption campaigner. A fresh recruit of the BJP (her enrollment was only a few weeks old), she was catapulted into local leadership of the party to compete against Arvind Kejriwal, the charismatic leader of the Aam Admi (Common Man) Party. A graduate of an Indian Institute of Technology, the forty-seven-year-old Kejriwal, a mustached man with a relaxed, smiling demeanor and rimless glasses, quit his job as an income tax commissioner in 2006 to participate in a grassroots movement to fight corruption by using the Right to Information Act. Both he and Bedi became part of the anticorruption campaign led by social activist Anna Hazare.[1]

In the grand electoral scheme of the BJP, Bedi was small fry. The party posters carried a large logo of a lotus, its election symbol, with the slogan

"Give Full Support to BJP" topped with "*Chalo chalen* Modi *ke saath*" (Let us go with Modi). It was hard to find a bus stop in Greater Delhi without the BJP poster. In addition, there was blanket advertising on radio and TV. To leave nothing to chance, full-page color wraparound ads in all leading English- and Hindi-language newspapers, each costing Rs 1 million ($20,000), would appear on the eve of the poll on February 7. The text in Hindi read: "To end 15 years of [Congress] corruption and bad governance / To rectify 40 years of bad administration / Press the lotus button today / Give full support to *Bhajpa*"—the initials BJP in Hindi.

Following the success of the BJP in the April–May 2014 parliamentary poll, the party had scored gains in the state elections in Haryana, Maharashtra, and Jharkhand. In Haryana, adjoining Delhi, the BJP's strength had soared from four seats to forty-seven, reducing the erstwhile ruling Congress Party to a rump of fifteen and in Jharkhand from nineteen to forty-three. In Jammu and Kashmir, the BJP's share in the State Assembly rose from eleven to twenty-five places, all of them in the Jammu region with a Hindu-Sikh majority. It would go on to form a coalition government with the People's Democratic Front with twenty-eight seats from the Kashmir Valley. It was the first time that the BJP came to share power in the only Muslim-majority state in India.

These gains were attributed to the "Modi wave." In the run-up to Delhi's Legislative Assembly poll, BJP leaders counted on Modi's prestige rising even higher as the imminent host of U.S. president Barack Obama during his three-day visit to Delhi starting January 25.

Barack's Sting in the Tail

Discarding his usual attire of waistcoat and tight pajamas, Modi decked himself out in a dark woolen suit with dull gold pinstripes and a checked pocket square to greet Obama and his wife, Michelle, at the airport. Close-up photographs revealed that the stripes on the tight-collar jacket and trousers formed the words "Narendra Damodardas Modi" embroidered in gold on the suit. Praising Modi's sartorial flair, Obama remarked, "He has style."[2] Little did Modi realize then that eliciting such a compliment from a U.S. president would cost his party dear in the ensuing election.

An off-the-cuff remark by an opposition supporter that "the levels of megalomania and narcissism [of Modi] are unparalleled" proved to be merely an appetizer. AAP leaders pilloried Modi for wearing a suit that cost more than Rs 1 million ($20,000) and attacked him for being insensitive and removed from the reality of life led by hundreds of millions of his fellow citizens. Such remarks resonated all the more when voters saw Kejriwal, wearing either a blue or red sweater and covering his head and neck with a woolen scarf (popularly called a muffler in India) both as protection from the cold and as a symbol of modesty, as he shook hands while mingling with the crowd surrounding him.

By and large the media focused on giving wall-to-wall coverage to the visit by Obama, who had been invited primarily to be the chief foreign guest at the annual military parade on India's Republic Day on January 26. It turned out to be a cold, wet day.

By contrast, the end result of Modi and Obama's talks the previous day had generated sunny headlines. These were centered on defense and trade relations, the 2008 Indo-U.S. civilian nuclear pact, and the subsequent 2010 Nuclear Liability Act of India, which was needed to enable U.S. nuclear reactor manufacturers to bid for building nuclear power stations in India. The contentious issue was over who would pay to repair the damage and compensate the victims in case of an accident: the U.S. supplier or the Indian operator? This was eventually resolved in Washington's favor when Modi agreed to set up an insurance pool, backed by India's public sector companies, that would indemnify American vendors and transfer liability to the Indian side. The two sides decided on increased cooperation on defense projects to cement an Indo-U.S. strategic partnership initiated by the previous Congress-led government.

The latter news item seemed like a cue for the start of the annual military parade, which is at the center of the two-hour-long Republic Day celebration. India showcased its military might with uniformed soldiers, some in colorful headgear, marching down Rajpath (Ruler's Avenue) in the center of New Delhi while specially invited guests watched, with gum-chewing Obama and colorfully turbaned Modi sitting inside a bulletproof glass enclosure to the right of Indian president Pranab Mukherjee. Tanks and missile launchers rolled down Janpath (People's Avenue), and paramilitary troops on motorbikes performed daredevil stunts. Helicopters showered petals through fog and drizzle on the huge crowds and thousands of security personnel as brass bands and dancers, dressed in kaleidoscopic costumes displaying the ethnic mosaic of India, filed past the guests.[3]

A day later Obama gave a town hall speech before two thousand students and human rights activists at the Siri Fort auditorium that was labeled a "parting shot" by Reuters. "Your Article 25 [of the Indian Constitution] says that all people are 'equally entitled to the freedom of conscience and the right freely to profess, practice and propagate religion,'" Obama said. "In both our countries—in all countries—upholding this fundamental freedom is the responsibility of the government, but it's also the responsibility of every person." After stating that "no society is immune from the darkest impulses of man," he added, "India will succeed so long as it is not splintered along the lines of religious faith." His applauding audience included Umar Ilyasi of the All India Imam Organization and Dominic Emmanuel from the Christian community.[4]

Rajnath Singh, the home minister with a Rashtriya Swayamsevak Sangh (RSS) background, diplomatically described Obama's remarks about a "religious divide" in India as "unfortunate."[5] But lesser leaders in the stable of groups fostered by the RSS—Vishwa Hindu Parishad (World Hindu Council, VHP), Bajrang Dal, and Dharm Jagran Samiti (Religious Awakening Association, JDS)—were furious. Surendra Jain, the joint general secretary of the VHP, called Obama a "stooge of the Church" and asked the Modi government to identify and weed out people in the Indian political class suspected to be batting for the Christian church.[6] This was a reflection of the belligerent confidence that had infected right-wing Hindu groups in the wake of the BJP's electoral victory.

Hindu Extremists Emboldened

On December 8, 2014, fifty-seven rag-picking Muslim families in an Agra slum had "re-converted" to Hinduism in a public ceremony jointly organized by the RSS, the Bajrang Dal, and the JDS. They were implementing a program called *ghar wapsi* (Hindi: returning home). The slum-dwelling Muslims were promised better accommodations, government ration cards for subsidized food grains, and schooling for children if they attended a ritual that turned out to be a ceremony for converting to Hinduism.[7]

When the story appeared in the media, the JDS chief in Uttar Pradesh said, "Our target is to make India a Hindu *Rashtra* [nation] by 2021. . . . The Muslims and Christians don't have any right to stay here. So they would either be converted to Hinduism or forced to run away from here." Elaborating on the JDS's plans, Champat Rai, the general secretary of the VHP, said,

"There are [only] a handful of [original] Muslims in India. Others within the Muslim community are actually Hindus. Their ancestors were converted to Islam forcefully." Rai revealed that the ghar wapsi had been an ongoing campaign of the VHP ever since its establishment in 1966 and that it had converted more than six hundred thousand Muslims and Christians to Hinduism so far. Stressing the independence of the VHP, he added, "We never ask Modi or any other BJP leader before chalking out our strategy. . . . We only expect them to speak for or against us to clarify their stand. But Modi is the Prime Minister. So his [current] silence means his approval. It is the right time for us to fulfill our agenda." A RSS leader told Delhi-based *Mail Today* that they have formed committees in every district of Uttar Pradesh to carry out conversions.[8]

Until the elevation of the BJP as the majority ruling party in the national Parliament, the hard-line Hindu groups had conducted their activities and disseminated their ultra-nationalist doctrine quietly. With Modi as the prime minister they started flexing their muscles with unprecedented confidence. But the leaders of the VHP, DJS, and RSS do not seem to have realized the enormity of their crusade. Leaving aside the 30 million Christians in India, converting the Indian Muslim population of 176 million—second in the world only to Indonesia's—within five years would be a gargantuan task, requiring 132,000 conversions a day. Moreover, achieving this aim would have meant destroying the secular constitution of India, not to mention dramatically reversing the principles, politics, and governing philosophy that had molded the Indian nation since its independence from Britain.

For the present, these alarming declarations by hard-line Hindu groups engendered communal tensions, much to the unease of the secular and leftist parties. Enjoying a comfortable majority in the Upper House of Parliament, they protested vehemently in the chamber and forced a debate, which started on December 16. They argued that since the recent conversions of Muslims and Christians to Hinduism had been achieved through fraud or inducement, they were illegal. They called on Modi to participate in the debate. When he refused, the united opposition caused the adjournment of the Upper House for four days. But Modi kept quiet.

Earlier Modi had also turned a deaf ear to the pleas of Christian leaders to condemn attacks on churches in Delhi. An arson attack on St. Sebastian Church in East Delhi during the night of November 31–December 1 gutted its entire interior, including the altar, a Holy Bible, and a cross. By the time the police arrived several hours later, the inside of the church still smelled of kerosene. Archbishop Anil Couto appealed to Modi to order a judicial enquiry, but in vain.[9]

On January 3, 2015, a crib set up on a table outside the Church of Resurrection in northwestern Delhi, consisting of twelve small electrified idols of Jesus Christ placed within a wooden frame, was burned in the middle of the night. Father Cyril Patrick alleged that the incident was a deliberate act to create panic among Christians. Eleven days later CCTV footage showed a man arriving on a scooter, breaking a stained glass window, and then upturning a statue of the Virgin Mary at Our Lady of Graces Church in West Delhi.[10]

The police's failure to apprehend the culprits reflected badly on the Modi government since the Home Ministry controlled the police force in the capital. Its inaction alienated the Christian and Muslim voters in the Legislative Assembly election.

Run-up to Polling Day

So confident was the BJP leadership of improving its strength from thirty-two in the dissolved Assembly of Delhi to an absolute majority that it never bothered producing an election manifesto. The Congress Party was too demoralized to offer a viable alternative. That role fell to AAP, which produced a twenty-point manifesto covering matters of daily concern to residents: clean water, uninterrupted power supplies, a corruption-free police force, and so on. Its candidates distributed modest flyers with the slogan "5 *Saal* Kejriwal" (5 Years for Kejriwal) and "Let us join hands to make Delhi a World Class city: Women's Safety; Electricity-Water; Education; Youth; Health and Trade." Though lacking blanket dissemination, these ads struck the right chord among voters.[11] With their talk of empowering communities and participatory politics, Modi compared AAP activists to anarchists and Naxalites.

In stark contrast, the BJP offered a "vision," putting its faith completely in the Modi magic. When the failure of its strategy started to show, the party's national leadership took charge of the campaign from the local hierarchy. It pressed almost the whole cabinet and 120 MPs into the campaign. They were backed by nearly 100,000 volunteers from the RSS and its family of organizations. Their efforts failed to neutralize the alienation that Muslims and Christians, forming 15 percent of voters, felt toward the BJP. The earlier collapse of the Congress Party in the parliamentary elections led Dalits, one-fifth of the electorate, to switch their votes to AAP.[12] Pollsters predicted a tight race between the BJP and AAP.

I was one of the millions of people in Delhi and elsewhere who could not believe the result announced on February 10. AAP scored sixty-seven seats, reducing the BJP to a rump of three. There was a record 67 percent turnout. Only nine months earlier, the BJP had garnered all the seven parliamentary seats allocated to Delhi. It was remarkable that AAP caused this political tsunami by spending only Rs 200 million—as revealed by AAP's national secretary, Pankaj Gupta—collected chiefly by online crowdsourcing.[13] That amount was a tiny fraction of the cash lavished by the BJP, which failed to report its election expenditure to the election commissioner of India. The trouncing of the BJP came three weeks before the presentation of the budget for fiscal 2015–16 by Finance Minister Arun Jaitley, a BJP luminary. Noting the drubbing his party received, he hurriedly decided to allocate an extra Rs 5,000 crore ($1 billion) to the National Rural Employment Guarantee scheme as a sop to the poor in order to balance his commitment to reduce the corporate tax from the current 30 percent to 25 percent within four years.[14]

Inflicting a humiliating setback on the BJP had a personal resonance for Kejriwal. He avenged the defeat he had suffered at the hands of Modi, his leading rival in the Lok Sabha election in Varanasi in 2014. Modi had beaten him by a margin of nearly 372,000 ballots. Neither of them was a resident of Varanasi, but an Indian citizen can contest an election to a Lok Sabha seat from anywhere in the country. A staunch secularist, Kejriwal had chosen to challenge Modi in Varanasi, where the BJP had won four mayoral contests since 2000.

Varanasi, the New Base of Modi

Located on the banks of the Ganges, which descended from the heavens in mythological tales, Varanasi is the holiest city for Hindus. According to the prevalent Hindu myth, Varanasi is the abode of Lord Shiva. Its popular temple dedicated to Lord Shiva is called Vishwanath (Sanskrit: Lord of the World). It is the site of eighty-four *ghats*—stairways to the riverbank—of which five are the most sacred, the foremost being the Dashashwamedh (Sanskrit: Ten Horses Sacrifice). It is at this ghat that a very theatrical religious homage, called *aarti*, is paid daily to the Holy Ganges at dusk.

To probe the appeal of Modi to the residents of Varanasi, in mid-February 2015 I spent a few hours at the entrance of the Vishwanath Temple, which is accessed through a narrow lane with small shops on both sides. My informal conversations with locals revealed that a large majority of Hindus had voted for Modi. The reasons were encapsulated by two men, Motilal Mishra and Krishan Kumar Shukla, both of whom sold marigold garlands at their hole-in-the-wall stalls to the pilgrims to honor the deities in the temple. A lean, mustached man of thirty-five with broken teeth, Mishra said, "I voted for Modi because all others did." His well-built, bespectacled neighbor in dark gray pants and a white shirt, Shukla, said, "I voted for Modi because he will make Hindus strong." Going by their surnames, both Mishra and Shukla were Brahmins.

At the other end of the Hindu caste system, I talked to the members of the outcaste community, called Doms, at the cremation ghat named Harish Chandra. To mask their pariah status in the Hindu hierarchy, Doms use Chaudhry as their surname. Some of them own shops along the street leading to the ghat where they stock dry logs in the open to be used for incarcerating a corpse. A group of Doms gathered at a nondescript temple, waiting to be picked up by the relatives of the deceased in order to initiate the cremation ceremony.

My conversation with this group showed that they had all backed Modi. This deviated from the widely prevalent view that backing for the BJP comes predominantly from Hindus of upper castes. One of the main reasons that Modi appealed to the Doms was his slogan "Clean Ganges" (aka Ganga); the river had become polluted from the untreated sewage and chemical waste factories discharged into it. Clean Ganges also implied cleansing the ghats, the Doms told me. "Prime Minister Modi appointed a committee of nine to supervise the Clean Ganga campaign," said Ramesh Chaudhry, a slim man of thirty with sunken cheeks and stubble, chewing paan. "None of them has visited this temple of ours. And our complaints about continued squalor at our ghat to local BJP officials do not get presented to the committee." Yet the mood had not turned sour. "Modi has been the prime minister for only eight months," said Rajan Kesari Chaudhry, a middle-aged man in a dhoti and a loose white shirt. "You have to give him more time."[15]

For his part, Modi lost no time in flying to Varanasi the day after the BJP's resounding victory in the parliamentary poll on May 16, 2014. After offering prayers at the Sankatmochan Temple and the Vishwanath Temple, he participated in the grand Ganga aarti at the Dashashwamedh Ghat. "I bow before the people of Varanasi for having so much faith in me," Modi said in his thanksgiving speech from a makeshift stage. "There's a lot of work that God has put me on this earth for."[16] This was a refrain of what he had told BJP workers during the election campaign. "There are some people who are chosen by God for undertaking difficult tasks," he said. "It occurs to me that perhaps God has chosen me to do this work."[17]

In reality it was RSS leaders who decided at their meeting in Jaipur on March 15, 2013, that the BJP's candidate for prime minister would be Narendra Modi, "a man of indefatigable and galvanizing energy," and that he would run from a constituency in Uttar Pradesh, the heartland of Hinduism. They thus elbowed out the foremost BJP leader, Lal Krishna Advani, who had served as deputy prime minister under Atal Bihari Vajpayee.[18] As prime minister, Modi displayed the same vigor that he had applied to electioneering. He provided a sharp contrast to his predecessor, Manmohan Singh, an inert and expressionless politician who had never contested a Lok Sabha election, relying instead on being elected to the Upper House by the members of the Assam State Assembly. Unfamiliar with social media, Singh communicated messages to the public during a crisis by inviting senior journalists to tea. By contrast, Modi was an avid user of social media. Following his elevation to premiership, the number of his Twitter followers doubled to more than 8 million.[19]

Modi's Pro-Business Stance

In quick order Modi announced a series of socioeconomic programs. The one that mattered most was the Make in India plan because it had the best potential for creating a cornucopia of new jobs, which Modi had promised in his election speeches. His grand goal was to turn India into a global manufacturing hub like the one that China had become, accounting for 21 percent of the world's manufactured goods—ten times the contribution that India made to this sector globally.[20] India's educated youths were flooding the labor ranks at the rate of one million a month. Even if half of them stayed in villages to work the land as their fathers had been doing, the labor market was set to swell by half a million a month. The enormity of achieving Modi's target was underscored by the fact that the average monthly increase in new jobs in 2014 was only 51,000.[21]

The GDP expansion rate during fiscal 2014, ending in March 2015, almost wholly under Modi's leadership, was 7.3 percent.[22] This was marginally better than the revised figure of 6.9 percent for the previous fiscal year, the last under the Congress-led government.

The Modi government quickly eased environmental and other regulatory rules to expedite clearances for mining and other industrial projects. Prospecting for minerals in forests was exempted from acquiring the consent of local village councils or settling tribal rights. This policy went hand in hand with putting pressure on environmental and civil right NGOs by labeling them as "anti-national" chiefly because of their opposition to a development model based on aggressive exploitation of coal and other minerals and on large hydropower and nuclear power schemes. In April 2015 the Modi administration froze the bank accounts of Greenpeace India.[23]

In the case of mines and minerals in general, the amended bill combined prospecting and mining rights and extended the leases from thirty years to fifty. It favored the mining companies further by reducing the contribution they had to make to the district mineral foundation for rehabilitating the displaced persons from the present 100 percent of the annual royalty they paid to the state government to 33 percent.[24]

After the Lower House passed a further amendment to the Mines and Minerals (Development and Regulation) (Amendment) Act 2011 in early March, it was debated in the Upper House on March 20. By agreeing to make it mandatory for the licensing state government to set rules for the district mineral foundation that accorded with the provisions of the earlier pro-Adivasi laws, it succeeded in dividing the multi-party opposition. That smoothed passage of the bill.[25]

As for the acquisition of land anywhere in India, the amendments to the Land Acquisition Act 2013 granted exemptions from the consent clause and the social impact assessment for the land acquired for national security, defense, rural infrastructure, industrial corridors, and social infrastructure. The consent clause in the 2013 act required private companies to secure consent from at least 70 percent of the affected farmers before their land could be bought. The social impact assessment clause mandated a survey to determine how the people in the area, including sharecroppers, would be affected by the loss of land.[26]

The Modi administration issued the amended bill as an ordinance on December 29, 2014. But the resistance to the amendments in the Upper House was so strong that it agreed to refer these to the joint parliamentary committee on March 20. Nonetheless, opposition outside Parliament built up. An April 19 protest rally organized by the Congress Party where Rahul

Gandhi spoke drew a crowd of one hundred thousand. Gandhi accused Modi of being beholden to big business at the expense of struggling farmers.[27] This led the committee to invite comments from public bodies and individuals. Appearing before it on June 10, leaders of five farmers' organizations described the proposed amendments as "alarming" and demanded the withdrawal of the bill.[28] This forced the government to reissue the bill as an ordinance. Its continued pursuit of this path will create the image of the BJP as an anti-farmer party, which will undercut its standing in villages, where most voters live.

As for the BJP's near-term prospects, commentators were divided on assessing the first year of the Modi government, which ended in late May 2015. His admirers praised his energy and strong leadership and viewed his frequent foreign jaunts as raising the status of India in the international community. His critics saw his almost monthly trips to foreign capitals as an exercise to wipe away the pariah status he had acquired abroad after the communal violence in Gujarat in 2002. They took heart from the stiff resistance he met in trying to alter the 2013 land acquisition law.

This underlined the long-established pattern of Indian politics. For a ruling party to maintain its popular base, it must balance its concession to the propertied classes with sops to the have-nots, who have increasingly come to realize the power of universal suffrage.

June 2015

Acknowledgments

A project such as this requires extensive field research, for which I needed the assistance of friends and associates based in India, Britain, and the United States. I wish to thank all those who volunteered to help as well as those who agreed to talk to me, most of whom appear in the book.

For all the assistance they provided me in making this book a reality, I am grateful (in alphabetical order) to Omair Anas, Suvojit Bagchi, Arijit Banerji, Bizeth Banerjee, Sumanta Banerjee, Sudha Bhardwaj, Lord Karan Bilimoria, Shaila Brijnath, Ishara Callan, Sumit Chakravaratty, Sena Gorih, Sir Thomas Harris, Jethmal Jain, Javed Jafar, Ranchod Ram Jangid, Mark Hutt, Aftab Kamal Pasha, Regi Phillips, Mahaveer Rathi, Khinv Raj, Rajendra Sail, Prince Jit Singh Sandhu, Bharat Sharma, Pulkit Sharma, and Mohan Tikku.

Notes

Preface

1. Ian Bremmer, "The New Cold War on Business," *Fortune*, October 8, 2014, http://fortune.com/2014/10/08/the-new-cold-war-on-business.html.

2. Stiglitz's full definition is as follows: "Fundamentally, it is the closer integration of the countries and peoples of the world which has been brought about by the enormous reduction of costs of transportation and communication, and the breaking down of artificial barriers to the flows of goods, services, capital, knowledge and (to a lesser extent) people across borders." In Joseph Stiglitz, *Globalization and Its Discontents* (New York: W.W. Norton, 2003), 9.

3. Vamsee Juluri, *Bollywood Nation: India Through Its Cinema* (New Delhi: Penguin Books, 2013).

4. "Production of India's Ambassador Car Suspended," BBC News, May 25, 2014, http://www.bbc.co.uk/news/business-27563784.

Introduction

1. Bernard Weinraub, "Economic Crisis Forcing Once Self-Reliant India to Seek Aid," *New York Times*, June 29, 1991, http://www.nytimes.com/1991/06/29/world/economic-crisis-forcing-once-self-reliant-india-to-seek-aid.html.

2. Manmohan Singh then got elected to the Rajya Sabha, the upper house of parliament, from the state of Assam.

3. When India's regulation required foreign automobile companies—specifically Ford Motor Company and General Motors, which had been assembling cars there since 1930—to undertake local manufacturing, they refused and left India in 1953.

4. Indian parliament consists of the Lower House (aka Lok Sabha, Hindi: People's Council) and the Upper House (aka Rajya Sabha, Hindi: States' Council). Members of

the Lower House are elected by voters. Of the 250 members of the Upper House, twelve are nominated by the president. The rest are allocated to the constituent states according to their population. The directly elected state lawmakers then elect the members to the Upper House. Its tenure is six years and a third of its members retire every two years.

5. S. Ramadorai, *The TCS Story . . . and Beyond* (Delhi: Penguin Books , 2011), 77–78.

6. Ibid., 75.

7. Amar K.J.R. Nayak, Kalyan Chakravarti, and Prabina Rajib, "Globalization Process in India: A Historical Perspective Since Independence, 1947," *South Asian Journal of Management* 12 (January 11, 2005), http://www1.ximb.ac.in/users/fac/visiting/vfac.nsf/23e5e39594c064ee852564ae004fa010/9372a1cbc985527e652573340023a8e5/$FILE/S1-SAJM.pdf.

8. Dilip Hiro, *After Empire: The Birth of a Multipolar World* (New York: Nation Books), 197.

9. "India Logs 8.2% Growth Rate in 2003–04," Rediff.com, June 30, 2004, http://www.rediff.com/money/2004/jun/30gdp.htm.

10. Septarishi Dutta, "India's Millionaire Tribe Set to Soar," *India Real Time* blog, *Wall Street Journal*, May 29, 2014, http://blogs.wsj.com/indiarealtime/2014/05/29/indias-millionaire-tribe-is-set-to-soar/.

11. Randeep Ramesh, "British Minister Defends £825 Million Aid," *The Guardian*, November 19, 2008, http://www.theguardian.com/world/2008/nov/19/britain-aid-to-india-825; and Somini Sengupta, "India Faces a Paradox in Its Ill-fed Children," *International Herald Tribune*, March 11, 2009.

12. Vivian Fernandes, "Gujarat Model or Modi Model? New Book Says There Is Only a Modi Style of Execution," *First Post*, April 11, 2014, http://firstbiz.firstpost.com/economy/gujarat-model-modi-model-new-book-says-modi-style-execution-81762.html.

13. FE Bureaus, "Modi Orders Inquiry into Nano MoU Note," *Financial Express*, November 11, 2008, http://archive.financialexpress.com/news/modi-orders-inquiry-into-nano-mou-note/383964/.

14. Megha Bahree, "Indian Billionaire Gautam Adani Finds a Savior in the Modi Govt," *Forbes* (Mumbai), July 17, 2014, http://www.forbes.com/sites/meghabahree/2014/07/17/adani-finds-a-savior-in-the-modi-govt/.

15. Rajeev Kumar, "Adani-Modi Nexus to Cost 23,625 Cr," *Gulail*, September 9, 2013, http://gulail.com/adani-modi-nexus-to-result-in-loss-of-rs-23625-crore-to-gujarat-in-one-deal-alone/.

16. Rohini Hensman, "Gujarat Model of Development: What Would It Do to the Indian Economy?," Countercurrents.org, March 19, 2014, http://www.countercurrents.org/rh190314.htm.

17. Harit Mehta, "Six-Year Banishment Led to Narendra Modi's Metamorphosis," *Times of India*, April 1, 2014, http://timesofindia.indiatimes.com/news/Six-year-banishment-led-to-Narendra-Modis-metamorphosis/articleshow/33040649.cms.

18. "UK Reads the Riot Act to Narendra Modi," *Times of India*, March 22, 2005, http://timesofindia.indiatimes.com/articleshow/1058718.cms; and "Gujarat Riot Death

Toll Revealed," BBC News, May 11, 2005, http://news.bbc.co.uk/1/hi/world/south_asia/4536199.stm.

19. A sting operation by the Delhi-based *Tehelka* magazine five years later would reveal testimonies by the killers explaining how the pogrom had been planned and implemented, and how Modi, senior BJP figures, and assorted police officers had been personally involved. Cited in Arundhati Roy, *Listening to Grasshoppers: Field News on Democracy* (London: Hamish Hamilton, 2009), 151.

20. Celia W. Dugger, "Religious Riots Loom Over Indian Politics," *New York Times*, July 27, 2002, http://www.nytimes.com/2002/07/27/world/religious-riots-loom-over-indian-politics.html.

21. Cited in Max Fisher, "Who Is Narendra Modi and Why Is the World Afraid of Him Leading India?," *War in Context*, April 10, 2014, http://warincontext.org/2014/04/10/who-is-narendra-modi-and-why-is-the-world-afraid-of-him-leading-india/.

22. "Narendra Modi Facts: Why Was Modi Denied a US Visa?," https://narendramodifacts.com/faq_visa.html.

23. Vinod Matthew, "Showcasing Gujarat, the Vibrant Way," *Hindu Business Line*, September 24, 2003, http://www.thehindubusinessline.in/2003/09/24/stories/2003092400010800.htm.

24. Fernandes, "Gujarat Model or Modi Model?."

25. Ehsan Jafri was hacked to death by a violent Hindu mob armed with swords, broken pipes, and kerosene, and his body parts were fed to the flames engulfing the housing complex of the Gulbarg Society in the Chamanpura neighborhood of Ahmedabad.

26. Saeed Khan and Himanshu Kaushik, "2002 Gujarat Riots: Clean Chit to Modi, Court Rejects Zakia Jafri's Plea," *Times of India*, December 26, 2013, http://timesofindia.indiatimes.com/india/2002-Gujarat-riots-Clean-chit-to-Modi-court-rejects-Zakia-Jafris-plea/articleshow/27968858.cms.

27. Dean Nelson, "British Decision to Lift Ban on Narendra Modi Criticized," *Daily Telegraph*, October 12, 2012, http://www.telegraph.co.uk/news/worldnews/asia/india/9605070/British-decision-to-lift-ban-on-Narendra-Modi-criticised.html.

28. "The Massacre of Gujarat, Narendra Modi: Sad as When an Animal Dies," *Asia News*, July 13, 2013, http://www.asianews.it/news-en/The-massacre-of-Gujarat,-Narendra-Modi:-Sad-as-when-an-animal-dies-28465.html.

29. Sachin Parashar and Kapil Dave, "Powell Meets Narendra Modi, Nine-Year-Old US Boycott Ends," *Times of India*, February 13, 2014, http://timesofindia.indiatimes.com/india/Nancy-Powell-meets-Narendra-Modi-nine-year-old-US-boycott-ends/articleshow/30329280.cms.

30. Uday Mahurkar and Kunal Pradhan, "Meet the Men Behind Modi's Audacious Election Campaign," *India Today*, February 14, 2014, http://indiatoday.intoday.in/story/narendra-modi-bjp-prime-ministerial-candidate-campaign-social-media/1/343517.html.

31. Priyanka Kaushal, "Overseas Friends of Modi?," *Tehelka* (Delhi), March 22, 2014, http://www.tehelka.com/tag/overseas-friends-of-bjp-ofbjp/. In Houston, Texas, some seven hundred nonresident Indians worked voluntarily to urge voters in India to back Modi.

32. "NRIs Set Up NaMo Tea Stall in Silicon Valley," *Indian Express*, February 11, 2014, http://indianexpress.com/article/india/india-others/nris-set-up-namo-tea-stall-in-silicon-valley-support-modi-for-ls-polls/.

33. Aditi Phadnis, "Modi to Woo Financial Elite Next Week," *Business Standard*, February 21, 2014, http://www.business-standard.com/article/current-affairs/modi-to-woo-financial-elite-next-week-114022000842_1.html.

34. Vijay Murty and Shailesh Sharma, "Move to Field Yashwant Sinha's Son Irks Party Workers," *Hindustan Times*, March 15, 2014, http://www.hindustantimes.com/india-news/ranchi/move-to-field-yashwant-sinha-s-son-irks-party-workers/article1-1195507.aspx.

35. Jessica Guynn, "Facebook's Mark Zuckerberg Latest Tech CEO to Visit India," *USA Today*, October 1, 2014, http://www.usatoday.com/story/tech/2014/10/01/facebook-mark-zuckerberg-india-internetorg/16533515/.

36. Dean Nelson, "'Magic' Modi Uses Hologram to Address Dozens of Rallies at Once," *Daily Telegraph*, May 2, 2014, http://www.telegraph.co.uk/news/worldnews/asia/india/10803961/Magic-Modi-uses-hologram-to-address-dozens-of-rallies-at-once.html.

37. Uday Mahurkar and Kunal Pradhan, "Meet the Men Behind Modi's Audacious Election Campaign," *India Today*, February 14, 2014, http://indiatoday.intoday.in/story/narendra-modi-bjp-prime-ministerial-candidate-campaign-social-media/1/343517.html.

38. Himani Chandra Gurtoo, "BJP's Advertisement Plan May Cost a Whopping Rs 50,000 Cr," *Hindustan Times*, April 13, 2014, http://www.hindustantimes.com/elections2014/state-of-the-states/advertisement-war-to-win-lok-sabha-elections-may-cost-bjp-whopping-rs-5-000-crore/article1-1207499.aspx.

39. Ibid.

40. "It Is Modi Driven Television Coverage," CMS Media Lab, May 8, 2014, https://cmsindiablog.wordpress.com/tag/cms-media-lab/.

41. Of the BJP's 482 candidates, only seven were Muslim. None of them got elected.

42. More than 36 million Muslims of Uttar Pradesh did not have a single representative in the Lok Sabha. The twenty-three Muslim MPs on the opposition benches were only a fraction of the seventy-six MPs that Muslims should have had to correspond to their proportion of the national population.

43. Frank Jack Daniel and Sanjeev Minglani, "Modi's Nationalist Foot Soldiers Take Centre-Stage in India," Reuters, May 27, 2014, http://in.reuters.com/article/2014/05/27/uk-india-politics-hindu-idINKBN0E70R020140527.

44. "Muslims Are Not Minorities, Parsis Are: Najma Heptullah," TNN, May 28, 2014, http://timesofindia.indiatimes.com/india/Muslims-are-not-minorities-Parsis-are-Najma-Heptullah/articleshow/35651799.cms.

45. Rajesh Kumar Singh and Aditi Shah, "India's Pro-Business Modi Storms to Historic Election Win," Reuters, May 16, 2014, http://www.reuters.com/article/2014/05/16/us-india-election-idUSBREA4E0XG20140516.

46. "Property Market Bullish After Modi Win," TGI News Service, May 19, 2014, http://www.theglobalindian.co.nz/modified-india-set-to-uplift-property-market/.

1. Gurgaon: Shining City with a Dark Underbelly

1. Rao Jaswant Singh, "Why Is Gurgaon So Neglected? Prime Minister Narendra Modi Asks," *Times of India*, October 12, 2014, http://timesofindia.indiatimes.com /home/specials/assembly-elections-2014/haryana-news/Why-is-Gurgaon-so-neglected -Prime-Minister-Narendra-Modi-asks/articleshow/44787781.cms.

2. Rana Kapoor, "Consolidation—A Critical Enabler for Efficient Farming," *Hindu Business Line*, May 15, 2011, http://www.thehindubusinessline.com/industry-and -economy/agri-biz/article2021516.ece.

3. Naazneen Karmail, "Mangal Prabhat Lodha Is India's Richest Property Baron as Kushal Pal Singh's DLF Tanks," *Forbes* (Mumbai), October 14, 2014, http://www .forbes.com/sites/naazneenkarmali/2014/10/14/mangal-prabahat-lodha-is-indias -richest-property-baron-as-kushal-pal-singhs-dlf-tanks/.

4. "IT Sector to Log 16–18% Growth in FY'12," ENS Economic Bureau, August 24, 2011, http://archive.indianexpress.com/news/-it-sector-to-log-1618—growth-in-fy-12- /836127/. During 2001–11, the business process outsourcing industry grew sixteen times, to $16.9 billion a year.

5. Delhi Development Act 1957, http://www.dda.org.in/tendernotices_docs/sept09 /rti/Delhi%20Development%20Act%201957.doc.

6. K.P. Singh with Ramesh Menon and Raman Swamy, *Whatever the Odds: The Incredible Story Behind DLF* (Noida: HarperCollins Publishers India, 2011), 90.

7. Ibid., 144.

8. Later, American Universal Electric (India) would be sold to GE Motors India Limited, part of the GE Group Global.

9. Simon Robinson, "Building a Dream," *Time*, August 17, 2007, http://www.time .com/time/magazine/article/0,9171,1653654,00.html.

10. T.N. Ninan, "How Sanjay Gandhi's Maruti Udyog Became Maruti Suzuki," *India Today*, December 18, 2006, http://indiatoday.intoday.in/story/how-maruti-udyog-became -maruti-suzuki/1/180152.html.

11. Dhiraj Nayyar, "India's Landlord: The Trials and Triumphs of K. P. Singh," *India Today*, November 18, 2011, http://indiatoday.intoday.in/story/whatever-the-odds-the -incredible-story-behind-dlf-by-k.p.singh/1/160593.html.

12. R. Sidharan, "Sultan of Suburbia," *Business Today*, February 3, 2002, http:// archives.digitaltoday.in/businesstoday/20020203/cover1.html.

13. Ibid.

14. For "discretionary powers," see chapter 8, 258–59.

15. Interviewed by the author, November 2011.

16. Interviewed by the author, October 2011. See also "Latest Property News on Real Estate Developers," *India Realty News*, February 2, 2012, http://www.indianrealtynews .com/category/real-estate-developers/. The Central Bureau of Investigation accused Emaar MGF of financial irregularities in the sale of plots at grossly undervalued prices in its 358-acre, joint-venture Emaar Hills Township Project in Hyderabad.

17. S.R. Bakshi, Sita Ram Sharma, and S. Gajrani, *Bansi Lal, Chief Minister of Haryana* (New Delhi: APH Publishing, 1998), 136–37.

18. The complex of 190 houses, surrounded by a high wall, was completed in 1993.

19. Interviewed by the author, October 2011.

20. Cited in Mark Tully, *Non-Stop India* (New Delhi: Allen Lane, 2011), and *India: The Road Ahead* (London: Rider Books, 2011), 14.

21. Interviewed by the author, October 2011.

22. "Dawn of the Indian Century," *Financial Express*, December 18, 2004, http://www.financialexpress.com/news/dawn-of-the-indian-century/122377/2.

23. Monique Perry Danziger, "New Report Finds Illicit Capital Flight out of India US $462 Billion," Global Financial Integrity, November 17, 2010, http://www.gfip.org/index.php?option=content&task=view&id=347.

24. Neeraj Chauhan, "How Did CBI Arrive at $500bn Black Money Figure?," *Times of India*, February 16, 2012, http://articles.timesofindia.indiatimes.com/2012-02-16/india/31066398_1_tax-havens-black-money-tax-evasion.

25. In 2005, GECIS transformed into an independent multinational company, Genpact, with its head office in Gurgaon. It offered customer services, IT, finance and accounting, sales and marketing analysis, debt collection, and actuarial and other insurance services.

26. General Electric was included in the Dow Jones Industrial Average in 1907.

27. Interviewed by the author, March 2011.

28. Interviewed by the author, October 2011.

29. Randeep Ramesh, "From Muddy Villages to Boomtown," *The Guardian*, January 13, 2007, http://www.guardian.co.uk/world/2007/jan/13/politics.india.

30. NASSCOM-McKinsey Report 2005 Summary, http://indiaoutsource.livejournal.com/129981.html.

31. Ramesh, "From Muddy Villages to Boomtown."

32. With assets of $2 trillion, JPMorgan Chase & Co. is the largest bank in the United States as measured by assets and market capitalization.

33. Interviewed by the author, March 2011.

34. Interviewed by the author, November 2011.

35. JPMorgan Chase Bank, N.A., operating as Chase, is the retail-banking subsidiary of JPMorgan Chase & Co., a financial services firm.

36. Interviewed by the author, November 2011.

37. "Unitech Espace Nirvana Country—Nirvana Country, Gurgaon (ID: J29097 0411)," http://www.propertywala.com/unitech-espace-nirvana-country-gurgaon. Outstripping this ad, its advertisement for the Uniworld City promised "the indulgence of Western architecture, the oriental charm of Asia and fine elements of American lifestyle."

38. Interviewed by the author, November 2011.

39. In Britain, a seventy-centiliter bottle of Ladyburn 1973 Vintage Single Malt Scotch Whisky sells for £550. At Leela Palace Kempinski in an upscale neighborhood of

New Delhi, the bar offered its special drink, the "Black Pearl," for Rs 125,000 ($2,500) a shot. Jason Burke, "Delhi's Food Revolution: Forget the Bhaji, Bring on the Risotto," *The Guardian*, January 20, 2012, http://www.guardian.co.uk/lifeandstyle/2012/jan/20/delhi-food-revolution.

40. Jim Yardley, "India's Way: In India, Dynamism Wrestles with Dysfunction," *New York Times*, June 8, 2011, http://www.nytimes.com/2011/06/09/world/asia/09gurgaon.html?pagewanted=all.

41. Interviewed by the author, March 2011.

42. The TCS Tower, the central office of Tata Consultancy Services, has five giant diesel generators on its roof, along with a twenty-thousand-liter diesel tank underground.

43. Raghav Ohri, "Have Sealed Over 442 Illegal Tube Wells, Gurgaon DC Tells Court," *Indian Express*, November 8, 2011, http://www.indianexpress.com/news/Have-sealed-over-442-illegal-tubewells—Gurgaon-DC-tells-court/872545/.

44. Interviewed by the author, November 2011.

45. A *paan* is made of betel leaf with areca nut, slaked lime paste, and brown powder paste. It is chewed by many Indians and considered a palate cleanser and breath freshener.

46. Interviewed by the author, November 2011.

47. Tanushree Roy Chowdhury, "Wazirabad Recreation Project Planned on Forest Land," *Times of India*, January 11, 2011, http://articles.timesofindia.indiatimes.com/2011-01-11/gurgaon/28379077_1_forest-land-leisure-project-acres.

48. Tanushree Roy Chowdhury, "SC Check on Land Acquisition a Blow to Government, Private Developers," *Times of India*, February 2, 2011, http://articles.timesofindia.indiatimes.com/2011-02-02/gurgaon/28359133_1_private-developers-panchayat-land-village-panchayats.

49. Ibid.

50. National Centre for Advocacy Studies, Pune, August 31, 2011, http://enwl.bellona.ru/pipermail/enwl-eng/attachments/20110916/aec7c553/recommendationsfromNCASPune-0001.pdf.

51. Most of the text on pages 49–51 is a compendium of interviews with assorted call-center employees living mainly in Delhi during my annual visits to India and the novel *One Night @ the Call Center* by Chetan Bhagat (New Delhi: Rupa Publications, 2005).

52. Jessica Marquez, "Report Cites Poor Working Conditions in India's Call Centers," *Workforce*, October 17, 2006, http://www.workforce.com/article/20061017/NEWS01/310179999.

53. "Are BPOs Adding Better Standard of Living for Youth in India?," Yahoo! Answers, http://in.answers.yahoo.com/question/index?qid=20070313095714AAAiUbq. See an earlier paper on the subject by Babu P. Ramesh, "'Cyber Coolies' in BPO: Insecurities and Vulnerabilities in Non-Standard Work," *Economic and Political Weekly*, January 11, 2004, http://www.jstor.org/pss/4414585.

54. An auto dialer, or automatic dialer, is an electronic device or software that automatically dials telephone numbers. Once the call has been answered, it either plays a recorded message or connects the call to a live person.

55. *Gurgaon Workers News*, newsletter no. 1, January 2007, https://gurgaonworkersnews .wordpress.com/gurgaonworkersnews-no1/.

56. Ninety-six percent of Pakistanis are Muslim.

57. P. Singh and A. Pandey, "Increased Empowerment, Declining Health for India's Female Call Centre Employees," *Economic and Political Weekly* 40, no. 7 (2005): 684–88.

58. Martinez Collins, "The Ongoing Story of Shopping Malls in Gurgaon," Articlesbase, November 10, 2008, http://www.articlesbase.com/cosmetics-articles/the -ongoing-story-of-shopping-malls-in-gurgaon-636112.html.

2. Britain: A Magnet for Indian Companies

1. Ewan C. Hewitt, *Rolling Around the World: An Autobiography* (Bloomington, IN: Xlibris, 2014), 97–98.

2. "Thomas Carlyle's Lecture in Manchester, 1867," http://www.tatasteel.com /corporate/heritage/images/landmark.xml.

3. "In 1902 J.N. Tata in Pittsburgh" and "In 1902, J.N. Tata Met Mr. Charles Page Perin, an Eminent Consulting Engineer in New York," http://www.tatasteel.com /corporate/heritage/images/landmark.xml.

4. "PM's Speech in Bangalore, India," July 28, 2010, http://www.number10.gov.uk /news/pms-speech-in-india/.

5. "India-UK Trade and Economic Relations; and UK Report 2007," http://hcilondon .in/economicreview.pdf.

6. "Same-Day Visa Service Launches in India," May 13, 2013, http://www.ukba .homeoffice.gov.uk/sitecontent/newsarticles/2013/may/41-spv-india.

7. Interviewed by the author, July 2012.

8. PTI, "India 2nd Largest Asian Investor in UK," *Times of India*, July 7, 2004, http:// articles.economictimes.indiatimes.com/2004-07-07/news/27410058_1_largest-asian -investor-mark-dolan-uk-trade-and-investment.

9. The previous world record was held by a $101.6 million sale for a residence in Hong Kong in 1997.

10. "Glimpsing a Fairytale Wedding," BBC News, June 22, 2004, http://news.bbc .co.uk/1/hi/3830009.stm.

11. Interviewed by the author, July 2011.

12. Cited in "Indian Companies Are on an Acquisition Spree: Their Target? US Firms," Knowledge@Wharton, December 13, 2006, http://knowledge.wharton.upenn .edu/article.cfm?articleid=1627.

13. Shri. Harun R. Khan, "Outward Indian FDI—Recent Trends & Emerging Issues," March 2, 2012, http://www.rbi.org.in/scripts/BS_SpeechesView.aspx?id=674.

14. Interviewed by the author, May 2011.

15. "Equitymaster Poll 2011 Results: Tata Most Trustworthy," http://www.equity master.com/poll/Most-trustworthy-financial-reporting/index.asp.

16. "A Tradition of Trust," http://www.tata.com/aboutus/articlesinside/A-tradition-of-trust.

17. Karl West, "Tata's British Empire," *Sunday Times*, September 23, 2012.

18. The tax year in India runs from April 1 to March 31.

19. James Hall, "UK Investment in India 'Way Too Little,'" *Daily Telegraph*, January 3, 2006, http://www.telegraph.co.uk/finance/migrationtemp/2809932/UK-investment-in-India-way-too-little.html.

20. Cited in "Indian Companies Are on an Acquisition Spree."

21. "Corus Accepts £4.3bn Tata Offer," BBC News, October 20, 2006, http://news.bbc.co.uk/1/hi/business/6068244.stm.

22. The lowest price—$154 per ton of steel—pertained to POSCO of South Korea. "The POSCO," *The Economist*, February 15, 2011.

23. Tata Steel, "Tata Steel to Acquire Steel Business of NatSteel, Singapore," press release, August 16, 2004, http://www.tata.com/article/inside/9dL0dP!$$$!j3Z4=/TLYVr3YPkMU, and "Tata Steel to Acquire Millennium Steel, Thailand," press release, December 15, 2005, http://www.tata.com/article/inside/xKXzTTzhgP8=/TLYVr3YPkMU.

24. However, as a son of Indira Gandhi, who was the daughter of Jawaharlal Nehru, Rajiv Gandhi considered himself, and was regarded by others, as a Brahmin Hindu.

25. Ratan Tata's interview with *The Economist*, February 15, 2011.

26. To highlight its faith in the financial strength of the Tata Group, Standard Chartered Bank provided a $375 million unsecured loan to Tata Steel UK. The Tata Group was at the top of the two hundred Indian companies this bank favored. See Incar Group, "News: Tata Readies to Knock Out CSN," press release, November 23, 2006, http://www.incargroup.com/news/2006/11/news-tata-readies-to-knock-out-csn.html.

27. CSN already owned 3.8 percent of Corus shares through previous purchases on the open market. While the deal was being negotiated, the merchant bankers of CSN purchased an additional 15 percent of Corus shares on the open market, underlining CSN's resolve in the deal. This turned out to be a profitable investment.

28. Prince Mathews Thomas, "CSN Sounds Out Banks for Bigger Play," *Economic Times*, January 20, 2007, http://articles.economictimes.indiatimes.com/2007-01-20/news/28415732_1_csn-uk-takeover-panel-corus.

29. Fiona Walsh and Randeep Ramesh, "Suitors Do Battle over Corus," *The Guardian*, January 30, 2007, http://www.guardian.co.uk/business/2007/jan/30/3.

30. Kenneth A. Tye and Jerrold M. Novotney, *Schools in Transition: The Practitioner as Change Agent* (Mumbai: Tata–McGraw Hill Education), 14, 38.

31. The earlier entries on the list were Indian corporations operating solely inside the country.

32. See chapter 7, 213–14.

33. Randeep Ramesh and Mark Milner, "Tata Celebrates Costly Victory in Corus Chase," *The Guardian*, February 1, 2007, http://www.guardian.co.uk/business/2007/feb/01/india.frontpagenews.

34. Often the buyer and the seller agree to an additional payment—called contingent consideration—based on the outcome of future events. It is typically based on revenue or earnings targets that the acquired company must meet after the acquisition date.

35. A non-recourse loan is one under which the collateral underwriting it is the ultimate source of repayment, and in case of default the lender can only seize and sell the collateral and must leave the non-pledged assets untouched.

36. The breakdown of Tata Steel's equity capital was $700 million from internal generation, $500 million of external commercial borrowings, $640 million from the preferential issues of equity shares to Tata Sons Ltd.—the parent company's holding firm—in 2006–7 and 2007–8, $862 million from a rights issue of equity shares to the shareholders, $1 billion from a rights issue of convertible preference shares, and about $500 million from a foreign issue of equity-related instruments. Tata Steel, "Management Discussion and Analysis," in *Tata Steel 100th Annual Report 2006–2007*, http://www.tatasteel.com/investors/tatasteelAR2006-07/html/discussion4.html.

37. Reeba Zachariah, "Tatas Unwrap Details on Corus Funding," *Times of India*, April 11, 2007, http://articles.timesofindia.indiatimes.com/2007-04-11/india-business/27876944_1_tata-steel-uk-corus-shareholders-bridge-loans. The loans were divided almost equally between the unsecured mezzanine and senior secured. Interest rates for senior loans were 0.200 to 0.225 percent above LIBOR (London Inter-Bank Overnight Rate), then 5.415 percent, and unsecured mezzanine loans were 0.400 to 0.500 percent above LIBOR.

38. Interviewed by the author, July 2012.

39. "UK Is Top Spot for Indian Business," July 29, 2008, http://www.contractoruk.com/news/003896.html.

40. Reserve Bank of India, "Weekly Statistical Supplement," July 4, 2008, http://rbi.org.in/scripts/WSSView.aspx?Id=12510; and Dilip Hiro, *After Empire: The Birth of a Multipolar World* (New York: Nation Books, 2010), 199.

41. C.P. Chandrasekhar, "The Importance of Public Banking," February 27, 2010, http://theeram01.wordpress.com/category/articles/page/13/.

42. Joe Nocera, "How India Avoided a Crisis," *New York Times*, December 17, 2008.

43. Heather Timmins, "In Global Crisis, India Finds Strength and Hope in Weakness," *International Herald Tribune*, February 28–March 1, 2009.

44. Sundeep Jain, "Dramatic GDP Growth Figures Baffle Economists," *India Real Time* blog, *Wall Street Journal*, August 30, 2012, http://blogs.wsj.com/indiarealtime/2012/08/30/dramatic-gdp-growth-revisions-baffle-economists/.

45. Karl West, "Tata's British Empire," *Sunday Times*, September 23, 2012; and "BAE Systems to Announce Nearly 3,000 Job Cuts," BBC News, September 27, 2011, http://www.bbc.co.uk/news/business-15063827.

46. Interviewed by the author, August 2011.

47. Interviewed by the author, September 2011.

48. S. Ramadorai, *The TCS Story . . . and Beyond* (Delhi: Penguin Books, 2011), 186–87.

49. Ibid., 87.

50. "Tata Consultancy Services Ltd. Company History," *Business Standard*, http://www.business-standard.com/company/tcs-5400/information/company-history.

51. Since then, there have been two stock splits of two for one, in June 2008 and June 2009. In August 2012, a stock price of Rs 1,280 meant that the stock had appreciated twelve-fold since its launch eight years earlier.

52. In Gurgaon, each division of TCS was housed in a different building. See chapter 1.

53. Interviewed by the author, November 2011.

54. Interviewed by the author, August 2011.

55. Between April and October 2011, outward foreign direct investment from India was more than $20 billion, with Singapore and Mauritius the preferred investment destinations. See http://www.deloitte.com/assets/Dcom-India/Localpercent20Assets/Documents/Budgetpercent202012/2012percent20Budgetpercent20Publication.pdf.

56. "PM's Speech in Bangalore, India, 28 July 2010," http://www.number10.gov.uk/news/pms-speech-in-india/.

57. Manubhai Madhvani and Giles Foden, *Tide of Fortune: A Family Tale* (New Delhi: Random House, 2010). Cited in a review by Mahadev Desai, *Atlanta Dunia*, http://www.atlantadunia.com/dunia/Features/F166.htm.

58. Andrew Bryson, "Britain's Richest Asians," *Daily Telegraph*, April 19, 2006, http://www.telegraph.co.uk/finance/2936997/Britains-richest-Asians.html.

59. Emma Midgley, "Slough's Wedding Season Brings Asian Gold Theft Warning," BBC News, April 14, 2012, http://www.bbc.co.uk/news/uk-england-berkshire-17567046.

60. Interviewed by the author, September 2012.

61. Kolkata, press release, July 6, 2002, http://ontrackindia.com/ontrackindia/index.php?option=content&task=section&id=101.

62. Interviewed by the author, September 2012.

63. "Contact Us," Ontrack Systems Limited, http://www.ontrackuae.com/contact.htm.

3. The Indian Diaspora in America's Valley of Fortune

1. Mayuri Chawla Saini, "Silicon Valley: Valley of Fortune," *Outlook* (Delhi), July 30, 1997, http://www.outlookindia.com/article.aspx?203952.

2. Prior to the 1964 immigration law, India inherited the British colony quota of one hundred people, as it was fixed prior to independence in 1947. During 1948–65, the number of Indian immigrants grew by a mere seven thousand. The excess of five thousand above the official quota was made up largely of those who qualified as spouses

of American citizens. See Brian Knowlton, "Immigrants from India Thriving in US," *International Herald Tribune*, October 30, 2006, http://www.nytimes.com/2006/10/29 /world/americas/29iht-indians.3322280.html.

3. To avoid confusion with American Indians, the Census Department called them Asian Indians.

4. Monica Whatley and Jeanne Batalova, "Indian Immigrants in the United States," Migration Policy Institute Spotlight, August 21, 2013, http://www.migrationpolicy.org /article/indian-immigrants-united-states.

5. Sean Randolph, "India to Silicon Valley and Back," *Asia Sentinel*, September 8, 2010, http://www.asianwindow.com/tag/indians-in-silicon-valley/.

6. Knowlton, "Immigrants from India Thriving in US."

7. Cited in Randolph, "India to Silicon Valley and Back."

8. In December 1958, a separate Indo-Soviet agreement was signed to help equip the planned ninety-eight laboratories at the Powai campus.

9. "Russian President Medvedev Visits IIT Bombay," December 22, 2010, http:// www.iitbombay.org/news/Current/medvedev-to-visit-iit-bombay.

10. Thomas Friedman, *The World Is Flat: A Brief History of the Twenty-first Century* (New York: Farrar, Straus and Giroux, 2006), 104–5.

11. Rebecca Leung, "Imported from India," *60 Minutes*, February 11, 2009, http:// www.cbsnews.com/8301-18560_162-559476.html.

12. Ramarao is the father of Nagavara, a Hindu, and "Narayana Murthy" is his subcaste.

13. Leung, "Imported from India."

14. Ibid.

15. Ibid.

16. See chapter 1, 37.

17. Mehul Srivastave, "Bangalore Express, a Networker's Paradise," *Businessweek*, March 8, 2012, http://www.businessweek.com/articles/2012-03-08/the-bangalore-ex press-a-networkers-paradise.

18. Tamal Bandyopadhyay, "Ajay Banga: He Can Sell Ice to Eskimos," Rediff.com, August 29, 2005, http://www.rediff.com/money/2005/aug/29banga.htm.

19. "Indra K. Nooyi Biography," http://www.notablebiographies.com/news/Li-Ou /Nooyi-Indra-K.html.

20. Dayamanti Datta, "PepsiCo Chief Indra Nooyi Sets Example, Says Supportive Husband Behind Success," *India Today*, December 25, 2006, http://indiatoday.intoday .in/story/pepsico-ceo-indira-nooyi-most-sucessful-and-super-achiever-woman-of-india -2006/1/180011.html.

21. Nandan Nilekani, "Personal Side of Indra Nooyi," *Times of India*, February 7, 2007, http://articles.economictimes.indiatimes.com/2007-02-07/news/28471801_1_indra -nooyi-nandan-nilekani-personal-side.

22. Ibid.

23. "Indra Nooyi: Simon Hobbs Meets the CEO and Chairman of PepsiCo," *CNBC* Magazine, June 2008, http://www.cnbcmagazine.com/story/indra-nooyi/452/1/.

24. "Shining Star: Indra Nooyi," DesiCEO, desiceo.com/shinning-star-indra -nooyi/.

25. "Indra Nooyi: Simon Hobbs Meets the CEO and Chairman of PepsiCo."

26. "PepsiCo Board Meet in India a Historic Event: Nooyi," *Economic Times*, November 11, 2009, http://articles.economictimes.indiatimes.com/2009-11-11/news/2842 1559_1_pepsico-board-global-board-ceo-indra-nooyi.

27. Leung, "Imported from India."

28. Built on a single chip, the Pentium P5's two microprocessors contained about 3.3 million transistors. It was available with microprocessor speeds of 60 to 200 MHz. It was superseded by faster and more powerful microprocessors in 1995 (Pentium Pro), 1997 (Pentium II), 1999 (Pentium III), and 2000 (Pentium IV).

29. Venture capital is the term used for the funding provided to new firms with the potential of high growth combined with high risk, often in the high-tech sector. A venture capitalist company gives money in return for a stake in the budding firm's equity, expecting to see its value rise with the success of the project, leading eventually to an IPO or sale of the firm to a bigger entity.

30. Saini, "Silicon Valley: Valley of Fortune."

31. Randolph, "India to Silicon Valley and Back."

32. Sonja Cheung, "Sequoia Capital Seeks Bigger Role in India's Maturing Venture Industry," *Venture Capital Dispatch* blog, *Wall Street Journal*, August 6, 2012, http:// blogs.wsj.com/venturecapital/2012/08/06/sequoia-capital-seeks-bigger-role-in-indias -maturing-venture-industry/.

33. Sean Randolph, "Silicon Valley Expats Spur Innovation in India," *YaleGlobal*, September 2, 2010, http://yaleglobal.yale.edu/content/silicon-valley-spur-innovation.

34. Srivastave, "Bangalore Express, a Networker's Paradise."

35. "Being an Entrepreneur Is 'Hot': Vinod Khosla," *DNA*, November 10, 2011, http://www.dnaindia.com/bangalore/report_being-an-entrepreneur-is-hot-vinod -khosla_1610298. Khosla had a knack for delivering memorable one-liners. At the same meeting in Bangalore, he said, "You grow old when you retire, not retire when you grow old."

36. "Tony Blair to Advise Khosla Ventures on Green Energy," BBC News, May 25, 2010, http://www.bbc.co.uk/news/10151221.

37. Ibid.

38. "Khosla Ventures Hires Former Top US Diplomat Condoleezza Rice," *Indian Express*, December 15, 2012, http://www.indianexpress.com/news/khosla-ventures-hires -former-top-us-diplomat-condoleezza-rice/1045506/.

39. Bala S. Manian, "Business Challenges Facing SME Sector," May 9, 2011, http:// www.sbf.org.sg/download/docs/eventsvc/event/event20110509slides.pdf.

40. Randolph, "Silicon Valley Expats Spur Innovation in India."

41. Ibid.

42. "The Entrepreneur of the Year Register; Employees: 678, Projected 1993 Revenues: $36 Million," *Inc.*, December 1, 1993, http://www.inc.com/magazine/19931201/3825_pagen_7.html.

43. Saini, "Silicon Valley."

44. Peter Galuszka, "Mastech Corp.: The Nabobs of Networking," *Businessweek*, May 31, 1999, http://www.businessweek.com/1999/99_22/b3631026.htm.

45. "Ashok Trivedi Talks to Amberish K. Diwanji," Rediff.com, October 24, 1998, http://www.rediff.com/computer/1998/dec/24sw.htm.

46. Silicon Valley Index, 2013, http://www.siliconvalleyindex.org/index.php/economy/income.

47. Infosys Technologies transferred to the New York Stock Exchange in December 2012.

48. "Story Behind Phaneesh's Resignation," *Times of India*, August 2, 2002, http://articles.timesofindia.indiatimes.com/2002-08-02/india-business/27291609_1_reka-maximovitch-sexual-harassment-infosys-and-murthy.

49. Fakir Chand, "Infosys Settles Sexual Harassment Lawsuit Out of Court for $3m," Rediff.com, May 11, 2003, http://www.rediff.com/money/2003/may/11infosys.htm.

50. iGate Corp (IGTE: NASDAQ GS), http://investing.businessweek.com/research/stocks/people/person.asp?personId=398034&ticker=IGTE.

51. India's top five IT companies by revenue were Tata Consultancy Services, Infosys Technologies, Wipro Technologies, HCL Technologies, and Tech Mahindra.

52. Patni Computer Systems Limited in 2007, http://www.123helpme.com/patni-computer-systems-ltd-view.asp?id=156520.

53. The deal set up iGate to win the M&A Atlas award for the Asia-Pacific region. "Asia Pacific Deal of the Year," M&A Atlas Awards, New York, April 28, 2012, https://www.globalmanetwork.com/presscenter/WINNERS%20CIRCLE%20MA%20ATLAS%20AWARDS%20Global%20Major%20Markets%202012.pdf.

54. "Business Process Outsourcing Newsletter, JANUARY-FEBRUARY 2011," Avendus Capital, http://www.avendus.com/upload/newsletter/avendus_outsourcing_newsletter_jan-feb_2011.pdf; and "iGate Completes Acquisition of Patni," *Economic Times*, May 13, 2011, http://articles.economictimes.indiatimes.com/2011-05-13/news/29540081_1_patni-board-integration-execution-patni-computers.

55. Shilpa Phadnis, "iGate Claims Damages from Phaneesh Murthy," TNN, March 3, 2014, http://timesofindia.indiatimes.com/tech/tech-news/iGate-claims-damages-from-Phaneesh-Murthy/articleshow/31298105.cms.

56. The name can be read as India Aluminum Company—"Hind" means India in Urdu, and "Al" is the symbol of aluminum in chemistry.

57. "India's Richest: Kumar Birla," Forbes.com, http://www.forbes.com/lists/2005/77/2X62.html.

58. Andrew Corn, "Indian Conglomerate Buys Novelis," *Seeking Alpha* newsletter, April 19, 2007, http://seekingalpha.com/article/32720-indian-conglomerate-buys-novelis.

59. Aman Srivastava and Rakesh Gupta, "Hindalco-Novelis Acquisition: Creating an Aluminum Global Giant," 11th Annual Convention of the Strategic Management Forum, May 8–10, 2008, http://www.iitk.ac.in/infocell/announce/convention/papers /Colloquium-04-Aman%20Srivastava,Rakesh%20Gupta%20final.pdf.

60. Cuckoo Paul, "Kumar Manglam Birla: A Man for All Seasons," *Forbes* (Mumbai), October 4, 2012, http://forbesindia.com/printcontent/33839.

61. This was exactly what Tata Steel was forced to fork out for Corus Group shares, but in that case there was a hostile bid by CSN.

62. Ruth David, "Hindalco to Buy Novelis for $6 Billion," *Forbes* (Mumbai), February 11, 2007, http://www.forbes.com/2007/02/11/mergers-acquisitions-aluminum-biz -cx_0211hindalco.html.

63. Later, a few other Indian companies, resorting to leveraged buyouts of Western businesses, would end up issuing bonds with high interest rates, thus building up a heavy aggregate debt burden.

64. Srivastava and Gupta, "Hindalco-Novelis Acquisition."

65. The banks included ABN Amro, Barclays Capital, Bank of Tokyo-Mitsubishi UFJ, Calyon, Citigroup, Deutsche Bank, HSBC, Mizuho Financial, and Sumitomo Mitsui Financial. Gagan Pareek, "Merger & Acquisition, Hindalco Novelis," August 27, 2010, http://www.slideshare.net/gagan3211/merger-acquisition-hindalco-novelis; and Hindalco Industries, "Directors Report," http://www.moneycontrol.com/annual-report /hindalcoindustries/directors-report/HI#HI. According to Hindalco's report for 2011– 12, its total assets were Rs 46,390 crore, or about $10 billion.

66. "Pepsi: Repairing a Poisoned Reputation in India," *Businessweek*, May 31, 2007, www.businessweek.com/stories/2007-05-31/pepsi-repairing-a-poisoned-reputation-in -indiabusinessweek-business-news-stock-market-and-financial-advice.

67. Melanie Warner, "How Do We Know PepsiCo Saved Huge Amounts of Water in India? It Told Us So," CBS News Money Watch, May 28, 2010, http://www.cbsnews .com/news/how-do-we-know-pepsico-saved-huge-amounts-of-water-in-india-it-told -us-so/.

4. The Scandalous Neglect of India's Agriculture

1. "Agriculture's Share in GDP Declines to 13.7% in 2012–13," *Economic Times*, August 30, 2013, http://articles.economictimes.indiatimes.com/2013-08-30/news/41618996 _1_gdp-foodgrains-allied-sectors.

2. "India Country Overview 2011," World Bank, http://www.worldbank.org/en /country/india.

3. R.V. Singh and Colleen Redcliffe, "Indian Government Seeks to Lower Official Poverty Line to 50 Cents Per Day," World Socialist Web Site, October 19, 2011, http:// www.wsws.org/en/articles/2011/10/pove-o19.html.

4. "A Wealth of Data: A Useful Way to Capture the Many Aspects of Poverty," *The Economist*, July 29, 2010, http://www.economist.com/node/16693283. The multi-dimensional poverty index (MPI) included health (child mortality and nutrition),

education, and living standards (cooking fuel, toilet, water, electricity, the size of the living space, and assets). In China, 12.7 percent of the population were MPI poor.

5. Rajeev Deshpande, "Govt Study Fixes Poverty Line at Rs 66 for Cities and Rs 35 for Villages," *Times of India*, April 29, 2012, http://articles.timesofindia.indiatimes.com /2012-04-29/india/31475601_1_poverty-line-population-expenditure.

6. *Panchayat*, a Sanskrit word, means "five persons." By tradition, an Indian village is represented by five wise men.

7. Interviewed by the author, March 2011.

8. Interviewed by the author, March 2011.

9. The term "Scheduled Castes" is used because these castes are listed in a schedule of India's constitution of 1950.

10. T. Haque, "Improving the Rural Poor's Access to Land in India," http://india governance.gov.in/files/improving-rural-poor-access-to-land-t-haque.pdf.

11. During the two decades preceding the NEP, the landless and marginal households rose by 9.3 percent, but in one post-NEP decade such households increased by 7.7 percent.

12. Named after Corrado Gini, an Italian statistician and sociologist, this index measures the inequality among values of a frequency distribution. A Gini Index of zero means perfect equality, where all values are the same with everyone having equal land or income. A Gini Index of 1.00 means one person has all the land or income.

13. Haque, "Improving the Rural Poor's Access to Land in India."

14. Biplab Dasgupta, *Globalisation: India's Adjustment Experience* (New Delhi and London: Sage Publications, 2005), 149, 170.

15. Vidya Sagar, "Suicide and Art of Living," *SR Magazine*, July–August 2006.

16. Interviewed by the author, February 2010.

17. The villagers' fallback position was to work the twenty-five hand-operated water pumps in the settlement, drawing water at a shallow depth.

18. Interviewed by the author, February 2010.

19. Interviewed by the author, March 2011.

20. P. Sainath, "The Largest Wave of Suicides in History," *Counterpunch*, February 12, 2009, http://www.counterpunch.org/2009/02/12/the-largest-wave-of-suicides-in -history/.

21. Binayak Sen, "The Coming Famine in India," *Mainstream*, November 3, 2012, http://www.mainstreamweekly.net/article3798.html.

22. Prasun Sonwalker, "Gujarat Has Lowest Farmer Suicide Rate: UK Study," *Hindustan Times*, April 19, 2014, http://www.hindustantimes.com/india-news/gujarat-has -lowest-farmer-suicide-rate-uk-study/article1-1209785.aspx.

23. Mark Tully, *Non-Stop India* (New Delhi: Allen Lane, 2011); *India: The Road Ahead* (London: Rider Books, 2011), 129.

24. P. Sainath, "The People Who Matter Most," *India Together*, http://www.india together.org/opinions/talks/psainath.htm.

25. Parwini Zora, "Indian Prime Minister Visits Rural Vidarbha," World Socialist Web Site, July 25, 2006, https://www.wsws.org/en/articles/2006/07/indi-j25.html.

26. Sainath, "Largest Wave of Suicides in History."

27. Markandey Katju citing NSSO round 66 (2009–10) in Kobad Ghandy, "Indian Economy: A Rocking Horse Galloping Forward—IV," *Mainstream*, June 2, 2012, http://www.mainstreamweekly.net/article3481.html.

28. Amruta Byatnal, "Lack of Irrigation Found to Be One of the Major Causes of Farmer Suicides," *The Hindu*, June 24, 2012, http://www.thehindu.com/news/national/article3563411.ece.

29. Andrew Malone, "The GM Genocide: Thousands of Indian Farmers Are Committing Suicide After Using Genetically Modified Crops," *Daily Mail*, November 3, 2008, http://www.dailymail.co.uk/news/article-1082559/The-GM-genocide-Thousands-Indian-farmers-committing-suicide-using-genetically-modified-crops.html.

30. Zora, "Indian Prime Minister Visits Rural Vidarbha."

31. "Study Questions Sustainability of Bt Cotton," *News from India*, June 24, 2012, http://www.gmwatch.eu/index.php?option=com_content&view=article&id=14024.

32. Zora, "Indian Prime Minister Visits Rural Vidarbha."

33. "Every 12 Hours, One Farmer Commits Suicide in India," *India Tribune*, http://www.indiatribune.com/index.php?option=com_content&id=5389:every-12-hours-one-farmer-commits-suicide-in-india.

34. "First Sight: Anusha Rizvi," *The Guardian*, August 12, 2010, http://www.theguardian.com/culture/2010/aug/12/first-sight-anusha-rizvi.

35. Rajeev Masand, "'Peepli Live' Is Engaging Picture," CNN-IBN, August 13, 2010, http://ibnlive.in.com/news/masand-peepli-live-is-an-engaging-picture/128807-47-84.html. Produced at the cost of $1.6 million, *Peepli Live* grossed $6.5 million at the box office.

36. "Vidarbha Reports Four More Farmers' Suicides in Last 72 Hours," Indian Agrarian Crisis, June 4, 2012, http://agrariancrisis.in/2012/06/04/vidarbha-reports-four-more-farmers-suicides-in-last-72-hours/.

37. Jayashree Nandi, "The Bt Show at 10," *Times of India*, April 1, 2012, http://articles.timesofindia.indiatimes.com/2012-04-01/special-report/31269811_1_bt-cotton-bt-technology-bt-crop.

38. "Maharashtra Bans Bt Cotton Seeds," *Times of India*, August 9, 2012, http://articles.timesofindia.indiatimes.com/2012-08-09/india/33118430_1_cotton-seeds-bt-cotton-cotton-growing-states.

39. "Karnataka Bans Mahyco's Bt Cotton Seeds After Crop Failure," GM Watch, March 28, 2014, http://www.gmwatch.org/index.php/news/archive/2014/15368-karnataka-bans-mahyco-s-bt-cotton-seeds-after-crop-failure.

40. Akash Bisht and Sadiq Naqvi, "Vidarbha: The Epicenter of Suicides," *Pratirodh, the Resistance*, November 25, 2012, http://www.pratirodh.com/politics-and-society-news/769-25-Nov-2012/vidarbha-farmer-suicide-maharastra-government-failure-agrarian-c.html.

41. Interviewed by the author, November 2011.

42. Interviewed by the author, November 2011.

43. Interviewed by the author, February 2010.

44. Interviewed by the author, November 2011.

45. Another solution lay in building dams where the land nearby did not require pumping, as in the case of a tube well. But the nearest one, called Khanda Dam, was thirty miles south of Kuri Bhagtasni.

46. Murali Gopalan, "Diesel Subsidy Down, but Free Pricing Some Time Away," *Hindu Business Line*, August 29, 2014, http://www.thehindubusinessline.com/features /smartbuy/automobiles/diesel-subsidy-down-but-free-pricing-some-time-away /article6363172.ece.

47. Dilip Hiro, *Inside India Today* (London: Routledge & Kegan Paul, 1976), 88.

48. Ibid.

49. Ibid.

50. Francine R. Frankel, *India's Green Revolution* (Princeton, NJ: Princeton University Press, 1972), 192–93.

51. G.S. Bhalla and Gurmail Singh, "Economic Liberalization and Indian Agriculture: A Statewise Analysis," *Economic & Political Weekly*, 44, no. 52 (December 26, 2009): 34–44.

52. "Population of India Over a Century," http://cyberjournalist.org.in/census/cenpop .html.

53. Bhalla and Singh, "Economic Liberalization and Indian Agriculture," 37.

54. Ibid.

55. Judith Renner, "Global Irrigated Area at Record Levels, But Expansion Slowing," Worldwatch Institute, November 27, 2012, http://www.worldwatch.org/global -irrigated-area-record-levels-expansion-slowing-0.

56. Somini Sengupta, "India Digs Deeper, but Wells Are Drying Up," *New York Times*, September 30, 2006, http://www.nytimes.com/2006/09/30/world/asia/30water2 .html.

57. K. Lakshmi, "Rain Water Harvesting Yields Rich Dividends," *The Hindu*, January 31, 2009, http://www.hindu.com/pp/2009/01/31/stories/2009013150010100.htm.

58. Tully, *Non-Stop India*, 120.

59. Anju Agnihotri Chaba, "Water Goes Down the Drain, Punjab May Go Dry in 20 Years," *Indian Express*, August 10, 2011, http://www.indianexpress.com/news/rain -water-goes-down-the-drain-punjab-may-go-dry-in-20-years/829524.

60. Ibid.

61. "A Brief History of Genetic Modification," Citizens Concerned About GM, http://www.gmeducation.org/faqs/p149248-20brief%20history%20of%20genetic%20 modification.html.

62. John P. Purcell and Frederick J. Perlak, "Global Impact of Insect-Resistant (Bt) Cotton," *AgBioForum* 7, no. 1–2 (2004), http://www.agbioforum.org/v7n12/v7n12a05 -purcell.htm.

63. "International Services for the Acquisition of Agri-Biotech Applications, ISAAA Brief 43-2011: Executive Summary Global Status of Commercialized Biotech/GM Crops: 2011," http://www.isaaa.org/resources/publications/briefs/43/executivesummary /default.asp.

64. "Kapas, 2007," Multi Commodity Exchange of India, http://www.mcxindia.com/SitePages/ContractSpecification.aspx?ProductCode=KAPAS.

65. M. Rajivlochan, "Farmers and Firefighters," *Indian Express*, August 28, 2007, http://www.indianexpress.com/news/farmers-and-firefighters————/213066/0.

66. "Report of the Expert Committee, (EC-II on Bt Brinjal Event EE-1)," Ministry of Environment and Forests, http://moef.nic.in/downloads/public- information/Report%20on%20Bt%20brinjal.pdf.

67. Open field trials for other food crops were permitted.

68. Rupashree Nanda, "Jairam Ramesh Defends Controversial BT Brinjal Decision," CNN-IBN, February 27, 2012, http://ibnlive.in.com/news/jairam-ramesh-defends-controversial-bt-brinjal-decision/233657-3.html.

69. For more on public interest litigation, see chapter 8, 273–74.

70. *Crop Protection Monthly*, no. 275, October 31, 2012, http://www.crop-protection-monthly.co.uk/Archives/CPMOct2012.pdf.

71. M. Sreelata, "Scientific Committee Advises Halt to Indian Bt Brinjal Trials," *Asian Scientist*, October 29, 2012, http://www.asianscientist.com/tech-pharma/scientific-committee-advises-halt-to-bt-brinjal-trials-2012/.

72. Mathieu von Rohr, "Vidarbha: 'They Build Cities and Neglect the Villages,'" August 13, 2007, http://vidarbha.wordpress.com/.

73. Dilip Hiro, *After Empire: The Birth of a Multipolar World* (New York: Nation Books, 2010), 191, 192.

74. Interviewed by the author, March 2011.

75. "Cause for Alarm," *Mainstream*, September 25, 2010, http://www.mainstreamweekly.net/spip.php?page=recherche&recherche=September+25+2010&debut_articles=10#pagination_articles.

5. Slums on the Rise

1. Interviewed by the author, March 2010.

2. "Delhi, Administrative Units," Geohive, http://www.geohive.com/cntry/in-07.aspx; and Neha Lalchandani, "Northeast District: Most Densely Populated," *Times of India*, April 1, 2011, http://articles.timesofindia.indiatimes.com/2011-04-01/delhi/29369878_1_yamuna-vihar-sq-km-population-density.

3. "Report on Construction Industry, 2006," Indo-Italian Chamber of Commerce and Industry, Mumbai, http://www.centroesteroveneto.com/pdf/Osservatorio%20Mercati/India/Ricerche%20di%20Mercato/2009/Construction%20Sector.pdf; and "Real Estate November 2011," India Brand Equity Foundation, http://www.ibef.org/download/Real_Estate50112.pdf.

4. "Cement Sector Analysis Report," *Cement*, November 7, 2012, http://www.equitymaster.com/research-it/sector-info/cement/Cement-Sector-Analysis-Report.asp; and "India Cement Production to Touch 320 Million Tonnes This Year," *Business Standard*, May 12, 2011, http://www.business-standard.com/article/companies

/india-cement-production-to-touch-320-mn-tonnes-this-year-111051200114_1
.html.

5. Randeep Ramesh, "India's Urban Poor Are Being Squeezed for Living Space," *The Guardian*, November 26, 2008, http://www.guardian.co.uk/world/2008/nov/26/india-national-survey-urbanisation-poverty.

6. Jason Burke, "Mukesh Ambani, India's Richest Man, Builds World's First Billion-Dollar Home," *The Guardian*, October 13, 2011, http://www.guardian.co.uk/world/2010/oct/13/mukesh-ambani-india-home-mumbai; and "Antilla—Mukesh Ambani and Nita's House at Altamount Road, Mumbai Photos," *Reporter 365*, November 29, 2012, http://reporter365.com/antilla-mukesh-ambani-and-nitas-house-at-altamount-road-mumbai-photos.html.

7. Ashish Ray, "It's Sad Mukesh Ambani Lives in Such Opulence: Ratan Tata," *Times of India*, May 22, 2011, http://articles.timesofindia.indiatimes.com/2011-05-22/india/29570930_1_corus-and-jlr-jlr-management-ratan-tata.

8. Arundhati Roy, "Capitalism: A Ghost Story," *Outlook* (Delhi), March 26, 2012, http://www.outlookindia.com/article/Capitalism-A-Ghost-Story/280234.

9. Katherine Boo, *Behind the Beautiful Forevers: Life, Death, and Hope in a Mumbai Slum* (New York: Random House, 2012), 140.

10. Bhavika Jain, "62% of Mumbai Lives in Slums: Census," *Hindustan Times*, October 17, 2010, http://www.hindustantimes.com/India-news/Mumbai/62-of-Mumbai-lives-in-slums-Census/Article1-614027.aspx.

11. Boo, *Behind the Beautiful Forevers*, 140.

12. "Slum Population in India," India Online Pages, http://www.indiaonlinepages.com/population/slum-population-in-india.html. In its report submitted in August 2010, an Indian-government committee came up with a revised estimate of 75.26 million, http://www.indiavision.com/news/article/national/98404/; and "India's Slum Population to Be Over 93 Million in 2011," IANS, September 3, 2010, http://www.daijiworld.com/news/news_disp.asp?n_id=84756&n_tit=India's+Slum+Population+to+Be+Over+93+Million+in+2011++.

13. "Report of the Committee on Slum Statistics/Census, 30 August 2010," http://mhupa.gov.in/W_new/Slum_Report_NBO.pdf.

14. "Urban Population Growth (Annual %) in India," Trading Economics, http://www.tradingeconomics.com/india/urban-population-growth-annual-percent-wb-data.html.

15. Mahendra Kumar Singh, "City of Dreams? Over 8m Slum Dwellers in Mumbai by 2011," *Times of India*, November 15, 2010, http://articles.timesofindia.indiatimes.com/2010-11-15/mumbai/28263181_1_slum-population-rajiv-awas-yojana-urban-poverty-alleviation-ministry.

16. "Capital Ranks Third in Per Capita Income," *Daily Pioneer*, November 21, 2012, http://dailypioneer.com/city/110108-capital-ranks-third-in-per-capita-income.html.

17. Somini Sengupta, "In Teeming India, Water Crisis Means Dry Pipes and Foul Sludge," *New York Times*, September 29, 2009, http://www.nytimes.com/2006/09/29/world/asia/29water.html.

18. Sunitha Rao R, "Every 3rd B'lorean Lives in Sub-human Slum," *Times of India*, March 17, 2011, http://articles.timesofindia.indiatimes.com/2011-03-17/bangalore/2913 7890_1_slum-population-slum-dwellers-urban-poverty.

19. "Ahmedabad Municipal Corporation to Upgrade 3,000 Shanties," DNA Agency, March 6, 2010, http://www.dnaindia.com/india/report-ahmedabad-municipal-corpo ration-to-upgrade-3000-shanties-1355874.

20. PTI, "ONGC Videsh Ltd Targeting 20 Mn Tonnes of Oil Output from Assets Abroad," *Economic Times*, August 18, 2011, http://articles.economictimes.indiatimes .com/2011-08-18/news/29900595_1_exploration-phase-greater-nile-oil-project-ovl.

21. "About Bihar," UNDP, http://www.undp.org/content/india/en/home/operations /about_undp/undp-in-bihar/about-bihar/.

22. Ujjwal Sur et al., "Identification and Mapping of Slum Environment Using Ikonos Satellite Data: A Case Study of Dehradun, India," Map India Conference 2004, http://www.gisdevelopment.net/application/environment/pp/pdf/mi04011.pdf.

23. Tripti Lahiri, "India Begins Releasing New Housing, Slum Data," *India Real Time* blog, *Wall Street Journal*, May 26, 2010, http://blogs.wsj.com/indiarealtime /2010/05/26/india-begins-releasing-new-housing-slum-data/.

24. Interviewed by the author, March 2011.

25. Interviewed by the author, March 2011.

26. Interviewed by the author, March 2011.

27. "Question No. 2," Department of Food & Public Distribution, http://dfpd.nic.in /?q=node/999.

28. Avantika Chilkoti, "Indian Slums and Their 'Enablers of Consumption,'" *Financial Times*, May 24, 2013, http://blogs.ft.com/beyond-brics/2013/05/24/indias-slum -dwellers-and-their-enablers-of-consumption/?Authorised=false#axzz2Y56R6HUk.

29. Jason Burke, "West Bengal Pledges Crackdown After Illegal Homemade Liquor Kills 140," *The Guardian*, December 15, 2011, http://www.guardian.co.uk/world /2011/dec/15/india-illegal-liquor-crackdown.

30. Interviewed by the author, November 2011.

31. Interviewed by the author, November 2011.

32. If a bet does not win, then the punter has the option of doubling it for the same number the next day and to keep doubling it until the payout, since one of the ten numbers is bound to come up.

33. Burke, "West Bengal Pledges Crackdown."

6. Sleaze Grows Exponentially

1. "A Rare Case of Arrest," *Hindu Business Line*, February 2, 2011, http://www .thehindubusinessline.com/industry-and-economy/government-and-policy/a-rare-case -of-arrest/article1150395.ece.

2. "Ex-Telecom Minister Sukh Ram Convicted in One More Case," *The Hindu*, November 19, 2011, http://www.thehindu.com/todays-paper/tp-national/extelecom-minister -sukh-ram-convicted-in-one-more-case/article2640956.ece; and Dhananjay Mahapatra,

"A Raja Made Rs 3,000 Cr in Bribes," *Times of India*, February 11, 2011, http://articles .timesofindia.indiatimes.com/2011-02-11/india/28545283_1_telecom-minister-raja -cut-off-date.

3. See chapter 2, 57.

4. See Dilip Hiro, *Inside India Today* (London: Routledge & Kegan Paul, 1976), 58–59.

5. Interviewed by the author in Kolkata, December 1970.

6. Shashi Bhushan, *Feroze Gandhi: A Political Biography* (New Delhi: Progressive People's Sector Publications, 1977), 162.

7. "Mundhra Scandal 1957," *Top Scams in India* blog, August 3, 2012, http:// topscamsindia.blogspot.co.uk/2012/08/the-mundhra-scandal-1957.html.

8. Arun Prosad Mukherjee, "Combating Corruption: The Indian Experience," *Dialogue*, October–December 2011, http://www.asthabharati.org/Dia_Oct%20011/a.p.%20 mukh.htm.

9. Kuldip Nayar, *India: The Critical Years* (Delhi: Vikas, 1971), 363.

10. The Companies Act officials went out of their way to inform large industrial houses that advertising was an admissible business expense.

11. Harinder Baweja, "Quattrocchi Had Free Access to Gandhis," *India Today*, January 5, 2011, http://indiatoday.intoday.in/story/%E2%AC%DCquattrocchi-had-free-access -to-gandhis%E2%AC%22/1/125661.html.

12. Brigadier Samir Bhattacharya, *Nothing But! Book 1* (London: Olympia Publishers, 2013), 93, http://olympiapublishers.com/authors/brigadier-samir-bhattacharya /nothing-but-book-1.html.

13. Columbia Journalism School, "1989: Scandal in India," citing *The Hindu* of April 8, 1988, http://centennial.journalism.columbia.edu/1989-scandal-in-india/.

14. Chitra Subramaniam-Duella, "The Bofors Story, 25 Years After," *The Hoot*, April 24, 2012, http://thehoot.org/web/home/story.php?storyid=5884&mod=1&pg=1 &sectionId=1.

15. Columbia Journalism School, "1989: Scandal in India."

16. Ibid.

17. The Watergate scandal refers to the illegal break-in of the Democratic Party office in one of the Watergate apartments in Washington, D.C., by the agents of Republican President Richard Nixon's close aides, with the chief executive's knowledge.

18. "Editorial: The Brothers Hinduja and the Bofors Scandal," *Frontline*, October 28–November 10, 2000, http://www.frontlineonnet.com/fl1722/17220200.htm.

19. "Bofors Scam," EkakiZunj, http://www.ekakizunj.com/Bofors_scam.

20. Aditya Chatterjee, "Harshad Mehta Is Dead," *Times of India*, December 31, 2001, http://timesofindia.indiatimes.com/india/Harshad-Mehta-is-dead/articleshow /788522579.cms.

21. Bharati V. Pathak, *The Indian Financial System: Markets, Institutions and Services* (Delhi: Penguin/Pearson Education, 2011), 106.

22. "The Securities Scam of 1992," CBI, http://cbi.nic.in/fromarchives/harshadmehta _nw/harshadmehta.php.

23. Pathak, *The Indian Financial System*, 107.

24. A comparatively new common law development, the Tort Act in India is supplemented by codifying statutes including those that deal with damages.

25. Edward A. Gargan, "India's Prime Minister Faces a No-Confidence Vote," *New York Times*, July 28, 1993, http://www.nytimes.com/1993/07/28/world/india-s-prime-minister-faces-a-no-confidence-vote.html.

26. Praveen Swami, "In Harshad Mehta's Wake," *Frontline*, January 15–February 1, 2002, http://www.frontline.in/static/html/fl1902/19020900.htm.

27. "A Rare Case of Arrest," *The Hindu*, http://www.thehindubusinessline.com/industry-and-economy/government-and-policy/a-rare-case-of-arrest/article1150395.ece.

28. Ranjit Bhushan, "Can Rao Survive the Urea Scam?," *Outlook*, June 26, 1996, http://www.outlookindia.com/article/Can-Rao-Survive-The-Urea-Scam/201597.

29. "D. Mallesham Goud vs State Through C.B.I. on 27 October, 1998," Delhi High Court, http://indiankanoon.org/doc/416586/.

30. At the NFL's board meeting on March 27, 1996, C.K. Ramakrishnan admitted that he had made no inquiries about the credentials of Karsan Limited and that he had relied exclusively on the verbal opinion of his marketing director, D.S. Kanwar.

31. Sudha Mahalingam, "On the Urea Deal Trail," *Frontline*, December 19, 1998–January 1, 1999, http://www.frontlineonnet.com/fl1526/15261040.htm.

32. A.G. Noorani, "The Law and Its Potency," *Frontline*, October 28–November 10, 2000, http://www.frontline.in/static/html/fl1722/17220990.htm.

33. Ranjit Bhushan et al., "Fitting the Pieces Together," *Outlook*, January 31, 1996, http://m.outlookindia.com/story.aspx?sid=4&aid=200690; and Sri Kanta Ghosh, *Indian Democracy Derailed: Politics and Politicians* (Delhi: APH Publishing, 1997), 332.

34. On the eve of his death, Harshad Mehta was convicted in only one of the many cases filed against him.

35. Sucheta Dalal, "Ketan Parekh: Delusions of Invincibility?," Rediff.com, March 31, 2001, http://www.rediff.com/money/2001/mar/31dalal.htm.

36. Lalatendu Mishra, "Who's Ketan Parekh and Why's He Bad for the Market?," *Mail Today*, July 15, 2012, http://indiatoday.intoday.in/story/ketan-parekh-stock-market-share-prices-sebi-k-10-stocks/1/208342.html.

37. "Ketan Parekh Scam," ICMR India, http://www.icmrindia.org/free%20resources/casestudies/ketan-parekh-scam3.htm.

38. Ibid. A later report by the Reserve Bank of India revealed that MMBC lent Rs 10 billion to stock markets, with more than Rs 8 billion going to Ketan Parekh and his firms.

39. Bharti Jain, "Jail Has Become Norm, Bail Exception!," *Economic Times*, November 4, 2011, http://articles.economictimes.indiatimes.com/2011-11-04/news/30359525_1_dmk-mp-kanimozhi-karim-morani-2g.

40. "Early History of Abdul Kareem Telgi," http://www.ksphc.org/stampit.info/Early%20history%20of%20telgi.htm.

41. The Bombay Stamp Act of 1958 listed sixty-two categories of documents to be legitimized through the use of a stamped paper. The fourteen different varieties of stamp papers were available in ten denominations.

42. Sayantan Chakravarty, "Stamp of Deceit," *India Today*, March 10, 2003, http://indiatoday.intoday.in/story/more-than-a-year-after-abdul-karim-telgi-arrest-rs-3300 -crore-worth-of-fake-stamps-seized/1/206881.html.

43. "Vilasrao on Telgi's Mind," *Times of India*, February 11, 2004, http://articles .timesofindia.indiatimes.com/2004-02-11/india/28324661_1_abdul-karim-telgi -stamp-scam-kingpin-stamp-papers.

44. "Mumbai Cop in Police Custody Till Feb 6 in Telgi Scam," *Deccan Herald*/UNI, February 3, 2004, http://archive.deccanherald.com/deccanherald/feb032004/update5 .asp.

45. "CBI Charges Mumbai Police Assistant Inspector," *Asian Age*, May 4, 2004, http://www.asianage.com/.

46. "Telgi Guilty Under Various IPC Sections," *The Hindu*, January 18, 2006, http://www.hindu.com/2006/01/18/stories/2006011817771700.htm.

47. When counterfeiting stamp papers, regulated at different stages, became increasingly risky, Telgi raised the output of fake revenue stamps.

48. Chakravarty, "Stamp of Deceit."

49. Ibid.

50. Sheela Raval with Sayantan Chakravarty, "The Swindler and His Rs 4,800 Crore Stamp Scam," *India Today*, November 24, 2003, http://archives.digitaltoday.in /indiatoday/20031124/crime.html.

51. "Telgi Unhappy with Mudrank," TNN, April 23, 2008, http://timesofindia .indiatimes.com/city/pune/Telgi-unhappy-with-Mudrank/articleshow/2973856.cms ?referral=PM.

52. "Stamp Paper Scam: Telgi Gets Life Term in 3 Cases; Jail for 3 Cops," *Indian Express*, March 1, 2012, http://www.indianexpress.com/news/stamp-paper-scam -telgi-gets-life-term-in-3-cases—jail-for-3-cops/918351/.

53. Chakravarty, "Stamp of Deceit."

54. The other three preeminent accounting and auditing firms were Deloitte, Ernst & Young, and KPMG.

55. "Satyam Stunner: Highs and Lows of Raju's Career," Reuters, January 7, 2009, http://ibnlive.in.com/news/satyam-stunner-highs-and-lows-of-rajus-career/82183-7 .html.

56. J.P. Sharma, "What Went Wrong With Satyam?" Institute of Directors, http://www.iodonline.com/Articles/Inst%20of%20Directors-WCFCG%20Global%20Cov ention-Paper%20Prof%20J%20P%20Sharma-What%20Went%20Wrong%20 With%20Satyam%20new.pdf.

57. Ibid.

58. Ibid.

59. Maytas is Satyam read backwards.

60. "Satyam Stunner."

61. "2G Spectrum Scam: Chronology of Events," *Economic Times*, May 20, 2011, http://articles.economictimes.indiatimes.com/2011-05-20/news/29564752_1_2g -spectrum-case-license-fee.

62. "CBI Scanning Transcripts of 5851 Calls," *The Telegraph* (Kolkata), November 23, 2010, http://www.telegraphindia.com/1101123/jsp/nation/story_13210307.jsp.

63. Ibid.

64. Jason Burke, "India's Rulers Lose £22bn in Massive Mobile Phone Scam," *The Guardian*, November 16, 2010, http://www.guardian.co.uk/world/2010/nov/16/india -corruption-government.

65. "2G Scam: Hot Tapes Expose Mediamen as Power Players," *India Today*, November 19, 2010, http://indiatoday.intoday.in/story/2g-scam-hot-tapes-expose-mediamen -as-power-players-/1/120436.html. For detailed conversation, visit www.openthemaga zine.com. After the first installment of 140 released tapes, *Outlook* magazine posted a further 800 tapes on its website.

66. Pankaj Mishra, "The Rotting of New India," *The Guardian*, December 1, 2010, http://www.guardian.co.uk/commentisfree/2010/dec/01/rotting-new-india-scandal.

67. Praful Bidwai, "A Who's Who of India Sleaze," *The Guardian*, December 26, 2010, http://www.guardian.co.uk/commentisfree/2010/dec/26/india-sleaze-corruption -economy.

68. Nira Radia managed to get her clients' favorite, Kamal Nath, appointed as minister of road transport and highways.

69. Clare Raybould, "The True Cost of the Commonwealth Games," MongaBay .com, September 30, 2010, http://news.mongabay.com/2010/0930-raybould_common wealth.html.

70. The term "red tape" originated in the eighty-plus petitions submitted by the English king Henry VIII (1509–47) to Pope Clement, each bound with the official red ribbon of the state, demanding the annulment of his marriage.

71. Nicola Smith, "Fake Safety Tests on Games Venues," *Sunday Times*, September 26, 2010, http://www.thesundaytimes.co.uk/sto/news/world_news/Asia/article 403922.ece.

72. Ravi Shankar and Mihir Srivastava, "Payoffs & Bribes Cast a Shadow on CWG," *India Today*, August 16, 2010, http://indiatoday.intoday.in/story/payoffs-&-bribes-cast -a-shadow-on-cwg/1/108072.html.

73. Besides Suresh Kalmadi, the CBI listed as accused two companies and eight people, including the Organizing Committee's former secretary general Lalit Bhanot and former director general V.K. Verma.

74. Minal Aswani was the daughter of an Indian businessman, Pessu Aswani, based in Lagos, who commuted between Nigeria and Britain. Her husband, Jack Sagrani, who also flitted between Lagos and London, went on to work for an Indian company in Saudi Arabia, where he served a jail sentence as a result of his involvement in a scam.

75. Michael Atherton, "Modi Masterminds India's Billion Dollar Bonanza," *Daily Telegraph*, April 9, 2006, http://www.telegraph.co.uk/sport/cricket/2335008/Modi-masterminds-Indias-billion-dollar-bonanza.html.

76. Cited in Samanth Subramanian, "The Confidence Man," *The Caravan*, January 2011, http://www.caravanmagazine.in/reportage/confidence-man.

77. "Lalit Modi Not in Hiding," *Dawn* (Karachi), November 4, 2010, http://archives.dawn.com/archives/24019.

78. Neeta Lal, "Indian Premier League: Not Quite Cricket," *Asia Sentinel*, April 20, 2010, http://www.asiasentinel.com/index.php?option=com_content&task=view&id=2419&Itemid=404.

79. Pradeep Thakur, "Black Money Is the Curse of India Shining," *Economic Times*, February 20, 2011, http://articles.economictimes.indiatimes.com/2011-02-20/news/28615247_1_hawala-trail-hawala-operators-hawala-dealers.

80. Rohit Mahajan and Arindam Mukherjee, "IPL Lalit Modi: Captain Crony Capital," *Outlook*, May 3, 2010, http://www.outlookindia.com/article.aspx?265185.

81. Vikas Bajaj, "Indian TV Network Sues Nielsen Over Ratings Data," *New York Times*, July 31, 2012, http://www.nytimes.com/2012/08/01/business/global/indian-tv-network-sues-nielsen-over-ratings.html.

82. Hemali Chhapia, "In Mumbai, Coaching Classes for Copying Too," *Times of India*, February 25, 2007, http://articles.timesofindia.indiatimes.com/2007-02-25/india/27883662_1_copying-coaching-classes-chits.

83. Gayatri Rangachari Shah, "Indians Hope to Raise Journalism Standards," *New York Times*, April 22, 2013, http://www.nytimes.com/2013/04/22/world/asia/22iht-educlede22.html.

84. S. Rukmini, "Pollsters Ready to Manipulate Surveys for a Price: TV Report," *The Hindu*, February 26, 2014, http://www.thehindu.com/news/national/pollsters-ready-to-manipulate-surveys-for-a-price-tv-report/article5726752.ece.

85. Aditya Menon, "The Whistle Blowing MP Who Shook the UPA Government by Exposing Coalgate Scam," *India Today*, September 2, 2012, http://indiatoday.intoday.in/story/the-whistleblowers-who-took-on-the-rich-and-powerful-so-that-they-do-not-get-away-with-corruption/1/215698.html.

86. Ibid.

87. S.N. Vijetha, "Probe Yeddyurappa's Role in Illegal Mining, Supreme Court Tells CBI," *The Hindu*, May 11, 2012, http://www.thehindu.com/news/national/article3407658.ece.

88. Saheel Makakr and Shasheer Yousaf, "CBI Files Chargesheet Against Yeddyurappa, JSW Steel," *Wall Street Journal*, October 16, 2012, http://www.livemint.com/Politics/re1ExbZsxZPntvGeeytknI/CBI-files-chargesheet-against-Yeddyurappa-JSW-Steel.html.

89. "Congress MP Naveen Jindal Blames Government for Coalgate," CNN-IBN, September 7, 2012, http://ibnlive.in.com/news/cong-mp-naveen-jindal-blames-govt-for-coalgate/289319-37-64.html.

90. Alam Srinivas, "Q&A: Five Things About India's Coal Scandal," BBC News, September 4, 2012, http://www.bbc.co.uk/news/world-asia-india-19463728.

91. Cited in ibid.

92. "Coalgate: SC Notice to Centre on Alleged Irregularities," September 14, 2012, http://www.webcitation.org/mainfram.php.

93. Vikas Bajaj and Jim Yardley, "Scandal Poses a Riddle," *New York Times*, September 15, 2012, http://www.nytimes.com/2012/09/16/world/asia/scandal-bares-corruption-hampering-indias-growth.html.

7. Maoists in the Mineral-Rich Heartland

1. Most of the wood from sal and teak trees was used for construction and accounted for nearly half of the forest sector's revenue.

2. Its full name is Counter Terrorism and Jungle Warfare College.

3. Dantewada is a derivative of Danteshwari.

4. The old Bastar princely state is now divided into five southern districts of Chhattisgarh: Bastar, Bijapur, Dantewada, Kanker, and Narayanpur.

5. Interviewed by the author, March 2011.

6. Dilip Hiro, *Inside India Today* (London: Routledge & Kegan Paul, 1976), 150.

7. Ibid., 159.

8. Cited in Gautam Navlakha, "Days and Nights in the Heartland of Rebellion," *Indian Vanguard*, April 2, 2010, http://indianvanguard.wordpress.com/2010/04/02/gautam-navlakha-days-and-nights-in-the-heartland-of-rebellion/. According to the police, 1,783 CPI (ML) supporters were killed in Greater Kolkata between March 1970 and August 1971. By 1973, more than 32,000 CPI (ML) leaders, activists, and supporters were imprisoned. Pamphlet, *Low Intensity Conflict*, CPI (Maoist) for internal circulation, publication date unknown.

9. Charu Mazumdar, an asthmatic, was probably denied medical treatment, which led to a heart attack.

10. The "Southern Land" referred to India, while the "Northern Land" was China.

11. "Left-Wing Extremist Groups: CPI India-Maoist (CPI-Maoist)," South Asia Terrorism Portal, http://www.satp.org/satporgtp/countries/india/terroristoutfits/CPI_M.htm.

12. Ibid.

13. The Gondi tribe was 7 million strong in 2010.

14. The evergreen ebony tree is the source of tendu (*Diospyros Melanoxylon*) leaves.

15. In 2010, it claimed more than one hundred thousand members. Suvojit Bagchi, interviewed by the author, February 2011.

16. Navlakha, "Days and Nights in the Heartland of Rebellion."

17. Sumanta Banerjee, ed., *Book of Naxalite Poetry* (Kolkata: Thema, 2009), 64, 31.

18. Prakash Singh, *The Naxalite Movement in India* (New Delhi: Rupa & Company, 1999), 122.

19. Sailendra Nath Ghosh, "Give the Adivasis a New Deal and Change the Development Paradigm," *Mainstream*, July 10, 2010, http://www.mainstreamweekly.net /article2195.html.

20. "List of Amending Acts," in *Mines and Minerals (Development and Regulation) Act, 1957*, Government of India Ministry of Mines, amended up to May 10, 2012, http://mines.nic.in/writereaddata/Filelinks/e342d686_MMDR%20Act%201957 .pdf.

21. The term "Scheduled Castes" is used because these castes are listed in a schedule of India's constitution of 1950.

22. Rema Nagarajan, "SC/STs Take Rapid Strides, Close Literacy Gap," *Times of India*, November 10, 2013, http://timesofindia.indiatimes.com/india/SC/STs-take -rapid-strides-close-literacy-gap/articleshow/25536193.cms.

23. The Dandakaranya Special Zonal Committee has eight divisions under it, which include Bastar in Chhattisgarh and Gadchiroli in Maharashtra. Abujhmad covers Narayanpur district and part of the old Bastar princely state.

24. Sudha Bharadwaj, "Gravest Displacement, Bravest Resistance: The Struggle of Adivasis of Bastar, Chhattisgarh Against Imperialist Corporate Land Grab," *Sanhati*, July 26, 2009, http://lalgarh.wordpress.com/2009/07/26/gravest-displacement-bravest -resistance-the-struggle-of-adivasis-of-bastar-chhattisgarh-against-imperialist-corpo rate-landgrab/.

25. The 1894 Act allows the government to forcibly acquire land from private landholders for projects of public purpose. "Land Acquisition Act, 1894," *Times of India*, March 12, 2012, http://articles.timesofindia.indiatimes.com/2011-03-12/lucknow/2868 3518_1_public-purpose-land-acquisition-act-bill-redefines-public-purpose.

26. To protect the environment, the Central Ministry of Environment and Forests had to clear a project before mining could be undertaken.

27. Interviewed by the author, February 2011.

28. "Naxalites Attack Koraput Town, Loot Police Stations," *Times of India*, February 7, 2004, http://articles.timesofindia.indiatimes.com/2004-02-07/kolkata/28340664 _1_koraput-district-police-station-crpf-jawans.

29. A few weeks later, a mass rally of some 150,000 people in Hyderabad welcomed the founding of the party.

30. "Maoist Documents: Party Programme," South Asia Terrorism Portal, http:// www.satp.org/satporgtp/countries/india/maoist/documents/papers/partyprogram .htm.

31. In Andhra Pradesh, Maoist cadres used their cell phones to order groceries, which were delivered by tractor or jeep, exposing them to informers and infiltration.

32. In 2009, Counter Terrorism and Jungle Warfare College in Kanker acquired a 1,300-meter airstrip.

33. In April 2008, the Supreme Court disapproved arming of private persons by the state government to tackle the Naxalite problem. "If private persons, so armed by the State government, kill other persons, then the State is also liable to be prosecuted for abetting murder," said a bench of Supreme Court judges. Dhananjay Mahapatra, "SC Takes Dim View of Arming Civilians to Fight Naxalites," *Times of India*, April 1, 2008, http://articles.timesofindia.indiatimes.com/2008-04-01/india/27771679_1_naxal-menace-salva-judum-arming.

34. Interviewed by the author, March 2011.

35. In 2005, the Indian government put the total number of PLGA guerrillas at 6,500.

36. Venkitesh Ramakrishnan, "Daring and Dangerous," *Frontline*, December 3–16, 2005, http://www.frontline.in/navigation/?type=static&page=flonnet&rdurl=fl2225/stories/20051216004103300.htm; and "Historic Jehanabad Jail Break," *People's March*, December 11, 2005, http://www.bannedthought.net/India/PeoplesMarch/PM 1999-2006/archives/2005/nov-dec2k5/edit.htm.

37. A booby trap is a device that triggers an explosive either by pulling a wire or releasing the tension on it, or applying pressure on an object by standing on it, or by releasing pressure by lifting or shifting something.

38. "Eight CISF Jawans Killed in Naxal Attack," *Times of India*, February 10, 2006, http://articles.timesofindia.indiatimes.com/2006-02-10/india/27822926_1_cisf-jawans-naxal-attack-explosive-depot.

39. In 2010, Rajendra Sail received the Hunter P. Mabrey Award for Social Justice for combining his Christian faith with social action.

40. Interviewed by the author, March 2010.

41. Sudha Bhardwaj, "Gravest Displacement, Bravest Resistance," *Sanhati*, June 1, 2009, citing Sanjay Ojha in *Times Network News*, September 13, 2008, http://sanhati.com/excerpted/1545/.

42. Karan Thapar, "What Is the Truth?," *Hindustan Times*, March 2, 2008, http://www.hindustantimes.com/editorial-views-on/KaranThapar/What-is-the-truth/Article1-279288.aspx.

43. Prem Shankar Jha, "The State as Landlord," *Outlook*, March 17, 2008, http://www.outlookindia.com/article/The-State-As-Landlord/236962.

44. It was not accidental that in 2006 the Maoist-led strikes and shutdowns cost the steel industry in Jharkhand sixty lost days, or nearly one-fifth of the working year.

45. Jha, "The State as Landlord."

46. See chapter 5, 141.

47. Interviewed by the author, March 2011.

48. No mention was made of the fact that the officers of its elite Greyhound police force were trained in Israel.

49. The constituents of the Central Armed Police Forces were the Central Reserve Police Force (CRPF), the Border Security Force (BSF), Border Security Organization (Hindi acronym: SSB), Indo-Tibetan Border Force (ITBF), and the Central Industrial Security Force (CISF). The CAPFs were 777,788 strong in May 2011.

50. "Status Paper on the Naxal Problem," tabled before Parliament on March 13, 2006, http://www.satp.org/satporgtp/countries/india/document/papers/06mar13_naxal%20 problem%20.htm.

51. "Naxal Management Division, Ministry of Home Affairs," Government of India website, October 16, 2006, http://mha.nic.in/uniquepage.asp?Id_Pk=540. The Review Group, the Coordination Center, and the Task Force, consisting of senior civil and police forces under the Standing Committee of the Chief Ministers of the Affected States, chaired by the central Home Minister, were focused primarily on bolstering the security forces and increasing center-state coordination.

52. Nandini Sarkar, "Insurgency, Counter-insurgency, and Democracy in Central India," http://burawoy.berkeley.edu/Public%20Sociology,%20Live/Sundar/Insurgency, %20Counter-insurgency%20&%20Democracy.pdf.

53. Policemen per 100,000 people: India (nationally), 122; Bihar, 57; Chhattisgarh, 133; Jharkhand, 98; Kashmir, 505; Orissa, 99; Punjab, 276; and Tripura, 591.

54. Nihad Nayak, "Naxalite Mayhem in Nayagarh," *IDSA* (Delhi), February 28, 2008, http://www.idsa.in/idsastrategiccomments/NaxaliteMayheminNayagarh_NNayak _280208.

55. Navlakha, "Days and Nights in the Heartland of Rebellion."

56. Ibid.

57. "Maoists Want to Overthrow Indian State by 2050: Pillai," *India Today*, March 5, 2010, http://indiatoday.intoday.in/story/Maoists+want+to+overthrow+Indian+state+by +2050:+Pillai/1/86882.htm.

58. Shelley Saha-Sinha, "India's New Mineral Policy Will Usher in Gloom for Adivasis," InfoChange News & Features, January 2009, http://infochangeindia .org/environment/analysis/indias-new-mineral-policy-will-usher-in-gloom-for-adivasis .html; and Keith Campbell, "Indian Mining Policy Overhaul Seeks to Stimulate Sector," *Mining Weekly* (Johannesburg), November 14, 2008, http://www.mining weekly.com/article/indian-mining-policy-overhaul-seeks-to-stimulate-sector-2008 -11-14.

59. Sudha Bhardwaj, "Gravest Displacement, Bravest Resistance," *Sanhati*, June 1, 2009, citing Chandra Bhushan, "Rich Lands of Poor People," http://sanhati.com /excerpted/1545/.

60. Diptendra Raychaudhuri, "The Danger of Fighting Maoists Without Knowing Who They Are," *Mainstream*, July 10, 2010, http://www.mainstreamweekly.net/article 2192.html.

61. "Development Challenges in Extremist Affected Areas," Report of an Expert Group to Planning Commission, April 2008, http://planningcommission.nic.in /reports/publications/rep_dce.pdf.

62. His successor was Shushil Kumar Shinde.

63. "India Is 'Losing Maoist Battle,'" BBC News, September 15, 2009, http://news .bbc.co.uk/1/hi/world/south_asia/8256692.stm.

64. Cited in Mark Tully, *Non-Stop India* (New Delhi: Allen Lane, 2011), 23–24.

65. Ibid., 24. Where actionable intelligence was available at the state level, as in Andhra Pradesh, the government had succeeded in curbing the Maoist movement.

66. Jim Yardley, "Maoist Rebels Widen Deadly Reach Across India," *New York Times*, November 1, 2009, http://www.nytimes.com/2009/11/01/world/asia/01maoist.html.

67. Cited in Tully, *Non-Stop India*, 13, 23–24. The offensives were part of an all-out drive against Naxalites.

68. The more appropriate name would have been Operation Red Hunt.

69. Jitendar of the People's Union for Civil Liberties, interviewed by the author in Raipur, February 2011.

70. Navlakha, "Days and Nights in the Heartland of Rebellion."

71. Some experts put the area under Maoist control at 23,180 square miles, divided into eight divisions and inhabited by 4.5 to 5 million people.

72. The Standing Committee did not include the heads of the public relations and justice departments.

73. Suvojit Bagchi, interviewed by the author, February 2011. Bagchi, a BBC correspondent in Delhi, spent five weeks in the Maoist-administered Dandakaranya zone in November–December 2010.

74. Suvojit Bagchi of the BBC, interviewed by the author, February 2011.

75. Navlakha, "Days and Nights in the Heartland of Rebellion.",

76. According to the Home Ministry, the Maoists party had the "hard core strength" of 8,600 in 2012. They were backed by 38,000 members of the People's Militia, armed with rudimentary weapons. Cited in Fakir Mohan Pradhan, "India—Maoists: Tactical Retreat," Offnews.info: *Intelligence y Segoridad*, March 13, 2013, http://www.offnews.info/verArticulo.php?contenidoID=44397.

77. Altogether, twenty-five Maoist publications were printed and distributed in the Dandakaranya forest region.

78. Suvojit Bagchi of the BBC, interviewed by the author, February 2011.

79. Mangal Pandey, regarded as a freedom fighter, was a private in East India Company's army before the outbreak of the Great Uprising of 1857. *Rang de Basanti* dramatizes corruption in the Indian military when a friend of a group of actors in a film about an Indian revolutionary gets killed in a fighter aircraft crash—an event that transforms these happy-go-lucky men into passionate partisans to avenge the tragedy.

80. These contractors cover the tax by over-invoicing the mining company.

81. *Prabhat Khabar* (Hindi: Dawn News), November 15, 2010.

82. Tully, *Non-Stop India*, 23.

83. Jason Miklian and Scott Carney, "Fire in the Hole," *Foreign Policy*, September–October 2010, http://www.foreignpolicy.com/articles/2010/08/16/fire_in_the_hole.

84. Supriya Sharma, "Industry Meets Insurgency," *Times of India*, October 9, 2011, http://timesofindia.indiatimes.com/home/stoi/special-report/Industry-meets-insurgency/articleshow/10284742.cms.

85. Yardley, "Maoist Rebels Widen Deadly Reach Across India."

86. Interviewed by the author, March 2011.

87. Ajit Kumar Singh and Sachin Bansidhar Diwan, "Maoists Extort Up to Rs 2,000 Crore Across India," Rediff News, April 28, 2010, http://news.rediff.com/slide-show /2010/apr/28/slide-show-1-drugs-extortion-violence-fund-maoists-movement.htm.

88. "Extortnomics: Maoists Raise Rs 2,000 Crore Every Year," *Times of India*, February 15, 2011, http://articles.timesofindia.indiatimes.com/2011-02-15/india/2854 1752_1_vishwa-ranjan-maoists-extortion.

89. Navlakha, "Days and Nights in the Heartland of Rebellion."

90. Ka Frank, "Chidambaram's Response: 'Maoists Must Abjure Violence for Talks,'" *Revolution in South Asia*, February 25, 2010, https://southasiarev.wordpress.com/2010 /02/25/chidambarams-response-maoists-must-abjure-violence-for-talks/.

91. Suvojit Bagchi, "Where the Maoist War Is Far from Won," BBC News, November 22, 2011, http://www.bbc.co.uk/news/world-asia-15716211.

92. Shoma Chaudhury and P. Chidambaram, "Halt the Violence! Give Me 72 Hours," *Tehelka*, November 21, 2009, http://archive.tehelka.com/story_main43.asp ?filename=Ne211109coverstory.asp.

93. Saha-Sinha, "India's New Mineral Policy Will Usher in Gloom for Adivasis."

94. The concept of corporate social responsibility was first mentioned by Lakshmi Mittal after his company acquired Arcelor in late 2006. He established the Arcelor Mittal Foundation to invest in social improvement programs focusing on the communities where it operated.

95. Interviewed by the author, February 2011.

96. Deepak Ranjan Patra, "A Tale of Prosperity . . . in the Vicinity of Terror," *Business & Economy*, 2008, http://www.businessandeconomy.org/21012010/storyd.asp?sid =4945&pageno=1.

97. Chaudhury and Chidambaram, "Halt the Violence! Give Me 72 Hours."

98. Purnima S. Tripathi, "Battle of Bastar," *Frontline*, April 21–May 4, 2012, http:// www.frontline.in/navigation/?type=static&page=flonnet&rdurl=fl2908/stories /20120504290803200.htm.

99. "West Bengal and Jharkhand, a Worry for Operation Green Hunt," Zee News/ PTI, February 22, 2010, http://zeenews.india.com/news/states/west-bengal-and -jharkhand-a-worry-for-operation-green-hunt_606214.html.

100. Gladson Dungdung, "Cleansing the Maoists?," Sanhati, April 5, 2010, http:// sanhati.com/articles/2256/.

101. Sibananda Das, "Tribals in Orissa Protest Against the Green Hunt," Orissa Diary TV, April 2, 2010, http://www.orissadiary.com/CurrentNews.asp?id=17638.

102. "Determined to Uproot Naxalism: Chidambaram," NDTV, April 5, 2010, http://www.ndtv.com/article/india/determined-to-uproot-naxalism-chidambaram -19240.

103. "Maoists Want to Overthrow Indian State by 2050."

104. This Maoist tactic was reminiscent of the Vietminh guerrillas in South Vietnam during the Vietnam War (1965–73) who planted grassy plots with spikes called

punji sticks, then ambushed the patrolling American soldiers, who took cover by throwing themselves on the grassy ground only to be injured or killed by the lethal sticks.

105. Yardley, "Maoist Rebels Widen Deadly Reach Across India."

106. "Azad's Assassination," *Sanhati*, July 25, 2010, http://sanhati.com/articles/2610/.

107. "Will Be Happy if Someone Can Do My Job Better: PC," *Zee News*, July 22, 2010, http://zeenews.india.com/news/nation/will-be-happy-if-someone-can-do-my-job -better-pc_642744.html.

108. Ajai Sahni, "Each State Is Doing Its Own Thing in War Against Naxals," *First Post*, June 20, 2011, http://www.firstpost.com/politics/each-state-is-doing-its-own-thing -in-war-against-naxals-31911.html.

109. Navlakha, "Days and Nights in the Heartland of Rebellion."

110. "Chhattisgarh Assessment 2012," South Asia Terrorism Portal, http://www.satp .org/satporgtp/countries/india/maoist/Assessment/2012/chhattisgarh.htm.

111. Bagchi, "Where the Maoist War Is Far from Won."

112. Ibid.

113. Ibid.

114. "Chhattisgarh Assessment 2012," South Asia Terrorism Portal.

115. Ibid.

116. Joseph John and Rashmi Drolia, "Maoists Kill Salwa Judum Founder Mahendra Karma Among Other Congress Leaders," *Times of India*, May 26, 2013, http:// articles.timesofindia.indiatimes.com/2013-05-26/india/39537550_1_congress -president-sonia-gandhi-mahendra-karma-bastar. A statement by the CPI (Maoist) said that Mahendra Karma and Nand Kumar Patel were its prime targets, and that it regretted the deaths of low-ranking Congressmen and other innocents.

117. Interviewed by the author in London, June 2013.

118. "Odisha Assessment 2012," South Asia Terrorism Portal, http://www.satp.org /satporgtp/countries/india/maoist/Assessment/2012/Orissa.html.

119. "MAC: Mines and Communities," *The National* (Dubai), October 25, 2011, http://www.minesandcommunities.org/article.php?a=11253.

120. Sayantan Bera, "Between Maoists and Mines," *Down to Earth*, April 30, 2012, http://www.downtoearth.org.in/content/between-maoists-and-mines.

121. Pradhan, "India—Maoists: Tactical Retreat."

122. Sharma, "Industry Meets Insurgency." The 150 villages and hamlets in the Bailadila area lacked electricity.

123. Bera, "Between Maoists and Mines."

124. Sudeep Chakravarti, "The Saranda Business Plan," *Live Mint*, March 14, 2013, http://www.livemint.com/Opinion/Z9J6UFpWST58bHjz8mLHFI/The-Saranda -Business-Plan.html?facet=print.

125. "7 Jawans, 2 Maoists Killed in Jharkhand Encounter," *Times of India*, January 8, 2013, http://articles.timesofindia.indiatimes.com/2013-01-08/india/36215723_1_jhark hand-jaguar-latehar-saranda-forests.

126. Pradhan, "India—Maoists: Tactical Retreat."

127. "Odisha Assessment 2012," South Asia Terrorism Portal.

128. "Maoists Blow Up Two Mobile Towers Ahead of Modi's Rally in Gaya District," *Daily Bhaskar*, March 27, 2014, http://daily.bhaskar.com/news/NAT-TOP -maoists-blow-up-two-mobile-towers-ahead-of-modi-rallies-scheduled-in-naxal-infes -4561886-NOR.html.

129. M.P. Prashanth, "Maoists See Tougher Days Ahead with BJP in Power," TNN, June 2, 2014, http://timesofindia.indiatimes.com/city/kozhikode/Maoists-see-tougher -days-ahead-with-BJP-in-power/articleshow/36411838.cms.

130. "11 Environmental Disasters Narendra Modi Blessed in His First 100 Days," *Quartz*, http://qz.com/255772/the-11-environmental-disasters-narendra-modi-blessed -in-his-first-100-days/.

131. Siddharth Varadarajan, "Modi's 100 Days: Biding His Time, Circling the Wagons," *Al Jazeera*, September 2, 2014, http://svaradarajan.com/2014/09/03 /modis-100-days-biding-his-time-circling-the-wagons/; "Corruption in NREGA Cannot Be Ignored: Sonia Gandhi," *Indian Express*, February 2, 2012, http://www .indianexpress.com/news/corruption-in-nrega-cannot-be-ignored-sonia-gandhi /907023/.

132. Vishwas Kumar, "Mission Possible," *India Legal*, September 2014, http://india legalonline.com/mission-possible/.

133. See chapter 7, 238.

134. Prashanth, "Maoists See Tougher Days Ahead with BJP in Power."

8. Innovations and Distortions of Indian Democracy

1. As early as 1966, the Administrative Reforms Commission recommended the establishment of the Lokpal institution.

2. Krishna Pokharel, "Who Is Anna Hazare?," *India Real Time* blog, *Wall Street Journal*, August 18, 2011, http://blogs.wsj.com/indiarealtime/2011/08/18/who-is-anna -hazare/.

3. "Anna Hazare," *Knowledge Point*, http://sumitkumarblogger.blogspot.co.uk/p /anna-hazare.html.

4. Rama Lakshmi, "India Agrees to Protesters' Demand on Graft Panel," *Washington Post*, April 9, 2011, http://www.washingtonpost.com/world/india_agrees_to _protesters_demand_on_graft_panel/2011/04/09/AFFyy05C_story.html.

5. "Jantar Mantar Turns into Carnival Site as Hazare Breaks Fast," *India Today*, April 9, 2011, http://www.ndtv.com/article/india/jantar-mantar-turns-into-carnival-site -as-hazare-breaks-fast-97398.

6. However, the UN Convention Against Corruption was not ratified by the Indian parliament.

7. A state government could refer certain serious cases to the CBI, whose normal jurisdiction extended to seven Union Territories, including Delhi.

8. Radhika Ramaseshan, "Hazare Runs into Civil Society Protest," *The Telegraph* (Kolkata), August 21, 2011, http://www.telegraphindia.com/1110821/jsp/nation/story _14404408.jsp.

9. Fasting for twelve days left Anna Hazare severely dehydrated, with a weight loss of seventeen pounds.

10. J. Venkatesan, "Setback to Modi as Supreme Court Upholds Lokayukta Appointment," *The Hindu*, January 2, 2013, http://www.thehindu.com/news/national/lokayukta -sc-rejects-gujarat-govt-plea/article4264450.ece.

11. The Modi government appealed to the Supreme Court but lost its case in January 2013. Pursuance of these cases in courts cost the taxpayers Rs 450 million ($900,000). "Lokayukta on Modi Govt: Can't Work with 'My Way or Highway' Mindset," Rediff .com, August 7, 2013, http://www.rediff.com/news/report/lokayukta-on-modi-govt-cant -work-with-my-way-or-highway-mindset/20130807.htm.

12. "Team Anna Questions Logic of RS Committee Looking into Lokpal," *Deccan Herald*, July 16, 2012, http://www.deccanherald.com/content/264789/team-anna -questions-logic-rs.html.

13. M.R. Biju, ed., *Development Issues in Contemporary India* (New Delhi: Concept Publishing Company, 2011), 272.

14. Yair Hussain, *Corruption Free India: Fight to Finish* (New Delhi: Epitome Books, 2011), 185.

15. Siddharth Pandey, "RTI Applications Now Expensive and Difficult, Will the Move Kill the Act," NDTV, April 29, 2012, http://www.ndtv.com/india-news/rti -applications-now-expensive-and-difficult-will-the-move-kill-the-act-479278.

16. Swati Mathur, "The Information Soldier," *Times of India*, January 8, 2011, http:// epaper.timesofindia.com/Repository/ml.asp?Ref=VENSTS8yMDExLzAxL zA4I0FyMDI3MDA=&Mode=HTML&Locale=english-skin-custom.

17. By January 2011, the 2G Spectrum scam details had become public knowledge.

18. Mathur, "Information Soldier."

19. Jason Burke, "Dying for Data: The Indian Activist Killed for Asking Too Many Questions," *The Guardian*, December 27, 2010, http://www.guardian.co.uk/world/2010 /dec/27/india-rti-activists-deaths.

20. Venkitesh Ramakrishnan, "Murder and Worse," *Frontline*, July 5–18, 2008, http://www.frontline.in/static/html/fl2514/stories/20080718251412700.htm.

21. Born in 1959 in Belgium, Jean Drèze graduated from Essex University in Britain and obtained his doctorate from the Indian Statistical Institute, Delhi. He settled in the capital, married an Indian researcher named Bela Bhatia, and lived in a one-room hut in a slum. He dressed like an Indian and rode a cycle, and lectured at the Delhi School of Economics. He became an Indian citizen in 2002.

22. Ramakrishnan, "Murder and Worse."

23. Ibid.

24. Manoj Prasad, "Lalit Mehta's Murderer Killed by Naxals: Police," *Indian Express*, January 6, 2009, http://www.indianexpress.com/news/lalit-mehtas-murderer-killed-by-naxals-pol/407000/,

25. Ramakrishnan, "Murder and Worse."

26. "Highest Marginal Tax Rate; Corporate Rate (%) in India," Trading Economics, http://www.tradingeconomics.com/india/highest-marginal-tax-rate-corporate-rate-percent-wb-data.html.

27. "Insight: How Sonia Gandhi Was Persuaded to Back India Reforms," Reuters, September 26, 2012, http://www.reuters.com/article/2012/09/26/us-india-gandhi-idUSBRE88P1NN20120926.

28. Tom Wright and Harsh Gupta, "India's Boom Bypasses Rural Poor," *Wall Street Journal*, April 29, 2011, http://online.wsj.com/article/SB10001424052748704081604576143671902043578.html.

29. Lydia Polgreen, "How the Poor Fight Corruption in Andhra Pradesh," *New York Times*, December 3, 2010, http://www.ndtv.com/article/india/how-the-poor-fight-corruption-in-andhra-pradesh-70273.

30. Ibid.

31. Ibid.

32. "Corruption in NREGA Cannot be Ignored: Sonia Gandhi," *Indian Express*, February 2, 2012, http://www.indianexpress.com/news/corruption-in-nrega-cannot-be-ignored-sonia-gandhi/907023/.

33. PTI, "Sonia Gandhi Appointed National Advisory Council Chairperson," *DNA*, March 29, 2010, http://www.dnaindia.com/india/1364896/report-sonia-gandhi-appointed-national-advisory-council-chairperson.

34. Special Correspondent, "Land Acquisition Must Respect Environment, Farmers' Rights: Sonia," *The Hindu*, September 2010, http://www.thehindu.com/todays-paper/land-acquisition-must-respect-environment-farmers-rights-sonia/article624392.ece.

35. "Cause for Alarm," editorial, *Mainstream*, September 25, 2010, http://www.mainstreamweekly.net/spip.php?page=recherche&recherche=September+25+2010&debut_articles=10#pagination_articles.

36. This dichotomy provided outsider analysts with evidence of the unique flexibility of the democratic process in India.

37. "Supreme Court Orders on the Right to Food: A Tool for Action," Right to Food Campaign, October 2005, http://www.righttofoodindia.org/data/scordersprimer.doc.

38. Heather Timmons, Hari Kumar, and Pamposh Rainba, "India Opens Door to Foreign Investment," *India Ink* blog, *New York Times*, September 14, 2012, http://india.blogs.nytimes.com/2012/09/14/india-opens-door-to-foreign-investment/.

39. Udit Misra, "The Good and Bad of the Food Security Bill," *Forbes India*, April 27, 2013, http://forbesindia.com/article/special/the-good-and-bad-of-the-food-security-bill/35135/1.

40. Ibid.

41. "Cabinet Clears Ordinance to Implement Food Security Bill," PTI, July 3, 2013, http://www.dnaindia.com/india/1856669/report-cabinet-clears-ordinance-to-imple ment-food-security-bill.

42. "Sonia Asks Union Ministers, CMs to Give Up Discretionary Powers," *The Hindu*, January 8, 2011, http://www.thehindu.com/news/national/sonia-asks-union -ministers-cms-to-give-up-discretionary-powers/article1072890.ece.

43. Amitav Ranjan, "Ministries Told to Frame, Reveal Discretionary Power Norms," *Indian Express*, April 18, 2012, http://www.indianexpress.com/news/ministries-told-to -frame-reveal-discretionary-power-norms/938481/.

44. Josy Joseph, "Antony Gives Up Discretionary Power on Defense Deals," *Times of India*, October 2, 2012, http://articles.timesofindia.indiatimes.com/2012-10-02/india /34217357_1_discretionary-powers-defense-minister-defense-secretary.

45. But it was the central government that owned fossil fuel resources. See also chapter 1, 30.

46. Jason Burke, "Indian Government Tried to Buy Votes, Says WikiLeaks Cable," *The Guardian*, March 17, 2011, http://www.guardian.co.uk/world/2011/mar/17/india-usa.

47. Sarah Hiddleston, "Cash for Votes a Way of Political Life in South India," *The Hindu*, March 16, 2011, http://www.thehindu.com/news/the-india-cables/article1541 302.ece.

48. See chapter 6, 149.

49. Hiddleston, "Cash for Votes a Way of Political Life in South India."

50. See chapter 6, 151.

51. "The Poor Rich Indian MPs," *Economic Times*, August 21, 2010, http://articles .economictimes.indiatimes.com/2010-08-21/news/27594515_1_crorepati-mps-bjp-mp -indian-mps; and Margherita Stancati, "Why Indians Are Getting Poorer," *India Real Time* blog, *Wall Street Journal*, October 12, 2012, http://blogs.wsj.com/indiarealtime /2012/10/12/why-indians-are-getting-poorer/.

52. Ruchika Singh, "Black Money and Elections: Who Will Bell the Cat?," *The Hindu*, April 30, 2014, http://www.thehinducentre.com/verdict/commentary/article 5959650.ece.

53. "MPLADS Funds Hiked to Rs 5 Crore," Express News Service, July 8, 2011, http://archive.indianexpress.com/news/mplads-funds-hiked-to-rs-5-cr/814422/. Funding this scheme would cost the central government Rs 3,950 crore a year.

54. Interviewed by the author, November 2011. The panchayat official in Tinwari, Rajasthan, (incorrectly) told me the figure was Rs 50,000 ($1,000).

55. Hanuman Ram Jangid, interviewed by the author in Kuri Bhagtasni, November 2011.

56. Ibid.

57. Soutik Biswas, "Why India Is in Dire Need of Electoral Reform," BBC News, June 28, 2011, http://www.bbc.co.uk/news/world-south-asia-13692575.

58. Sunanda K. Datta-Ray, "Assets—Real or Otherwise: It's Discrepancy That Matters," *The Tribune*, April 16, 2014, http://www.tribuneindia.com/2004/20040426/edit .htm#5.

59. "Munde Admits Spending Rs 8 Crore in 2009 Polls," *The Hindu*, June 28, 2013, http://www.thehindu.com/news/national/other-states/munde-admits-spending-rs-8-crore-in-2009-polls/article4857676.ece/

60. Paranjoy Guha, "Now Candidates Can Spend Up to 60% More on Polls," Rediff News, February 24, 2011, http://www.rediff.com/news/column/now-candidates-can-spend-upto-60pc-more-on-polls/20110224.htm.

61. "EC Differs with Govt on Funding of Political Parties," *Times of India*, March 31, 2013, http://articles.timesofindia.indiatimes.com/2013-03-31/india/38162854_1_law-ministry-law-commission-political-parties.

62. IANS, "Every Third Newly-Elected MP Has Criminal Background," *Times of India*, May 18, 2014, http://timesofindia.indiatimes.com/news/Every-third-newly-elected-MP-has-criminal-background/articleshow/35306963.cms.

63. "The Representation of the People Act, 1951," India Ministry of Law and Justice, http://lawmin.nic.in/legislative/election/volume%201/representation%20of%20the%20people%20act,%201951.pdf.

64. "Disclosure of Income Tax Returns of Political Parties," Central Information Commission, New Delhi, April 29, 2008, http://web.archive.org/web/20130120161454/http://adrindia.org/sites/default/files/CIC-Political%20Parties%20Income%20Tax%20Returns.pdf.

65. Central Information Commission, New Delhi, April 28, 2008, http://web.archive.org/web/20130120161454/http://adrindia.org/sites/default/files/CIC-Political%20Parties%20Income%20Tax%20Returns.pdf.

66. Ibid.

67. "Black Money Funds Political Parties: Rahul Bajaj," *Economic Times*, February 4, 2011, http://articles.economictimes.indiatimes.com/2011-02-04/news/28432802_1_black-money-bajaj-family-rahul-bajaj. Rahul Bajaj was elected to the Rajya Sabha from Maharashtra with the backing of the BJP.

68. "Corporates Made 87% of the Total Donations from Known Sources to National Parties Between FY 04-05 and 11–12," Association for Democratic Reforms, Report Year 2014, http://adrindia.org/research-and-report/political-party-watch/combined-reports/2014/corporates-made-87-total-donations-k.

69. See "Political Parties Act (Parteiengesetz, ParteienG)," published July 24, 1967, amended January 31, 1994, http://www.iuscomp.org/gla/statutes/ParteienG.htm.

70. PTI, "Government Clears Election Commission Proposal, Candidates Can Spend More on Campaign," *Economic Times*, February 28, 2014, http://articles.economictimes.indiatimes.com/2014-02-28/news/47774542_1_rs-8-lakh-40-lakh-rs-25-lakh.

71. "Elections to Give Rs 60,000 Crore GDP Boost to Economy: ASSOCHAM," Associated Chambers of Commerce and Industry of India, 2014, http://www.assocham.org/prels/shownews-archive.php?id=4421.

72. Himani Chandra Gurtoo, "BJP's Advertisement Plan May Cost a Whopping Rs 50,000 Cr," *Hindustan Times*, April 13, 2014, http://www.hindustantimes.com/elections2014/state-of-the-states/advertisement-war-to-win-lok-sabha-elections-may-cost-bjp-whopping-rs-5-000-crore/article1-1207499.aspx.

73. Sudhir Suryawanshi, "Congress Rs. 700 Cr Ad Blitzkrieg to Revolve Around Rahul Gandhi," *DNA* (Mumbai), February 15, 2014, http://www.dnaindia.com/india /report-congress-rs700cr-ad-blitzkrieg-to-revolve-around-rahul-gandhi-1962172.

74. When questioned about the use of Adani corporate airplanes of the Adani Group, Gautam Adani said that Narendra Modi had been a regular charter flight customer since 2009 and that he paid fully for the flights, though he did not reveal the fares. If the conglomerate's charges were the same as those of the competing charter services, then Modi would have been well advised to opt for another charter service company.

75. Tony Munroe, "Billionaire Adani Prospers as Modi Stresses Development," Reuters, April 11, 2014, http://in.reuters.com/article/2014/04/10/india-election-adani -modi-idINDEEA3908220140410.

76. "Environment Ministry Slaps Rs 200 Crore Fine on Adani Group," *Economic Times*, September 4, 2013, http://articles.economictimes.indiatimes.com/2013-09-04 /news/41765520_1_environment-minister-jayanthi-natarajan-adani-group-mundra-port.

77. Siddharth Varadarajan, "Modi's 100 Days: Biding His Time, Circling the Wagons," *Al Jazeera*, September 2, 2014, http://svaradarajan.com/2014/09/03/modis-100 -days-biding-his-time-circling-the-wagons/.

78. "India: More NGOs, Than Schools and Health Centres," *Indian Express*, July 7, 2010, cited in http://southasia.oneworld.net/news/india-more-ngos-than-schools-and -health-centres.

79. Many NGOs monitor violations of existing laws, such as the Environment Protection Act of 1986, applicable throughout India, by state governments and private corporations. Most of these breaches pertain to environmental conservation and the legal rights of the tribal people.

80. Bharat Sharma, interviewed by the author in Dehradun, March 2011; and Bharat Sharma, e-mail message to the author on May 30, 2011.

81. Bharat Sharma, interviewed by the author in Dehradun, March 2011.

82. National Alliance of People's Movements, December 1996, http://www.proxsa .org/politics/napm.html.

83. "Supreme Court Ruling," Friends of River Narmada, http://www.narmada.org /sardar-sarovar/sc.ruling/.

84. Saritha Rai, "Protests in India Deplore Soda Makers' Water Use," *New York Times*, May 20, 2003, http://www.indiaresource.org/news/2003/4125.html.

85. Georgina Drew, "From the Groundwater Up: Water Rights in India," *Development* 51 (2008): 37–41, http://www.conflicts.indiawaterportal.org/sites/conflicts.india waterportal.org/files/Asserting_Water_Rights_in_India.pdf.

86. Michael Levien, "India's Double-Movement: Polanyi and the National Alliance of People's Movements," *Berkeley Journal of Sociology* 51 (2007), http://michaellevien .files.wordpress.com/2012/07/07-indias-double-mvmt-v51.pdf.

87. Swati Mathur, "National Alliance for People's Movement Demands Political Dialogue and End to Militarization," *Times of India*, May 27, 2013, http://timesofindia .indiatimes.com/city/lucknow/National-Alliance-for-Peoples-Movement-demands -political-dialogue-and-end-to-militarisation/articleshow/20285258.cms.

88. Article 226 of the Indian constitution states, "Every High Court shall have power . . . to issue to any person or authority . . . directions, orders or writs . . . for the enforcement of any of the rights conferred by Part III [of the Constitution] and for any other purpose."

89. Article 32 of the Indian constitution grants the right to move the Supreme Court by appropriate proceedings for the enforcement of the rights conferred by Part III. "The Supreme Court shall have power to issue directions or orders or writs . . . for the enforcement of any of the rights conferred by this Part." "Article 32 (Remedies for enforcement of rights conferred by this Part III)," see "Constitution of India: Part III, Fundamental Rights," http://lawmin.nic.in/olwing/coi/coi-english/Const.Pock%202Pg.Rom8Fsss(6).pdf.

90. Pavan K. Verma, "Courts Also Need a Lokpal," *Times of India*, May 16, 2013, http://timesofindia.indiatimes.com/home/opinion/edit-page/Courts-also-need-a-Lokpal-Without-judicial-reform-one-of-the-pillars-of-our-democracy-will-continue-to-crumble/articleshow/20073405.cms.

91. Mumbai Kamgar Sabha, "Bombay vs M/S Abdulbhai Faizullabhai & Ors on 10 March 1976," Supreme Court of India, http://indiankanoon.org/doc/191016/.

92. T.R. Andhyarujina, "Disturbing Trends in Judicial Activism," *The Hindu*, August 6, 2012, http://www.thehindu.com/opinion/lead/disturbing-trends-in-judicial-activism/article3731471.ece.

93. "The Powers of the American President," History Learning Site, http://www.historylearningsite.co.uk/pres1.htm.

94. See chapter 6, 165.

95. See chapter 6, 172.

96. See chapter 6, 178.

97. See chapter 6, 190.

98. "PM Inaugurates the 17th Commonwealth Law Conference at Hyderabad," Press Information Bureau, Government of India, February 6, 2011, http://pib.nic.in/newsite/erelease.aspx?relid=69623.

99. "India—Literacy Rate," Index Mundi, http://www.indexmundi.com/facts/india/literacy-rate. According to a survey by the "Support My School" program of the Coca-Cola Foundation and NDTV, by the end of primary education at the age of eleven, one-third of the pupils dropped out, and by the end of junior secondary education at fourteen, an additional one-third quit.

100. P. Sawant, "The Secretary, Ministry of . . . vs Cricket Association of Bengal & . . . on 9 February, 1995," Supreme Court of India, http://indiankanoon.org/doc/539407/.

101. Rishab Aiyer Ghosh, "Indian Supreme Court Ends State Control of the Airwaves," *Electronic Dreams*, February 10, 1995, http://www.hartford-hwp.com/archives/52a/020.html.

102. Shilpa Kannan, "India's 150 Million-Home Digital Switchover Begins," BBC News, October 30, 2012, http://www.bbc.co.uk/news/business-20121024.

103. "Internet World Stats," http://www.internetworldstats.com/asia/in.htm; and "India Is Now World's Third Largest Internet User After US, China," BBC News,

October 30, 2012, http://www.thehindu.com/sci-tech/technology/internet/india-is-now
-worlds-third-largest-internet-user-after-us-china/article5053115.ece.

104. Press Release No. 66/2014, Telecom Regulatory Authority of India, October 14, 2014, http://www.trai.gov.in/WriteReadData/WhatsNew/Documents/Press%20Release%20Aug-14.pdf. Of these, 545 million were urban users and 380 million rural.

105. Dilip Hiro, *After Empire: The Birth of a Multipolar World* (New York: Nation Books, 2010), 195.

106. "Executive Summary," Telecom India, http://www.imaginmor.com/telecom -india.

107. Mansi Tiwari, "Mobile Penetration Impacts Economic Growth: Study," *Economic Times*, January 18, 2009, http://articles.economictimes.indiatimes.com/2009-01 -18/news/28450352_1_penetration-mobile-telephony-mobile-connections.

9. Perspectives from the Grassroots

1. Interviewed by the author, March 2011.

2. Interviewed by the author, March 2011.

3. "Much of Rural India Still Waits for Electricity," Phys.org, November 4, 2013, http://phys.org/news/2013-11-rural-india-electricity.html.

4. As in the rest of India, electricity supply was plagued by outages.

5. Interviewed by the author, March 2011.

6. *Ashiana*, a Persian word meaning "nest," is the generic name for all the housing colonies constructed by Ansal all over India.

7. See http://www.ashianahousing.com/ashiana_projects.php?txt_search=Jodhpur.

8. Interviewed by the author, November 2011.

9. Interviewed by the author, March 2011.

10. E-mail message to the author from Bharat Sharma on December 20, 2012.

11. Ibid.

12. "Haridwar Election Results, 2014," Elections.in, May 16, 2014, http://www .elections.in/uttarakhand/parliamentary-constituencies/hardwar.html.

13. Interviews by Bharat Sharma of the Friends of Doon NGO, October 2014.

14. See chapter 1, 47; and chapter 5, 132.

15. Interviewed by the author, February 2010.

16. Interviewed by the author, March 2010.

17. "Chhattisgarh: Naxals Kill 12 Cops, Civilian," *Indian Express*, May 12, 2009, http://www.indianexpress.com/news/chhattisgarh-naxals-kill-12-cops-civilian/457619/.

18. Ibid.

10. Overview and Conclusions

1. Dilip Hiro, *Inside India Today* (London: Routledge & Kegan Paul, 1976), 70.

2. Ibid.

3. "Lok Sabha Polls to Cost More Than US Presidential Election," *Live Mint*, March 1, 2009, http://www.livemint.com/Politics/sFrNtS4yTgirv7rY0y8CHO/Lok -Sabha-polls-to-cost-more-than-US-presidential-election.html.

4. "The Poor Rich Indian MPs," *Economic Times*, August 21, 2010, http://articles .economictimes.indiatimes.com/2010-08-21/news/27594515_1_crorepati-mps-bjp-mp -indian-mps; and "The Cost of India's MPs," Infochange Governance, September 20, 2010, http://infochangeindia.org/governance/features/the-cost-of-indias-mps.html.

5. See chapter 6, 181, 189.

6. B.G. Shirsat and Ashok Divase, "Jindal Retains Top Positon in India Inc's Salary Sweepstakes," *Business Standard*, February 2, 2012, http://www.business-standard .com/article/companies/naveen-jindal-retains-top-position-in-india-inc-s-salary-sweeps takes-112020200046_1.html.

7. "Making Political Parties Accountable," Association for Democratic Reforms, Ajit Ranade, June 17, 2013, http://adrindia.org/media/adr-in-news/making-political-parties -accountable.

8. Interviewed by the author in London, June 2013.

9. Nayan Chanda, *Bound Together: How Traders, Preachers, Adventurers and Warriors Shaped Globalization* (New Haven, CT: Yale University Press, 2009), 317.

10. "CEO-to-Worker Pay Cap in the United States," AFL-CIO, 2014, http://www .aflcio.org/Corporate-Watch/CEO-Pay-and-You/CEO-to-Worker-Pay-Gap-in-the -United-States.

11. "U.S.-India Bilateral Trade and Investment," Office of the United States Trade Representative, May 9, 2014, http://www.ustr.gov/countries-regions/south-central-asia /india.

12. "Statistics of Overseas Indian Population," NRIOL, http://www.nriol.com /indiandiaspora/statistics-indians-abroad.asp.

13. Sadanand Dhume, "What Is the Natural Political Home of Indian-Americans?," *The American*, August 29, 2012, http://www.american.com/archive/2012/august/what -is-the-natural-political-home-of-indian-americans; and "Silicon Valley Index, 2013," http://www.siliconvalleyindex.org/index.php/economy/income.

14. Dilip Hiro, *After Empire: The Birth of a Multipolar World* (New York: Nation Books, 2010), 195.

Epilogue

1. See chapter 7, 238.

2. Khaleda Rahman, "Worried He Wouldn't Know Who You Were? Indian PM Meets Obama Wearing a Suit with His Own Name Repeatedly Sewn into It," *Daily Mail*, January 26, 2015, http://www.dailymail.co.uk/news/article-2926935/Indian-PM -meets-Obama-wearing-suit-repeatedly-sewn-it.html.

3. BBC News, "Obama in India Joins Modi at Delhi Republic Day Parade," January 26, 2015, http://www.bbc.co.uk/news/world-asia-india-30978148.

4. Frank Jack Daniel and Roberta Rampton, "In Parting Shot, Obama Prods India on Religious Freedom," Reuters, January 27, 2015, http://in.reuters.com/article/2015 /01/27/india-obama-idINKBN0L00F720150127; "Remarks by President Obama in Address to the People of India," Office of the Press Secretary, White House, January 27, 2015, https://www.whitehouse.gov/the-press-office/2015/01/27/remarks-president-obama -address-people-india; and Dan Roberts and Jason Burke, "Barack Obama Challenges India on Religious Tolerance and Women's Rights," *The Guardian*, January 27, 2015, http://www.theguardian.com/us-news/2015/jan/27/obama—india-womens-rights -religious-intolerance-delhi

5. Pradeepkumar Kadkol, "Reference to Religious Divide 'Unfortunate', but I Endorse Obama's Statement: Rajnath Singh," *The Hindu*, February 2, 2015, http://www.thehindu .com/news/national/karnataka/obamas-reference-to-religious-freedom-really -unfortunate-rajnath-singh/article6848368.ece.

6. Deeptiman Tiwari, "VHP Hits Back at Obama, Calls Him 'Stooge of Church,'" *Times of India*, February 7, 2015, http://timesofindia.indiatimes.com/india/VHP-hits -back-at-Obama-calls-him-stooge-of-Church/articleshow/46151122.cms.

7. New Delhi Correspondent, "Christmas Season Brings Christianity Under Renewed Attack in India," *Morning Star* (London), December 23, 2014, http:// morningstarnews.org/2014/12/christmas-season-brings-christianity-under-renewed -attack-in-india/.

8. Piyush Srivastava, "We Will Free India of Muslims and Christians by 2021," *Daily Mail*, December 19, 2014, http://www.dailymail.co.uk/indiahome/indianews /article-2879597/We-free-India-Muslims-Christians-2021-DJS-leader-vows-continue -ghar-wapsi-plans-restore-Hindu-glory.html.

9. "Press Statement by Archbishop of Delhi on the Church Burning in Delhi," December 1, 2014, http://christianpersecutionindia.blogspot.co.uk/2014/12/press -statement-by-archbishop-of-delhi.html. The press release referred to the officials in the BJP-ruled Chhattisgarh ordering Catholic priests to install the statues of Sarswati, the Hindu goddess of knowledge, in their schools.

10. Katki Angre, "Church Vandalized in Delhi, Archbishop Says There Is a Pattern in Attacks," NDTV, January 14, 2015, http://www.ndtv.com/india-news/church -vandalized-in-delhi-archbishop-says-there-is-a-pattern-in-attacks-727179.

11. Election literature collected by the author, January–February 2015.

12. "10 Reasons for the AAP Tsunami," *Times of India*, February 11, 2015, http:// timesofindia.indiatimes.com/listshow/46194170.cms.

13. Vidya Venkat, "Paisa, Power and Politics," *The Hindu*, February 11, 2015, http:// www.thehindu.com/opinion/op-ed/paisa-power-and-politics/article6879362.ece.

14. "Budget Highlights of Union Budget 2015," *The Hindu*, February 28, 2015, http://www.thehindu.com/business/budget/highlights-of-union-budget-2015 /article6944752.ece.

15. Interview on February 12, 2015.

16. Kartikay Mehrotra and Rakteem Katakey, "Narendra Modi Prays to Ganges in Varanasi; Promises to Clean Up India," *Live Mint*, May 17, 2014, http://www.livemint

.com/Politics/9hg7dRctK6FpL17VlYRpxN/Narendra-Modi-arrives-in-Varanasi-to-offer-prayers-to-Gange.html.

17. "I Have Been Chosen by God: Modi," *The Hindu*, April 24, 2014, http://www.thehindu.com/news/i-have-been-chosen-by-god-modi/article5944125.ece.

18. Patterbuzz, "An Election Diary," *Hard News* (Delhi), January 2015, https://patterbuzz.com/web/fullArticle?type=4&articleId=14268, citing Harish Khare, *How Modi Won It* (New Delhi: Hachette India, 2015).

19. "Modi Crosses the 8 Million Followers Mark on Twitter," *Indian Express*, November 21, 2014, http://indianexpress.com/article/technology/social/pm-narendra-modi-crosses-the-8-million-followers-mark-on-twitter/. This figure rose to 12.6 million at the end of Modi's first year in power in May 2015. Nicola Smith, "'Tax Terrorism' Returns to India," *Sunday Times*, May 31, 2015, www.thesundaytimes.co.uk/sto/business/Economy/article1562300.ece.

20. Abhirup Bhunia, "Why India Must Revive Its Manufacturing Sector," *The Diplomat*, February 25, 2014, http://thediplomat.com/2014/02/why-india-must-revive-its-manufacturing-sector/.

21. Surabhi, "Job Growth Falls in India, Down to Lowest in 3 Quarters," *Financial Express*, April 17, 2015, http://www.financialexpress.com/article/economy/job-growth-falls-in-india-down-to-lowest-in-3-quarters/64420/.

22. "Govt Cheers Data Showing 7.3% GDP Growth in 2014–15," *Times of India*, May 30, 2105, http://timesofindia.indiatimes.com/business/india-business/Govt-cheers-data-showing-7-3-GDP-growth-in-2014-15/articleshow/47477836.cms.

23. Praful Bidwai, "Indian Government Sanctions Greenpeace to Send a Menacing Message," *The Ecologist*, April 23, 2015, http://www.theecologist.org/News/news_analysis/2841481/indian_government_sanctions_greenpeace_to_send_a_menacing_message.html.

24. Brinda Karat, "Glass Half Empty for Adivasis," *The Hindu*, May 2, 2015, http://www.thehindu.com/todays-paper/tp-opinion/a-glass-half-empty-for-adivasis/article7162997.ece.

25. FE Bureau, "Mining Bills Clear Rajya Sabha Test, No More Coalgates Now," *Financial Express*, March 21, 2015, http://www.financialexpress.com/article/economy/mining-bills-clear-rs-test-no-more-coalgates-now/55922/.

26. Rajesh Roy and Anant Vijay Kala, "Indian Government Amends Land Acquisition Bill," *India Real Time* (blog), *Wall Street Journal*, December 30, 2014, http://blogs.wsj.com/indiarealtime/2014/12/30/indian-government-amends-land-acquisition-bill/.

27. AFP, "India's Rahul Gandhi Set to Lead Protest Against Modi's Land Law," *Daily Mail*, April 19, 2015, http://www.dailymail.co.uk/wires/afp/article-3045200/Indias-Rahul-Gandhi-leads-protest-against-Modis-land-law.html.

28. Express News Service, "Joint Parliamentary Committee: Land Bill Provision 'Alarming', Drop Them, Farmers Tell Panel," *Indian Express*, June 10, 2015, http://indianexpress.com/article/india/india-others/joint-parliamentary-committee-land-bill-provisions-alarming-drop-them-farmers-tell-panel/.

Select Bibliography

Bardhan, Pranab K. *Awakening Giants, Feet of Clay: Assessing the Economic Rise of China and India*. Princeton, NJ: Princeton University Press, 2010.

Basu, Debashis, and Sucheta Dalal. *The Scam: Who Won, Who Lost, Who Got Away. From Harshad Mehta to Ketan Parekh*. Columbia, MO: South Asia Books, 1993.

Boo, Katherine. *Behind the Beautiful Forevers: Life, Death, and Hope in a Mumbai Slum*. New York: Random House, 2012.

Bouquet, Tim, and Byron Ousey. *Cold Steel: Britain's Richest Man and the Multi-Billion Dollar Battle for a Global Empire*. London: Little, Brown, 2008.

Bremmer, Ian. *The End of the Free Market: Who Wins the War Between States and Corporations?* New York: Portfolio, 2010.

Chakravarati, Sudeep. *Red Sun: Travels in Naxalite Country*. New Delhi: Penguin Books, 2008.

Chanda, Nayan. *Bound Together: How Traders, Preachers, Adventurers and Warriors Shaped Globalization*. New Haven, CT: Yale University Press, 2009.

Chenoy, Anuradha M. and Kamal Mitra Chenoy. *Maoist and Other Armed Conflicts*. New Delhi: Penguin Books, 2010.

Danim, Rodnick. *The Globalization Paradox: Democracy and the Future of the World Economy*. New York: W.W. Norton, 2011.

Dasgupta, Biplab. *Globalisation: India's Adjustment Experience*. New Delhi: Sage Publications, 2005.

Eichengree, Barry. *Globalizing Capital: A History of the International Money System*. Princeton, NJ: Princeton University Press, 2008.

Frankel, Francine R. *India's Green Revolution*. Princeton, NJ: Princeton University Press, 1972.

French, Patrick. *India: A Portrait*. New York: Vintage, 2012.

Ghosh, Sankar. *The Naxalite Movement*. Calcutta: Mother India Press, 1975.

Hiro, Dilip. *After Empire: The Birth of a Multipolar World*. New York: Nation Books, 2010.

————. *Blood of the Earth: The Battle for the World's Vanishing Oil Resources*. New York: Nation Books, 2006.

————. *Inside India Today*. London: Routledge & Kegan Paul, 1976/New York: Monthly Review Press, 1977.

Kapoor, Sanjay. *Bad Money, Bad Politics: The Untold Hawala Story*. Delhi: Har Anand, 1996.

Kapur, Akash. *India Becoming: Portrait of Life in Modern India*. New York: Riverhead Books, 2012.

Luce, Edward. *In Spite of the Gods: The Strange Rise of Modern India*. New York: Anchor, 2008.

Nadeem, Shahzad. *Dead Ringers: How Outsourcing Is Changing the Way Indians Understand Themselves*. Princeton, NJ: Princeton University Press, 2011.

Nagpal, C.S. *Indian Agriculture*. New Delhi: Anmol Publications, 2004.

Navlakha, Gautam. *Days and Nights in the Heartland of Rebellion*. New Delhi: Penguin Books, 2012.

Nayar, Kuldip. *India: The Critical Years*. New Delhi: Vikas, 1971.

Nilekani, Nadan. *Imagining India: The Idea of a Renewed Nation*. New York: Penguin Books, 2010.

Oza, B.M. *Bofors: The Ambassador's Evidence*. New Delhi: Konak Publishers, 1997.

Pathak, Bharati V. *The Indian Financial System: Markets, Institutions and Services*. New Delhi: Pearson Education, 2011.

Ramadorai, S. *The TCS Story . . . and Beyond*. New Delhi: Penguin Books, 2011.

Ray, Rabindra. *The Naxalites and Their Ideology*. New Delhi: Oxford University Press, 1988.

Singh, K.P., with Ramesh Menon and Raman Swamy. *Whatever the Odds: The Incredible Story Behind DLF*. Noida: HarperCollins Publishers India, 2011.

Singh, Prakash. *Kohima to Kashmir: On the Terrorist Trail*. New Delhi: Rupa and Co., 2001.

Sodhi, J.S., ed. *Tracking Globalization: Debates of Development, Freedom and Justice*. New Delhi: Viking, 2011.

Sooryamoorthy, R. and K.D. Gangrade. *NGOs in India: A Cross-Sectional Study*. Jaipur: Rawat Publications, 2006.

Tully, Mark. *Non-Stop India*. New Delhi: Allen Lane, 2011.

————. *India: The Road Ahead*. London: Rider, 2011.

von Braun, Joachim, and E. Díaz-Bonilla, eds. *Globalization of Agriculture and Food: Causes, Consequences, and Policy Implications*. New Delhi: Oxford University Press, 2008.

Index

Publishing in the Public Interest

Thank you for reading this book published by The New Press. The New Press is a nonprofit, public interest publisher. New Press books and authors play a crucial role in sparking conversations about the key political and social issues of our day.

We hope you enjoyed this book and that you will stay in touch with The New Press. Here are a few ways to stay up to date with our books, events, and the issues we cover:

- Sign up at www.thenewpress.com/subscribe to receive updates on New Press authors and issues and to be notified about local events
- Like us on Facebook: www.facebook.com/newpressbooks
- Follow us on Twitter: www.twitter.com/thenewpress

Please consider buying New Press books for yourself; for friends and family; or to donate to schools, libraries, community centers, prison libraries, and other organizations involved with the issues our authors write about.

The New Press is a 501(c)(3) nonprofit organization. You can also support our work with a tax-deductible gift by visiting www.thenewpress.com/donate.